AFRICAN STUDIES SERIES

Editorial board

The African Studies Series is a collection of monographs and general studies which reflect the interdisciplinary interests of the African Studies Centre at Cambridge. Volumes to date have combined historical, anthropological, economic, political and other perspectives. Each contribution has assumed that such broad approaches can contribute much to our understanding of Africa, and that this may in turn be of advantage to specific disciplines.

THE LIONS OF DAGBON:
POLITICAL CHANGE IN NORTHERN GHANA

BOOKS IN THIS SERIES

THE LIONS OF DAGBON: POLITICAL CHANGE IN NORTHERN GHANA

MARTIN STANILAND

Lecturer in Politics, University of Glasgow

CAMBRIDGE UNIVERSITY PRESS

CAMBRIDGE

LONDON · NEW YORK · MELBOURNE

Published by the Syndics of the Cambridge University Press
The Pitt Building, Trumpington Street, Cambridge CB2 1RP
Bentley House, 200 Euston Road, London NW1 2DB
32 East 57th Street, New York, NY 10022, USA
296 Beaconsfield Parade, Middle Park, Melbourne 3206, Australia

Library of Congress Catalogue Card Number: 74–16989

ISBN: 0 521 20682 0

First published 1975

Photoset and printed in Malta by St Paul's Press Ltd

TO MY MOTHER AND
THE MEMORY OF MY FATHER

CONTENTS

MAPS, FIGURES, AND TABLES

This our business has nothing to do with
writing and you keep trying to put it down
and in the process you ruin it for us.

– An elder of the Ya-Na

PREFACE

'The Lion of Dagbon' is a praise-title of the paramount chiefs, the Ya-Nas, of the Dagomba people in northern Ghana. This study is concerned with the political history of the Dagomba kingdom, notably during the last seventy years when the kingdom has been subordinated to governments, successively colonial and national, in Accra and Tamale. Its purpose is to examine the policies which the overlords of Dagomba have adopted in order to preserve, exploit, and assimilate the pre-colonial structure of authority and also to consider changes in local politics which have come about, at least partly, through the action of these external authorities. The concluding chapters deal with the origins and character of a major dispute within the kingdom, the conflict which has come to be known in Ghanaian politics as 'the Yendi skin dispute'.

My original interest in northern Ghanaian politics arose from earlier work on central–local relations in the Ivory Coast. It seemed to me, from field-work in the Ivory Coast, that relations between the national capital and the outlying, underdeveloped districts of the north involved a distinctive pattern of patronage–clientage and a distinctive set of attitudes towards government. After reading other studies (notably that by Dunn and Robertson in this series), I now regard the narrowness of patronage–clientage and the syndrome of dominance-cum-ingratiation to be found in the northern Ivory Coast as extreme forms of general phenomena rather than as regional peculiarities.

They are, nonetheless, interesting and I felt that it would be useful to explore a comparable case in northern Ghana. In the event, it was impossible to find a situation which was economically and geographically exactly comparable. Instead, I decided to explore a case in which there was the most apparent political interest in Ghana and an almost notorious involvement of 'brokers', namely, the Yendi skin dispute.

The research took me into a scene thickly inhabited by impassioned octogenarians and feuding bureaucrats, a fading but still quite colourful world which at times is reminiscent of Shakespeare or Sergei Eisenstein, at others of Cary and Waugh. I have tried, I hope not laboriously, to pass on some of the surrealist flavour produced by this mixture. After my reading of an infinite quantity of minutes and memoranda, the colonial encounter in Africa still seems to me a cultural mystery of the first order. Some sense of this mystery is conveyed by novelists like Cary and Orwell, both of whom had a special understanding of the intimate absurdities of colonialism. But the colonial encounter has not, on the whole, had the imaginative treatment it deserves. On the one hand, we have the rather undiscriminating celebrations of the colonial service produced by Heussler and memoirists from the profession; on the other, we have the Punch and Judy spectaculars beloved of some members of the Left. Both seem to lack an appreciation of the larger tragi-comedy which the colonial encounter involved.

As a study of African politics, the Dagomba case is interesting, both because of the sophisticated and elaborate nature of the pre-colonial state and because of the importance of the Dagomba people in present-day Ghana. Numbering rather over a quarter of a million, they constitute the largest group in the north and, until the 1972 *coup*, controlled six seats in the National Assembly. The Dagomba kingdom also provides a good case study in colonial government, since between the wars it attracted the attentions of an energetic and articulate team of 'indirect rule' administrators, whose programmes and correspondence are meticulously preserved in the Tamale archives.

As regards the theoretical implications of the study, these lie in the debatable ground between theories of international underdevelopment and the self-contained literature of tribal and community studies. This is certainly not a study of 'political modernisation' or 'development' in the conventional sense; nor is it, I hope, only a chronicle of court politics. In the perspective formed by development theory, the case study is, presumably, of limited interest, since it concerns an area of the neo-colonial hinterland which was relatively untouched by the dynamic processess of social and economic change under colonialism. Nor can it be said to exemplify the unequivocal onset of 'modernity'.

The Dagomba case does, however, exemplify very well the consequences of uneven development. I have argued that during a considerable part of this century the major – at times the only – area of innovation has been in the political and administrative spheres. There has thus been change but, in C. S. Whitaker's phrase, it has been a 'dysrhythmic' process – that is, an erratic and uncoordinated pattern of development, from which certain sectors emerge more transformed than others. Even in the political sphere, modernisation has been, to say the least, ambiguous in its effects. Northern Ghana came late into national politics and it did so with a structure of local government which was still dominated by the chiefs and their elders. The result has been the uneasy amalgamation or coexistence of several types of authority and persistent 'boundary problems' between them. There are at least three, ultimately incompatible principles of legitimation to which appeal may be made in Dagomba politics: the traditional, grounded in the authority of myth and precedent; the bureaucratic, deriving from the sovereignty of central (or, in some instances, royal) government; and the democratic, based on the representation of majorities.

This diversity is not, of course, unique to northern Ghana or to Africa but it is evident there to an extreme degree, because of the tempo of formal institutional change in the area during this century. The overall outcome is a pattern of politics which is often bizarre, occasionally violent, and generally confused. All of these characteristics amply feature in the Yendi dispute, which would yield neither clarity of argument nor consistency of position even to the most sophisticated of analytic techniques. That it would not is, however, further evidence of the incoherence of relations between centre and periphery and between chiefly, elective, and administrative institutions in contemporary Ghana.

Concerning approach, this book is perhaps, in the worst sense, interdisciplinary (more, possibly, sub- or extra-disciplinary). It may seem to some readers to be a disquieting mixture of history, political science, and anthropology, but I think that, at the risk of infuriating specialists, it is essential to bring the materials and ideas of these disciplines together if we are to make articulate sense of what is happening politically in African countries, and by extension elsewhere. Nevertheless, there are costs and these, I suspect, will be particularly evident to anthropologists. While preparing this book, I did not live in a village compound and my knowledge of Dagbane is, to put it mildly, reticent. I deliberately sought out, and have depended on, written materials, principally from the archives. As a result, the book probably lacks a well-informed sense of attitudes and values at village level and I regret that this is so. But I decided that, with the time and money at my disposal – not to mention my own lack of training in certain fields – I should concentrate on a particular set of relationships, those between members of the Dagomba ruling class and the representatives of suzerains.

One somewhat fortuitous limitation on the research should be mentioned, if only to explain the lack of certain details in the chapters concerned with politics in the fifties and sixties. It had been my intention to interview a wide range of politicians and chiefs involved with the parties, but shortly after I had started my programme of interviews, the then Regional Commissioner, Colonel Iddissah, decided that investigations touching upon the Yendi dispute might, unintentionally, have an inflammatory effect on the participants and I was asked, very courteously, to desist, which I did. I do not, therefore, regard the account given in Chapters 8 and 9 as much more than an outline and I hope that some day an energetic (and tactful) research student will probe further into party history in the area.

I was, indeed, given every assistance by government officials while engaged in fieldwork and I would like in particular to acknowledge the considerable kindness and material help I received from Mr R. A. Karbo, at the time District Administrative Officer for Tamale. I owe special gratitude also to Canon H. A. Blair of Truro who gave up a large amount of time to talk to me about colonial government in the thirties and who lent me some invaluable material, notably his unpublished memoirs. I have a particular debt to Bill and Anne Johnson who put me up in Oxford for the best part of a term. Of the many others who helped me during my research work, I would like to thank especially R. I. Alhassan, A. B. Baba, Tony Berrett, A. Tarponee Cobla, John Dunn, Elizabeth Hook, Dassana Iddi, Yahaya Iddi, Fisata Kabache, J. S. Kaleem, Christine Oppong, Charles and Gillian

Raab, Yaw and Fanny Saffu, Agnes Samuel, S. M. Sibidow, Terry and Anne Smutylo, Tia Sulemana, B. A. Yakubu (former Gushie-Na), and Salifu Yakubu. For their many kindnesses while I was writing this book, I am indebted to a host of friends, among them Brian and Jean Barr, Andrew and Anne Lockyer, Simon and Fanny Mitchell, Karin Reilly, Michel and Diane Verdon, and Stephen and Ishbel White. Among the librarians who gave me advice and assistance, I would single out for special thanks those at the Institute of Commonwealth Studies and at Rhodes House in Oxford, at the Manuscripts Department of the University Library, Cambridge, and at the Northern Region Library in Tamale. Finance for the project was provided by the Social Science Research Council, the administration of which was most understanding of the problems which inevitably arose in the course of fieldwork. The Court of the University of Glasgow gave me leave of absence to pursue the research as well as a grant to cover typing expenses. The staff of the Cambridge University Press and the editors of this series gave me a great deal of help in preparing the work for publication and Jean Beverly, Sheila Hamilton, and Charlotte Logan assisted in the revision of the draft. Lastly, I should express my warm appreciation of the skill and efficiency of Mrs Jean Clydesdale, who produced an immaculate typescript out of a tangle of stapled and amended pages. To all of these, my sincere thanks. The defects which remain are, without exception, all my own work.

Glasgow   M.S.
July 1974

ABBREVIATIONS AND GLOSSARY

Principal abbreviations used in the text and the notes

C.C.N.T.	Chief Commissioner, Northern Territories
C.P.P.	Convention People's Party
C.R.O.	Chief Regional Officer
D.A.O.	District Administrative Officer
D.C.	District Commissioner
D.P.O.	District Political Officer
G.A.	Government Agent
M.A.P.	Moslem Association Party
N.A.	Native Authority
N.A.G.A.	National Archives of Ghana, Accra
N.A.G.T.	National Archives of Ghana, Tamale
N.A.L.	National Alliance of Liberals
N.L.C.	National Liberation Council
N.P.P.	Northern People's Party
N.T.	Northern Territories
N.T.C.	Northern Territories Constabulary
P.C.	Provincial Commissioner
P.P.	Progress Party

Principal Dagbane terms used in the text

baga	soothsayer
dagbandaba	the commoner estate (lit. slaves)
dang	clan, kindred
fong	town or quarter of a town
gbonlana	regent of a king or a divisional chief
kambonse	state musketeers
katini duu	the hut in which a king is enskinned
kpamba	elders, counsellors to a king or a chief
kpanalana	elder to a divisional chief
limam	imam
na-bihe	the royal sons; senior members of the royal family eligible for the skin of Yendi

xii

nam (pl. *nama*)	skin
na-yanse	royal grandsons
tindana	
(pl. *tindamba*)	fetish priest
wulana	senior elder to divisional chief
yidana	head, husband
yili	house, compound
zuliya	male line of descent

In this work 'District' and 'Region' refer to the administrative units of colonial and post-colonial government; 'district' and 'region' refer to geographical areas.

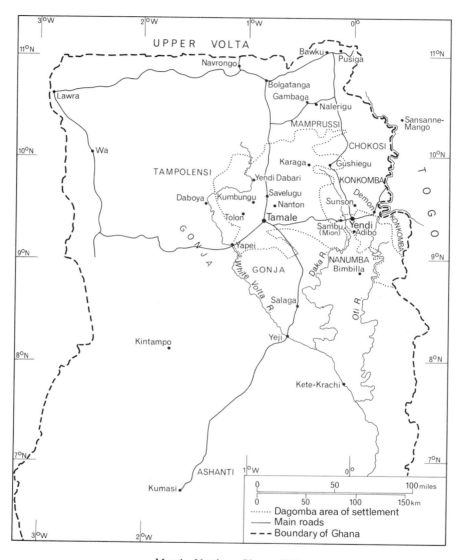

Map 1. Northern Ghana, 1965

CHAPTER 1

THE COUNTRY AND THE PEOPLE

When the British moved their administration to Tamale in 1907, it was a village of 1,435 people. Now it is a sprawling town of 80,000, and the morning plane from Accra swings down to land over shimmering iron rooftops, concrete offices, and a web of asphalt roads, masts, and aerials. Around Tamale stretches the flat orchard savannah of northern Ghana, a thinly populated land across which the main north road to the Upper Volta border runs as smooth and straight as the drive of a country park. To reach Dagomba villages in this country might now take as little as eight hours by jet from London: when the British first came to Tamale, the journey took a month or more.

At the time of colonial partition the Dagomba kingdom spread over some 8,000 square miles of the savannah plains.[1] The kingdom had then been in existence for about four hundred years, ruled over by the paramount chief, the Ya-Na, from his capital at Yendi, sixty miles east of Tamale. On the eastern edge of the kingdom lay the Konkomba, a stateless people, treated as subjects of the Dagomba.[2] The Mamprussi to the north and the Nanumba to the south were related to the Dagomba: they migrated into the area at the same time and retained myths of common origin. The other neighbours of the Dagomba – the Gonja, Tampolensi, and Chokosi – were of entirely different stock, although the principal chief of the Chokosi (the Chereponi-fame) had become, and still is, a member of the Dagomba State Council.[3]

In 1960 the total population of Dagomba origin enumerated in Ghana was 217,640, of whom 186,970 were at that time actually resident in the Northern Region (in which the whole area of Dagomba settlement now lies).[4] It is impossible to give precise figures for the growth of Dagomba population in this century. The 1931 census indicated a total population of 191,956 for the two Dagomba districts (although this figure included the adjacent Nanumba). In 1948 the Dagomba population of the then Gold Coast was estimated at 172,379, roughly 150,000 of whom were living in the Dagomba administrative district. The most useful recent figures are perhaps those given for the six main Dagomba constituencies by the Siriboe commission on electoral and local government reform in 1967: these suggest a total population of 267,907.[5]

As large towns, Tamale and Yendi are quite distinct from the majority of Dagomba settlements. Indeed, Tamale is more an administrative and commercial centre within Dagomba than a Dagomba town.[6] Yendi, although a market town, has not changed to the same extent as Tamale: it has a moderately large population (around 16,000) but lacks many of the facilities

1

of a developing urban centre, such as banks and chain stores. Yendi only acquired a secondary school in 1970: it is still essentially the royal capital of pre-colonial times, with modern amenities added to but not supplanting the traditional structure of the town.[7]

In Dagomba generally population density is low and villages are typically small. The average population density is roughly 31 persons per square mile: it is highest in the west, around Tamale.[8] Yet it has been calculated, by Christine Oppong, that of 382 settlements in western Dagomba, 285 (74.6 per cent) have less than 200 inhabitants.[9] The larger villages are, for the most part, also the capitals of divisional chiefs under the Ya-Na. It is, in fact, interesting that these capitals, such as Savelugu, Kumbungu, Sambu, Gushiegu, and Karaga, have kept their pre-eminence under colonial and post-colonial government, though in no case has population risen dramatically. Their continuing importance is a result of administrative policies concerned with chieftaincy and local government in the area, policies which preserved or restored earlier spheres of authority and gave new functions to those vested with authority.

The main features of Dagomba economy and social structure are discussed in Chapter 2, but some general characteristics may be pointed out here. The predominant activity of the Dagomba is still subsistence agriculture: in 1960, 82 per cent of Dagomba men were classified as engaged in 'farming, fishing, and hunting'. Conversely, only 0.2 per cent were in occupations described as 'administrative, executive, and managerial' and only 1.1 per cent in those classed as 'professional, technical and related'.[10] The Dagomba are, moreover, known as skilful farmers, and successive governments, noting the apparent availability of land in the area as well as the rising demand for foodstuffs in the towns, have looked upon this part of the north as a potential granary for Ghana.

Yet Dagomba has no obvious advantages as an environment for agriculture, let alone for intensive cash-crop farming. It lies within the Sudanese climatic zone. Rainfall is moderate, highly seasonal, and unreliable: water supply has been a chronic problem, especially in western Dagomba.[11] Although there has not yet been a detailed soil survey, it is clear that the top-soil is thin and the sub-soil lateritic. Yields are not high in any of the major crops and, as Levtzion remarks, 'neither cereal nor root crops are very successful'.[12] Finally, the Dagomba farmer has not been compelled, by shortage of land, to abandon shifting cultivation. Thus, while easy access to an urban market has stimulated farmers to sell surplus foodstuffs (and even to increase acreages in order to produce a surplus), there is as yet no question of cash-crops assuming priority. At present, the major initiative in the area of extensive commercial agriculture seems to be coming from civil servants and merchants in the local towns rather than from village farmers – understandably enough, given the comparative advantage of the former in respect of capital. Some chiefs have also moved into large-scale farming, but the basic unit of Dagomba economy remains the subsistence family farm, producing millet, maize, guinea-corn, and yams.

2

Nor has migration been a factor of sufficient importance to bring about significant change in the local economy. Unlike, for example, the Frafra of north-eastern Ghana, the Dagomba have not been encouraged to migrate because of overcrowding on the land. Only 10 per cent of the Dagomba population has moved south, compared with 18 per cent of the Frafra.[13] There has not been any substantial exodus from the land on account of schooling and the search for non-agricultural employment. For until very recently the level of literacy was very low and there were very few schools in Dagomba. In 1960 only ten male Dagombas in the age-groups over 25 had received secondary or post-secondary education (another eighty in the younger age-groups were at that time passing through post-primary courses).[14] Further, the Dagomba have not been one of the 'military tribes' from which soldiers and policemen have been recruited by central government. At the time of the 1960 census, only 460 Dagomba were enumerated as resident in 'service barracks, army and brigade camps', compared to 3,050 from the Frafra, Buinsa, and 'Grusi' of the Upper Region – groups which in total represented only 3.6 per cent of Ghana's population, as against 3.2 per cent made up by the Dagomba alone.[15]

DAGOMBA HISTORY

The Dagomba kingdom was one of a cluster of states created by groups of migrant cavalrymen moving south and imposing themselves as a ruling class on established stateless peoples.[16] Of the latter, little is known: they spoke a language belonging to the Gur group and had earth priests (*tindamba*).[17] The indigenous people figure in Dagomba myth as 'the Black Dagomba'. Although the name 'Dagomba' itself may have been that of the indigenous people, assumed by the invaders, the great body of mythology is clearly that of the migrants and in this sense 'Dagomba' history is that of the kings since the fifteenth century.[18]

The migrants who established Dagomba were part of a movement which, as I have noted, also led to the creation of the Mamprussi and Nanumba states, as well as to the formation of the Mossi kingdoms now within Upper Volta. The mythology of all these states refers to a common ancestor, Tohajie, 'the Red Hunter', whose grandson Na Gbewa, settled at Pusiga, near Bawku, in north-eastern Ghana. The migrants seem to have been pagans of Hausa origin, possibly from Zamfara, one of the old Hausa 'Banza Bokwoi' states located in the area of Nigeria to the north of Borgu.[19] According to Fage, they moved westwards and for a time supported themselves by raiding the towns of the Niger valley. This period is symbolised in Dagomba history by the story of the hunter who helped the king of Mali in war. The raiders were pushed south in the fifteenth century by the Songhai kings Sonni Ali and Askia Muhammed.[20]

Thus we arrive at the settlement of Na Gbewa at Pusiga. Na Gbewa is said to have had seventeen children, the eldest being Zirile who succeeded him. According to Phyllis Ferguson, in the period following Zirile's accession,

3

the other brothers moved away from Pusiga, Tohagu to found the Mamprussi dynasty at Nalerigu and Sitobu to establish the branch which subsequently controlled Dagomba. The Mossi kingdom of Ouagadougou was created by the offspring of Yantaure, a daughter of Na Gbewa. There followed an extended campaign of conquest, led by Sitobu's son Nyagse, at the conclusion of which Nyagse was invested by his father with the regalia of the new kingdom. Nyagse then established a capital at a place now known as Yendi Dabari, some twenty-nine miles north of Tamale.[21]

The conquest of western Dagomba was undertaken by the Dagomba cavalry, who killed or removed the indigenous *tindamba* and replaced them by members of the royal dynasty and captains of the army. Younger brothers of Sitobu were installed in (or took) divisional chiefdoms: one, Biemone, became Karaga-Na, while another, Biyumkomba, became Mionlana, and a third, Bojyeligu, became Sunson-Na. The first Kuga-Na (an important court elder) is said to have been yet another brother of Sitobu, Sibie, who became soothsayer (*baga*) to Nyagse.[22] The two most important non-royal chiefdoms established during the conquest were those of Tolon and Kumbungu: the Tolon-Na is traditionally head of the king's army and the Kumbung-Na commander of the archers.

Although a large number of *tindamba* were killed by the Dagomba, the institution itself was not destroyed. Indeed, in a few places the *tindana* was allowed to remain as village chief under a Dagomba divisional chief. An important example is Tamale, where the chief, known as the Dakpema, seems to be descended from the earlier *tindana*. Moreover, the imposition of new chiefs did not destroy the jurisdictions of the *tindamba*. According to some writers, the Dagomba chiefs assumed some of the authority of the earth priests – the Ya-Na himself wearing regalia taken from them. The Dagomba state was certainly not strongly centralised, at this or any other period, and the survival of the *tindana* divisions may have helped the emergence of a federal structure.[23]

The conquest of eastern Dagomba took place later than that of the west and apparently with less slaughter of earth priests. The final settlement of this area may have occurred in the seventeenth century when the capital was moved towards present-day Yendi.[24] The Dagomba pushed back the Konkomba and established divisional chiefs among them. The main towns, such as Nakpali and Zabzugu, had the character of outposts, strategically located on the east bank of the River Oti. Despite this assertion of suzerainty, the Dagomba kingdom seems never to have exercised close control over the Konkomba: administration took the form of slave raiding and punitive expeditions. The Konkomba were by no means assimilated. Relations between them and the Dagomba were distant and hostile: there was little, if any, mixing by marriage.[25]

The wars with Gonja and Ashanti

In the early seventeenth century Gonja was invaded by a conqueror of 'Mande' origin, Sumaila Jakpa.[26] Like Sitobu and Nyagse in Dagomba,

4

Jakpa moved across country installing his relatives as chiefs. He came into conflict with the Ya-Na when he seized control of Daboya, north-west of Tamale, and made himself overlord of the Tampolensi. Daboya had been a useful asset to Dagomba as a salt-producing centre and the Ya-Na had claimed suzerainty over the Tampolensi in the area. Having appointed his son as chief of Daboya, Jakpa moved south to attack the Dagomba, defeating (and killing) Na Dariziegu in battle at Yapei. Subsequently Jakpa caused the trade in kola nuts to be directed through the town of Salaga, which, under his patronage, became an important caravan centre. Raiding continued, with Konkombas being taken as labourers to grow food for Gonja chiefs.[27]

There seems to have been an appreciable economic element in the Dagomba wars with Gonja and, indeed, in the subsequent clash with Ashanti. For example, Phyllis Ferguson argues that the Dagomba, in competition with the Gonja, had been drawn eastwards in search of iron ore and slaves: the Gonja had then moved into the vacuum formed in western Dagomba.[28] Further, the 'Ashanti hinterland' was the meeting point of two important caravan routes. One went north-west from Begho (in the present Brong–Ahafo Region) via Bondoukou and Kong (in the Ivory Coast) to Djenne on the Niger; the other went north-east from Salaga via Sansanne-Mango in Togo and Nikki in Dahomey to Kano. These routes were linked at their northern ends to the trans-Saharan caravans and along them passed kola nuts, gold, salt, and other goods, not to mention the creed of Islam. The rulers of Gonja and Dagomba were naturally anxious to profit from control of this trade and it is probable that competition for control was an important factor in the wars of the seventeenth and eighteenth centuries.[29]

For Dagomba, an important consequence was the movement of the capital eastwards to Yendi (originally a Konkomba town called Chare). The movement seems to have taken place under Na Luro, the twelfth Ya-Na, though the oral ('drum') history of Dagomba attributes it to his successor, Tutugri.[30] From Yendi, as Tamakloe writes, 'Na Luro found it easy to drive the Ngbanye [Gonja] away from some of the Dagbamba towns occupied by them.'[31] The final eviction of the Gonja from Dagomba, however, only occurred in the early eighteenth century, under Na Zangina. The Gonja had mounted a new campaign against western Dagomba under Kumpati. Zangina, who was old, apparently had difficulty persuading his divisional chiefs to lead troops against Kumpati and few of the eastern Dagomba chiefs took part in the campaign, which lasted about seven years. Finally, Andani Sigili, chief of Kpoge, with the assistance of the Yo-Na (chief of Savelugu), killed Kumpati. Zangina was remembered by the Dagomba as 'the man who loosed the ropes from their necks' (Andani Sigili succeeded him as Ya-Na).[32]

Zangina is also remembered as the king who brought Islam into Dagomba (having, according to some accounts, travelled as a trader to Timbuktu and Hausaland as a young man). Islamisation was no doubt assisted by the location of Yendi on the trade route from Salaga to Kano. Although

5

Phyllis Ferguson sees the introduction of Islam as marking the start of 'the Second Kingdom' of Dagomba, Islam was by no means universally adopted, even at court: the generality of Dagombas remained pagan and the Ya-Na himself never developed into a theocrat. Indeed, his regalia and the ritual surrounding his office kept a substantial pagan element.[33] The significance of the Na's conversion was that it entailed the attachment of Muslim officials (*limamnema*) to the court at Yendi and to the courts of lesser chiefs. The *limam* could be a powerful figure in the court not only because of his spiritual authority but also because, as Northcott wrote, 'he is able to read and write, and etiquette forbids that any member of the royal family should compass these accomplishments'.[34]

Another contribution of Islam to Dagomba culture is said to have been the wearing of clothes. The 'drum history' records this innovation: 'At that time everyone wore skins as clothing. When Zangina became chief, he went to the Mosque at Sabali and prayed that God might grant the Dagomba clothing. It was thereafter that God enabled the Dagombas to know the art of weaving clothing.'[35]

Very soon after the Gonjas had been expelled from Dagomba, the kingdom became subject to raids from Ashanti. These raids may have been spread over a period of as much as fifty years (as Fage suggests).[36] They culminated in an episode which reveals the same kind of internal disunity as had been evident in the Gonja wars. The chief of Kpatina, Ziblim (a son of Andani Sigili and grandson of Zangina on his mother's side) is alleged to have invited the Ashanti to attack Na Gariba. Gariba, deserted by all the major western Dagomba chiefs, was captured by an Ashanti army and was to have been taken to Kumasi. However, he was released en route, at Yeji, following an appeal by some of the Dagomba princes.[37] In return, the Ya-Nas were required to send a fixed number of slaves, cattle, sheep, and some cloth to Kumasi each year.[38] In addition, an Ashanti representative was stationed at Yendi. The payments continued irregularly until 1874, when they ceased with the decline of Ashanti power.

There was thus a period of perhaps 130 years during which Ashanti was a strong influence in Dagomba. Historians disagree about the strength and character of this influence. Wilks and Fage have said that it amounted to the creation of a protectorate, the payments being a form of tribute; Tamakloe described Dagomba as a 'vassal state'.[39] Not surprisingly, the Dagomba 'drum history' minimises Ashanti influence, declaring that the incident of the capture and release of Gariba 'was the only occasion that the Dagombas came under the Ashantis', though it admits that payments to Kumasi continued for some years.[40]

Duncan-Johnstone and, more recently, Iliasu have argued that the Ashanti influence was more limited and symbolic and that the relationship between the states was mutually beneficial. Duncan-Johnstone reported that 'the Ashanti always treated Dagbon with respect as a powerful kingdom although tributary to their King'.[41] Iliasu sees the relationship as one of 'politico-economic symbiosis rather than conquest'. In his view, the

Asantehene did not interfere with the internal affairs of Dagomba and the payments made were not 'tribute' but rather instalments of the ransom paid for the return of Gariba. Iliasu further remarks that the Ashanti presence was 'highly profitable to both sides'.[42] Yendi was on the north-eastern caravan route which became more important in the late eighteenth and nineteenth centuries (the result of troubles disrupting trade on the route via Kong).

Contemporary descriptions seem to confirm Iliasu's interpretation. Dupuis, writing in the 1820s, commented: 'Yandy forms no part of the [Ashanti] empire, but it is true that Ashantee influence carries great weight in the councils of the sovereign of Dagomba.'[43] Bowdich, travelling at the same period, gave a vivid, if second-hand, picture of Dagomba:

Yahndi is described to be beyond comparison larger than Coomassie, the houses much better built and ornamented. The Ashantees who had visited it told me they frequently lost themselves in the streets ... The markets of Yahndi are described as animated scenes of commerce, constantly crowded with merchants from almost all the countries of the interior. Horses and cattle abound, and immense flocks are possessed even by the poorer class.[44]

Bowdich saw Dagomba's submission to Ashanti as the result of intelligent calculation:

As it was, [the Ashantis] still respected her resources, and were content to secure him [the Ya-Na] as a tributary. A triumph of policy was in the view of the King of Dagwumba, equivalent to the small diminution of personal dignity; and at the expense of an inconsiderable tribute, he established a commercial intercourse which, his markets being regularly supplied from the interior, was both an advantage and a security to him.[45]

For the internal politics of Dagomba, one consequence of Ashanti influence was the creation of a wing of Ashanti-trained musketeers within the state army. It is unclear whether these musketeers (*kambonse* in Dagbane) were originally trained in Kumasi or were trained in Yendi by Ashanti 'technical assistance'. In either case, the result was the formation of five chieftaincies (the *kambon naanema*), within which the titles of offices and organisations show marked Ashanti influence – the chiefs, for example, sitting upon stools rather than the skins used by Dagomba chiefs.[46]

While the establishment of the *kambonse* obviously increased the military power of Dagomba, it also added another potential force for instability. The *kambonse* became notoriously independent-minded and could easily have developed the role of a Praetorian Guard manipulated by factions within the royal family.

The Ashanti presence seems to have stimulated such factionalism. Iliasu suggests that the annual tribute was a significant factor in factional competition and remarks on

the immense opportunities the annual payments afforded for intrigues against the paramountcy. Unsuccessful candidates to the paramountcy, chiefs and princes who desired to court favour in Kumasi and others who, for a variety of reasons, wanted to score points against the paramount chief, invariably sneaked out to Kumasi where, with little difficulty, they were able to persuade the Asantehene to be more assiduous in demanding slaves from Yendi.[47]

The nineteenth century

On at least one occasion in the nineteenth century, intervention came about in exactly this way[48] and in general Dagomba was seriously affected by the movement of events further south. After 1874 Ashanti control of its hinterland declined. This decline, though relieving the Yendi authorities of the obligation to send tribute, removed the imperial protection which traders had enjoyed. Ashanti merchants and officials were killed or imprisoned and both Salaga and Yendi lost their prestige as commercial towns.[49] By 1890 there was apparently no security on the route from Ouagadougou to Salaga, as Binger reported: 'The chiefs are extremely rapacious. The traders frequently alter the routes they use ... the wisest course to take is to get on good terms with the strongest tribes, this is the only way of getting through.'[50]

The British had tried to supplant Ashanti as a southern trading partner for Dagomba and to this end a Travelling Commissioner, Dr Gouldsbury, had visited Yendi in 1876. But, though the Ya-Na was willing to arrange for the dispatch of ivory to the coast, Ashanti power was still sufficient to stop the establishment of a really substantial trade by-passing Kumasi.[51]

Politically, the middle and late nineteenth century was a period of endemic dispute in Dagomba.[52] The character of the disputes will be examined in the next chapter, since they are only intelligible when related to an analysis of the dynamics of pre-colonial politics and are certainly of no intrinsic interest, being complex and often quite obscure.

Broadly, what seems to have happened was a weakening of the authority of the Ya-Na over his divisional chiefs. Phyllis Ferguson and Ivor Wilks argue that the intensification of conflict over the Yendi skin in fact reflected a rise in the prestige of the office, caused by the development of a court bureaucracy which provided 'a new and powerful executive instrument' for the paramount.[53] Certainly there was no real suggestion in any of the disputes of a movement in favour of partitioning the kingdom. But on several occasions the Ya-Na went to war with divisional chiefs over disputed successions and one Ya-Na was killed by a rival from another branch of the royal family.[54] Further, many of the wars arose from princes seizing chiefdoms, without or against the authority of the Ya-Na.

In a system of indeterminate succession, such as obtained in Dagomba, the king was almost bound to act as a partisan in quarrels over succession. For in most cases his own side of the royal family would have some interest in the settlement – some hope of gain, however trivial, or some fear of loss, however remote. It does, however, seem that contests were more frequent in the nineteenth century and that the divisional chiefs were readier than before to defy their paramount.

The instability of nineteenth-century Dagomba may have been partly due to the withdrawal of Ashanti, though, as noted above, the relationship with Kumasi could as well undermine the paramount as reinforce him. Another factor was the availability of mercenaries. Probably in the early 1860s, Ya-Na Abudulai began to employ a number of Zabarima horsemen from the region of Fada N'Gourma in Upper Volta, to help in capturing people to make up the annual consignment of slaves for the Asantehene.[55] According to Cardinall, the Zabarima were difficult to get rid of. They eventually settled to the north of Dagomba, in the 'Gurunsi' area, where they continued raiding.[56] From time to time, says Cardinall, 'their services were in request by petty Chiefs of the Dagomba or Moshi blood who were endeavouring to set themselves up in the old way'.[57] 'The old way' was the use of force in defiance of Yendi and the rulings it imposed. It was a procedure sanctioned by many precedents, though obviously not one formally embodied in tradition.

Fish from the sea

Shielded by Ashanti from the coast, the rulers of Dagomba knew little about Europeans until the 1890s, when German, French, and British expeditions began criss-crossing over their territory, bringing with them flags, treaties, and offers of protection. Their innocence persisted until the very day of military defeat, 4 December 1896, when a Dagomba army of 7,000 was routed by a tiny German force of 100, at Adibo, south of Yendi. Ya-Na Andani had told his soldiers to go out and capture the Europeans, encouraging them with the words, '*Sereminga yi-la kuom-na, o-nye la zaham*' ('The white man is come from the water, he is a fish').[58] On 5 December the Germans marched into Yendi and burnt it; the Ya-Na himself was smuggled out of the town and went into hiding.

The Germans had first laid claim to Togo in 1884, when Nachtigal landed near Lomé and declared a protectorate. Their occupation was accepted by the other powers and, unlike the French in Dahomey and the British on the Gold Coast, their progress was not impeded by a powerful African state behind the coastline. In 1886, and again in 1888, German expeditions were sent north. The first, under Krause, passed through Savelugu in July 1886 on its way to Ouagadougou, and the second, led by Captain von François, visited Yendi, Salaga, Gambaga, Karaga, and Nanton between March and May 1888, getting the chiefs to accept German protection.[59]

Unfortunately for von François, his own government had by this time reached agreement with the British for the establishment of a 'neutral zone' in the area. The zone was to extend northward from the Daka–White Volta confluence as far as 10°N. and westward from 0°33'E. as far as 1°27'W. Within these limits the powers agreed 'to abstain from acquiring protectorates or exclusive influence'. This 'neutral zone' survived, in principle, until 1899.[60]

The next move came from the British. Under pressure from commercial interests at home, the Government in 1892 authorised the dispatch of a mission, led by G. E. Ferguson, to arrange treaties with the 'native authorities' in Dagomba, Gonja, 'Gurunsi', and Mossi. The treaties were mainly commercial in character. In 1894 Ferguson was sent north again and he arrived in Yendi on 17 August. Ferguson reported that conditions in the north were unsettled:'In all the countries mentioned, there are frequent civil wars between rival claimants for regal ascendancy ... In many cases, however, they are willing to submit their feuds to arbitration ... the numerous princes who seize goods from traders are a pest to the community and put restrictions on trade.'[61] The question of trade also arose in his advice to the Governor on dealings with the Germans. Concerned about suggestions of a partition of the 'neutral zone', he remarked: 'Considering the political condition of the people, the arrangement is unfavourable to the civilization of our Hinterland ... The strip of country which is owned by Dagomba and Bimbla [sc. Nanumba] between the eastern boundary of the Neutral Zone and the Oti River, is of the greatest strategic importance.'[62] Ferguson warned that concessions to Germany might result in the cutting of communications between the Gold Coast and British territories on the Niger and would give the Germans command of 'the principal caravan route from the Hausa countries to Salaga and the neutral zone'.

During the next eighteen months two more German expeditions visited Yendi. In December 1894 the Ya-Na accepted protection from Germany (adding to that he already had from the British) and in February 1896 von Carnap-Quernheimb passed directly across the neutral zone to Gambaga.[63] Although he was recalled following protests from London, it was clear that a partition was imminent. Negotiations between the two powers on a possible boundary (leaving Yendi to Germany and Salaga to Britain) had broken down in November 1895.

The final impetus to partition was provided by the occupation of Kumasi in January 1896. Worried by the German expeditions (and by a French mission which had crossed from Dahomey to Kong in the Ivory Coast in 1895), the Colonial Office decided on an effective occupation of the Ashanti hinterland.[64] The partition finally took place in a rush at the end of 1896, with British, French, and German expeditions converging on the neutral zone in the last weeks of December. The German force, under Gruner and von Massow, moved up from Kete-Krachi, defeated the Dagomba at Adibo, and then went on to occupy Sansanne-Mango before a French mission could get there. The French arrived too late, on Christmas Day. But when a German detachment moved on to Gambaga, they in turn found that a British expedition under Captain Stewart had arrived there before them.[65] The French withdrew to the east, while Stewart entertained the German commander over Christmas.

For the Dagomba, however, the agony continued throughout 1897. A band of Zabarima, under Babatu, entered Dagomba from the north, having been pushed south by French and British troops. The Zabarima joined forces with a number of western Dagomba princes who were in revolt against Ya-Na Andani – the latter having taken the view that his allegiance to Ashanti must be transferred to the British, as conquerors of Ashanti. An extended campaign began between the British occupying forces and the dissidents, the Dagomba villages of Pigu, Singa, and Karaga being destroyed in the course of 1897 and 1898.[66] Finally, as Tamakloe writes, 'The insurgents . . . ran away [from Karaga] through some Gushiago villages into Yendi – where the Zabarimas now settled peacefully, built houses and farmed for their maintenance.'[67]

In 1899 the occupying powers met to tidy up frontiers. The major concern of the British seems to have been that of securing the entire Mamprussi area. Chamberlain agreed to a boundary running north from the Daka–White Volta confluence as far as 9°N., its course thereafter to follow on-the-spot settlement by a mixed commission of British and German officials. The actual convention, signed on 14 November 1899, provided that the frontier should be drawn 'in such a manner that Gambaga and all the territories of Mamprussi shall fall to Great Britain, and that Yendi and all the territories of Chakosi shall fall to Germany'.[68]

This arrangement was apparently disappointing to the German colonial interest, which (according to Cornevin) felt that the British had got the better deal, with all of Gonja, Salaga, and the greater part of Dagomba going to their side.[69] The British government had in fact got less than its original demand, which included the Chokosi territory.

But the Ya-Na had had his kingdom sliced in half. As Chamberlain remarked: 'It will be seen that the boundary proposed . . . will divide the Dagomba country in two parts, of which the western portion would be British, while the eastern one (including the chief town, Yendi) would be German.'[70]

On the German side, the partition was followed by the establishment of a post at Yendi in 1901 and the incorporation of eastern Dagomba into the Sansanne-Mango administrative division. Also in 1901, the British established, by Order-in-Council, 'the Protectorate of the Northern Territories' under a Chief Commissioner answerable to the Governor of the Gold Coast.[71] The Northern Territories were divided into three provinces, North-Eastern, North-Western, and Southern: the latter consisted of three districts, Eastern Gonja, Western Gonja, and Western Dagomba (also known as Tamale District). The Dagomba District was to comprise 'all lands subject to the Divisional Dagomba Chiefs of Savelugu and Karaga and to the Gonja Chiefs of Kawsaw, Daboya, and Busunu'.

Colonial rule lasted in the Dagomba area for fifty-six more years and underwent two major rearrangements. The first was the reunification of the German and British sections after World War I. Under the terms of the Milner–Simon Agreement of July 1919, the British were given Eastern Dagomba (and other parts of ex-German Togo) under League of Nations mandate and were given permission to administer the northern areas as integral parts of the Northern Territories Protectorate.

The second rearrangement involved the introduction of indirect rule in

11

the thirties. Initially the Yendi mandate section was administered as a separate district, the Eastern Dagomba District, but from 1932 there was a single Dagomba District, with headquarters at Yendi and with boundaries which were made to fit as closely as possible those of the kingdom. The shift to indirect rule led also to the establishment of a Dagomba Native Authority, presided over by the Ya-Na, and of Subordinate Native Authorities, headed by divisional chiefs. Direct taxation was imposed in the late thirties, so as to provide a financial basis for 'native self-government'.

'Indirect rule' officially died in 1952, when nine Local Councils and a Dagomba District Council were set up in accordance with the Local Government Ordinance of 1951. In 1953/4 the elective principle was extended beyond local government and five single-member constituencies were created for elections to the Legislative Assembly in Accra. Shortly after independence Dagomba became part of the Northern Region of Ghana and political appointees replaced Europeans at regional and district levels.

With this general overview of the physical, demographic, and historical background of Dagomba in mind, we may now examine in more detail the social and political structure of the kingdom.

CHAPTER 2

DAGBON

> Idleness and frivolous gatherings around the king or a chief to
> prattle and to 'flatter' him seem to be the delight and duty of the
> nobility in the eyes of the Dagbambas, so much so that in Yendi,
> any grown-up men are all chiefs in their own estimation . . . unless
> a stern regime prevails, these frivolous noblemen would remain
> truculent and mock at authority.[1]

This chapter is concerned with the structure and dynamics of Dagomba
politics in the pre-colonial age. As an exercise in reconstructing 'traditional'
society, it is liable to produce an excessively rigid and formalised model,
since it is so hard to distinguish in retrospect between what was important
and what was trivial and flexible. Further, although the intervening period
of colonial rule did bring about a great increase in foreigners' knowledge
of pre-colonial government, the 'conservationism' practised by some
administrators led to a certain fossilisation of 'traditional' politics, to a
mummification of the body politic in a wrapping of ethnography. The
'indirect rulers' sometimes killed the thing they loved: that is, they destroyed
the essential dynamics of 'archaic' societies by heavily administered efforts
to preserve formal institutions and procedures. For, as Peter Lloyd writes,
'In the colonial territory and the modern independent state it is often the
rituals and ceremonies which have survived, while the traditional decision-
making processes have been irrevocably changed.'[2]

In depicting Dagomba political organisation we are immediately involved
in conceptual problems which are familiar to political anthropologists.
Among these problems are the definition and isolation of 'the political
sphere' and the characterisation of the traditional state.

In most societies, and particularly in African societies, it is difficult
to distinguish 'the political sphere' at all rigorously, because of the over-
lapping of roles, the multi-functional nature of institutions, and (in some
African cases) the lack of specialised structures of government. Fortunately,
Dagomba society has at least had a clear, formalised structure of authority,
giving rise to relations of the kind that Maquet describes as 'political' –
those involving 'command-sanctioned-by-coercion'.[3] It is this structure
which is concerned with what most authorities would accept as the basic
political functions: the defence of the society against external threats; the
assurance of internal order by the formulation and enforcement of law
(which in turn depends upon an ultimate monopoly of force); and 'the
control and coordination of those activities deemed to affect the welfare

of the society as a whole or large sections within it'.[4] Those controlling such a structure will also have to make provision for the material sustenance of government and will normally see to its legitimation among its subjects (although Maquet argues that such legitimacy is 'a secondary phenomenon' which is not intrinsic to the maintenance of government).[5]

On closer examination, we shall see that the Dagomba structure justifies the label 'state'. It possessed territorial sovereignty; it had 'a centralised machinery of government' undertaking the maintenance of law and order; and it manifested 'the existence of a specialised privileged ruling group or class separated from the main body of the population'.[6] Its characteristics were, of course, more specifically those of a kingdom ('a sovereign political group, headed by a single leader who delegates authority to representatives in charge of the territorial units into which the country is divided').[7]

We shall now consider, in turn, the social structure of Dagomba, the offices, procedures, and functions of the state, the resources upon which it depended, and the tensions and crises to which the political system was prone.

THE SOCIAL ORDER

Like many kingdoms, Dagomba originated, as we have seen, in conquest. The result was the imposition of a ruling class upon the indigenous population, which became the commoner estate (*dagbandaba*). This class has remained distinct in several respects. With the exception of the elders and some chieftaincies held by descendants of the earth priests (*tindamba*), political office is monopolised by descendants of the invaders. The lineage structures of the two classes are somewhat different; and the ruling class is more Islamised than the commoner estate. But there has certainly been intermarriage and, although the chiefly class dresses more grandly than the commoners, there is little visible evidence of the existence of separate strata. Indeed, it seems to have taken the British a long time to realise that 'the Dagomba' were not homogeneous.

Dagomba society, high and low, is based on a patrilineal system of kinship.[8] The ruling class has a concept of bilateral descent which may be invoked for some purposes or in certain contexts, but not usually as a basis for claims to chieftaincy. The household (*yili*) is made up of two or more men, related agnatically, with their wives and other dependants: that is, father and son (or sons), grandfather with married son (or sons), or brothers with their dependants. The senior man acts as household head (*yili yidana*) and in this role exercises authority in such matters as agricultural work, negotiations over marriage, and prayer to the ancestors.[9]

The household is part of a wider patrilineal unit, the maximal lineage, defined by Manoukian as 'the most extensive group of individuals tracing descent from a single common ancestor'.[10] Normally, descent would be traced back over eight or ten generations. The components of the maximal lineage have their own heads and may on occasion act as independent units, subject to the overall authority of the senior lineage head.[11] The latter undertakes arbitration in disputes, but otherwise has only functions of ritual and moral leadership. In the ruling class, the kinship group involves descent traced through relations on both maternal and paternal sides, the male and female children of one grandfather or great-grandfather. This unit of 'bilateral descending kindred' (known as the *dang*) is usually no more than four generations deep. Within such a system, an individual may be a member of up to four kindreds, none of which is likely to be confined to one village or town. But while claims to succession in chieftaincy are sometimes founded on maternal connections, the normal practice in this respect is to follow the strict agnatic line (*zuliya*) and to prefer those favoured by it.[12]

A Dagomba village typically consists of quite closely grouped circular compounds, with the chief's domed hut standing out above the rest. The village is divided into wards (*fona*, sing. *fong*), each being identified by its head or by the specialist group dominating it. There may be a chief's quarter (*nayilifong*), an imam's quarter (*limamfong*), a quarter for the soldiers, one for the butchers, another for the drummers, and so on. The commoner population distributes itself throughout the village, not being concerned in the distinctions of status indicated by the naming of wards, and there is no physical segregation of the commoners from the ruling class, though there is a clear protocol governing access to the chief and the treatment of his relatives.

The village was, materially, a 'global society', depending on the 'compound farms' encircling it and the bush farms, up to several miles away, kept by each family.[13] Most of the work on the farms was done by the younger men of the family, the women helping with the harvest and threshing. For tasks which needed a bigger supply of labour (such as the building of yam mounds and the harvesting of crops), the family head could get assistance from other men in the village or from outside. Such labour was paid for with food and drink (generally the local beer, *pito*).[14]

Land was controlled by the *tindamba* (earth priests), each of whom had authority over a particular area. The *tindana* sanctioned the use of land and received in return an annual tithe with which he acquired sheep for sacrifice to the spirit of the land.[15] He does not seem to have had secular political functions: as Eyre-Smith writes, 'His was a purely spiritual office. He was not a ruler but a priest, a mediator between the people and their god.'[16] The title to land given by the *tindana* was normally permanent, being heritable within the family. It provided use but not ownership of the land: the concept of land as an alienable commodity was unknown to the 'black Dagomba'.[17]

With the conquest in the fifteenth century, the right to dispose of land was claimed as the prerogative of the Ya-Na and it was in principle delegated to the divisional and village chiefs. In reality, a complementary relationship seems to have grown up in many places between the old *tindamba* and the new rulers. The village chief was, politically, an agent of the paramount and of his divisional chief, and the majority of his functions were administrative and judicial. The *tindana*, as a fetish priest, continued to perform sacrifices and to care for shrines recognised as those of the spirits of the land. He would be provided with food and with animals for sacrifice by the chief. Moreover, the *tindana* still controlled the apportionment of land, as H. A. Blair (the most knowledgeable of British D.C.s in Dagomba) remarked:

> Right of control is vested in the Ya-Na, for the decision of boundary dispute between Chiefs, but not for the apportionment of land outside Yendi sub-division. Similarly sub-divisional Chiefs have no right to apportion land to persons except within their own towns ... The Chief does not grant farming land to individuals. He is considered not to have any right of control over farms ... *Tindamba* have still power over Chiefs and are feared.[18]

A similar duality can be found in religious beliefs. The social structure of Dagomba was sustained by religious sanctions which reportedly were particularly strict in regard to rights of seniority in the lineage and to all matters affecting the dignity of ancestors.[19] Animism and the cult of ancestors thus permeated Dagomba culture, but they were partially complemented or supplanted by Islam. More recently, the 1960 census indicated that 42 per cent of Dagombas were animists and 53 per cent Muslims.[20] But it is clear that Islam is still strongest in the towns and at the courts of the king and his chiefs: it has not penetrated village culture to the same extent, and even within the ruling class the two forms co-exist and blend. It is, obviously, impossible to assess the strength of religious belief as a framework of social behaviour, at least insofar as many acts explained locally as due to 'fear of the gods' can be explained alternatively by reference to values which, superficially, lack religious sanction – concern with social disgrace, fear of losing patronage, or ambition for office. Certainly, the 'drum history' gives evidence of a surprising pragmatism with regard to the fetish and its demands.[21]

THE DAGOMBA STATE

The sovereignty of the Dagomba state was vested in the person of the Ya-Na, resident in Yendi. He was the commander of the Dagomba army; he was the highest judicial authority; he appointed chiefs and elders, who conducted the administration of the state. The Ya-Na was also lineage head of the dynasty, head of the royal patriclan, and a figure surrounded by rituals of avoidance and deference.

Under the monarch lay several hierarchies of chiefdoms and a complex network of dynastic politics. The kingdom was divided into three provinces, Karaga, Mion, and Savelugu, ruled by royal 'dukes'. There were also smaller units, the twelve divisions, ruled by the dukes, other senior royals, or independent commoner chiefs. Each division in turn consisted of a number of villages, each village having a chief under (or, as the British liked to put it, 'following') the divisional chief.

The various categories of chieftaincy are examined in greater detail below, but it is important to mention here the ground rules of office-holding, since these rules provided the framework of dynastic politics, affecting the king and his subordinates. Perhaps the most distinctive feature of Dagomba chieftaincy was its system of promotion. Young men of the blood royal usually started on the ladder of promotion by appointment to small villages, moving upwards until they reached divisional capitals and ultimately, if they were qualified and fortunate, the paramount chieftaincy itself. Promotion and competition for office were limited above all by one rule: that no man could rise higher than his own father. The most important implication of this rule was that only the sons of a Ya-Na could become Ya-Na. But, of course, this provision did not eliminate competition: it merely structured the field. There were always several qualified candidates, even for Yendi. For all chieftaincies under Yendi the choice ultimately lay in the discretion of the paramount: even the highest degree of eligibility did not confer the *right* to a skin.[22]

At any time numerous members of the royal family were engaged at different levels in the pursuit of advancement and the search for preferment. Each hoped to reach his 'terminus', as defined by his father's ultimate rank. The prospects of his own sons were involved with, indeed dependent on, his success: the rank and honour of the line were thus at stake in each generation. So, while Yendi was the prize *par excellence*, others were as vital to more junior royals.

Moreover, although the target was fixed individually for each candidate, he did not necessarily seek it in isolation. Kinship and patronage provided the bases of alliance and opposition. The selection of a Ya-Na affected the outcome of various other contests, at divisional level or even at an obscure village level. The higher chiefs often had relatives or protégés engaged in struggles for minor chieftaincies. Every contest or dispute was thus kaleidoscopic, revealing on closer study an apparent infinity of patterns, perspectives, highlights, and shades.

The politics of chieftaincy were further complicated by the existence of interests and offices outside the royal family. There were divisional and village chieftaincies held by commoners (generally descendants of the captains and ministers of earlier kings). These, too, were objects of competition and were also in the gift of the king. There were also the offices of the various councillors, not only to the Ya-Na but to the divisional and village chiefs as well. For every chief had a court, a group of elders, warriors, and attendants, which moved with him as he made his way along the *cursus honorum*. The elders were commoners, but in certain cases they could appoint to chieftaincies or themselves be appointed. They had (as we shall see) immense power at court, as advisers, judges, and patrons. Patronage was, indeed, one of the resources which fuelled and sustained the Dagomba political system: others, making up the economic substructure of the state, will be considered towards the end of the chapter, when we examine the dynamics of Dagomba politics.

(a) Succession

Since the foundation of Dagbon, there have been over thirty paramounts. We shall use here the most recent sequence, established by Phyllis Ferguson, which varies only in minor details from earlier lists provided by Tamakloe and Tait.[23] According to Fage's calculations, the average length of reign is roughly fourteen and a half years.[24] Between 1900 and 1967 there were five kings: the longest reign was seventeen years, the shortest five, and the average was 12.2 years (allowing for interregna – one of which lasted for three years).

All Ya-Nas have been descendants in the male line from Sitobu and Nyagse: all have been sons of Ya-Nas. But this does not mean that every Ya-Na has been succeeded by his eldest son.[25] Since the death of Na Zirile, there have been only nine cases in which a Ya-Na has been followed directly by his eldest son and twelve in which younger brothers have succeeded.[26] In the remaining cases, the skin has passed to collaterals (nine cousins of different degrees, five nephews, and one uncle). When there has been conflict over succession, it has generally been between, on the one hand, the deceased's younger brothers and, on the other, sons of the deceased or of previously deceased elder brothers – in other words, the Shakespearian pattern of uncle versus nephew or cousin, but rarely brother versus brother.[27]

In confronting the universal problem of succession, the Dagomba have adopted formulae which, while limiting competition (and therefore vulnerability to conflict and instability), still leave an element of uncertainty and a capacity for choice. Like any other system, the Dagomba system manifests characteristic crises and patterns of conflict.[28] In order to minimise the disturbance caused by conflicts within the dynasty, the Dagomba had to develop rules which both imposed stricter limits on eligibility and allotted to non-royals the responsibility for making the selection. Such rules became necessary quite soon, for after a few generations in power the consequences of polygyny made themselves felt, in the form of large numbers of eligible sons.[29] As Goody points out, this problem is common to many dynasties:

In agnatic systems ... the effects of polygynous marriage can mean a rapid growth of the dynasty over a very few generations ... Such growth complicates the process of selection, because the larger the number of eligibles the more difficult they are to handle. Where the support of such a large dynasty is not required, one solution is to lop off the unwanted branches ... Homicide apart, the dynasty can only be cut down in size by shedding whole segments (i.e. lineages) whose claim to the throne has now become distant.[30]

TABLE 1   *Ya-Nas, 1500–1974*

Name	Entitlement	Relationship to predecessor	Dates (approximate)
1. NYAGSE	Son of Na Sitobu	Son	
2. ZULANDE	Son of Na Nyagse	Son	
3. NAGALOGU	Son of Na Zulande	Son ⎫	
4. DATORLI	Son of Na Zulande	Brother ⎬	
5. BURUGUYOMDA	Son of Na Zulande	Brother ⎭	
6. ZOLIGU	Son of Na Datorli	Nephew	
7. ZONMAN	Son of Na Zoligu	Son ⎫	
8. NINMITONI	Son of Na Zoligu	Brother ⎪	
9. DIMANI	Son of Na Zoligu	Brother ⎬	
10. YANZO	Son of Na Zoligu	Brother ⎭	
11. DARIZIEGU	Son of Na Zonman	Nephew	
12. LURO	Son of Na Zoligu	Uncle	*c.* 1660
13. TUTUGRI	Son of Na Luro	Son ⎫	
14. ZAGALE	Son of Na Luro	Brother ⎪	
15. ZOKULI	Son of Na Luro	Brother ⎬	
16. GUNGOBILI	Son of Na Luro	Brother ⎭	
17. ZANGINA	Son of Na Tutugri	Nephew	*c.* 1700
18. ANDANI SIGILI	Son of Na Zagale	Cousin	
19. ZIBLIM BUNBIOGO	Son of Na Zangina	Second cousin ⎫	
20. GARIBA	Son of Na Zangina	Brother ⎬	*c.* 1740
21. ZIBLIM NA SAA	Son of Na Andani Sigili	Third cousin	
22. ZIBLIM BANDAMDA	Son of Na Gariba	Fourth cousin ⎫	
23. ANDANI	Son of Na Gariba	Brother ⎬	
24. MAHAMA	Son of Na Ziblim Bandamda	Nephew	
25. ZIBLIM KULUNKU	Son of Na Andani	Cousin	*c.* 1820
26. SUMANI ZOLI	Son of Na Mahama	Second cousin	
27. YAKUBA	Son of Na Andani	Second cousin	*c.* 1850
28. ABUDULAI	Son of Na Yakuba	Son ⎫	
29. ANDANI II	Son of Na Yakuba	Brother ⎬	*d.* 1899
30. DARIMANI (KUKRA ADJEI)	Son of Na Yakuba	Brother ⎭	1899 (deposed)
31. ALHASSAN	Son of Na Abudulai	Nephew	1900–17
32. ABUDULAI II	Son of Na Alhassan	Son	1920–38
33. MAHAMA II	Son of Na Andani	Second cousin	1938–48
34. MAHAMA III	Son of Na Alhassan	Second cousin	1948–53
35. ABUDULAI III	Son of Na Mahama III	Son	1953–67
36. ANDANI III	Son of Na Mahama II	Distant cousin	1968–9
37. MOHAMADU ABUDULAI IV	Son of Na Abudulai III	Distant cousin (son, if Andani III ineligible)	1969–74

NOTE: Darimani (30) and Andani III (36) are disputed. Some accounts list Mahama (24) as successor to Ziblim Bandamda (22), instead of Andani, and cite a Ya-Na Sumani as immediate predecessor of Andani. For this and other details of royal chronology, see Ferguson (1973), pp. 3–17, and Benzing (1971), pp. 214–15.

The rule that sons only could succeed served to some extent the function of 'dynastic shedding': whole lines were cut out by the failure of their heads to secure the Yendi skin. But the problem of succession nevertheless quickly became acute and it was therefore necessary further to distinguish between royals who might be eligible for Yendi and others who would be eligible for lesser chieftaincies (i.e. to create a nobility). For even the category of royal sons was becoming uncomfortably large. For example, all five of Na Zoligu's sons succeeded to Yendi and they had all together twenty sons: again, five became king and they produced thirty-one sons.

Not surprisingly, after another generation there was a crisis. On the death of Na Gungobili, there were nine contestants (eight of them sons of Na Tutugri and one, Andani Sigili, a son of Na Zagale). As Duncan-Johnstone and Blair write: 'All the *Na-bihe* [royal sons] . . . wished to succeed and no decision could be arrived at.'[31]

It seems that the elders preferred Zangina, but he was the youngest of the candidates and had no title, whereas at least two of his elder brothers were divisional chiefs. Fearing civil war if they appointed Zangina, the elders referred the selection to the Na-yiri, paramount of the Mamprussi: 'The elders having secretly sent messengers to the King of the Mamprussis in Nalerigu to inform him of their opinion, begged him to act in their favour, and advised the contending claimants to defer their claims to the King of Mamprussi.'[32] According to the 'drum history', the Na-yiri staged a competition between the claimants, each being required to prove his wisdom by the choice of a proverb. Tamakloe says that considerable bribes were given by the candidates (including Zangina who, according to Phyllis Ferguson, had in his previous career as a trader 'accumulated sufficient capital virtually to buy his way into the *nam* against all opposition').[33] In any case, the Na-yiri chose Zangina, the youngest contestant.

More important than his actual choice of candidate was the Na-yiri's alleged edict concerning selection for the Yendi skin. This edict limited the range of eligibles to those already occupying three 'gate' skins. To be a candidate for Yendi, a royal had first to be Karaga-Na, Yo-Na (divisional chief of Savelugu), or Mion-lana: only occupants of these skins could be considered. All authorities agree that these were the skins selected as 'gates' and on the whole the rule has been followed.[34] Thus, of the last ten paramounts, eight were occupants of one of the three gate skins immediately before their accession. The other two were regents, who succeeded in circumstances to be considered later in the book.

There does not seem to have been any dispute about the identity of the gate skins, although it has recently been asserted that the regency itself constitutes a fourth gate. One problem, however, has been that of whether there is an order of precedence of the royal 'dukes', one having a superior right to succeed to Yendi. Some writers and participants hold that the Mion-lana is the senior of the three. Manoukian, citing David Tait as her authority, argues that 'the choice commonly falls on the Mionglana, who is, in fact, the heir presumptive'.[35] Certainly, five of the last ten paramounts

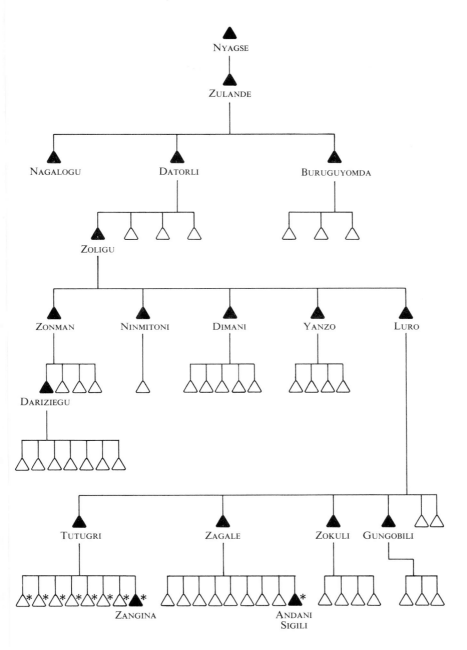

* Candidate for succession after death of Na Gungobili

▲ Ya-Na

Fig. 1. Royal genealogy from Na Nyagse to Na Zangina

21

have come directly from Mion; two came from Savelugu, and one from Karaga. But these figures do not necessarily reveal the operation of a rule of precedence: there could be other ways of explaining the frequency of transition from Mion to Yendi.

Those supporting the right of the Mion chief claim, however, that he has a specific prerogative which invariably gives him the right to Yendi. The prerogative in question is that of supervising the funerals of Ya-Nas. According to a Dagomba sociologist, Dassana Iddi, 'the one chief occupying a gate skin who is responsible [for carrying out the funeral] is the Mion-lana. Customarily the chief who performs the Ya-Na's funeral becomes the next man on the skin.'[36] Iddi further states that usually the Mion skin was occupied by the eldest son: the right of the Mion-lana and that of the eldest son thus generally coincided.[37] But there have been occasions when the eldest son was not Mion-lana at the time of his father's death. In these circumstances, the normal practice has been for the Mion-lana to succeed and for the eldest son to move on to the vacant Mion skin, in anticipation of succeeding next time. Finally, Iddi argues, the Mion-lana's seniority is demonstrated by the fact that he, alone of the gate chiefs, comes to Yendi to act as protector of the kingdom during an interregnum.[38]

There has been no persistent claim for seniority on behalf of the Karaga-Na and Yo-Na – although the present Karaga-Na, Adam, told Iddi that he had precedence over the others and that the Mion-lana was 'the youngest of us'.[39] The Yo-Na, equally, does not admit that the Mion-lana has any special rights. Perhaps all one can say is that, on the whole, the Mion-lana is more likely than his peers to become Ya-Na; one cannot say with any certainty that there is an active rule which prescribes that he should.

THE YA-NA

(b) Selection

The actual procedure for selecting and enskinning a Ya-Na, though complex, does not seem to have been in dispute until recently. There were, of course, disputes about the rights of candidates to be enskinned, and pressures of various kinds were undoubtedly applied to the selectors. But in present circumstances it is virtually impossible to talk about a 'proper' procedure, since there are conflicts over several crucial elements of selection.[40] Because of these difficulties, I have cast the account which follows in the past tense, although the ceremonies concerned still take place. I have also described the ceremonies in some detail, not only because of their symbolic interest, but also because of the significance they have assumed in the recent dispute.

Generally, as much as a year could elapse between the death of a Ya-Na and the installation of his successor. The death of a paramount was not regarded by the Dagomba as a natural result of ageing; there was a strong tendency to suspect poisoning or witchcraft, inspired by rivals or enemies. For a considerable period after a death, the kingdom was held to be in a state of fallen grace and the processes of nature upset: the land was 'hollow' and the water 'spoilt'. Such disarray continued until a new king was chosen.[41]

During an interregnum Dagomba was initially in the charge of the Kuga-Na, an elder of Yendi, and the Mion-lana. The Kuga-Na made the first proclamation of the death of the king, at the house of a colleague, the Gullana. A more general announcement was made later, also by the elders, once the senior chiefs had been informed and the eldest surviving son had arrived in Yendi.[42] The announcement was phrased euphemistically, since it was taboo to say the king was dead; instead, he was said to have 'gone to the farm'.

At this point, usually about a month after the king's death, the regent (normally the king's eldest son) took over, with the title of *gbonlana* (literally, 'owner of the skin').[43] Within a few days of the death of the king, divination began, in order to establish the identity of the successor. But divination might continue for some months, and the funeral would be postponed until agreement had been reached on the succession.

The choice of a new Ya-Na was entrusted to a group consisting of three elders of Yendi (Kuga-Na, Tuguri-nam, and Gomli), plus the Gushie-Na (the chief of Gushiegu and a senior commoner divisional chief).[44] Only the elders took part in the divination, which involved sacrifice to the spirits of former kings. In principle, it was the latter who chose the new king, although in practice many diviners might be consulted, the elders sometimes shopping around until they could be sure of obtaining an oracular declaration favourable to the candidate they actually preferred. Certainly, they were seen as responsible for finding a chief with appropriate qualities. Thus one elder told Iddi that the spirits tended on the whole to favour the candidate 'whose reign will bring sufficient material gains, one who will feel himself bound by the advice of the elders'.[45] The elders had to discover any physical defect (such as blindness or malformation) which would make a candidate ineligible.

The process of selection was bound up with the cycle of ritual leading to the funeral of the deceased Ya-Na. Any gate chief wishing to 'apply' for the Yendi skin was expected to present (to the king's relatives) a set of objects for burial with the corpse. Presentation of this 'burial kit' (consisting of the skins of a lion and a leopard and clothes in which to dress the body) was regarded as a tacit declaration of the donor's wish to be considered as a successor; and rejection of it was regarded as rejection of his claim.[6] The prerogative of accepting or rejecting these gifts lay with the king's relatives, who also had, at least formally, the right to decide who should perform the funeral.[47] In reality, these powers seem to have provided another way for the elders to influence or even determine the selection of a new paramount.

When divination had been completed, the funeral could be carried out. The ceremony involved the removal of the corpse, upright and dressed, through a hole in the wall of the royal compound to a grave in the royal burial chamber. On the way, the king was 'walked' over the body of a live cow.[48]

The actual burial was accompanied by further sacrificial slaughter and by the ritual cleaning of the king's wives, who were subsequently released from the household, to remarry if they wished. The corpse was washed and dressed; it was then buried along with the leopard's and lion's skins. Food was left in the burial chamber for the dead king and the other royal spirits.

Meanwhile, the elders responsible for selection would meet the Gushie-Na at Sakpiegu, north of Yendi, and confer with him about the succession. The decision they reached would be communicated to the principal divisional chiefs not in line for Yendi and the approval of these chiefs was sought – indeed, it was essential if the new king was not to become involved in civil war. The Gushie-Na then proceeded to Yendi where he rode ceremonially three times around the burial chamber and then entered it, to emerge demonstrating grief. His action was regarded as the final declaration that the previous reign was over and that the regency was also at an end. From the burial chamber, the Gushie-Na went to the royal court (*yili bla*). Here, after a symbolic display of resistance by the royal bodyguard, the Gushie-Na seized three pieces of straw from the palace roof and handed one to the successful candidate. Then the Gushie-Na left Yendi, custom forbidding him to spend the night in the town after indicating the identity of the new king.[49]

The Ya-Na designate was taken to a hut (the *katini duu*) where he was adorned with the insignia of paramountcy – a gown and hat (both said to have belonged to Tohajie), beads, a calabash, a gourd, a club, and a set of spears. Each piece of regalia was guarded by a particular chief or elder as was the royal stool (*gbolon*) on which the king was required to sit three times while in the *katini duu*. Only the elders and chiefs who had already reached their 'termini' were allowed to be present in the hut when the installation was taking place. Subsequently, the new Ya-Na was led to the house of an elder, Zohe-Na, where he was formally kept as a 'prisoner' for a week, during which period Kuga-Na ruled the state. After another few days' staying with Mbadugu (the king's linguist), the Ya-Na was taken to the court where Muslim prayers were said and homage was paid by other chiefs and by commoners, the king sitting on the lion skin of a Ya-Na.[50]

Such seems to have been the usual procedure for the burial of a Ya-Na and the selection and enskinment of his successor. The account is summary. It is also based on other people's investigations and, as a result, it may tend to overformalise the process and exaggerate the ritual element. Nevertheless, it is clear that there was ritual and that the symbolism was like that of many other coronations.

DIVISIONAL AND VILLAGE CHIEFS

The provincial, divisional, and village courts were, in many respects, miniatures of the royal court.[51] Succession to chieftaincy was, however, determined by the king, though nominations to village chieftaincies were generally made by the dukes, subject to the king's approval and to his receiving some of the money paid by candidates. As we noted above, no candidate could ultimately claim the right to a skin, but the eldest son of a former chief was usually recognised as deserving prior consideration. Promotion was, of course, limited by the rule that no man could rise higher than his father, though he had no assurance of ever reaching his father's terminal rank.

Many offices were ranked in seniority and there was even a certain ranking of the three royal provinces. The western province was known as 'Toma' and was ruled from Savelugu by the Yo-Na: it was the largest and reputed to be the richest of the three (Savelugu itself was, indeed, referred to as 'the Yendi of the west' ('Toma-naya')).[52] The next largest was Karaga, Mion being a very small province.[53] The most easterly section of Dagbon (including the predominantly Konkomba divisions) was ruled from Yendi.

Chiefly offices can be classified either in terms of their level in the

TABLE 2   *Classes of chieftaincy*

ROYAL CHIEFDOMS (*ya-na-bihe-nama*)

(a) Doo-bihe-nama

Eligibility	Generally sons of Ya-Nas: may be occupied by grandsons but latter will not thereby become eligible for Yendi skin
Chiefdoms	MION, SAVELUGU, KARAGA, Bamvim, Galiwe, Gbungbaliga, Kpatinga, Kunkon, Kutun, Nyon, Pigu, Sakwe, Sanerigu, Sang, Sanpiemo, Sun, Tampion, Tibung, Tidjo, Tong, Tugu, Viluli, Voggo, Yamalkaraga, Zakpalse, Zangballon, Zoggo, Zugu, Zulogo

(b) Yanse-nama

Eligbility	Generally for 'grandsons of (Ya-) Nas whose own fathers have never reached the position of Na'.[a] Royal sons may be appointed to these skins but they are usually terminus skins
Chiefdoms	(Include) DEMON, KWORLI, *SUNSON, *YELZORI, *NANTON, Bago, Danyo, Dzenkunyili, Gnani, Kpunkpano, Kubalem, Kushebihi, Nasa, Nbatena, Nyamalega, Nyankpala, ?Pisigu, Sakpiegu, Salenkuga, Vokpia, Woriboggo, Yashegu, Zagbana, Zakule, Zoya

(c) Ya-na-bipunsi-nama

Eligibility	Usually for daughters of Ya-Nas
Chiefdoms	Gundogo, Kpatuya, Kukulogo, Yimahego, Sasagele

(d) Paga-bihe-nama

Eligibility	For sons of women of the royal house (e.g. sisters of the Ya-Na)
Chiefdoms	No standard appointments: normally minor village chiefdoms

ELDER CHIEFDOMS (*kpamba-nama*)

Eligibility	For court elders and other commoners
Chiefdoms	GUSHIEGU, TOLON, GULKPEOGU, KUMBUNGU, Dalon, Dipali, †Gbirimani, Gbulun, Kasoriyili, Kpugi, Langa, Langona, Lungbunga, Mogola, †Nyankpala, Singa, Tali, Zandua

MION = Divisional chiefdom.

[a]Rattray (1932), vol. 2, p. 576.

*   = In principle, an 'elder' chiefdom; but invariably held by a royal.

†   = Known to have been held by royals.

NOTE: The list above includes chieftaincies named in standard sources; it is by no means exhaustive and at best indicates only the more important posts.

political system (provincial, divisional, or village) or in terms of the status of those entitled to occupy them. In respect of the latter, there were two broad categories: offices generally reserved for members of the royal patriclan and offices open to commoners (including elders). 'Royal' chiefdoms were reserved for those who could claim descent in the male line from Nyagse, but not all claiming descent achieved office, even at village level.[54] Younger sons suffered from the preference accorded their elder brothers and if a man had failed to achieve office, his sons in turn were excluded.[55] They ceased to be members of the dynasty for all effective purposes and fell to the ranks of the *taremba* (people not of the royal blood).

Within the class of royal chieftaincies (*ya-na-bihe-nama*), there was a distinction between posts generally restricted to sons of Ya-Nas (*doo-bihe-nama*) and those usually restricted to grandsons of Ya-Nas (*yanse-nama*). The distinction seems to express historical convention rather than any rigid and explicit rule: the Ya-Na retained ultimate freedom of choice in appointment. Thus grandsons and great-grandsons could reach even the royal dukedoms, though they were ineligible to go on to Yendi – and, indeed, attracted the hostility of royal sons, for blocking access to the paramountcy. In general, as Tait remarks, grandsons (*yanse*) were regarded as a 'great nuisance', since they tended to make demands for skins to which they were not entitled.[56] Equally, royal sons occupying divisional skins, such as Demon or Kworli, were resented by nobles in line for these posts, which were normally 'terminus' posts. (Another convention was that Sunson, Yelzori, and Nanton, in principle commoner skins, were invariably held by *ya-na-bihe*.)[57]

In addition to the two major classes of royal chiefdoms, there were five posts reserved for women of the royal house, generally for the daughters of paramounts. These were ranked in seniority, the eldest daughter usually holding Gundogo, the daughter occupying Kpatuya being her heir-presumptive. Women became eligible for these posts only after having passed the menopause.[58]

The four remaining divisional chiefdoms and a number of village posts were reserved for elders and other commoners. Appointment again lay in the discretion of the Ya-Na, although in practice Gushiegu was the preserve of one commoner patrilineage.[59] Indeed, Gushiegu and Gulkpeogu were posts conferring a distinct ritual status on their occupants, who had important responsibilities in connection with the selection of paramounts and with the maintenance of the royal ancestor cult. Tolon and Kumbungu were military posts, situated (like most of the commoner chiefdoms) in Western Dagomba, having been established soon after the conquest when the capital was still at Yendi Dabari.[60]

The commoner chieftaincies were ranked in seniority, Tolon and Gushiegu being the two senior posts. The Tolon-Na was head of the state cavalry, senior elder to the Ya-Na, and senior of the *worizahonema*, the twelve royal linguists. The Gushie-Na had an equivalent, ritual importance to Tolon-Na, and in this sense, given their different roles, it is hardly meaningful to say that one was 'senior' to the other. According to Tait, Sunson, Yelzori, and Nanton came next in seniority (all in practice were, however, held by royals).[61] After the divisionals came the various village 'elder' chiefdoms.

DAGOMBA GOVERNMENT

In many monarchies the process of differentiation within the royal lineage is accompanied by a differentiation between the interests of 'the state' and those of the dynasty. This is not to say that the two are necessarily opposed but only that the requirements of government cannot always be met by reliance upon kinsmen. Further, the hierarchical properties of the state are ultimately incompatible with the corporate character of the lineage.[62] Differentiation within the latter tends to generate tensions which may be relieved by delegating authority to the junior stratum of the dynasty (the nobility); but equally they may lead the king to rely on personnel and resources acquired independently of the kinship network. This development is partly a matter of expediency (of setting the king apart from the rest of the lineage) but is related to another problem of descent-based organisations, that of the uncertainties of inheritance in regard to the distribution of ability.

Hence the emergence of bodies of appointed officials, chosen by and responsible to the monarch. In Dagomba the emergence of an administrative class, the elders, helped, as Wilks points out, 'to differentiate the king *in role*, and not as hitherto only *in rank*, from other members of the ruling group'.[63] Many of the various offices of elder and councillor to the Ya-Na seem to have been created at the time of the conquest, although the institution of new titles went on until at least the middle of the eighteenth century. However, the class of elders became more important and more powerful after the introduction of the rule limiting accession to the throne to the three royal dukes. The problem then was that the nobility (especially those who had achieved divisional chieftancies) tended to act independently. Indeed, they are still said to be more powerful than the royal dukes: the latter must preserve their good names at Yendi if they are to become king, but the grandson divisional chiefs have little more to hope for. The royal administrative class was strengthened (Wilks argues) to control – or at least to watch – the activities of this nobility.

The difficulty about such officials has often been that they seek to establish a hereditary right to their posts. Like many other kingdoms, Dagbon solved this problem by recruiting eunuchs or, more exactly, by creating them: the original Balo-Na, Kum-lana, Mba Malle, Gullana, and Zohe-Na were all, according to the 'drum history', young men castrated on the orders of the king and then taken into his service.[64] The one major exception is the very important office of Kuga-Na which supposedly was first held by a younger brother of Na Sitobu and has been hereditary since then.[65] But for the rest, as Wilks again remarks, their reliability and their dependence on royal patronage were 'ensured by recruiting them from non-princely circles; the

27

TABLE 3 *Elders of Yendi*

KUGA-NA
Instituted by
Functions and prerogatives

Intermediary for
Appoints to
Comment

Ya-Na Sitobu
Principal adviser to Ya-Na; administrator of state during interregna; guardian of royal shrine; member of traditional selection committee for Yendi skin; had prerogative of interceding on behalf of condemned prisoners
Chiefs of Singa and Gbetobo
Chiefdoms of Bagele, Gbalga, Tanyeli, Nandoli, Taloli
Allegedly descends from Sibie, brother of Na Sitobu

ZOHE-NA
Instituted by
Functions and prerogatives
Intermediary for

Comment

Ya-Na Sitobu
Principal counsellor of Ya-Na; regent in wartime
Yo-Na, Karaga-Na, Mion-lana, Kumbung-Na, Gushie-Na, Demon-Na, Sunson-Na, Yelzori-lana, Kworli-Na, Bamvim-lana; chiefs of Voggo, Lungbunga, Zogu, Langa, Boggo, Namashiegu, Zosali, Tugo
Eunuch

KUM-LANA
Instituted by
Functions and prerogatives

Intermediary for

Comment

Ya-Na Ninmitoni
Counsellor of Ya-Na; attends funerals on his behalf; responsible for making arrangements for Ya-Nas' funerals
Zangballon-Na; Bimbilla-Na; chiefs of Galiwe, Sakpiegu, Dalon, Sangule, Taganomo, Bago, Yimahego, Zanduli, Kpunkpano, and Gbungbaliga; and representatives of other kings
Eunuch; title originally meant 'owner of death'

BALO-NA
Instituted by
Functions and prerogatives

Intermediary for

Comment

Ya-Na Nyagse
Counsellor; attends chiefs' funerals for Ya-Na; in charge of Balogo quarter of Yendi
Sanerigu-Na; Sang-lana; chiefs of Timbungu, Diari, Gbirimani, Kpatinga, Sanpiemo, Kutun, Pigu, Sun, and Pion; also *kambonse* officers in Yendi district
Eunuch

MBA MALLE
Instituted by
Functions and prerogatives

Intermediary for
Appoints to
Comment

Ya-Na Zangina or Ya-Na Andani Sigili
Counsellor and personal attendant of Ya-Na; in charge of royal household and Nayili quarter of Yendi; responsible for relations with Muslim dignitaries in kingdom and for their installations;[a] officiates at enskinment of Ya-Na
Chiefs of Sankune, Nasa, Gbanbaya, Woriboggo;
Chiefdoms of Balogo and Ga
Eunuch; said to be normal successor to Balo-Na

MBA BUNA[b]
Instituted by
Functions and prerogatives

Ya-Na Zangina
Counsellor to Ya-Na; officiates at enskinment of Ya-Na and at Ya-Na's funeral; head of quarter of Yendi

Intermediary for	Nanton-Na, Tolon-Na, Kalebila-Na
Comment	Eunuch

GAGBINDANA
Instituted by   Ya-Na Gariba
Functions and prerogatives   Counsellor to Ya-Na; officiates at enskinment of Ya-Na
Intermediary for   Chiefs of Tibung and Kushingo
Comment   Eunuch

MBA KPAHIGU
Instituted by   ?
Functions and prerogatives   Counsellor of Ya-Na; occasional judicial role; officiates at enskinment of Ya-Na
Intermediary for   –
Comment   Eunuch

GULLANA
Instituted by   ?
Functions and prerogatives   Counsellor of Ya-Na; personal attendant
Intermediary for   –
Comment   Eunuch

MBADUGU
Instituted by   Ya-Na Ninmitoni
Functions and prerogatives   Ya-Na's official linguist, conducting all audiences of Ya-Na; controller of royal treasury; supervisor of cooking in royal household; responsible for announcing births and other events to Ya-Na
Intermediary for   Chiefs of Gnani, Danyo, Kushebihi, Zagbana, Zanga, Zakule, Kamshiegu; Gundo-Na; all persons seeking audience of Ya-Na
Comment   Eunuch but not member of Council of Elders

TUGURI-NAM
Instituted by   Possibly fetish priest under Na Gbewa
Functions and prerogatives   One of elders responsible for selecting Ya-Na and present at enskinment of Ya-Na
Intermediary for   –
Comment   Apparently no regular administrative function at court

GOMLI
Instituted by   Possibly fetish priest under Na Gbewa
Functions and prerogatives   One of elders responsible for selection of Ya-Na and present at enskinment
Intermediary for   –
Comment   Apparently no regular administrative function at court

SOME MINOR OFFICIALS
Dambale (or Nano-lana) – the Ya-Na's staff-bearer and spokesman
Zanko-lana – apparently no specific function
Brafo – the Ya-Na's executioner (an Akan title)
Kyere-lana – defunct in this century (last occupied under Ya-Na Andani II)

[a]See Ferguson (1973), pp. 196–9.
[b]Also referred to as 'Bunga' and 'Bung-lana'.
PRINCIPAL SOURCES: Manoukian (1952), pp. 56–8; Rattray (1932), vol. 2, pp. 570–4; Tamakloe (1931), pp. 11, 15, 60–2; Tait 'A'; Tait 'B'.

descendants of Na Gbewa, in other words, were in general barred from such offices'.[66] Whereas relations between the king and the nobles often bore an element of reciprocity, those between the king and the elders were those of master and servant (admitting all the familiar qualifications about formal and informal power in such relationships).[67]

The general role of the elders was to maintain, protect, and enhance the authority of the royal court, both in day-to-day government and in supervising arrangements for the succession. The more specific functions of elders may be seen in the accompanying table: some were judicial, others ceremonial, and others again domestic. There was a treasurer who was at the same time the mouthpiece of the Ya-Na (Mbadugu). The elders were also responsible for bringing up the royal children. The latter were given only a limited Muslim education, or none at all (a similar disdain towards or suspicion of European schooling was shown later by the officials of the Yendi court).[68]

However, the real power of the elders rested, first, on their membership of the royal councils and, secondly, on their role as intermediaries between the nobles and the king. The Ya-Na did not normally leave Yendi and his movements were generally restricted by taboos. The government of Dagomba was therefore carried on from the royal court, notably through the Council of Elders, made up of nine officials and the king.[69] Apart from administrative matters, this council dealt with judicial cases, the Ya-Na acting as judge and the elders as assessors. Minor cases were often judged by a smaller tribunal, consisting of Zohe-Na, Mba Malle, and Kum-lana, plus Mbadugu, the king's mouthpiece. In major cases the council could impose a range of penalties, including enslavement and death (the Ya-Na alone had the right to authorise executions, although, subject to his approval, the death sentence could be imposed by divisional chiefs). The Council of Elders also advised the king on appointments to chieftaincies.[70]

The nine elders were members of the larger State Council, which was attended as well by the twelve divisional chiefs and the Chereponi-fame (paramount of the Chokosi). This body met only on very important occasions, such as the outbreak of war. There was no regular consultation of the divisional chiefs by the paramount, legislation (such as it was) being formulated and enacted by the Council of Elders.[71]

The more important elders acted as intermediaries between the chiefs and the king and derived both money and political power from doing so. Every divisional chief, even a royal duke, had to approach the king through the elder who was his patron at court. This relationship was symbolised by the fact that, no matter what his status, the chief normally addressed his court patron as '*ba*' ('father'). Tamakloe observes that when chiefs come to Yendi,

they have to lodge with these eunuchs according to their rank as has been arranged. These administrators then charge the chiefs certain fees which are probably left to the judgment of the visitors, before leading them to the king, who would then listen to their remonstrances, without them, no chiefs – whoever they are – can approach the king, and an attempt to defy these orders results in a severe mulct or even a destoolment of a chief.[72]

The elders made money from at least two other sources. One was revenue from justice. People bringing cases before the Council of Elders frequently had to take an oath on one of the king's ancestors and for this the Ya-Na charged a fee (*pore ligidi*), part of which went to the elders.[73] Income from summons fees and fines was also given in part to the elders (the remainder going into the king's treasury). The other source was money paid by candidates seeking appointment to chieftaincy (the fee known as *nam ligidi*). Kuga-Na himself appointed to certain village chieftaincies and received money direct from candidates for these posts.[74] In other cases, where the nominations were sent in by the divisional chiefs, part of the fee was also taken by the elders of Yendi, the remainder being divided between the royal treasury, the divisional chief, and the divisional chief's elders.[75]

Elders were eligible for promotion, both within the court and to chieftaincies outside. For example, it is said that when Balo-Na dies or is promoted, he is generally succeeded by Mba Malle. Both divisional and village-level commoner chieftaincies were within their grasp: those most commonly allotted to elders of Yendi seem to have been Tolon, Gulkpeogu, Kumbungu, and Lungbunga. Here again there appear to have been certain standard routes of promotion: Mbadugu, for instance, was normally regarded as heir to the divisional skin of Gulkpeogu.[76]

Each divisional chief had a court which resembled in its essentials the court of Yendi. Collectively, his elders and servants were known as *nazonema* ('the chief's friends'). Like the Ya-Na's elders, they were generally eunuchs of slave origin (or the earliest were). As at Yendi, they were ordered in a titled hierarchy. The senior officials were the *wulana* (literally, 'chief spear-bearer') and the *kpanalana* ('spear-bearer'). The *wulana* was a functional equivalent of Kuga-Na at Yendi: the senior adviser to the chief, his representative in dealings with other chiefs, an arbitrator in disputes, and a judge or assessor in the court. He was also an administrator, supervising the work of subordinate officials and allotting duties to them. The *kpanalana* was *wulana*'s deputy, his range of functions being broadly similar. Again, the elders took the role of patron for chiefs visiting the capital, in this case for village headmen.[77] As at Yendi, there was a council of elders to deal with disputes, offences, and more general questions concerning the division: the council was usually made up of the divisional chief, his *wulana* and *kpanalana*, and the various titled heads of wards in the town. There was apparently no equivalent to the State Council at divisional level. Instead, subordinate chiefs came in to salute their superior (usually on Mondays or Fridays) and problems were sorted out individually, with the elders advising the divisional chief. Divisional elders shared in the revenue from court cases and from appointments of chiefs, although, as has been noted, some part of this revenue usually found its way to Yendi.[78]

The range of offices in the divisional chief's court was probably smaller than that in Yendi, but its hierarchy and functions were practically identical.

The divisional court was held together by a similar flow of money and patronage, and the whole was borne along by the chief, himself involved in a wider network of clients and rivals. Christine Oppong describes graphically the complexion of politics at divisional level:

When a chief travels on the ladder of the political hierarchy, he does not go alone, but takes with him servants, musicians, advisers, and relatives ... These join the followers of his predecessors, who may have been serving his line for two or more generations of rulers ... Exchanges of services and favours, rights over women and children tend to bind the chief as royal patron to his followers, with the result that he has a considerable monopoly of professional services, trained labour, goods, and women. The chief may give female wards in his charge to his followers in return for their loyal services and they in turn may later give him the offspring of such marriages; the girls to be given in turn by him in marriage; the boys perhaps to come and serve him either as grooms, personal servants, or musicians.[79]

MUSLIMS AT THE COURT

None of the Yendi elders had spiritual authority, though Kuga-Na acted as guardian of the royal shrine at Bagele. Religious offices were performed either by the paramount himself or by the Muslim functionaries attached to the court. Although Islam only became the court religion in the eighteenth century, with the conversion of Zangina, at least one of the principal Muslim families, the Yidan Kambara, was prominent at the time of the move to Yendi, that is, in the reign of Na Luro.[80] This family, of Hausa origin, became responsible for washing the corpses of paramounts and other chiefs. This office is hereditary, like that of *limam*.[81] There were, in fact, several imams in Yendi – one a chaplain to the Ya-Na (*nayiri limam*), another chaplain to Zohe-Na (*zohe limam*), and a third serving the Muslims of the town.[82] By the time of colonial occupation, the latter official had come into being, under the control of another of the older Muslim communities, the Baba.[83] There were a number of families who provided incumbents for the hierarchy of Muslim offices at the courts of Yendi and at those of divisional chiefs.

Nevertheless, Dagomba never became theocratic. Islam was introduced well after the political structure of the kingdom had developed most of its essential features: 'the Muslims had therefore to be accommodated within an essentially non-Islamic system'.[84] Yendi was not a major centre of learning. The royal children did not receive a full Koranic education and the *limam* to the paramount chief did not need to be especially well versed in the Koran. As Tamakloe succinctly puts it: 'The Imamship ... in Yendi, is not for the service of God, but for the king.'[85]

THE DAGOMBA ARMY

The military organisation of a pre-colonial state is of interest for two reasons: first, because ultimately the identity of any state depends on its ability to claim a monopoly of 'the means of destruction'; secondly, because of the interaction between social structure and military organisation.[86]

In military terms, Dagomba can be placed firmly in the category of 'cavalry states'. The foundation and reputation of Dagbon depended on its use of horses. The kingdom was surrounded by peoples on the savannah and in the hills who did not have a sophisticated political or military organisation. The Dagomba were therefore able to dominate (or at least intimidate) their neighbours by dispatching armed horsemen across the flat, open countryside of the north. Their raiding was checked only by the hills to the east and the forest to the south.

The Mossi and Mamprussi kingdoms, relations of Dagomba, developed their power by similar means. It was, as Wilks says, a power

based firmly on the possession of horses and a knowledge of the techniques of cavalry warfare. Using their heavy armoured cavalry for defensive purposes, the real strength of the savannah kingdoms lay in their employment of light cavalry for long-range raiding. Penetrating country where organised opposition was seldom encountered, battles were correspondingly rare; planners were concerned more with strategic than with tactical matters.[87]

The further development of the Dagomba army came about as a result of encounters with 'organised opposition' (Gonja and Ashanti) in the seventeenth and eighteenth centuries. The principal change was the formation of companies of foot musketeers (the *kambonse*), with the assistance of the Ashanti. Each of the five major *kambonse* companies was headed by a *kambon-na*, with a commander-in-chief (*kambon-kpema*) drawn in turn from each of the villages near Yendi where the *kambonse* lived.[88]

Ashanti influence was marked in the organisation and the titles adopted by the *kambonse*. Rattray, always keen to find traces of Akan culture in the north, noted enthusiastically:'we are here dealing with institutions which have been copied from the Akan, and not vice versa'.[89] He pointed out that many forms had been adopted: for example, the title '*safohene*' ('war chief') which appeared among the *kambonse* in a Dagbane corruption, '*sapasene*', and the term '*adonten*' ('centre') which the Dagomba altered to '*dantene*'. In this respect at least, Rattray is supported by other writers. Tait remarks that 'out of 45 principal titles . . . 27 to 30 of them appear to be Twi words' and he goes on: 'the extensive use of Twi terms . . . suggests that a deliberate effort was made, not only to get guns and gunpowder, but also to learn something of the organisation that had made Ashanti so powerful'.[90] The divisional chiefs followed the example of Yendi, establishing their own companies of infantrymen which in wartime had positions allotted to them under particular divisional chiefs.

The *kambonse* supplemented the military resources of Dagomba, but they did not replace the mounted bowmen and spearmen on which it had previously relied. The cavalry was organised into companies, provided for the national army by the divisional chiefs, each of whom had a prescribed position in its order of battle. Under the Tolon-Na, who was overall commander of the cavalry, were the head of the spearmen and the chiefs commanding the bowmen (the Kumbung-Na and Diari-Na).[91] Under them again were the company leaders, for the most part village chiefs.

The Ya-Na himself did not usually command the army in the field (although he seems occasionally to have led raiding parties). He had to rely on the skill and support of his divisional chiefs for success in all major campaigns: only the *kambonse* at Yendi were in any sense his own troops. It is possible that the formation of this force served an ulterior purpose – that of strengthening the position of Yendi *vis-à-vis* the divisional chiefs. But since the king's example was followed by the divisional chiefs, any marginal advantage he had thus gained over them was presumably lost.

DYNAMICS OF THE TRADITIONAL STATE

So far we have discussed the Dagomba state largely in terms of functions, rules, rights, and duties. In the concluding section I shall try to draw these elements together and to relate them to certain broader questions, with a view to developing a comprehensive model of the dynamics of pre-colonial politics.

First of all, we should ask how the political system was related to its environment. The economic setting was one of low-productivity subsistence agriculture and the population was thinly spread over the kingdom. Though the ruling class could extract some wealth from levies on trade, slave-raiding, and the exploitation of resources such as iron-ore and salt, the limits of appropriation were set essentially by the constraints of meagre agricultural production and a low level of technology.[92]

One consequence of this situation was that land was not a scarce commodity. Indeed, it was not a commodity at all. As Goody points out, 'under such conditions neither individuals nor kin groups bother to lay specific claims to large tracts of territory, since land is virtually a free good'.[93] Political domination based on the right to allocate and withdraw the use of land therefore made no sense, and, as we have seen, the Dagomba chieftaincy was on the whole indifferent to control of the land: there was no question of 'feudalism' in the European sense.[94]

Another implication was that, with so little surplus available, there was equally little scope for the development of extreme forms of economic inequality and social differentiation. As Gluckman puts it, one man can eat only a limited amount of porridge: 'There was little trade and luxury, so even a conqueror could not make himself more comfortable than he had been before. One cannot build a palace with grass and mud, and if the only foods are grain, milk, and meat, one cannot live much above the standard of ordinary men.'[95] Eyre-Smith made precisely this point about the savannah chiefs: 'Their wants from their people would be, of necessity, few, though undoubtedly their subjects would bring them presents annually and help to make their farms ... There was little scope for material aggrandisement.' He went on to identify the really important resource in establishing power: 'It was the numbers of his men that connoted the power of a chief and not his territorial possessions ... the impregnability of a state or community lay in the number of the inhabitants rather than in the extent of its territory.'[96]

The principal resources which the Dagomba ruling class required were, in fact, foodstuffs and manpower. Tribute in kind was paid to the local chiefs and the Ya-Na: subjects also worked on their chiefs' farms. The amount and frequency of tribute in either category cannot now be estimated with accuracy. As we shall see, the colonial government undertook an investigation of the subject in the 1930s, for the purpose of establishing taxation (the level of which was to be equivalent to that of the tribute previously given). The administration concluded that,

prior to the European occupation of the Northern Territories, there existed a well defined system of tribute from the people to their chiefs. A prescribed quantity of yams, corn and other foodstuffs was paid by the head of a compound to the local chief who retained his share and sent the remainder to the divisional chief. The latter, in his turn, took his portion and transmitted the residue to the paramount chief. In this way the Dagombas recognised the right of their chiefs, as rulers on behalf of the community, to a share of the usufruct of the land.

Furthermore, the chiefs were entitled to and received the free assistance of their people in the cultivation of their farms, as well as in the building and maintenance of their houses.[97] According to the British estimates, the annual value of tribute in kind was roughly 1.5 per cent of the average annual 'income' of an adult male: the value of tribute labour was assessed as equivalent to under 0.5 per cent of income, though the calculation was of very dubious relevance.

Further supplies of labour were obtained through slave-raiding, conducted in the Konkomba area and, occasionally, in the north-west. Some of the slaves were kept to grow food for the royals, while others were sent to the south.

Trade provided another source of wealth for the Dagomba state. As we noted earlier, one of the main caravan routes from Ashanti to Hausaland passed through Yendi, and it is clear that the Dagomba paramounts were always anxious that commerce should continue and grow. Apart from the indirect benefits, their treasury profited greatly from the tolls levied on the roads and in the markets. Indeed, the Ya-Nas accepted a mild degree of subservience to the Asantehene, recognising the prosperity which the Ashanti connection had brought to the kingdom.[98] Politically, it seems that the rise of the administrative class in Yendi coincided with this period of prosperity and, conversely, the weakening of the king's authority appears to have followed the collapse of Ashanti power and the resulting disruption of commerce.[99] The process of dislocation was to a certain extent cumulative: the less control Yendi exercised, the more divisional chiefs were tempted to loot the caravans, and the less inclined the merchants became to use the Yendi route. Certainly, by the time of the partition, there had been severe fighting within the kingdom, and travel through the area was generally regarded as hazardous.[100]

The process of government itself yielded revenue to the Ya-Na and his subordinates. Court fees and fines provided one source; payments by candidates for appointment to office were another. The elders, of course, siphoned off some of this income, in addition to the gifts they received from the chiefs for whom they acted as friend at court.

In considering the 'inputs' sustaining the political system, we are inevitably brought back to the factors of military support and political allegiance, which in turn lead to an examination of the distribution of power. It is clear that the Dagomba monarchy did not dispose of a powerful, centrally controlled army (such as the Dahomean king, for example, commanded). Apart from its intermittent slave-raiding, Dagbon was not an especially aggressive state and when it was attacked (as by Gonja and Ashanti) its capacity for self-defence was not particularly impressive. The use of mercenaries in the latter part of the nineteenth century was a striking revelation, as Northcott observed, of 'the poverty of the potentates in the country ... and their consequent inability to maintain a standing army ... the result of a pitched battle is that the commonality returns at once to their ordinary avocations, accepting with more or less resignation the rule of the victor'.[101] But, as he suggested, such weakness was a characteristic, not just of the monarchy, but of all political authority, and it had a benevolent aspect in that violence could not be maintained for long in internal conflicts. Just as in medieval England (at least as seen by Macaulay),

resistance was an ordinary remedy for political distempers, a remedy which was always at hand, and which, though doubtless sharp at the moment, produced no deep or lasting ill effects ... Regular army there was none. Every man had a slight tincture of soldiership, and scarcely any man more than a slight tincture. The national wealth consisted chiefly in flocks and herds, in the harvest of the year, and in the simple buildings inhabited by the people ... The calamities of civil war were confined to the slaughter on the field of battle, and to a few subsequent executions and confiscations. In a week the peasant was driving his team and the esquire was flying his hawks.[102]

There was, in fact, a 'low-level equilibrium' between the central government and any force which arose to resist or overthrow it – one resulting from the general condition of poverty and a rudimentary technology.[103] Furthermore, the use of cavalry meant that the king was dependent on the support of other members of the dynasty and, as Goody suggests, this dependence was probably a major factor underlying constitutional development: a broad distribution of offices was the condition for assured military support.[104] And the corollary was that once the king no longer needed military support, he would no longer need to be so solicitous towards other members of the dynasty.

As it was, however, Dagbon had many of the features of Southall's 'segmentary state'.[105] The capacity of the central government to control outlying centres of power was limited; the king did not have an effective monopoly of force; and the institutions of government were replicated at lower levels. In this sense, the structure was 'pyramidal' rather than 'hierarchical'. Rattray, indeed, described Dagbon as a 'loose federation of semi-independent provinces': 'Each of these Divisions' (i.e., provinces) 'is under a ruler who in his own state is a Na. Each Division has an almost identical organization, the only distinction between them being that the Yendi Division is regarded as a kind of *primus inter pares*, with its Na also nominally Na over all the others.'[106] Eyre-Smith was equally emphatic about the weakness of Yendi: 'the Paramount Chief had little or no executive authority in the government of the semi-independent states and . . . received little or nothing other than perhaps slaves from his distant sub-chiefs'.[107] And Manoukian writes: 'decentralization was the rule in the original native administration: the divisional chiefs were left to manage their own divisions with little interference from the Ya-Na, and they in turn left the local affairs of the villages in the hands of sub-chiefs and headmen'.[108]

There are several recorded occasions on which divisional chiefs or dissident royals either took up arms against the king or called on outside powers to intervene. The procedure for selecting the Ya-Na implicitly recognised this danger by providing for consultation of divisional chiefs before the successor was publicly nominated. In principle, once a Ya-Na was appointed, he could neither abdicate nor be deskinned. But at least one Ya-Na (Sumani Zoli) was killed by a rival and others were threatened by intrigue and open rebellion.

Yet, in a familiar paradox, the instability of the state was also the key to its survival: the disputes which afflicted it both arose from and validated its structure. For, 'where a large dynasty is involved in the military and civil government of a country, an element of ambiguity, of uncertainty, in the selection of a successor not only provides a spur to effort, but gives expression to the "corporate" character of the royal kin group'.[109] Disputes over succession were structurally prescribed: the rule that the king should be chosen from three contenders produced competition, and the rule that no man should rise higher than his father added urgency to it.

The result was persistent tension between senior and junior generations – between uncles, anxious to secure a title for their lines, and nephews, determined to succeed their fathers. This pattern was evident, in the nineteenth century, in the struggle between Na Yakuba's sons and their uncles (the Mion-lana, Yo-Na, and Sunson-Na) and in the ensuing combat between Na Abudulai's son (Karaga-Na Alhassan) and his uncles and cousins.[110] The same pattern necessarily occurred at lower levels, in competition for divisional and even village skins. These were the dynamics of competition within the dynasty, supplementing (and to some extent coinciding with) the dynamics of tension between central government and the peripheral centres of power.

But conflict and rebellion seem to have had the overall effect of supporting the fundamental order through resolving the recurrent crises characteristic of the system, in the manner classically analysed by Max Gluckman.[111] The factional leaders were intent, not on destroying the paramountcy, but on acquiring it for themselves. The Ya-Na himself could deploy considerable resources of patronage; his person was surrounded by the sanctity attaching to his office and to his status as senior member of the royal patriclan; and he disposed of an, admittedly marginal, administrative and military advantage as head of state.[112] But he was restrained from destroying or altogether defying his subordinates by his lack of an assured military and political superiority, by the practical necessity of delegating authority, and, perhaps not least, by the ties of clientage and kinship which bound together the king and the nobility (not to mention the nobility and their clients).

As for the commoners, it may well be (as Maquet claims) that their rulers took more than they gave and that they did not pay for their privileges.[113] There was some redistribution of wealth in the form of individual largesse, festivals, and relief in times of scarcity. Otherwise, the services of government were limited to external defence, justice, and spiritual leadership: most needs were, in fact, met from within the village. Even there, the chief was generally a transient figure, set on moving up to higher office and taking his courtiers with him when he did so.

But the demands of the ruling class (at least as they have been recorded) were not enormous and, indeed, whatever sentiments of relative deprivation they may have provoked, the standard of living of the chiefs could not have been much higher than that of their subjects. In any event, it was not internal revolution which upset the finely stressed equilibrium of Dagomba politics, but the impact of a political system sustained by immeasurably greater military, economic, and technological resources: colonialism.

CHAPTER 3

COLONIAL RULE, 1899–1930

> ... power is like the wind: if it rises there is no-one who can stop it,
> it must die down of itself.[1]
>
> ... the natives are a very conservative pig-headed race.[2]

In this chapter we shall examine the problems, structure, personnel, and policies of the British administration in Dagomba from the time of the partition down to the advent of 'indirect rule' in the 1930s. We shall also explore aspects and consequences of the isolation of the Northern Territories from the rest of the Gold Coast: this isolation. I shall suggest, led to the entrenchment in power of a group of officers whom, on account of their cohesion and independence, I shall refer to as 'the northern interest'. These officers also had a distinctly pragmatic view of 'native administration', a topic to which we shall return in Chapter 4.

The partition of the Dagomba kingdom was formalised on 14 November 1899 by the signing of a convention concerned with 'the settlement of the Samoan and other questions'. An earlier agreement delimiting British and German spheres of influence had made an equally magnificent sweep of the imperial globe: an agreement, as its title grandly stated, 'respecting Africa and Heligoland'. With similar panache, the British then created, by Order-in-Council, the Protectorate of the Northern Territories, the boundaries of which recognised local geography or social organisation only to the extent of following the line of a river, the Black Volta, along part of its southern border.[3] By such drawing of lines on maps, some 30,000 square miles of hills and savannah were transformed into an administrative unit. Later, they took on a political identity, an identity developed by colonial administrators and sharpened by political organisers in the 1950s.

But, for at least the first thirty years of colonial rule, the expression 'Ashanti hinterland' suggests more accurately the status of the area, in the eyes of the Gold Coast central administration. The 'N.T.' had been acquired (at great cost) not because of any intrinsic value they possessed, but because it was strategically undesirable to let the French or the Germans take them. They were occupied not in a fit of absent-mindedness, nor even in a spasm of avarice, but rather in the course of a general epidemic of jealousy, of which the Protectorate was a memento.

· The government quickly realised that the N.T. had very few of the assets which made colonialism elsewhere such an uplifting and profitable enterprise. It therefore concentrated its resources, such as they were, on the more

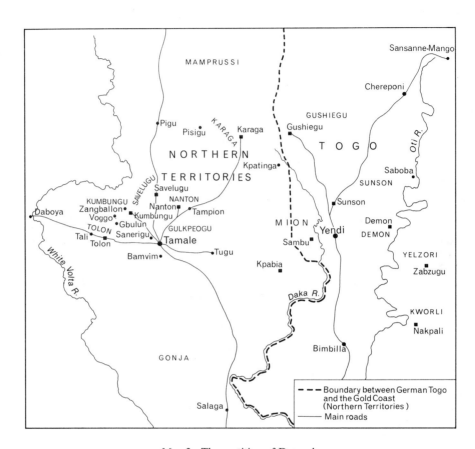

Map 2. The partition of Dagomba

obviously wealthy Ashanti and coastal regions.[4] Economically, the Protectorate became a satellite of the southern economy. Even so, the relationship of north and south was marked more by indifference than by aggressive exploitation (such as occurred in the corresponding districts of the Ivory Coast).

Both the N.T. and the northern Ivory Coast were, indeed, subject to demands for labour and for cash-crops (notably cotton and foodstuffs). But the British in the N.T. were always more resistant to such demands and less whole-hearted in seeking to satisfy them than the *commandants* of Ivory Coast. Ultimately, in the mid-twenties, they largely stopped putting pressure on their subjects, at least in respect of labour recruitment and food production. Thereafter, the British administration adopted a philosophy of explicit isolationism, which, under the title of 'indirect rule', was intended to dissipate any tendency which might have existed towards an assimilation of the north into a southern-dominated Gold Coast.

This doctrine of 'indirect rule' was highly effective in keeping northerners outside the main currents of politics in the Gold Coast, at least until the 1950s, when they were pushed abruptly (and, in some instances, protestingly) into a wild and dazzling world of polling booths, election manifestos, and parliamentary procedure.

ADMINISTRATION AND JUSTICE

The isolation of the north was partly a consequence of an administrative and judicial system which treated the Gold Coast as three separate units: the Colony, Ashanti, and the Northern Territories. Within each unit, authority was concentrated in a Chief Commissioner who was a delegate of the Governor, and in the hinterland the Governor alone had power to legislate.[5]

The Chief Commissioner of the Northern Territories (C.C.N.T.) was effectively a viceroy, uncontrolled by elective or representative bodies. Indeed, he only became a member of the Gold Coast Executive Council (a consultative body) in 1934 and of the Legislative Council in 1946 (the incumbent C.C.N.T. was, in fact, silent in the Council until its dissolution in 1951).[6] The Legislative Council never contained any N.T. representative apart from the Chief Commissioner, since before 1951 the administration held that northerners were insufficiently 'mature' to have non-official representation at this level. Indeed, the Legislative Council itself only obtained the right to legislate for the entire Gold Coast in 1934, and even then such legislation required specific promulgation by the Governor in order to take effect in the N.T. (this was, in fact, a continuation of earlier practice by which ordinances had to be separately enacted for each of the three areas of the colony). Thus, in the period covered by this chapter, the N.T. were under a strict 'administocratic' regime: as David Kimble says, 'there was . . . no constitutional method whereby N.T. affairs could be publicly debated'.[7]

Although there was a single budget for the Gold Coast, each of the three units had a particular history in regard to taxation. Each, moreover, had its own judicial system. In the N.T. the Chief Commissioner presided over his own court: other courts were held by Provincial Commissioners and District Commissioners. The courts heard both civil and criminal cases. Yet until 1934 barristers and solicitors were excluded from all courts in the N.T. (and Ashanti), the Governor arguing that the introduction of lawyers 'would be speedily fatal to the social and economic well-being of the native population'.[8] During the early years, the C.C.N.T. was not required to consult the Governor before the execution of death sentences; and even after this prerogative was removed, there was no provision for appeal in criminal cases tried before the C.C.N.T.'s court.

Under the C.C.N.T. the north was divided into a number of provinces and districts, ruled by Provincial Commissioners and District Commissioners (or at times, in Northern Togoland, District Political Officers). Originally, the N.T. were under a direct military administration with headquarters at Gambaga, in Mamprussi. Officers of the Gold Coast Regiment served as commissioners until 1907 when civil administration took over, headquarters were moved to Tamale, and the army was replaced by the Northern Territories Constabulary (N.T.C.) as the agency of law-enforcement.

The territorial organisation of the N.T. went through several phases between 1902 and 1932. Until 1921 it consisted of three provinces (Southern, North-Eastern, and North-Western), subdivided into ten districts.[9] Between 1921 and 1932 there were two provinces (Northern and Southern), comprising, at different times, eight or ten districts.[10] During the partition of Dagomba (1899–1914) the British section was governed from Tamale, where both the D.C., Western Dagomba (sometimes called D.C., Tamale District), and the Provincial Commissioner, Southern Province, had their headquarters. In 1914 the British took over Yendi, which ultimately became the headquarters of an 'Eastern Dagomba' district. From 1914 until 1932 there were two D.C.s for Dagomba, one at Tamale, the other at Yendi (administering the former German section).

The Provincial Commissioner had the role of overall coordination and supervision. The mainspring of colonial government was, however, the D.C. whose function covered a wide range of administrative and technical tasks. The D.C. was responsible for law and order and held his own court. He had to regulate and report on the behaviour of chiefs as well as on that of his own subordinates; he had charge of the police in his district. The original instructions to District Commissioners (circulated in 1899) further required the D.C. to report on economic and political developments in his district, to encourage and protect trade, to establish personal contact with chiefs and people in the villages, and to initiate and supervise public works schemes.[11] All forms of social development (such as health services and schools) came within the purview of the D.C. and depended on his interest and abilities. So, too, did agricultural development (notably the encouragement of cash-crop production) and the control of urbanisation.[12]

In principle, the D.C. was allowed 'all possible freedom of action'. Indeed, given the slowness of communications and the pressure of work on all officials, it was natural that he should have a wide degree of autonomy. What is perhaps surprising, in view of the smallness and isolation of the colonial community, is the degree to which the protocols of hierarchy were maintained by officials and the extent to which disciplined formality prevailed, at least on paper.[13] Moreover, autonomy was tempered by a requirement that D.C.s should write, and submit for comment, 'informal diaries' recording each day's work, as well as more general observations.

Apart from liberty of action, the D.C. was given substantial positive powers. These included the power to effect summary justice; the power to collect taxes approved by government; and the power to require the provision of communal labour. The judicial sanctions of the D.C. were exercised through his court (formally a branch of the C.C.N.T.'s court). At their widest (in the period before 1910) these sanctions included the right to inflict sentences of up to three months' imprisonment (with or without hard labour), floggings of up to thirty-six lashes, and fines of up to £20. Indeed, his powers went rather further, as one passage in the 1899 circular indicates: 'In no circumstances whatever will a sentence of death be carried into effect until approved by the [Chief] Commissioner.'[14] The D.C. could also carry out punitive expeditions against villages. Indeed, as late as 1929 the D.C., Eastern Dagomba, burnt compounds and foodstuffs in Konkomba villages which had been involved in fighting each other. He had argued that 'the only way to stop these fights is to burn all the compounds and food, [sic] I made a very thorough job of it yesterday . . . I hate these fine men to kill each other when I am convinced that by burning their compounds fights would very soon stop'.[15]

Nor were chiefs immune to the harsher side of colonial justice. The 1899 circular prescribed that 'especial care [was] to be taken to foster the authority of native chiefs, and to avoid wounding the religious susceptibilities of the inhabitants'. But it also stated: 'No chief or headpriest is to be flogged without previous reference to the Officer Commanding the District'.[16] This was scarcely the spirit of indirect rule, nor was it meant to be.

GOVERNMENT FINANCES

Until the 1930s, the financial resources on which D.C.s could draw were very small. This was due partly to the lack of taxable income in the north and partly to the reluctance of the Gold Coast government to spend money on the N.T. The government's view was stated with brutal simplicity on a number of occasions. Thus Governor Hodgson declared in 1899:

I cannot too strongly urge the employment of all the available resources of the Government upon the development of the country south of Kintampo . . . I would not at present spend upon the Northern Territories – upon in fact the hinterland of the Colony – a single penny more than is absolutely necessary for their suitable administration and the encouragement of the transit trade.[17]

Thorburn reiterated this policy in 1912: 'until the Colony and Ashanti have been thoroughly opened up and developed, the Northern Territories must be content to await their turn'.[18]

The best hope for raising money locally seemed to be by taxes on the 'transit trade', that is, the caravans traversing the N.T. from the north towards Kumasi. Caravan tolls were introduced in 1899, with fixed charges for head-loads and donkey-loads of trade goods, as well as for livestock on the hoof. Officers were, however, instructed not to tax foodstuffs in transit, since the administration wanted to encourage production for the Accra and Ashanti markets.

Northcott (the first Commissioner of the N.T.) wished also to impose direct taxation, writing: 'The essence of easy rule over natives in West Africa is the existence of some convincing proof of paramountcy.'[19] The dominance of pre-colonial rulers had been symbolised, he believed, by their receipt of tribute from their subjects and Northcott proposed to exploit this custom, substituting a 'maintenance tax' for tribute. In this respect, he anticipated the formula used in the establishment of direct taxation in the thirties.

It was hoped to raise as much as £875 from the maintenance tax and the Commissioner toured the N.T. explaining the rationale of the tax, and the benefits to flow from it. Unfortunately, inquiries showed that only the Dagomba were familiar with the idea of an annual tribute (in kind) to their sovereign. The collection of the tax was costly and created discontent, since the chiefs (who were responsible for collection) tended to take a portion for themselves. The maintenance tax was therefore dropped in 1901 by Northcott's successor, Major Morris, and direct taxation was not in fact introduced to the N.T. until the late thirties. In Kimble's words, 'the Government failed to observe Lugard's principle that "The inauguration of British rule is the moment at which to lay the foundations" of a tax system'.[20]

In 1907 the Government abolished the caravan tolls, which had become the main source of revenue for the N.T. It did so for fear that these levies would discourage merchants from bringing their goods through the N.T. to the railhead at Kumasi. The protection of the 'transit trade' thus took priority over the development of the N.T.; and, indeed, for some officials, the existence of the trade was the only reason for continued British presence there.

The immediate consequence of the abolition of caravan tolls was an enormous drop in the revenue of the Protectorate which took twenty years to regain its level in 1907.

Table 4 shows quite clearly why the N.T. were regarded as a wasteful possession. In the twenties the Protectorate was self-supporting only to the extent of between 9 and 11 per cent of its expenditure. District administration was even more dependent: on the eve of the First World War, the Western Dagomba district provided, as tax revenue, only 1.3 per cent of the government funds spent in the area. All local revenue came from indirect taxation and from fines, fees, and rents.[21]

TABLE 4 *Northern Territories: revenue and expenditure (selected years)*

Year	Northern Territories		Southern Province		Western Dagomba District	
	Revenue £	Expenditure £	Revenue £	Expenditure £	Revenue £	Expenditure £
1906/7	18,046					
1907/8	3,500					
1911/12			1,632			
1912/13			1,980		80[a]	4,319[a]
1913/14			2,976			
1922/3	6,446					
1923/4	8,852	87,736				
1924/5	8,222	85,300				
1925/6	9,201	100,792				
1926/7	19,027	118,097			1,137	52,904
1927/8	22,286	111,868				
1930/1	24,574	140,132				

[a]Revenue/expenditure for one quarter only.

SOURCE: Ferguson and Wilks (1970), p. 334; *Annual Report on the Southern Province*, 1912, 1913, and 1914 (N.A.G.A., ADM. 56/1/466; ADM. 56/1/470); *Quarterly Report, Southern Province*, second quarter, 1914 (N.A.G.A., ADM. 56/1/474); *Annual Report on the Western Dagomba District for the quarter ending 31 March 1926* [sic] (N.A.G.A., ADM. 56/1/506); *Annual Report of the Northern Territories*, 1925/6, 1926/7, 1927/8, 1930/1 (N.A.G.T., ADM. 1/97; ADM. 1/127).

FORCED LABOUR

For lack of revenue, the D.C. had to rely on the only other resource his district could provide – labour. Compulsory labour took two main forms, carrier service and road-building. Apart from its moral aspects, forced (or communal) labour had two unhappy consequences. One was its effect on relations between the chiefs and their subjects, for the administration relied on the chiefs to provide labourers. The damage entailed by this dependence will be considered in the next chapter. Forced labour was also admitted to be harmful to the local economy: it represented both a heavy drain on the labour supply of the districts and a very inefficient use of the labour.

The administration recognised these facts but could see no alternative. In principle, every adult male in the north was liable to do six days' work on the roads each quarter. In addition, he could be drafted into service as a bearer. (Whether or not he was recruited for either purpose in reality depended on the standing of his chief and also, not least, on how near his village was to a road.) Western Dagomba alone provided 3,730 labourers in 1909, 3,558 in 1910, and 3,976 in 1912.[22] Those recruited as carriers by the chiefs were paid less than a third of the rate paid to those hired in the market-place by the government. Thus a carrier received, in 1917, the sum of four shillings for a journey from Yendi to Salaga and back (a distance of at least 140 miles) and three shillings for a return trip from Tamale to Yendi (120 miles).[23]

The wastefulness of carrier transport was not lost on the D.C.s. The Provincial Commissioner, Southern Province, wrote in 1910: 'The method is probably more primitive than that adopted by the ISRAELITES, when proceeding to the PROMISED LAND. Until boats or wheels are at the disposal of the Protectorate, transport must remain as it is.'[24] Relief finally came with the appearance of motor vehicles in the twenties. Until then, however, forced labour was used in great quantities, to the detriment of agricultural development. The P.C., Southern Province, argued that rising food prices in 1914 could be attributed to 'our calls for carriers at all times of the year, as not alone does this practice deplete certain country sides at critical farming times but also the young men are inclined to leave the country on account of it'. He continued: 'In the Tamale district alone over 4,000 boys were taken from their farms for periods varying from four to thirty days, and when we calculate the total male population who can work on farms this drain must be very heavy on a population which is purely agricultural.'[25]

In the immediate postwar period, demand was still heavy. The D.C., Western Dagomba, recruited 1,344 carriers in 1920 which, as his Provincial Commissioner pointed out, meant 'the loss of over ten thousand man-days to the agricultural and industrial development of the district'.[26] In 1926, however, the number of carriers employed was down to 5 per cent of the figure in the postwar years and by 1930 the use of bearers had virtually ceased: the Protectorate had over 500 miles of all-weather roads and, as the Chief Commissioner said, 'where motors can pass, carriers are not required'.[27]

STAFF

Colonial administration was in form bureaucratic, but in practice it was personalised, at times even proprietorial. The effectiveness of the administration was conditioned by the powers and resources available to its agents, but the direction and impact of colonial government depended, to a greater extent than in other systems, on the personalities of its field officers, 'the men on the spot'.

Administrative personnel in the north consisted of members of the Political Service (the commissioners and Political Administration clerks) and the technical services (Education, Health, and, eventually, Public Works). This establishment scarcely represented Miss Perham's 'iron grid of administration', as the recurrent complaints about overwork and understaffing make quite plain. The official establishment, on the political side, was 20 between 1908 and 1921 and 27 thereafter.[28] It was rarely, if ever, up to strength and was further depleted by illness and absences on leave. In 1922, of a total of 89 political officers in the Gold Coast, 21 were attached to the N.T. administration.[29] Expressed as a ratio of officials to population, this figure represented one official to 34,204 subjects (compared to one to

17,425 in Ashanti and one to 27,253 in the Colony). The difference is perhaps more striking when expressed in terms of areas to be covered. With the addition of northern Togoland during the war, the average area per administrative officer in the N.T. was 1,953 square miles (as against only 593 square miles in the Colony and 1,006 in Ashanti). Manpower for carrying out even basic law-enforcement functions was fairly small: by 1930 the total strength of the N.T. Constabulary was around 280, of whom 120 were stationed in the Southern Province, at Tamale and Yendi.[30]

Shortage of staff led to a fairly high turnover in posts, and it also sharpened conflicts of duty – notably the conflict between the demands of office work and the requirement of keeping personal contact with the villages, something which received heavy normative emphasis in memoranda and other instructions. In both respects, the general result was to reduce the effectiveness of the administration.

From an administrative point of view, Dagomba was rather better placed than, for example, the north-western districts. It benefited from the importance of Tamale as headquarters of the Protectorate and it lay across both the old and the new lines of communication. Even so, the post of D.C. (or D.P.O.) at Yendi had forty-one incumbents between August 1914 and July 1944.[31] The average tenure of a D.C. at Yendi was eight months, but some officials had exhaustingly long tours, largely because of staffing difficulties.[32] High turnover was a problem even at Tamale (the Western Dagomba District changed hands eleven times between April 1924 and January 1931).

As for 'trekking', it is clear that the number of days spent by D.C.s in visiting the divisions and villages went down in the middle years of colonial rule. Such decline did not necessarily indicate a weakening of contact, however, since motor transport enabled officials to get round more quickly than before.[33] There was, nevertheless, persistent complaint about the conflict between office work and touring. The latter always occupied a high place among the categorical imperatives of imperialism. It was constantly urged on junior officers by their seniors, thus: 'On assuming the administration of the Yendi District you should make it your duty to get in touch as quickly as possible with the Chiefs and people of the District by travelling constantly and by making yourself personally acquainted with every village, however small or remote.'[34] A tremendous effort was, indeed, made in Eastern Dagomba after the occupation.[35] But in 1921 the D.P.O. complained that the district, as reconstituted after the 1919 settlement, was 'now so big that it [was] impossible for one Commissioner . . . to control it'.[36]

Even so, the D.C. at Yendi still managed to spend over four months a year on trek in the mid-twenties. His counterpart at Tamale was less successful, having to deal with the larger volume of paperwork and court cases accompanying processes of economic and social change around Tamale. The D.C., Western Dagomba, wrote in a quarterly report for 1921: 'No travelling was done by the District Commissioner Tamale and it is impossible for him to run the District alone. An Assistant is necessary for there is enough work in Tamale alone to keep a District Commissioner fully employed.'[37] The staffing position in Tamale was in fact quite favourable relative to that which obtained after the Slump when the administration was subject to retrenchment. But in 1928 the D.C. alleged that a decline in the authority of divisional chiefs was 'largely due to the fact that the Western Dagomba District is not trekked as much as it should be, the District Commissioner is not able to get away from Tamale for more than a day or two unless he has an Assistant District Commissioner owing chiefly to the large increase in Court work'.[38]

What kind of people were the colonial administrators? Within what I referred to earlier as 'the northern interest', there were in fact two generations. One consisted of men who, for the most part, had originally come to the Gold Coast as colonial soldiers and had then become administrative officers. Table 5 lists the more important members of this group who impinge on Dagomba history (it includes, with minor exceptions, only officers who still held a post in the N.T. in the late twenties).

TABLE 5 *Northern Territories: principal administrative officers with service dating from 1914 or earlier*

Name	Educated	Military rank	Entered Gold Coast service	First served in north	Comments
ARMITAGE, C. H.	?	Captain (D.S.O.)	1894	1897	C.C.N.T., 1910–20
WALKER-LEIGH, A. H. C.	Cheltenham	Major	1898	1907	C.C.N.T., 1924–30
POOLE, G. A. EVERED	?	Captain	1899	1907	D.P.O., Yendi, 1916–20
PHILBRICK, A. J.	Rugby and Cambridge	–	1901	1921	C.C.N.T., 1921–4
BRANCH, H.	?	–	1902	1912	Intermittently D.C., Western Dagomba; P.C., Southern Province
RATTRAY, R. S.	?	Captain	1907	–	Anthropologist
WHITTALL, P. F.	Felsted	Colonel	1907	1907	D.C. and P.C., largely Northern Province
CASTELLAIN, L.	Eton	Captain	1909	1909	P.C., Southern Province, in twenties
CUTFIELD, A. J.	Epsom	Captain	1910	1917	P.C. in twenties
CARDINALL, A. W.	Winchester	–	1914	1916	D.P.O., Yendi
RAKE, E. O.	Bradfield and Cambridge	–	1914	1914	D.C., Western Dagomba, and headmaster in twenties

SOURCES: *The Gold Coast Civil Service List*, 1908–36; personal communications. I am most grateful to Canon H. A. Blair and Mrs Elizabeth Hook for their generous assistance in obtaining information about the background of colonial officers.

The second generation began to arrive in 1919 and consisted of men who had served in the war. The majority held commissions and a number had won decorations. In general, their background was similar to that of the first generation, although obviously the experience of trench warfare was very different from that of colonial soldiering.[39] There were few products of the major English public schools at this or any other time (or, for that matter, in any West African colony at any time). Table 6 lists officers of this group who served as D.C. in Eastern or Western Dagomba during the twenties.

Most of these postwar entrants were sent directly to the north and were apparently assimilated without stress into the small world of N.T. administration. Their arrival did not lead to any new direction in policy or methods, which only came at the end of the twenties, with the retirement of Walker-Leigh, the Chief Commissioner, the posting of several D.C.s, and the appointment of Jackson, Duncan-Johnstone, and others sympathetic to the establishment of an indirect rule regime. Indeed, the hostility of the in-direct rule administrators was particularly felt by several of the postwar entry, such as Gilbert, Moreton, and Rutherford.

TABLE 6 *Northern Territories: post-1918 administrative entry (selected members)*

Name	Educated	Military rank	Entered Gold Coast service	Age on entry	First served in north	Comments
GILBERT, W. E.	Lutterworth G. S.	Captain (M.C.)	1919	34	1920	D.C., Eastern Dagomba, in twenties
MORETON, P. R. C.	St John's, Leatherhead	Major (D.S.O.)	1919	33	1920	Served at Yendi and Tamale
SUMNER, R. C.	Lancing	Lieutenant	1920	33	1920	Intermittently D.C., Western Dagomba
BUTLER, C. O.	Tollington Park College	Lieutenant	1921	25	1921	Briefly D.C., Western Dagomba
PARKER, G. O.	Trinity College, Dublin	Lieutenant	1921	26	1921	
RUTHERFORD, P. W.	Brighton College	Captain (M.C.)	1921	25	1924	D.C., Western Dagomba, in late twenties
BROCKMAN, A. D.	King's, Canterbury	Served; rank n.a.	1923	31	? 1925	Headmaster, Yendi Trade School and acting D.C.
ARMSTRONG, J. A.	?	Captain	1924	32	1924	D.C., Eastern and Western Dagomba

SOURCES: See Table 5.

COLONIAL SOCIETY

It is difficult now to evoke the social world of the official class in the north. Numerically, it was certainly small: in 1928 there were only twenty-eight European residents in the Western Dagomba District, all of them officials or relatives of officials. Although the north was vaguely reputed to be healthier than the Colony and Ashanti, there was a substantial amount of illness from malaria and other diseases. Several officials died of yellow fever and blackwater fever, and there were periods when Tamale was put into quarantine to stop these diseases from spreading.[40]

Naturally, these conditions tended to discourage the emigration of wives and families so that, at least in the earlier period, the north had the characteristics of a bachelor society. D.C.s often led a solitary existence in which, as their diaries reveal, visitors were a precious treat, to be looked forward to and warmly entertained. The Christmas trip to Tamale provided another greatly appreciated break. Other public holidays were scrupulously observed, though sometimes the population failed to show the same enthusiasm as its rulers, as the D.P.O., Eastern Dagomba, noted on the occasion of Empire Day in 1920:

The Chief and his people turned up nearly an hour late for the march past ... Gave a short address on the Empire and reasons of the salute etc., in the Court house after parade ... Held races in the afternoon. Found nearly the whole town too lazy to come and except for small boys, too lazy to run, so the whole thing was rather a farce.[41]

In Tamale there was a social club for Europeans, a polo club, and also (particularly after the arrival of Duncan-Johnstone, the bagpipe-playing Provincial Commissioner) a Caledonian Club, which in 1929 had nine members.[42] Sport was actively pursued, at least in its conventional forms; there were hare-and-hounds races, promoted by an institution known as 'the Tamale hunt'.[43]

Otherwise, spare time tended to be spent on pet projects and obsessions, such as the D.C. Yendi's Kulpeni bridge, perpetually under construction and as perpetually swept away. There was also the universal passion for resthouse building. The main responsibility for constructing and maintaining resthouses lay with the chiefs, but when visiting villages the D.C. often showed particular interest in the state of the local resthouse. Yendi district alone had forty-two resthouses by the late twenties.[44] After reading diaries of tours, one is sometimes tempted to think that if independence had been delayed for another ten or fifteen years, the entire surface of the N.T. would have been covered with resthouses, chicken-runs, and half-completed bridges.

There were, in fact, two expatriate communities in the north. For as well as the Europeans, there was from the beginning a community of 'coast Africans', southerners working as clerks for the government or for the few commercial firms which had branches in the north. Given the lack of educated northerners, the government had to rely on strangers and such dependence, apart from raising problems of language and custom, involved extra cost, since the government had to pay inducement allowances of up to thirty shillings a month to keep clerks in the north. They were isolated physically and socially, as Kimble remarks: 'the little community must have lived like expatriates, with their own amusements and church services, few of them spoke local languages'.[45] They did not seek assimilation into northern society, but equally they were not accepted into European expatriate society. European officials were often wary of southerners, fearing that they might be vectors for 'progressive' ideas and organisers of 'agitation'. An explicit preference for the 'simple' or 'loyal' northerner sometimes appears in official correspondence. Thus Governor Thorburn commented that northerners were 'much more easy to deal with than their compatriots on the coast. They willingly make the most excellent roads, culverts, and rest-houses for small "dashes."'[46]

It is not, then, surprising to find that most officials were completely unsympathetic to efforts by the southern community to establish separate institutions. In 1911 the Acting Commandant of the N.T.C. reported that his clerks and some N.C.O.s objected strongly to being required to appear before the chief of Tamale for judgement when they were involved in legal cases. The Commandant asked that his subordinates, many of them southerners, should have the option of trial in the commissioners' courts.[47] When this arrangement was rejected, the southerners set up their own association. The Twi Foreigners Arbitration, and requested the Chief Commissioner to give official recognition to tribunals formed by this society. Such recognition was refused, although the Chief Commissioner said that he did not object to southerners forming a friendly society under this name.[48]

The wish of 'coast Africans' to escape from the jurisdiction of northern chiefs was never met by the administration which, indeed, was later outraged by the attempts of southern clerks to get themselves exempted from direct taxation, when it was introduced as part of the indirect rule system in the thirties. The stranger community did, however, get recognition for its own elected chief, whose authority extended to Ga, Adangbe, Akwapim, and Ayigbe residents of Tamale.

The southern community also produced one of the most assiduous collectors of local history and folklore, in the person of E. F. Tamakloe, an Ewe, who began his career as interpreter to two German students of the north. He joined government service before the First World War and undertook his own research, which culminated in the publication of his *Brief History of the Dagbamba People* in 1931. This work, and his Dagbane dictionary and grammar, prepared in association with Blair, came into their own as the British went about establishing indirect rule and they remain important records of Dagomba history and culture.[49]

ECONOMIC POLICY

Development policy in the N.T. was, broadly, concerned with three objectives: the promotion of trade; the encouragement of cash-crop farming; and last (and least) the recruitment of migrant labour for work in the south.

We have already noted the overwhelming importance of commerce as a reason for British presence in the north. The 1899 *Instructions to Officers* stated: 'especially it is desired that suggestions should be made with a view to the development of trade'. Officers were to encourage Africans to use the markets and 'they should impress on them the necessity of greater industry in order that they may obtain money with which to make purchases'.[50]

The promotion of British commerce depended on exclusion of trade goods from non-British sources and on a continuing expansion of cash incomes locally. Initially, a large proportion of the goods in northern markets were of German origin: this was stopped by a strengthening of the preventive service on the Togo border. Some increase in cash and income was provided by the movement of the administration from Gambaga to Tamale and the growth of wage labour around the main administrative centres as a result of governmental activity. By 1914 such activity had levelled off and trade was stagnating. The war itself produced a further decline in local commerce.[51]

The major hope for developing a monetary economy lay, therefore, in encouraging cash-crop agriculture, the only alternative being remittances from migrant labourers. But, to a great extent, these sources were mutually exclusive, especially as local forced labour was proving such a drain on the agricultural work force. For this reason, P.C.s and D.C.s were generally reluctant to help labour recruiters from southern mining companies in finding workers in the N.T., since in so doing they would be undermining their own efforts to develop the production of cotton and foodstuffs for sale.

Such efforts began effectively with the establishment of civil administration. Great enthusiasm was put into a campaign to introduce cotton between 1908 and 1914: the administration had a ginnery and a press in Tamale by 1909 and in later years representatives of the British Cotton Growing Association toured the area distributing seed and urging farmers to expand the acreage under cotton.[52] Despite spasms of optimism, the administration was generally disappointed with the results of its campaign. The P.C., Southern Province, reported in 1910:

Every effort was made by Commissioners to induce the natives to take the question of cotton growing seriously, and the benefit to be derived from so doing was constantly impressed on them. Up to the present the results have been rather disappointing than otherwise. There is no doubt that the natural antagonism towards innovation of any kind, amongst the natives, and the small price at present offered – ½d per lb – have a distinct effect.[53]

This statement was unusually disparaging of the Dagomba as a farmer. For, whatever other faults they attributed to him, the British were generally complimentary about his skill and productivity.[54] The real causes of failure were to do with low prices, the cost of transport, and competing claims on local labour, as the D.C., Tamale, noted: 'till this demand for manual labour is decreased, it is impossible to have any hopes of this country ever being able to export produce in large quantities'.[55] Indeed, so far from there being a marketable surplus, a shortage of foodstuffs appeared by 1914 (as we have noted earlier), prompting the Provincial Commissioner to ask: 'Are we demanding too much of the people in the matter of transport etc. and making the people neglect the most important task of producing food?'[56]

The arrival of the lorry in the twenties eased the burden of porterage and during this period the work of road-building became less onerous. Trade flourished, and the governor, Sir Gordon Guggisberg, was enthusiastic about the economic prospects of the N.T.: 'there can be no doubt that at some future time the produce of the Northern Territories will be a considerable factor in the trade of the whole country'.[57]

With the improvements in transport and a continuing growth in urban demand (both from Tamale and from southern towns), the production of foodstuffs for sale grew quite satisfactorily during the twenties. But cotton, the administration's first priority, was little more successful than before the war. A new scheme was launched in Western Dagomba in 1926 and again large quantities of free seed were distributed: 7,827 lbs of cotton were produced for ginning in the district in the 1927/8 season.

But yields were low, soils were poor, and the price offered by European companies was unattractive, compared to the prices paid locally. The C.C.N.T. reported: 'There does not appear to be a great prospect for cotton here.' And he added: 'From what I can gather the present population around Tamale is hardly able to supply the necessary foodstuffs to meet the local demand, this being the case, how on earth can we expect them to produce cotton for export?'[58] The Governor accepted his argument but replied: 'the crop is so important that we must prove its failure definitely before giving it up'.[59] In 1930 the administration decided that failure had been proved and the cotton campaign was stopped, pending the discovery of a suitable type of seed for the N.T.

After 1930 the economic development of Dagomba was focussed on the development of trade in foodstuffs and, to a certain extent, on the cattle trade. There was also some labour migration but, as with cash-crop agriculture, there was a reaction against government direction in this field during the inter-war years.

Labour recruiting in the north for the mines in the Tarkwa–Prestea area began in 1906, when the Chamber of Mines approached the C.C.N.T., Watherston, about the possibility of getting workers from the Protectorate. Despite initial suspicions, recruitment was undertaken and continued until 1924, when the Secretary of State for the Colonies intervened, on account of increasing complaints about the high rates of death and illness among mine workers.[60] Indeed, despite the support given by Philbrick, as C.C.N.T., in the early twenties, there was growing opposition by D.C.s in the Dagomba area to the recruiting activities of the mines. The D.C.s argued that agriculture and public works were being deprived of a precious resource, and they objected to the suffering caused to the labourers and their families. When the Secretary of State authorised recruitment to recommence, under more stringent conditions and without official sponsorship, the mining companies found, as Kimble remarks, 'that organised recruiting would be so expensive that it was no longer worth their while. So the Administration was relieved of its major responsibility in this field.'[61]

EDUCATION

In the sphere of education, however, the administration never relaxed its control. Schooling developed very slowly in the north: by 1930 there were only five government primary schools and two technical schools in the N.T.[62] In Dagomba there were only two institutions in this period: the Tamale primary school, opened in 1909, and the trade school, started at Yendi in 1922 and transferred to Tamale in 1927. The number of pupils grew only gradually: Tamale primary had 44 pupils in 1909, 72 in 1919, 112 in 1925, and 122 in 1929.[63]

Although the D.C. enthused about 'the marvellous strides' made by the Tamale school, it was soon apparent that the Dagomba were less enthusiastic. One or two divisional chiefs' sons were enrolled, but other chiefs sent the children of slaves or commoners, fearing that the European schools would turn their sons into labourers or stewards.[64] More generally, parents saw no economic advantage in sending their children to school: to do so was to reduce a family's labour force, without any assurance of an ultimate benefit in the form of highly remunerated or esteemed employment. As Bening remarks,

Before the introduction of Native Authorities and the imposition of direct taxation in the Northern Territories in 1936, there were very limited opportunities for paid employment, even for literates. The rank and file of the constabulary was illiterate and service with the political administration as clerks or interpreters was naturally restricted.[65]

The administration, for its part, saw the schools as instruments for producing literate chiefs and 'Clerks and Assistant Storekeepers'. Before 1918 all teachers were southerners who did not speak local languages and the curriculum was of a formal literary kind, neatly exemplified by the programme for the Tamale school Prize Day in 1915 which included four songs, entitled 'Hurrah! hurrah! for England', 'Our home is the ocean', 'The Union Jack', and 'The Bay of Biscay'. There was little effort to produce local teachers: only in 1917 were three boys sent for teacher-training in Accra.[66]

In the twenties, Guggisberg's administration produced a reaction away from literary education and towards a more 'practical' and traditionally oriented curriculum. Sir Gordon himself said at Yendi on 8 March 1921:

When we give a Dagomba man a European education we do not want him to forget the customs of his own country. We do not want to make him into a European. We want to teach him to remain a good Dagomba. If you want good trade, and to have a fine country, it is necessary that you should all be good Dagombas and stick together and not try and break up. That is why we are going to be very careful about the European education that we give you.[67]

The establishment of the Yendi trade school in 1922 was prompted by the Mandates Commission's criticisms of the lack of schools in the Togoland mandate area. Nevertheless, as a vocational institution, it was in line with Guggisberg's policy, which was further elaborated in a memorandum he issued after a visit to the north in 1925.

In his memorandum Guggisberg declared that the N.T. were 'fifty years behind Ashanti and the Gold Coast Colony in progress from a primitive to a higher state of civilisation'.[68] He believed (unlike his subordinates) that there was an 'appreciable' demand for education in the north, largely due to the experiences of migrant workers as reported back to the villages. The backwardness of the north, he said, represented an opportunity to create a system which did not repeat the errors committed in the south, one which did not uproot children and make them contemptuous of inherited concepts and values.

Guggisberg's programme involved the creation of a 'central institution' (in Tamale) as a 'model for infant and primary schools in the N.T.s'. It would cater almost entirely for northerners and in time, with the provision of a teacher-training centre at Tamale, all teachers would also be northerners.[69] In order to ensure the development of a coherent 'northern' system, the administration should have control of all schools in the north, to which end a body of inspectors would be required.[70] There should be one education officer for the north to ensure controlled development of education. Guggisberg continued: 'It is essential that we should pass an Ordinance in the Northern Territories which will prevent any system of education being started by the missions and growing up without control, with the inevitable result that we should have to destroy later.'[71]

The 'central institution' was the Tamale Senior School, which alone was to provide education to the level of Standard VII. Launched in April 1927, the school was intended to produce 'capable and self-reliant citizens', educated farmers and artisans, rather than clerks; later in the year the trade school was transferred to Tamale so as to increase facilities for technical instruction. At the same time, a Superintendent of Education for the Northern Territories, the Reverend A. H. Candler, was appointed and made answerable directly to the Colonial Secretary in Accra, instead of to the Education Department. Under Candler's administration, the schools outside Tamale ceased to offer education above the level of Standard IV and only a small number of pupils were allowed to go for further schooling in Tamale. Candler also decided in 1928 that it would be premature to set up teacher-training facilities in the north.[72]

The preoccupation of the government seems to have been to avoid the creation of an unemployable educated group, with the political consequences they feared this would entail. Access to advanced schooling was to be rigorously controlled and primary education would be strictly related to the requirements of the agricultural economy. As the Provincial Inspector of Schools later wrote:

Agriculture was made the central feature of school life and instruction, and craft-work of all sorts was given a front place in the school curriculum. While realising the necessity of training suitable lads for employment in the Government departments, Government kept before it the aim of a localised education which was to fit the average lad for a fuller village life. Every pupil was to be trained to be a handyman, to make and use simple tools, to build hygienic houses of an improved local type, to farm with his head as well as his hands, and to realise the relation of cause and effect.[73]

This philosophy of education was entrenched by the establishment of indirect rule, which was founded on the same moral and political assumptions and which tended in the same direction, namely, towards the creation of a neo-traditional elite, an elite of educated chiefs and aristocratic clerks. In this sense, the character of Dagomba politics in the period after 1945 was formed in the inter-war years by an official policy of partial and selective modernisation.

CHAPTER 4

DAGOMBA DIVIDED AND UNITED, 1899–1930

The King of Yendi refused to sign a treaty in 1894, since he feared
the eventual partition of his territory: 'Did you ever see two men
riding one donkey?' he asked.[1]

The advent of colonial rule was doubly traumatic for the Dagomba ruling
class. For not only was the kingdom deprived of sovereignty and the rights
and powers attaching to sovereignty, but it was also physically divided between two colonial overlords, the British and the Germans. This chapter is
concerned, first, with the exercise of colonial authority in relation to the
chiefs; secondly, with the effects of partition upon chieftaincy; and, thirdly,
with the politics of reunification following the British invasion of Togo in
1914.

Colonial rule was legitimated, internationally, by the 1899 convention
and earlier agreements with France and Germany. Locally, it rested on
treaties of protection signed with the Ya-Na and other chiefs in the 1890s.[2]
The British refused any recognition to the paramount, forbade chiefs in
their domain to have any relations with him, and vested authority instead
in the persons of the Karaga-Na and the Yo-Na, both of whom found themselves in British Dagomba. In 1901 the British Commissioner, Major Morris,
simply 'informed an assembly of twenty-two Western Dagomba chiefs that,
since the Ya-Na was now in German territory, he and not the Ya-Na was
henceforth their Head Chief'.[3]

Between 1899 and 1928 native administration involved reliance on the
chiefs. But such reliance, while officially recommended, was pragmatic
rather than doctrinaire in spirit. It derived from a recognition of necessity,
not from any positively elaborated philosophy of political development.
Traditional authority had instrumental rather than normative value: that
is, it was useful insofar as it aided the achievement of colonial objectives,
but those exercising it were not seen as having intrinsic or inalienable rights
or as entitled to assert interests of an independent kind.

However, the phrase 'direct rule', sometimes applied to this period, is
misleading to the extent that it implied a similarity to French colonial
policy or, more specifically, to the alleged wish of French administrators to
destroy systematically the 'feudal' rule of chiefs. The British in the N.T.
before 1930 did not accord even such negative consideration to the question
of native authority. They were largely indifferent to the moral and political
character of such authority and, apparently, quite uninterested in its historical origin. We do not find in the N.T. between 1900 and 1930 'scholar-

administrators' of the type so common in French territories at this time (men such as Delafosse and Tauxier). Although towards the end of 'direct rule' administrators like Cardinall did begin to take an interest in African history and institutions, the general level of cheerful ignorance revealed by casual entries in administrators' diaries is sometimes quite startling.[4]

But the official prescription for native administration did not, in fact, require any detailed enquiry into or knowledge of pre-colonial institutions. It simply laid down that the chiefs should 'exercise the jurisdiction heretofore exercised by them in the same measure as such jurisdiction has been heretofore exercised'.[5] The 1899 instructions (as we have seen) also recommended use of the chiefs: 'As regards the natives, Officers will act through the native chiefs as far as possible for the suppression of minor offences, and will support them in securing execution of sentences.'[6] The civilian commissioners took a similar view. In his handing-over report of 1909, Irvine, P.C., Southern Province, advised his successor: 'As it is impossible to govern the country successfully except through the chiefs, every endeavour should be made to strengthen their hands in their dealings with their people as far as it is compatible with equity and good governance.'[7]

With time the concept of rule through chiefs became more refined. Thus Nash, P.C., Southern Province, wrote in 1914 that the D.C.

must keep a light hand on [the] Chief's politics, knowing everything, and yet doing little, and saying almost nothing. If he is autocratic and deputes power to no-one, he will have quiet, obedient, but *furtive* Chiefs. Under such circumstances Chiefs are positive danger [sic], as they possess no responsibility and merely regard their Office as an avenue to misdemeanour. On the other hand if Chiefs are allowed unlimited authority a District Commissioner is not master in his own District.[8]

A similar appreciation of the role of chiefs was shown when the British occupied German Dagomba in August 1914. The Governor told the O.C. Togoland Force that 'in the administration of native affairs you should make as much use as possible of the services of the native Chiefs and Headmen, and should afford as much latitude as you may think expedient to such Chiefs and Headmen in disposing of matters in dispute among their people'.[9]

Under the governorship of Sir Gordon Guggisberg in the twenties, support for native administration became official policy. In March 1921 Guggisberg declared:

Our policy must be to maintain any Paramount Chiefs that exist and gradually absorb under these any small communities scattered about. What we should aim at is that some day the Dagombas, Gonjas and Mamprusi should become strong native states. Each will have its own little Public Works Department and carry on its own business with the Political Officer as a Resident and Adviser. Each state will be more or less self-contained.

He concluded: 'I would like the Chief Commissioner to draw up and submit to me in due course a policy for the Northern Territories showing a definite scheme for fostering the formation of these big states without compulsion.'[10]

Guggisberg's vision of indirect rule was not adopted in the N.T. until after his departure in 1927 and then in a slightly different fashion. Indeed, although in 1928 the Chief Commissioner, Walker-Leigh, asserted that in the north there had always 'been a system of indirect rule', the first thirty years of colonial government undoubtedly had a harmful effect on the status of the chiefs. The very existence of a suzerain government, the powers which it reserved, and the controls which it exercised weakened the authority of the chieftaincy and limited its jurisdiction. Although the inherited procedures of selection were not formally abolished, the Ya-Na's right of appointment was curtailed and the tenure of chiefly office at all levels was made conditional on government's approval. The British placed all newly appointed chiefs on a year's probation before confirming them in office.[11] Even after completion of the probationary period, chiefs could be (and were) dismissed. The overall principle of 'working through the chiefs' did not protect them if they failed to provide help in implementing specific colonial policies.

In this respect, the administration's demands for labour had a particularly damaging effect on the standing of the chiefs. As Ferguson and Wilks remark, it was the abolition of caravan tolls (and the consequently increased dependence of the government on forced labour) which marked the beginning of 'the era of "sergeant-major" chiefs'.[12] Pressure on chiefs to provide labourers sometimes caused them to lose the respect and loyalty of their subjects, either because of the exactions they in turn imposed or because of the humiliations (such as fining, suspension, or imprisonment) they suffered as a result of failing to give satisfaction to their masters.

Not even the royal dukes and senior divisional chiefs were immune to such penalties. Thus in 1913 the Yo-Na was fined £10 for failing to supply labourers for work on the Tamale–Savelugu road; in 1916 the Tolon-Na was fined £5 for allowing a road and several resthouses to fall into disrepair; and in 1919 the Gushie-Na was twice fined, once for neglecting a resthouse and once for failing to come out to greet the D.P.O., Yendi, when the latter was, approaching Gushiegu.[13] Guggisberg's declarations of reverence for traditional institutions did not cause the N.T. officers to become noticeably more tender towards the senior chiefs. Thus the P.C., Southern Province, recorded in his diary for August 1923: 'KARAGA and SAVELUGU are not pulling their weight in the matter of supplying guinea corn ... have ordered the Chief of KARAGA to supply 30 loads by the 28th inst. failing the supply of which I shall bring him to be dealt with.'[14] Rutherford, in his handing-over notes for Western Dagomba in 1924, was equally forthright: 'The Chief of KARAGA needs keeping up to scratch. He is liable to get above himself and when sent for generally takes much more time than necessary to come in. This being a sign of disrespect should be punished.'[15]

There are, however, not many recorded instances of chiefs being deposed and most of them occurred before the war and involved political offences. The Yo-Na, Mahama, was deposed and imprisoned in 1910 and Abudulai, 'Kpabia-Na', was treated similarly in 1914: in both cases their offence was political, that of continuing to recognise and have dealings with Yendi.[16]

After the war the main problem seems to have been the refusal of village chiefs to acknowledge the authority of divisional chiefs and for this the Kaduri-Na, Mahama, was deposed in 1928, at the behest of the Karaga-Na.

The chiefs were deprived of both their coercive and their judicial powers. They lost the right to use or command armed force and, indeed, they were required, in wartime, to find recruits for the colonial army. All criminal cases went to the commissioners' courts and 'native tribunals' were left with the more trivial matrimonial and land disputes. The administration declined to regularise the status and powers of these tribunals, despite an appeal by the P.C., Southern Province, in 1917. He reported to the C.C.N.T. that he could 'find nothing laid down in writing' concerning the scale of fines which chiefs could impose in matrimonial cases, though he had heard that a predecessor had adopted a range of penalties. The Provincial Commissioner continued:

I think that the time has come when it should be very definitely laid down what the powers of a Chief are, and what disputes he can hear and determine; what punishments he can inflict on persons who refuse to attend or to obey his final order, what Chiefs should be granted such powers and many other details relative to his fees etc.

He pointed out that people frequently refused to attend the Tamale native court, 'and the Chief is quite powerless to enforce [their] attendance, doubtless this is the case elsewhere'.[17]

The C.C.N.T. shrugged off the issue. After writing to other field officers, he announced that it was unnecessary to make rules for the native tribunals, since it was generally understood that anyone aggrieved with a judgement by a tribunal could appeal to a commissioner's court – before which, in any event, all important cases were heard.[18] The latter could hardly have expressed more clearly the practical indifference of the British to the sensibilities of native rulers – an indifference which shocked and dismayed the 'indirect rule' administrators of the next generation. Cardinall, a true believer, reported in 1928 on the calamitous state of native institutions:

The Native Courts of the Southern Provinces have taken no real part in the administration. As to the constitution of the Native Courts or Tribunals, nothing is on record. The system of direct rule has been so intense that how a court is formed, of whom it consists, what officers are attached to it, the nature of its procedure, have never been recorded or even considered.

Cardinall's verdict on the standing of chiefs under British rule was equally gloomy. The Dagomba had a sophisticated political structure but, he continued,

in spite of this well-defined system, the Administration in the past has interfered many a time in its working and almost succeeded in breaking it down to replace it with the sergeant-major type ... in reality the chiefs are practically powerless; they have neither revenue nor authority; they have tended to become mere sergeant-majors through whom the Administration can address the rank and file.[19]

But it was not altogether true that the chiefs were impoverished under 'direct rule'. Although they had, in a sense, to pay tribute to the colonial authority, they nevertheless still received tribute from their own subjects. Some chiefs actually took advantage of their backing by the government to enrich themselves. The chief of Sandule, in Eastern Dagomba, was dismissed for 'calling in labour in the D.P.O.'s name and using the men to work on his farm'.[20] Other forms of manipulation were also practised for economic gain, as Eyre-Smith pointed out:

Material wealth and possessions are becoming the criterion of power, so that in some cases we find a Chief using his 'magical' power over the people to aggrandise himself. [People] are afraid to complain of injustices for fear of the evil powers of the magic a Chief possesses striking them . . . this magical power enables these Chiefs to make exactions on their subjects for their personal aggrandisement . . . On every hand one is able to observe the steady growth of affluence in all that appertains to such a Chief and his immediate entourage.[21]

Abuse of office, when it occurred, was all the more serious because, short of action by the government, there was no procedure for removing an unsatisfactory or tyrannical chief (except, of course, poison). In general, the administration tended to take the chief's side in disputes, since, in its view, he represented 'authority'. But the endorsement of a chief by the administration did not automatically enhance his reputation and it certainly cannot be said that in this period the administration did much to enhance the status of chieftaincy as an institution.

THE EFFECTS OF PARTITION

The division of the kingdom between two European powers provided the occasion for opportunism of a different kind. For fifteen years, the Ya-Na was officially denied authority over his chiefs in the west and, in fact, over the greater part of his kingdom. He found himself in the Mango–Yendi district of Togo, along with the Gushiegu, Sunson, Kworli, Demon, and Yelzori divisions (all largely peopled by Konkombas).[22] The dukedoms of Savelugu and Karaga came under British control, as did Tolon, Gulkpeogu, Kumbungu, Nanton, and the best part of Mion province – a highly unfortunate situation from the point of view of royal government, and one rich in possibilities of intrigue.

The immediate beneficiaries were the two western dukes. In British Dagomba, the Yo-Na (chief of Savelugu) and the Karaga-Na were recognised as paramounts, although (as we have noted) royal dukes had previously been rather ineffectual figures in the government of Dagbon. Duncan-Johnstone and Blair remarked how, in consequence, 'the Divisional Chiefs of Tolon, Nanton, and Kumbungu found themselves put arbitrarily into the Savelugu Division under the Na of Savelugu, with whom they were of equal rank'.[23] (To appreciate the humiliation involved, it should be recalled that the Tolon-Na and the Kumbung-Na were the king's principal war chiefs and the former was also his principal elder.)

The Yo-Na exploited his good fortune to the full. As Blair later pointed out, the royal duke 'suffered much from hubris and stole a large number of Gulkpe-Na's villages and established a suzerainty over Kumbungu, etc. Even Nanton now pays a nominal allegiance to Savelugu, owing to his numbers of people, though in the old days, Nanton was much greater than Savelugu, and still ranks higher at the court of the Na.'[24] Savelugu's arrogance eventually led to protests by his neighbours, when in 1911 he nominated a new Kumbung-Na, against the wishes of the sub-chiefs of Kumbungu and 'without reference to the Commissioner'.[25]

The Yo-Na's ability to steal villages from the Gulkpe-Na was due to another piece of confusion. The Gulkpe-Na (divisional chief of the Tamale area) was in Yendi at the time of the conquest and he stayed there for the duration of German rule. The *dakpema* (headman) of Tamale, then a small village, 'seized the opportunity to increase his own power and importance, actually making a journey to Gambaga, the then Government Headquarters, to invite the Government to build a station in his town where there was plenty of water'.[26] The British accepted his offer and in fact moved the headquarters of the entire N.T. administration to Tamale. They quickly found that there was not 'plenty of water' in the area. But they only discovered the falsity of the *dakpema*'s claims to paramountcy in the district at the end of the twenties, during investigations connected with the establishment of indirect rule. Such opportunism was not unusual and I have cited here only the more prominent examples. For, as Cardinall wrote afterwards, 'Ambition to be kings was roused in the hearts of the most petty of chieftains and the prevarications to establish such claims made a confusion in administration which seems almost incredible.'[27]

DYNASTIC POLITICS

The partition created still greater confusion in dynastic affairs – which had been complicated enough even before the British and the Germans arrived on the scene. Through the confusion, however, we can see the shape of the present dispute between two branches of the royal family beginning to form and beginning to emerge as a public issue, albeit a minor one.

The starting-point is some forty years before the partition, in the reign of Ya-Na Yakuba. Yakuba had well over thirty sons, but only the two eldest, Abudulai and Andani, actually became king. Abudulai succeeded his father; Andani in turn succeeded him and was on the Yendi skin at the time of the European conquest. The descendants of these two kings have become known colloquially as 'the Abudu gate' and 'the Andani gate' respectively.

Andani died in August 1899 and a complex series of manoeuvres followed. A group of western Dagomba chiefs (notably the eldest sons of Andani, Iddi

(Tugu-Na) and Bukari (Pigu-Na)) campaigned initially to get one of their own number (by preference Bukari) accepted for Yendi. Bukari was not on a gate skin, however, so they transferred their support to the Yo-Na Darimani (also known as 'Kukra Adjei'), the twelfth son of Yakuba. An opposing faction wavered between Abudulai's son, Karaga-Na Alhassan, and the Mion-lana Salifu (the sixth son of Yakuba). It finally settled on Alhassan and the competition thus assumed the classic form of uncle versus nephew (see Fig. 2).[28]

By negotiation, the two factions agreed on Yo-Na Darimani (the uncle). As he moved up to Yendi, an Andani candidate (Iddi) moved to Savelugu, leaving the Abudu gate in occupation of Karaga, with an uncle (Salifu) at Mion. Both sides of the royal family thus had a candidate on a gate skin should Yendi become vacant.[29]

But this vacancy occurred rather more quickly than might have been expected. For the supporters of Darimani had offended both the Germans and the British: in 1898 they had joined up with the Zabarima leader, Babatu, in defying both the British and Ya-Na Andani, who had decided to cooperate with the invading power. The Germans were also anxious to eliminate the local opposition and in April 1900 they sent a force into Dagomba, killing Yo-Na Iddi and deposing the paramount Darimani, after he had been on the skin for only seven weeks. The German authorities then installed Karaga-Na Alhassan, the defeated candidate, at Yendi. Alhassan proceeded to appoint his cousin, Bukari Narkaw, to Karaga and to put his younger brother, Kalim, on the Mion skin (replacing Salifu, his earlier rival). Another supporter, Alhassan's uncle Bukari, was appointed to Savelugu, in place of the deceased Iddi; when Bukari died (in the early 1900s), he was replaced by one of Alhassan's brothers, Mahama.[30] There was thus not one son of Andani on a gate skin.

Between 1900 and 1917 (when Alhassan died) aristocratic politics in a sense marked time. The Ya-Na himself was cut off from his subordinates and was a German *protégé*. He was treated with little respect by his patrons, as Tamakloe points out:

though the Germans were his benefactors, their settlement in Yendi did him no good. For he was deprived of all his authority as a king, and was caused to be utterly rejected and despised by his own people, and the country was, after its partition ... ruled directly by the Germans first, and sometimes through the agency of the king's own ministers to whom only the German [sic] talked.[31]

The paramount had little opportunity to advance the position of his own branch, the Abudu gate. His brother at Savelugu, Mahama, fell from favour with the British and was removed in 1910 and jailed after he had been found to be in communication with Yendi. Mahama's treatment of his subordinates was described as 'very arbitrary' and despite their earlier opposition, these subordinates came to be regarded as 'British' chiefs.[32] The Andani gate was powerful in Western Dagomba. When Mahama was deposed, the British appointed Andani's second son, Bukari, to Savelugu,

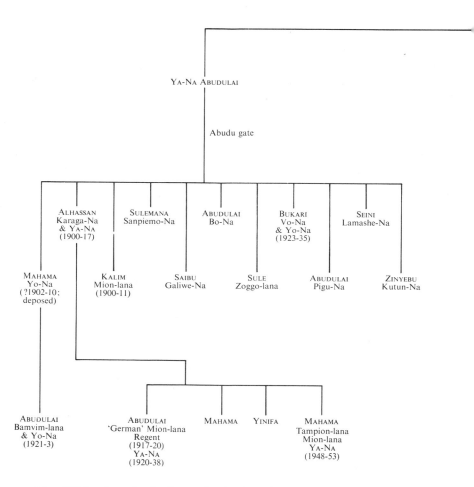

and by 1915 other Andani sons had taken the skins of Sanerigu, Tampion, Zangballon, and Kpatinga – all important royal chiefdoms on the way to Yendi.[33]

Further division within the royal house was caused by the behaviour of Alhassan's cousin, the Karaga-Na Bukari Narkaw. The latter accepted the orders of Tamale to cease communication with Yendi and, despite an initial aloofness towards the British, he became in time so cooperative that he was described by the Chief Commissioner as 'one of the most loyal

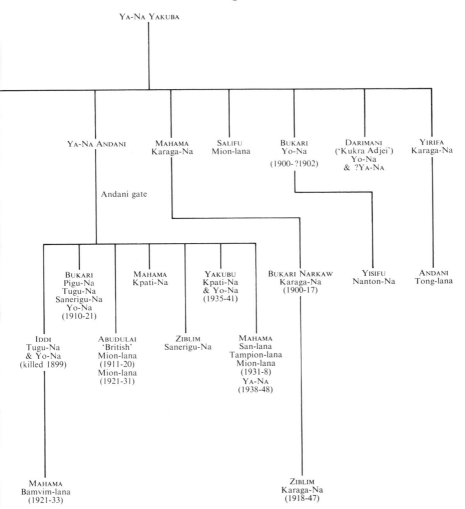

Fig. 2. Some descendants of Na Yakuba

adherents to this Administration'.[34] It was through exploiting his position that Bukari Narkaw got into bad odour at Yendi, in particular through his action in appointing a new Mion-lana.

The Mion skin, as we saw earlier, had some claim to be next to Yendi, and it was therefore greatly coveted by ambitious royals. Unfortunately, of the three provinces, Mion was the most severely affected by the partition. The villages of the province lay close to Yendi and the provincial capital, Sambu, was within the German sphere. But the majority of the villages

65

were in British Dagomba, and one of them, Kpabia, became a substitute capital. Until 1910 the British did not bother to appoint a Mion-lana for the British side: Alhassan's brother Kalim held the title until his death in 1911 or 1912, though he lived at Sambu.

On Kalim's death, the Karaga-Na, in his assumed capacity as 'Paramount Chief' of British Dagomba, took the initiative of appointing Ya-Na Andani's third son, Abudulai, to the Mion skin. At the same time, Ya-Na Alhassan appointed his eldest son, Abudulai, to the same skin. There were thus two Mion-lanas, both called Abudulai. One, belonging to the Andani gate, resided in the west and was recognised by the British. The other (the presumptive regent) lived in Togo and was backed by what were later described as 'the Yendi legitimists', that is, Alhassan's chiefs and elders, who asserted the continuing authority of Yendi throughout the kingdom.[35]

Even before the British invaded Togo, this situation was a cause of trouble for the N.T. administration. Led by the village headman of Kpabia, as many as eight village chiefs refused to accept the 'British' Mion-lana and crossed the frontier into Togo. The headman was dismissed and jailed for his part in the revolt and the village chiefs were replaced. But once Yendi had been occupied the dispute spread to the administration itself and indeed became entangled with wider diplomatic manoeuvres.

THE OCCUPATION OF TOGO

The actual invasion of northern Togo in August 1914 was a very straightforward military operation, carried out, as Cornevin puts it, by *'de pittoresques détachements entraînés par les administrateurs'*.[36] A small force of N.T. Constabulary, led by Major Marlow, crossed the frontier and occupied Yendi, without meeting opposition. Ya-Na Alhassan submitted to the British on 22 August and he and other chiefs are said to have welcomed the invaders. Alhassan's son, the 'German' Mion-lana, Abudulai, 'was the first to welcome and supply with food and carriers the British Troops'.[37] In return, the king and his family wanted the junction of the two parts of Dagbon, restoring Yendi to its former authority and certain 'British' nobles to their previous obedience.

But there was a diplomatic problem, however much the Governor and local officials might sympathise with the Ya-Na. London and Paris had agreed to the establishment of provisional governments in the occupied zones, but, as the Governor, Sir Hugh Clifford, told the Legislative Council, these arrangements were 'for immediate purposes only and without prejudice to any settlement which [might] hereafter be arrived at'.[38] Clifford informed the Secretary of State that he had received from the C.C.N.T., Armitage, a document which comprised 'a petition for protection and for the unification, under British rule, of the Dagomba country'. While recognising the impossibility of satisfying this demand, Clifford thought that it should ... be noted for future reference, that any attempt once more to divide the Dagomba country in a manner which is opposed to the ethnological distribution of the native population, will be keenly resented by the chiefs and people both in the Northern Territories and in the Sansanne-Mangu district of Togoland.[39]

The Colonial Secretary in Accra enlarged on the officials' dilemma in a rather exasperated letter to Armitage:

His Excellency fully appreciates the strong desire of the Dagomba people to be united once for all under British rule, and he is strongly representing this matter to the Secretary of State. During the continuance of the European War, however, and until some final and formal settlement is reached the portion of the Dagomba country hitherto administered by the Germans must continue to occupy the somewhat anomalous position which His Majesty's Government has decided to assign to it. The Governor appreciates the fact that you and your officers may experience some difficulty in making the native population understand this necessity.[40]

In the event, Armitage had even more difficulty than the Colonial Secretary predicted, partly because of his own tactlessness, and partly because his own 'man on the spot' refused to accept the necessity of deferring appointments.

Suppressing his own sympathies, the C.C.N.T. evidently decided to adopt an uncompromising stance and he forbade any assertion of the Ya-Na's authority in Western Dagomba.[41] Armitage declared his position forcefully in a speech to the chiefs at Yendi in June 1916:

I told them [he reported afterwards] that England had given the whole of her manhood to preserve the freedom of the world and that there was not a single family that did not mourn the loss of a husband, a son, brother or relative, and pointed out how grateful they ought to be when, in the midst of such worldwide misery, they were sitting peacefully in their villages protected by the power of the British Empire. All other matters dwindled, and were eclipsed by the Titanic struggle now being waged in Europe ... all minor considerations, such as a re-united Dagomba, must await its advent ... We were out to slay the German Beast and when that had been accomplished, and not until then, could any final partition of its carcass be made. The 'King' ... said he would make no further reference to his longing to see Dagomba re-united under him until the end of the war.[42]

Crushingly Olympian as this speech was, it failed to squash dynastic politics and it also concealed a rather less lofty element in the Chief Commissioner's thinking. With the death of Alhassan on 16 January 1917, a fresh controversy broke out, in the course of which it became clear that Armitage was, to some extent, concerned with advancing British interests in the occupied territory in anticipation of negotiations. He had, indeed, revealed this concern when, only four months after the speech cited above, he pointed out to Cardinall, acting D.P.O. at Yendi, that there were a number of Dagomba villages in the French-controlled area. Armitage continued: 'At the end of the War we must have a case ready prepared to be put forward for the return of these villages and lands to their rightful owners'.[43]

When Alhassan died, his son Abudulai became regent. Somewhat unwarily, Cardinall suggested that while Abudulai was regent at Yendi, his place at Sambu (as Mion-lana) should be taken by another Abudu gate chief, Zinyebu (a junior son of Na Abudulai and Kutun-Na). This man was to act as regent for Mion. The acting C.C.N.T. replied that the British administration already recognised Andani's son Abudulai as Mion-lana, that Sambu was not the capital of Mion province, and that 'neither Yendi nor Sambu had the right to appoint the Chief of Miong before the War and any claim he [presumably the regent of Yendi] makes to do so now cannot be entertained'.[44]

Cardinall maintained, however, that 'the skins of Mion are at Sambu which for long past has been the residence of the Chiefs of Mion'. He also pointed out that, in any case, the Karaga-Na had had no right to appoint Andani's son as Mion-lana, especially as Bukari Narkaw had been only a grandson of a paramount and therefore junior 'in blood rank' both to the Yo-Na and to his own appointee.[45]

With the return of Armitage and Evered Poole (the D.P.O.), both men of imperious and irascible temper, a battle royal commenced. Poole found that the chiefs and elders of Yendi were anxious to have a new king appointed, because seven months had elapsed since Alhassan's death. Poole sympathised with them: 'It is the expressed wish of the whole country, and in my opinion desirable that the Chief of Yendi be appointed now. While there is no King in Yendi the whole Dagomba administration is dislocated'. He accepted that such an appointment would 'not of course affect British Dagomba', but remarked that there were several skins vacant, including that of Mion. The regent at Sambu (Zinyebu) carried 'no weight with the people'.[46]

Armitage was having none of this. He replied:

You do not appear to realize that if British and Togoland Dagomba are re-united at the end of the War the appointment of the Paramount Chief of Dagomba will rest largely with the Chiefs of Karaga, Savelugu and Miong, and that it is not improbable that one of our Chiefs will be elected. If, on the other hand, Togoland is returned to Germany the Paramount Chief would probably have to fly for his life, and the whole of native procedure would be upset.

As for the Mion skin,

the Chief of Miong, recognised by this administration, lives near Kpabia, and I am surprised that you do not appear to recollect that the Chief of Sambu, who is now Regent at Yendi, was appointed to the same stool by the late King of Yendi but was never recognised by us, nor do we recognise the acting Chief mentioned in ... your letter.[47]

The regent Abudulai would, said Armitage, continue in that capacity till the end of the war and would rule only in the ex-German section.

Unchastened, Poole returned to the charge with a petition, signed by the five senior elders of Yendi, which declared:

WE are greatly disappointed at being made to wait for such a long time for a King. It is against DAGOMBA CUSTOM for a KING not to be appointed within five months of the death of the late RULER, and that time has now passed.

The present GBONLANA ABUDULAI is the man of our choice, and we crave permission to enstool him with the ceremonies as performed by the CHIEF of GUSHIEGO, to take over the position as held by his late father ALHASSAN:[48]

Poole followed up the petition with two letters in which he reported on the strength of feeling at Yendi ('I might almost call it "bitter"'). He went on to argue that nobody on the British side was eligible for the paramountcy. The Yo-Na was now blind and would therefore be unacceptable; Karaga was a grandson (he in fact died in September). Andani's son Abudulai would have been eligible 'had he been appointed Chief of Mion constitutionally'. The D.P.O. concluded: 'If you consent to this man [the regent] being enstooled for this side only the concession will mean nothing but will do a lot of good.'[49] Armitage's response was blistering: 'I wish you to understand, once and for all, that this administration recognises "Abudulai of Kpabia", as you still choose to call him, as Chief of Miong . . . this administration recognised N'Dani's sons by that title and will continue to do so.'[50] As for the petition, Armitage believed it to be the work of 'a small minority' which had found itself in the German section, 'owing to the mistaken policy of the late King Abudulai and his advisers at the time of the occupation'. He criticised Poole's 'lack of foresight' in recommending the appointment of a new king, 'before our hope to see British and Togoland Dagomba re-united under our rule has been realized'. Everybody hoped that the war would soon finish but it was not in his power to end it, 'to meet the requirements of a very insignificant body of natives whose villages you describe elsewhere as "full of old and useless people"'.[51]

However, Armitage was agreeable to the regent's being appointed 'Chief of Yendi', on condition that this was not attended with 'the ceremonies attached to the enstoolment of a "King of Dagomba"' and that Abudulai signed a document promising not to 'interfere with affairs on this side of the Boundary'. The arrangement was to be provisional, pending the election of a king when the war was over.

On 4 October 1917, therefore, a meeting was held at Yendi, as Poole reported: 'On the sodden ground a large crowd assembled and listened while the conditions were stated upon which the Election of the King could take place.'[52] An affidavit containing the terms of Abudulai's appointment was prepared and signed by the regent himself, three divisional chiefs, two junior royals, and the five senior elders of Yendi. With this, the dispute subsided, except that Poole was once more reprimanded (for using the term 'king').[53]

THE ADMINISTRATOR–PARAMOUNT

During this period an interesting and amusing phenomenon began to appear in dynastic politics, namely, a propensity on the part of chiefs and elders to

69

evade involvement in decision-making. This was a completely logical and prudent reaction to the colonial government's assumption of paramountcy: if the British wished to assume the royal prerogative of appointing and dismissing, then the chiefs would ensure that the British alone bore moral and political responsibility in this area – and if possible in most other areas as well. However, such tactical disengagement by no means excluded lobbying: if anything, it made lobbying rather easier. In the course of time, members of the ruling class grew bolder and actively started to involve officials in the conflicts and intrigues surrounding high office.

This phenomenon of tactical self-denial first appeared in the selection of a new Tolon-Na in the summer of 1917. The P.C., Southern Province, went to Tolon in the expectation that the chiefs would choose and approve their own candidate. But instead he found that 'no headman would record his vote, they all said that they would follow whoever was appointed'. The Provincial Commissioner decided to give democracy another try, and held a further meeting on 25 August. He heard all the candidates again and once more asked the chiefs to give their opinion. But they still refused to vote, saying they would follow 'whoever the P.C. appoints'. In some irritation, Nash referred the matter to Armitage, asking him to 'see the claimants and elect one for appointment to the stool of Tolon'.[54]

An even more impressive display of abdication occurred in the spring of 1918, when the selection of a new Karaga-Na took place. Bukari Narkaw had died in September 1917, in the midst of attempts to effect a reconciliation between himself and the 'Yendi legitimists'.[55]

The selection of a replacement was a delicate matter, because it involved a Yendi gate skin and because the political situation in Dagomba was so fluid. All of the eleven candidates were from British Dagomba, but they represented both Abudulai and Andani gates as well as a couple of noble families descended from Na Yakuba.[56] The question of reunification was thus to some extent involved, in that the British had to weigh their debts of loyalty against the imperatives of getting support in the east (which might be useful in making claims to keep 'Togoland Dagomba' after the war). Jealousy between the Abudus and the Andanis was already apparent. When the P.C., Southern Province, met the claimants from the Tamale area, Abudulai (a younger brother of Na Alhassan) remarked: 'Andani's sons have always been getting the senior appointments.'[57]

Since the regent, Abudulai, was forbidden to appoint chiefs in British Dagomba, the selection was to be carried out by the Western Dagomba chiefs. But it soon became clear that, given the uncertainties about the outcome of peace negotiations, the chiefs and headmen were not going to commit themselves to any dynastic faction. On 13 May 1918, the unfortunate Provincial Commissioner therefore found himself once more confronted by a happily indecisive electorate: 'All the Chiefs and Headmen stated that they wished the appointment to be made direct by the Government.' Again the P.C. took the matter to his superior, remarking that he felt that Bukari Narkaw's son Ziblim might be the best man for the job: 'He informed me that if he was elected ... he would as he expressed it "do all in his power to follow in the footsteps of his father" who was extremely loyal to the Government'.[58] On 15 May the Chief Commissioner met the non-committal voters and told them

that it had always been my policy to interfere as little as possible with native customs and that I had learnt with some regret that they had been unable to bring forward a candidate for the Karaga stool on their own initiative. The Chief of Savelugu replied that in the old days the Claimants to a Stool appeared before the big Chiefs, presided over by the King of Yendi, and their choice was final. Nowadays it was their wish that the Chief Commissioner should appoint new Chiefs.[59]

Armitage then

asked if it were not a fact that in the old days the man who brought most money in his hands when claiming a Stool was, as a rule, the successful candidate. There was a general burst of laughter at this, which continued when the Chief of Savelugu made a gallant, if unsuccessful, attempt at equivocation by stating that even a poor man *might* be elected to a stool if he were a good man.

The C.C.N.T. said that the chiefs had placed on him 'a heavy burden of responsibility' and required them to 'promise loyally to abide by' his 'decision'. The promise was given ('immediately and unanimously') and Armitage reviewed the candidates. He rejected Mahama, the ex-chief of Savelugu (deposed in 1910), and said that he 'could never again expect to be appointed a Chief'. He turned down all the Western Dagomba candidates, on the grounds that it was 'inadvisable in existing conditions' to move a western chief out of his area. Finally, Armitage declared that Ziblim, son of Bukari Narkaw, was his choice: 'I had watched him for some years and had found him to be an energetic and just man, and one whose loyalty to the Government was beyond dispute.'[60] The Karaga stool was thus kept out of the grasp of either the Andanis or the Abudus, all of whose candidates had been rejected.

In July 1920 the Gushie-Na Bukari died. Evered Poole (still D.P.O., Yendi) talked to the regent and 'Chief of Yendi', Abudulai, about successors and then went to Gushiegu to conduct his own selection. The candidates there, he reported,

brought me the most lavish dashes, for which I expressed my thanks but said that I dare not accept anything ... They all laughed and went off very happy. It was amusing to have secret visits paid me when it was dark by certain claimants who each assured me that he was the man most fitted for the post, etc.[61]

From an entry in the D.P.O's diary, it seems that Poole did nominate the new Gushie-Na, after further consultations at Yendi.

'UNITED DAGOMBA'

Under Article 119 of the Treaty of Versailles, Germany renounced all claims to overseas possessions, including Togo. Even before the official signing of the agreement, France and Britain had been authorised to devise a suitable division of Cameroon and Togo between themselves and to make proposals for the administration of these territories under international mandate. The boundary between British and French Togoland was fixed by the Milner–Simon Agreement of July 1919 and three years later the official document conferring a mandate was issued by the League of Nations, though the effective period of British administration began in July 1919.[62]

The Milner–Simon Agreement gave Britain a mandate area of 13,000 square miles, of which 10,597 square miles lay in the 'Northern Section', including the ex-German parts of Dagomba and Mamprussi. The League's mandate stated (Article 9) that territory under mandate should 'be administered in accordance with the laws of the Mandatory as an integral part of his territory'.[63] The British government, by an Order-in-Council of 11 October 1923, therefore proclaimed that the Northern Section of British Togoland should be 'administered as if it formed part of the Protectorate' of the Northern Territories.[64] The ex-German section thereafter became the 'Eastern Dagomba District', administered as part of the N.T. by a D.C. responsible to the Chief Commissioner at Tamale.

In this way, the ambitions of Clifford and Armitage to see the Dagomba and Mamprussi kingdoms reunited under British rule were fulfilled. The Gold Coast administration had, in fact, made some effort to collect from chiefs in northern Togo statements of opinion favouring this outcome. In April 1918 Clifford had told Walter Long, Secretary of State, that 'the people of Togoland' had, with 'practical unanimity' and 'frankness', expressed 'a strong aversion from German methods, and an equally strong preference for British rule'. Clifford enclosed a long list of the vices of the Germans: among them were 'the imposition of a head tax' and 'forced labour, and the restrictions which were thereby placed upon the ability of the people to earn their livelihood'. The Germans, it seems, had also sought 'to make trade as far as possible a European monopoly' and had imposed a criminal code under which the people 'were liable to floggings, imprisonment, etc.'[65]

With the status of Togoland Dagomba established for the foreseeable future, the way was clear for the election of a new Ya-Na, one whose domain would extend over the whole area of the kingdom. The regent Abudulai, erstwhile 'Chief of Yendi', had by this time served a satisfactory apprenticeship under British rule. So when it became known that Armitage had been asked to settle the Yendi succession before leaving the N.T., Poole wrote to him setting out the regent's qualities:[66]

I trust that the claims of Chief Abudulai of Yendi will receive your great influence, insofar as such support can in justice be pressed.

I would advance the following claims on his behalf:–

a. He has occupied the position of Chief of Yendi for three years in a befitting manner.
b. He was the first to welcome and supply with food and carriers the British Troops on their entry into German Togoland Dagomba.
c. He is the son of a deceased Yendi King so is in the running for the appointment.
d. He is well acquainted with the people and their palavers in this District, and

72

such knowledge will be most useful now in administering the new Sub Districts of Segbiri and Sansugu.

e. He is well known and trusted by the Konkombas, which is the most important and virile tribe in this District.

f. He has supplied 678 men and women for Government work on the coast and 92 for the mines.[67]

But Abudulai was not the only candidate. Further, the N.T. administration could not easily renege on the 'British' chiefs whose interests Armitage had so vocally defended in 1917. At least three other chiefs had some semblance of a claim (bearing in mind the rule that Savelugu, Karaga, and Mion were the 'gates' to Yendi). They were the Yo-Na, Bukari, son of Ya-Na Andani; the new Karaga-Na, Ziblim; and the 'British' Mion-lana, Abudulai, another son of Andani. The Yo-Na's credentials were impeccable; but he had become blind and was very old. The Karaga-Na, though occupying a gate skin, was not the son of a paramount: he was only a great-grandson (of Na Yakuba). Andani's son Abudulai was eligible, but his claim to be Mion-lana was, of course, contested by the regent and the Yendi elders, who could be expected to have some role in the election. So the administration was again faced with a delicate problem of diplomacy.

The elders did not, in fact, take any part in the selection of the new Ya-Na. There was no attempt to comply with 'traditional' procedures. The Chief Commissioner summoned the chiefs and elders to Tamale for a meeting on 20 November 1920. When the meeting opened, Armitage gave a speech, pointing out the historic importance of the occasion, 'for it saw their country re-united and an arbitrary and unjust boundary, which cut Dagomba into two portions, done away with'.[68] He appealed to the chiefs to forget their resentment of Karaga, the late chief of which had 'loyally carried out our instructions by discontinuing all communication with Yendi'. The C.C.N.T. then asked the chiefs to consider the candidates and give him their decision on 22 November.

When the meeting convened again, Armitage asked for their nomination. What happened next can best be described in the words of his own report:

the Chief of Miong, acting as their spokesman announced that the old Chief of Savelugu had been unanimously elected to the stool of Yendi, as 'King of Dagomba'. This was exactly what I had hoped and wished for, as the Chief of Savelugu's election was in strict accordance with Native Custom and satisfied everybody. I congratulated the Chiefs warmly on their choice and confirmed it.

I then informed the Assembly that although Bukari, Chief of the Dagombas' old age and failing health (he is stone blind and partially paralysed) rendered him unfitted to perform the onerous duties attached to that office, I should consider it an act of cruelty to remove Bukari from Savelugu, where he had spent so many years of unswerving loyalty to the Government, far from his old associates and friends, and that I wished him to spend his declining years peacefully and full of honours at Savelugu.

I called upon the old man to state what he wished to do, when as I had anticipated, he placed his resignation of the 'Kingship' of Yendi in my hands. I called upon the assembly to applaud Bukari's decision, which had been taken in the interests of the country and had set a crown upon a life's work devoted to duty and to loyalty towards the Government. I said that a permanent record would be kept of his having been unanimously elected to the Stool of Yendi and that he should have the honour of nominating his successor. I then went on to say that it was essential that a Chief should be appointed to the Yendi Stool who knew, and was known to, the Natives of that District; one who had gained the confidence of the wild Konkomba Tribe and who could travel everywhere and would be able to consolidate re-united Dagomba. In my opinion, there was no one who [was] better equipped with these qualifications than was Abudulai, present Chief of Yendi, and son of Allassan, late 'King of Dagomba', and I confidently recommended him to Bukari as his successor. The old man assented readily and was followed by all the other chiefs.[69]

This account is worth quoting in full because it so clearly reveals the extent to which Armitage directed, even stage-managed, the assembly's deliberations, taking the initiative both to secure Bukari's abdication and to nominate a replacement, without waiting to hear the old man's views.

The C.C.N.T. did not stop at appointing a new king, but seized the opportunity to impose a solution to the problem of the Mion skin. His report continued:

I ... told the new 'King' what was expected of him and begged him to disabuse his mind of all suspicions that he might hitherto have entertained against the British Dagomba Chiefs, who had simply obeyed our instructions by severing themselves from all communication with German Yendi. I made it a condition to his appointment that Abudulai should hand over the 'Skin' of Miong to our Chief, who, if he wished, would now take up his residence at Sambu. Abudulai very frankly stated that he would immediately hand over to Abudulai, the British Chief of Miong, all the paraphernalia connected with the Miong skin and Miong stated that he would take up his residence at Sambu. I told the assembly that I could now leave the N.T.s, happy in the knowledge that one of my last acts [had] been to re-unite British and Togoland Dagomba and begged the Chiefs to dismiss the past from their minds.[70]

Contented though he was with his day's work, Armitage noticed that the Karaga-Na and his followers 'did not look best pleased at the turn events had taken'. And it was, in fact, Karaga-Na Ziblim who made, intentionally or not, the shrewdest comment on the proceedings. For next day Armitage presented various gifts to the chiefs, among them 'a large mirror in a gilt frame' to both Ziblim and the Yo-Na. The Karaga-Na gazed at his present and then remarked that 'when he looked in his mirror, he would see, not himself, but the Chief Commissioner'.[71]

YA-NA ABUDULAI

The reunification of the kingdom did not greatly affect relations between the government and the Dagomba chieftaincy, although the administration expressed a wish to build up the authority of the king (which was in accordance with the Guggisberg policy of creating 'strong native states'). The

D.C. at Yendi made it 'a strict rule that all orders to the Sub-Chiefs and their people are to go through the Head Chief'.[72] The government also made occasional efforts to assert Yendi's authority over the divisional chiefs. In 1927 the acting P.C., Southern Province, asked the D.C., Western Dagomba, to instruct 'the Chiefs of SAVELUGU and KARAGA to visit the NA and pay him their respects ... When the Chiefs have paid their respects they must see that their Sub-Chiefs do likewise in accordance with custom.'[73]

The Ya-Na's prestige was bolstered in other ways. When the exiled Asantehene returned from the Seychelles in 1925, the D.C., Eastern Dagomba, persuaded Abudulai to defy the taboo which forbade Dagomba kings to cross the Volta and dispatched him (along with several wives and a number of retainers in two lorries) to Kumasi to greet Prempeh. In 1928, the D.C. began to agitate for a grant from the government to help the Ya-Na buy a lorry, pointing out that the king had 'practically no revenue' and relied entirely on gifts which were 'not in any sense a regular form of taxation'.[74] The request was met, but Abudulai was sadly disappointed with his new vehicle. (He had assumed that when he bought the lorry, the firm concerned would provide him, as a matter of course, with a permanent, free supply of oil and petrol.)

While it often claimed to have a policy of non-intervention in chieftaincy matters, the administration still kept the right to confirm and to terminate appointments. Although the Ya-Na was responsible for selection, the earlier rule about probation still applied to newly installed chiefs. Further, the reinstatement of the paramount did not stop candidates for office from seeking the D.C.'s favour and it did not lead notables to abandon the agreeable habit of leaving decisions to the government. The government, for its part, did not altogether abandon the use of gentle pressure when an important appointment came up.

An interesting case in point was the selection of a successor to the old Yo-Na, Bukari, who died early in 1921. The new Chief Commissioner. Philbrick, announced that once Bukari's funeral had been completed, he would arrange a meeting at Yendi at which he would expect the chiefs to 'put forward the selected man' for the king's approval.[75] Shortly afterwards, the Bamvim-lana appeared in the office of Walker-Leigh (at this time Provincial Commissioner) and made it clear that he believed ('erroneously') that Leigh 'had some influence in the Savelugu election'.[76]

In fact, it seems that, although he had chosen the wrong official, the Bamvim-lana was right in assuming the existence of an official view and correct in believing that it would find its way to Yendi. The following letter, from Philbrick to Guggisberg, seems to bear out both assumptions:

19 June 1921

Dear Gen. Guggisberg,

Your letter re the succession to the Stool of Savelugu reached me last night.
The candidate from the English side is the Chief of Bamvim. He had Armitage's support, and has that of all the men up here, who know.

The H[ead] C[hief] himself will certainly try to put one of the German candidates on the Stool, and he will have a certain amount of plausibility on his side, as Bamvim's title, though strong, is not so strong as those of one or two others.

The English Dagombas refused to attend the election at Yendi unless I went with them. I deputed Walker-Leigh with whom they are quite satisfied. (I thought this was an ideal job for a Deputy.)

He will go to Yendi with them in about a week's time, and has already my instructions to use all possible influence with the H.C. to get Bamvim elected.

The Government has the power of refusing to approve their nominee, but I don't think it wise to exercise this too arbitrarily. It will be, I think you will agree, better to put what pressure is necessary on before or during the election.

You will remember the H.C. tried to get at you during your visit to Yendi for some promise. He is very crafty and all his movements have had the object of aggrandizing himself and his immediate entourage. He has not yet absorbed the 'United Dagomba Nation' idea, but hopes to increase his own importance in lowering that of those who were previously big men on this side.[77]

Abudulai of Bamvim was, indeed, selected as the new Yo-Na.

COLONIALISM AND POLITICAL CHANGE

What had colonial government done to the Dagomba kingdom in its first thirty years? More, perhaps, than it had done to the Dagomba people; more, certainly, than it had done to the Dagomba economy.

The really important effect of colonial rule was to be found in the political sphere. The principal and immediate consequence of the European presence was to change the locus of sovereignty and to alter the source, if not the use of authority. Responsibility for the basic political functions – external defence, maintaining internal order, and regulating matters 'affecting the welfare of the society as a whole' – was appropriated by the colonial administration. At the same time, the administration expressly claimed the various powers attached to these functions: the power to tax; the power to legislate; the power to administer justice; the power to appoint and dismiss officials; the power to regulate the economy; the power to command labour; and the power to coerce.

The Dagomba political structure was, however, neither destroyed nor systematically incorporated into the colonial bureaucracy. The latter did not command manpower or money sufficient to enable it to exercise its authority in any but the most general and superficial manner. As a result, chiefly authority survived. Though reduced to a conditional existence, and sometimes impaired by the abuses and exactions of individual chiefs, it was still the basis upon which the day-to-day government of the divisions and villages was conducted.[78]

Many aspects of social life were, indeed, practically untouched by the presence of a colonial government. Colonial officials generally did not wish to bring about fundamental change in Dagomba society in the short term or, in some respects, at all. The number of people whose lives were drastically affected was small and the material consequences for the great

76

majority were trivial. For the ordinary Dagomba family, colonial government meant, at most – and if it was unlucky – six days each quarter working on the roads or carrying stores for the administration. Perhaps – if it was very unlucky – it meant also the absence of one member of the family for some months working at the mines; probably it also involved the occasional harangue by a visiting D.C., urging people to grow more yams or cotton. These were the only points of contact required by particular policies.

What occurred in Dagomba was a process of change which was, in this period, overwhelmingly political in character: a process which was initiated by outsiders and one which, *pace* 'modernisation' theorists, did not entail inevitable and consequential changes in other spheres. In northern Ghana (as in northern Nigeria) we are confronted with what C. S. Whitaker has dubbed 'dysrhythmic change' – change in one sector which is not accompanied by change in other sectors or which produces a symbiosis so ambiguous or equivocal as to defy categorisation by a simplistic framework of 'tradition versus modernity'.[79] In the present case, there was no inexorable, unfolding progression towards 'modernity', but rather a jerky and unpredictable process of adaptation, redefinition, and manipulation.

This was a particular (though not unique) form of response to 'modernisation'. It is one which can only be understood by reference to the dynamics of pre-colonial politics and one which involved manipulation of those responsible for 'modernisation'. I shall, indeed, try to show in succeeding chapters the validity for Dagomba of the proposition which Whitaker puts forward after looking at a rather similar process in northern Nigeria – the proposition that 'subjected to potentially transformative political change, a society previously characterized by political domination presents special opportunities for "manipulative response" that limits the impact of that change'.[80]

CHAPTER 5

THE BATTLE OF WATHERSTON ROAD

Every system of Government if it is to be permanent and progressive must have its roots in the framework of indigenous society.[1]

Native Administration will cause a system of graft to be born like unto which Tammany Hall is an infant.[2]

August 1928 saw the beginning of a short and bitter conflict between the 'die-hards' of Tamale and the supporters of 'indirect rule'. The first casualty of the war was the newly arrived acting Chief Commissioner, Major F. W. F. Jackson (deputising for Walker-Leigh, who was absent on leave). Jackson was disturbed by the coolness of his reception in the offices and bungalows strung out along Watherston Road, Tamale, and noted in his diary that he had been made to feel 'like a Thief in the Night'. Relations between Tamale and Accra had, indeed, reached a critical point, as another 'southern' officer observed: 'there was . . . in the Northern Territories a definite attitude of hostility to the Coast emanating from the N.T.s headquarters and permeating the whole of its soil. Officers were allowed to speak and write openly of "Accra" (the name by which all authority was known) in a most contemptuous way.'[3] The war raged around the question of indirect rule – what it meant, whether it was necessary, how it should be applied – until, effectively, December 1929, when Walker-Leigh left, preceded, and followed, by several of his equally die-hard supporters. Thereafter Tamale was firmly in the hands of newly appointed officers, mostly 'southerners' and all enthusiastically dedicated to the application of the doctrines of Lugard and Cameron to the unsuspecting Northern Territories.

The dispute was set in train by the removal of Guggisberg from the governorship in April 1927. Guggisberg saw himself as a supporter of indirect rule, but (as Wraith points out in his biography of Sir Gordon) his understanding of the concept appeared to his successors (notably Slater and Thomas) both vague and incomplete: 'In fact there had never been any clear thinking on this subject in the Gold Coast, for indirect rule, though largely assumed, had never been expressly enunciated. Various expedients had been allowed to congeal into a more or less workable system, but the system, such as it was, lacked the very essence of indirect rule.'[4] That 'essence' consisted in giving real financial and executive responsibility to 'native authorities', accompanied by positive and thorough devolution. Guggisberg's last measure of indirect rule (the 1927 Native Administration (Colony) Ordinance) fell far short of this standard; it failed to provide chiefs with their own treasuries and sources of revenue and it did not give them real 'local government' functions to perform. It was, as Wraith notes, 'the shadow of indirect rule'.[5]

In the Gold Coast, indirect rule was an imported doctrine, but it had, in the eyes of its apostles, various merits in the local context (though individual officers naturally ordered these merits differently). The material advantages were quite apparent, given the lack of staff and shortage of money from which colonial government suffered. Indirect rule would enable the government to transfer a number of responsibilities from its own shoulders (and those of the D.C.) onto the shoulders of the chiefs.

Such a transfer became more attractive, and indeed necessary, in the early thirties, for two reasons. First, the Slump led to a severe retrenchment in colonial expenditure and personnel: it was therefore imperative to use local resources to the maximum. Secondly, the Geneva convention on forced labour, adopted in 1930 after a conference sponsored by the International Labour Office, obliged those colonial governments which ratified the convention to abolish the more important forms of compulsory labour service, such as porterage and work on road construction.[6]

When Lord Passfield, Secretary of State for the Colonies, wrote to colonial administrators about the convention, the Governor of the Gold Coast replied: 'the financial prospects of this Government are extremely poor . . . The adoption of the new labour policy would involve additional expenditure to the extent of £150,000 per annum at least. In present circumstances it is quite impossible to find this from Government revenue.'[7] The solution, as the C.C.N.T. remarked to the P.C., Northern Province, was to introduce some kind of levy on native communities and at the same time to establish native treasuries for handling the funds collected and for financing local development. The imposition of a tax did not, of course, require the creation of native administration authorities. But, following the Aba riots in Eastern Nigeria, colonial governments were nervous about introducing direct taxation, unless local cooperation could be engineered.[8] The administration of assessment, collection, and expenditure by 'native authorities' was thought to be one way of ensuring such cooperation.

There was, then, a sound, indeed compelling, administrative rationale for indirect rule. But this alone does not account for the zeal of many officials on its behalf, a zeal which, as several writers have remarked, often achieved a theological, even mystical form of devotion. Although Cameron himself found this exaltation of indirect rule 'a rather mysterious business', for its more fervent advocates it was less an administrative expedient than a philosophy of development, one combining a belief in tradition, a preference for gradualism, and a faith in local government.[9] To political officers, indirect rule appealed as a doctrine which both satisfied their desire to provide administrative education for local leaders and enabled the D.C. to control the technical services, ever liable to escape the tutelage of the political service. Indirect rule was an altogether splendid ideology, making up in rhetorical grandeur for much that it lacked in precision and coherence, and concealing, under its broad normative umbrella, a wealth of ambiguities and contradictions. It engendered, moreover, the enthusiasm appropriate to a great cause. For true believers, indirect rule was good in itself. It was an agency of uplift rather than an administrative device – not so much a policy, in fact, as a way of life.

THE NORTHERNERS' DEFENCE

While the details of the struggle between the established northern officers and 'the indirect rule team' make a fascinating study in bureaucratic warfare, it is perhaps more useful to focus here on the issues raised and the positions taken up in the course of the battle. We shall begin by examining the arguments put forward by Walker-Leigh and his supporters.

The initiative was, necessarily, taken by their opponents. It was embodied in a minute written by the acting Governor, Shenton Thomas, after a visit to Tamale in July 1928. In his minute, Thomas declared: 'So far as I can ascertain, this Government is completely in the dark as regards the Native Administration policy of the Northern Territories: there seems to be no clear-cut statement of policy: we do not know what is being done or what our administration is intended to bring forth.'[10] This was, of course, also an attack on the autarchy of N.T. government: officers in the N.T., said another Secretariat spokesman, were 'prone sometimes to administer in accordance with their own desires'.[11] The northerners, for their part, accepted that there should be 'one Government and one Governor', but most would have agreed with Cardinall when he declared that 'there should be two systems and two services to direct these systems'. They were particularly hostile to the importation of officials from the south, as Cardinall again made clear: 'it would be impolitic to introduce, into the Northern Territories Administrative staff, officers trained in and imbued with the ideas and customs prevalent in the Colony and Ashanti'.[12]

In any case, they protested, the N.T. did have a policy and that policy was, indeed, a policy of indirect rule, tempered by considerations of efficiency, native welfare, and the capacity of the chiefs. Senior officers, such as Gilbert (D.C., Eastern Dagomba) and Walker-Leigh, believed that by issuing orders through the chiefs and leaving them to get on with their execution, they were practising indirect rule, which they understood as pragmatic reliance on native rulers. Gilbert was typical in reacting to the assault from Accra with pained surprise: 'Indirect Rule . . . has been my policy ever since I have been stationed here, all civil cases and all orders concerning the Dagomba country have been sent to the Na, so that the proposed innovation under the heading Indirect Rule will be a change in detail only.'[13] Walker-Leigh backed up his officers vigorously. Why, he asked, was more responsibility for chiefs thought desirable when, under the existing 'quasi indirect' system, revenue had gone up, communications had improved, crime had not 'unduly increased', and the people were 'contented and happy'?[14] Rutherford (D.C., Western Dagomba) took the same view: 'Indirect rule is an established fact and has been so for years . . . [the] present system does not require any great alteration but only regulation and strengthening. The people are at present enjoying life under a benevolent autocracy and this surely is the best and certainly the most paternal form of government.'[15]

In the light of these advantages, the dangers involved in giving more responsibility to native authorities were all too clear. Even northerners who were sympathetic to indirect rule (as, for instance, were Cardinall and Whittall) insisted that progress would 'necessarily be very slow and cautious', and on this point at least they were reassured by Accra. Nothing sudden was intended, Thomas said: 'I have never imagined that a system of indirect rule can be introduced into the N.T. in a moment . . . I said that a definite policy should be laid down without delay so that, *when the time is ripe*, a system of indirect rule can be introduced.'[16]

Northern officers pointed to a number of specific factors which, in their view, meant that full-scale indirect rule was impractical (or, at least, 'premature') and, in any event, risky. The major factor was the lack of education in the north: the chiefs were universally illiterate in English and there were too few educated commoners to staff the native authorities adequately. For that reason, wrote Walker-Leigh, until there were enough 'educated N.T.s people' to staff the authorities, indirect rule was 'condemned not to be anything but a failure . . . to have non-natives of the N.T.s on this work is unthinkable'.[17] To rush ahead with taxation and the establishment of native treasuries would, in the circumstances, merely lead to corruption and extortion. Under the existing system, the C.C.N.T. observed, the Chiefs had become poorer 'and the people better off and happier, thus shewing that graft on the part of the Chiefs [had] been lessened'.[18] Any devolution of authority would, he declared, just stimulate 'the inherent graft of the Native' and the chiefs were the worst of all: 'some of the biggest are the worst grafters'.[19]

Walker-Leigh was especially opposed to the introduction of direct taxation for, he argued, this would involve 'a breach of faith with the natives'. They had been promised, during the 1921 census, that census returns would never be used for taxation purposes and to bring in taxation would therefore 'break the word of the Government'. In any case, no tax at a realistic level for the north could sustain adequately staffed native authorities and most of the revenue would be absorbed by salaries. Regarding the effect of taxation on labour supply, Leigh had two mutually contradictory objections: first, that it would cause accelerated emigration, through people seeking to avoid the new burden; secondly, that it would curb migration, since the availability of paid local government work in the north would discourage labourers from going to the coast.[20] (In the event, taxation seems to have made little difference either way.)

Under pressure from Accra, Walker-Leigh made one concession but, curiously, the result was to illuminate more sharply the difference in assumptions between the two sides. In October 1929, after ten months of implacable campaigning by the old guard in Tamale, Slater (the Governor) apparently decided to make a final attempt to persuade Walker-Leigh of the merits of indirect rule. In a rather heavily tactful letter, the Colonial Secretary therefore informed the C.C.N.T. that 'the Governor would regard it as a fitting climax to your long and faithful service in the Protectorate if a Native Administration Ordinance could be enacted as a proof of the confidence reposed by you in the ability of certain Chiefs to exercise a limited measure of increased authority'.[21] Grumbling that there was 'not nearly enough time to make anything but a hash of such an important measure', Leigh had produced, not a draft ordinance (as required), but a set of rules to govern the operation of native tribunals. These rules were rejected by Accra because they failed to comply with a basic canon of indirect rule philosophy, namely that such tribunals possessed 'certain inherent rights of jurisdiction'. What Accra wanted, as the Colonial Secretary said, was an ordinance 'to define and to regulate the exercise of these powers and jurisdictions and not rules which purport to confer jurisdiction on them'.[22]

The difference of approach was fundamental. The northerners judged native authorities ultimately according to their contribution to the efficiency of government and, in judging, reserved the prerogative of granting or withdrawing authority from the chiefs. The ideologists of indirect rule asserted (though not always recognising in practice) the existence of an ultimate and distinct authority stemming from local custom. For one school, efficiency was the final test; for the other, authenticity. The paternalism of one could not, in the last resort, be reconciled with the traditionalism of the other. In reality, however, pragmatism was common to both: the principles and the policy of indirect rule were significantly different from each other.

Indeed, somewhat perversely, there was occasionally a vein of traditionalism in the northern case. Thus both Rutherford and Gilbert objected to the idea of paying salaries to chiefs on the grounds that this

would change them from tribal rulers to the equivalent of minor Government officials. They would [Rutherford argued] lose the confidence of their people and would themselves be more apt to consider how any actions would affect their standing with Government than whether such action would be good or bad for their people. In other words, the Chiefs must be taught to work for their people and not as Government hangers-on.[23]

This statement was paradoxical in at least two respects. First, it actually represented a criticism of the *policy* of indirect rule from the point of view of its first principles. For, indeed, it was accepted by the indirect rule team that the chiefs would become 'an integral part of the Government machinery'.[24] Secondly, Rutherford was here on common ground with the African nationalists, who equally mistrusted the bureaucratising effects of indirect rule. The real point, to be explored further, is not that the *philosophy* of indirect rule led to bureaucratisation: it was the *political relationship* through which it found expression that did so.

It was, of course, this relationship which inspired suspicion on the part of the African intelligentsia. In Tamale, the latter was mainly represented by southerners and they were most hostile to the new policy. When Duncan-

Johnstone (the most passionate of 'indirect rulers') spoke to a meeting of school-teachers in the town, a teacher from Cape Coast got up and asked, in Duncan-Johnstone's words, 'why we were doing this and was it not true that we were following out our policy of "divide and rule" splitting the country up into Native States so that the Gold Coast could never become a nation'.[25] But the indirect rule team were quite equal to such arguments: they had their own theory of political development. It was a theory of doubtful propriety, relevance, or accuracy, but it blazed with words like 'progress' and 'responsibility'. Truly, a theory for the age of the wheel and the motorised missionary.

DUNCAN-JOHNSTONE AND DAGBON-BIA

One of the main reasons for the independence, not to say the intransigence, of the N.T. administration was that it had for so long been controlled by the same officers. Most had either served in the north since before 1914 or served there continuously since their arrival in the postwar years. Walker-Leigh had been in the north since 1898; Whittall (P.C., Northern Province) had been there since 1907; Cardinall and Rake, both senior D.C.s, had spent most of their fifteen years in the Gold Coast in northern posts; Armstrong, Gilbert, Moreton and Rutherford had served in the N.T. for nearly ten years.[26] The introduction of indirect rule was therefore accompanied by a wholesale change in staff. By the end of 1930, all the officers most closely identified with the Walker-Leigh regime had been transferred or had retired (as in the case of the Chief Commissioner himself). Of the new men, three were of particular importance: H. A. Blair, A. C. Duncan-Johnstone, and W. J. A. Jones.

Blair, the son of a missionary of the Society for the Propagation of the Gospel and himself an Oxford graduate, had entered the Gold Coast in 1928 at the age of twenty-seven. He was appointed D.C., Western Dagomba, in February 1929 and stayed in Tamale and Yendi for almost ten years. He was, in fact, the first D.C. to have both a close acquaintance with Dagomba culture and history and a fluent knowledge of Dagbane, to such an extent that he acquired the complimentary nickname 'Dagbon-bia' ('son of Dagbon'). As his successor remarked, by the time of his departure Blair 'had come to be regarded as a Dagomba institution'.[27]

Duncan-Johnstone was a very different personality. A Scot, educated at Glenalmond and Sandhurst, he had been in the Gold Coast since 1913, serving mainly in the Colony. The career and reputation of Duncan-Johnstone had advanced considerably during the twenties: he had become engaged to a niece of Lady Guggisberg, and in 1924 had been entrusted with the task of bringing the exiled Asantehene home from the Seychelles. By 1928 he had become Provincial Commissioner for the Central Province of the Colony and in August 1929 he arrived in Tamale as P.C., Southern Province. He remained in the N.T. until 1933, becoming after reorganisation Assistant C.C.N.T.[28]

Jones was not appointed to the north until 1933, when he became Chief

Commissioner. Nevertheless, he was an important figure in the establishment of indirect rule in the N.T. because in the summer of 1929 he became Secretary for Native Affairs. His influence and support were therefore essential to the success of the new administrators in Tamale and, both as Secretary for Native Affairs and as C.C.N.T., Jones was a very active propagandist in the cause of indirect rule.[29]

For the purpose of Dagomba history, the 'indirect rule team' consisted of Duncan-Johnstone, Blair, and several energetic D.C.s, notably Armstrong, Cockey, and Miller. It was not an egalitarian team, at least in respect of Duncan-Johnstone's role: the archives are replete with imperious and ill-tempered memoranda from the Provincial Commissioner to his subordinates.[30] The first months of his rule were especially tumultuous and his diary resounds with outrage at the 'sloppiness' and 'apathy' of N.T. administrative life. Within a few days he had reprimanded the Postmaster for 'the slovenly appearance of his staff', sorted out the financial affairs of the African Club, and told off the Yo-Na for the scruffiness of his capital.[31] Duncan-Johnstone also set about the hapless remnants of the old guard with great vigour, developing a particular animus against Rutherford, D.C., Western Dagomba. Rutherford was soon reprimanded for, among other things, 'his objectionable habit of sitting on the bench in his shirt sleeves minus a tie, which [the P.C.] told him was not conducive to the dignity of the law'.[32]

Yet there was a striking complementarity between the indirect rule officials. Blair provided the intellectual and cultural foundations of indirect rule, Duncan-Johnstone provided the drive and authority which ensured its implementation, and the other officers put it into operation with both energy and patience. In the remainder of the chapter we shall consider what they sought to do and what they achieved.

THE IDEOLOGY OF INDIRECT RULE

The basic charter of indirect rule in the Southern Province was the set of *Notes on Policy and Standing Orders* which Duncan-Johnstone issued early in 1930. Here he defined his policy as 'Indirect Rule through Native Administration. Native Administration is itself based on the principle of recognising and developing native institutions, subject to Government control so as to prevent abuses'.[33] The vision of 'development' entertained by Duncan-Johnstone involved the gradual evolution of a Gold Coast nation through the creation of progressively larger monarchies: ultimately the Colony, Ashanti, and the N.T. would, independently, reach the point of administrative maturity where they could fuse into 'one or two big kingdoms'.[34]

Maturity was to be achieved through local government, a point frequently made by Jones. Like so many others, up and down Africa, then and later, Jones held 'that local government was the only school in which the people could learn self-administration'.[35] In a necessarily long evolution, the British government would exercise a control which, given Jones's metaphors, should perhaps be called 'maternalist' rather than 'paternalist'. The

84

Dagomba, he said, were 'like children in the matter of government' and thus far it had been necessary for the administration to carry and care for them. But it was time for a change: 'The time has now come for Government to put the Dagomba on the floor so that they may learn first to crawl, then to take a few steps, supported and guided by the Administrative Officers and eventually, it is hoped, to stand by themselves.'[36] The nursery stage would be difficult, he warned, since even the British, who had 'been governing backward races for hundreds of years', were not yet satisfied that their methods were 'entirely correct'.

To those who regarded the Dagombas' ascent to toddlerdom as premature, Duncan-Johnstone said that to prevent change would require placing a fence around the N.T. As it was, every northerner who went south returned as 'a potential educationalist, if not always of the right kind'. At all costs, he declared, they must avoid a re-enactment of the situation in the Colony, where direct rule, accompanied by uncontrolled educational and social development, had created 'a large and discontented body of educated natives': 'And so with disgruntled chiefs, detribalised people and a discontented educated class the soil becomes really ripe for the seed of the agitator.'[37] In reality, the Provincial Commissioner continued, the government would always have to rely on 'native subordinates' and it was better that these should be traditional chiefs rather than strangers 'bound by no custom, tradition, or fear of public opinion'.

Given the premises of indirect rule, the immediate tasks were to discover the real character of the pre-colonial political structure, to repair the harm done by direct rule, to reinstate lost suzerainties, to put usurpers in their place, and generally to build up the self-respect of the N.T. chiefs. These chiefs, remarked Jones, had often been treated with 'a rather contemptuous attitude':

they were regarded as 'bushmen' dressed up in a peculiar garb covered with all sorts of charms and talismans, seated on prancing steeds, followed by a ragged retinue of one or two drummers and a violin player, and a small rabble of flatterers, who rent the air with howls of adulation of their ruler. Few realized the real administrative capacity of some of these rulers and it was years since it had been put to a severe test.[38]

The first job was 'to ascertain the customs and habits of the people' so that improvements and reforms might be effected 'without destroying any of their reverence for the past'.[39] To this end, Cardinall had proposed in 1928 that Rattray, the government anthropologist, should be invited to carry out a survey of native constitutions – a proposal across which Walker-Leigh had wearily scrawled, 'God help the N.T.s'.[40] Nonetheless, Rattray was commissioned to make the survey which eventually appeared as *The Tribes of the Ashanti Hinterland.* Blair also undertook enquiries with the aim of devising a Dagomba constitution which would 'attain as nearly as possible to a point in the natural and normal development of any tribal constitution, to which can be added improvements which a civilised people realise to be such'.[41]

Apart from avoiding 'Westernisation', Blair was particularly intent on re-storing the authority of the Ya-Na, who, he said, had come near to being ousted from his position 'by the arrogance and intractability of Savelugu and Karaga'. The first step towards re-establishing that authority, and towards setting up the new structure of native administration, was the convening of a conference of chiefs and elders at Yendi.

NATIVE AUTHORITIES

The Dagomba conference opened on 24 November 1930, in the presence of some 6,000 people and after meticulous preparations by the administrative officers. Before the conference, Blair and Duncan-Johnstone met Ya-Na Abudulai and informed the king of the government's hopes that 'Dagomba Chiefs would gradually come to acquire greater powers, and more adminis-trative scope'.[42] Blair had already impressed on the Western Dagomba chiefs their obligation to obey instructions and summonses issuing from Yendi and had arranged for a Yendi elder, the Zankolana, to act as his mouthpiece when on trek, so that administrative orders appeared to be delivered in the name of the king.

At the conference, which lasted for several days, the acting C.C.N.T. announced that it was intended to give 'a more particular acknowledgement than ... heretofore, to the standing and authority of Chiefs over their people; and to clothe them with powers, enforceable by law, which they have not previously exercised'.[43] Subsequently a detailed statement of the history, boundaries, and constitution of Dagomba was secured from the Ya-Na, the chiefs, and the elders. The chiefs were required to sign docu-ments acknowledging the paramountcy of the Ya-Na, listing the various classes of chieftaincy and the order of precedence within each, specifying the elders of Yendi and the members of the State Council and the Judicial Council, and stating the procedures and qualifications relating to royal succession.

With regard to succession, they accepted that only chiefs occupying the skins of Karaga, Mion, and Savelugu could be considered eligible for Yendi. Also, the chiefs and elders in effect excluded Ya-Nas' grandsons from the paramountcy by formally adopting 'the general rule that a son may never rise higher than his father' – although an affidavit explicitly laying down such exclusion was not produced by the conference.[44] The participants further agreed that the Gushie-Na, Kuga-Na, Tuguri-Nam, and Gomli formed 'the committee of selection' for Yendi and that in selection, 'recourse is made to the spirits of the dead Chiefs'.[45] The proper successor was indicated by 'the results of a sacrifice'. Finally, it was confirmed that all appointments to chieftainships were made by the paramount and that 'the holder of a chieftainship cannot be deprived of his office except by death'.[46]

On the basis of these proceedings and of 'the unmistakable desire of the Chiefs and people for the restoration of the old Dagomba Kingdom', the administration made plans to establish a Dagomba Native Authority and to adjust district boundaries so that they would coincide with those of native states (for Gonja and Dagomba in the Southern Province and eventually for other districts, as native authorities were set up elsewhere in the N.T.). The first step was to draft a Native Authority Ordinance, which came into effect on 30 January 1932 and was followed by Orders constituting a Dagomba Native Authority (the Ya-Na and his council) and thirteen Subordinate Native Authorities (the various divisional chiefs and their elders).[47]

The Native Authority Ordinance empowered the C.C.N.T., with the Governor's approval, to constitute Native Authority areas and to 'appoint any chief or other native or any group of natives to be a Native Authority for any area'.[48] Such appointment was revocable and the Ordinance laid down penalties for any person who might profess 'to exercise administrative functions' or to be a Native Authority without the approval of the Governor or of a Native Authority. The Ordinance also prescribed the functions and powers of Native Authorities. These included the duty of maintaining order, and all natives, irrespective of origin, were required to comply with rules issued in this and other respects. A Native Authority had the right of arrest and of imposing penalties not exceeding £10 or two months' imprisonment on any person obstructing or interfering 'with the lawful exercise by a Native Authority of any power conferred by' the 'Ordinance'. For conspiring against or attempting 'in any manner to undermine the lawful power of any Chief or Native Authority', penalties not exceeding £100 or one year's imprisonment were prescribed, although the consent of the Governor was required before prosecutions could take place under this section.[49]

Native Authorities were empowered to issue rules on a wide range of matters, including firearms, liquor, markets, sanitation and infectious diseases, and others 'generally providing for the peace, good order, and welfare of the natives of' an 'area'.[50] They could hire employees and could impose charges for services provided. However, the government retained rights of supervision and direction: a D.C. could order an Authority to issue rules, could cancel them, or could enact them himself, and he could fine an Authority up to £50 for neglecting its duties or ignoring his directions.

Indeed, the crucial question is: how far did this Ordinance embody the spirit of indirect rule? To what extent were the chiefs really independent of the government? What degree of direction could officers exercise? For at least one D.C. argued that, whatever custom might say about chiefs being irremovable, it would be irresponsible of the government to abandon altogether the right to dismiss a chief. He pointed to the case of Savelugu, where the royal duke controlled some 30,000 subjects. But he was firmly contradicted by the acting P.C., who remarked that, since it was policy 'to respect and support Native Custom', it would be impossible to ask the Ya-Na to depose one of his subordinates.[51]

In reality, however, the Ordinance provided an effective solution. For, without infringing any customary procedure or denying to any chief 'traditional' standing, the government could curtail the powers of a chief simply by withdrawing recognition from him as an approved Native Authority, a status conferred at discretion by the Crown. As Jones put it:

the position of a chief in the Protectorate is that he holds office as a native authority ... by the wish of the people indicated in his appointment by their representatives, but at the will of the Crown, signified in the Orders made by its representative the Governor. If the support of the Crown is withdrawn by revocation of the Orders, the executive powers and jurisdiction of the chief in question cease.

The government did not wish to interfere with the right of people to elect a chief, much less to dictate whom they should appoint, but, Jones said,

in the interests of justice and good administration Government must reserve to itself the right in each instance to decide whether rule-making and judicial powers under the Ordinances shall or shall not be entrusted to the headchief or chief so elected.[52]

By providing such legal and administrative distinctions in regard to status and functions, the government managed to keep its ultimate control without abandoning the concept of 'inherent rights' at the heart of indirect rule.

Nevertheless, the Ordinance left a large area of uncertainty where the working relationship between the D.C.s and the chiefs was concerned. By chance, an especially awkward test-case arose when, in July 1930, a young wife of the Yo-Na limped into Tamale, with her legs in irons, seeking sanctuary with the government after having been severely beaten by her husband. Duncan-Johnstone acknowledged that this incident raised 'a very delicate question indeed', namely, how far indirect rule required an uncritical acceptance of custom. He recorded the dilemma in his diary:

although to our ideas it is repugnant to see a woman in leg irons, it is not so to the native, and according to Native Custom the Chief of Savelugu was acting within his rights. To have given way to natural indignation at the sight of a woman hobbling through Tamale with her feet in leg irons and to have taken action against Savelugu would have served no good purpose, on the contrary it would probably have succeeded in antagonising the Chief and would not have been in accordance with the Policy of Ruling Indirectly.[53]

His solution to the immediate problem was to refer the matter to the Ya-Na, warning him that 'Government views such practices on the part of the Chiefs with grave disapproval' and asking that he summon the Yo-Na for reprimand. He was further led to expatiate on the general question of relations with chiefs: 'the Political Officers of this Province will act as sympathetic advisers and counsellors to the Paramount Chiefs, keeping in the background as far as possible so as not to lower the Chiefs' prestige or cause them to lose interest in their work'. This said, it must be understood that

under Indirect Rule the Chiefs or Native Authorities are not *independent* rulers, they are the delegates of the Governor. The advice therefore of the Political Officers must be followed, although the Chiefs will issue their own instructions to their Divisional Chiefs ... everything must be done to redeem the Chiefs and their people from practices which are unhealthy or degrading while cherishing at the same time all local associations and traditions which are good.[54]

Whether or not this advice helped the D.C.s, it certainly brought out more clearly the ambiguity of indirect rule policy (as distinct from indirect rule philosophy). There was, as Austen rightly says, a paradox at the heart of indirect rule: 'the incompatibility of the decentralization implied by Indirect Rule with the centralizing tendencies of all bureaucracies'.[55]

For the administration itself, the major change resulting from indirect rule was the amalgamation of Eastern and Western Dagomba into one district, with headquarters at Yendi.[56] The new Dagomba District came into existence in 1933, when the retrenchment of the Gold Coast service was at its most severe; at the same time the post of Provincial Commissioner was abolished in the N.T. Duncan-Johnstone and others approved of the reform as a logical consequence of indirect rule, since throughout the N.T. it brought about a situation in which no major group was divided between two districts, though in some cases there was more than one N.A. in a district.

NATIVE TRIBUNALS

The indirect rule team naturally wished to restore judicial powers to the chiefs. This was an area in which, as we have seen, the previous regime had treated native institutions fairly harshly. It was also one which presented the basic dilemma of indirect rule in an acute form: the dilemma of how to balance, on the one hand, respect for custom and 'inherent rights' against, on the other, encouragement of social change and the exercise of a degree of political control. The question, as ever, was one of so defining a relationship that the D.C. had a working minimum of rights and duties while the chiefs had a real measure of independent authority.

A particular obstacle to the reform of justice was the division between the N.T. and Togoland, which meant that, because of the different legislation applying to the two areas, the king was more powerful in the east than in the west. In Western Dagomba the sub-chiefs (divisional and village) enjoyed considerably greater judicial rights than their paramount – an anomaly which, Duncan-Johnstone believed, could be ended by establishing and asserting the king's inherent rights of jurisdiction throughout the kingdom.[57] But then the question would arise, whether or not the king, or other chiefs, should have the power of life and death. Cardinall, at least, thought that there was 'no reason at all why so important a ruler [as the Ya-Na] should not have in reserve the power of life and death over his subjects. The execution of such sentences can always be restricted by the Chief Commissioner.'[58] In saying this, Cardinall placed himself at the permissive extreme of the indirect rule spectrum: the Native Tribunals Ordinance of 1932 was much more inclined towards safeguards and regulations.

The Ordinance was, like the Native Authorities measure, a compromise between administrative prerogative and customary right, but it kept even more power in the hands of government. For in 1930 Jones had persuaded Jackson and Duncan-Johnstone that they need not carry out their intended enquiry into 'inherent rights' of jurisdiction, since, he noted, 'all we required was to decide the extent of the powers which we were prepared to allow the Chiefs to exercise'.[59] Under the Ordinance the government did, indeed, reserve complete discretion in deciding on whom judicial powers should be conferred and what jurisdiction they should enjoy. As Jones wrote (of the 1935 legislation which superseded the 1932 Ordinance):

the principle embodied in the Native Courts Ordinance is that the right of jurisdiction flows from the Crown, and is not the corollary of a chief's election by the people. The Governor, by Order, nominates the president and members of a native court and assigns to such court the powers which it is deemed fit to exercise without any regard for the rank of the chief or the area for which it is established . . . [Members of courts] are under no delusion as to the source of their power; they lay no claim to inherent rights of jurisdiction but appreciate that their courts are British courts, deriving their authority from the Crown.[60]

The government thus retreated from the initial position of Cardinall (and others), that indirect rule implied a full restoration of the jurisdiction exercised by the chiefs before 1902. The Ordinance of 1932 (and its successor) empowered the government to establish Native Courts as it saw fit, to specify by Order the members of courts, and to suspend both courts and members if necessary.[61] The courts were to administer 'native law and custom' obtaining in the area specified, except insofar as law and custom were 'repugnant to natural justice or morality' or were inconsistent with the provisions of existing ordinances. In addition, the Governor could confer on Native Courts the power of enforcing specified ordinances.

The jurisdiction of the courts was hedged by administrative controls. The commissioners had a right of access to all courts and to their records at all times, and the Governor could exclude persons or classes of persons from their jurisdiction. The commissioners' courts remained in existence to try criminal cases brought by the police and to hear appeals from Native Courts in both criminal and civil matters. The D.C. could, in fact, order the transfer of a case from a Native Court to his own, magistrate's court. However, the highest grade of Native Court (in this case, the Ya-Na's tribunal) had appellate jurisdiction for cases heard in subordinate tribunals, though again with provision for appeal to administrative courts.

Under the 1935 Ordinance, Native Courts were graded into three categories. Those in category A (in Dagomba the tribunals of the Ya-Na and the Bimbilla-Na) had jurisdiction in civil matters to a maximum of £50 or imprisonment not exceeding six months; for those in category B (two divisional tribunals), civil jurisdiction was limited to £25 and penalties in criminal cases were restricted to £25 or three months' imprisonment; for those in category C (fourteen divisional and urban courts) civil jurisdiction was restricted to £10 and penalties to £5 or one month's imprisonment.[62] All courts could impose corporal punishment on juveniles but in no case on adults.

90

The administration moved rather cautiously in applying the Ordinance, partly because there was a shortage of both suitable buildings and trained clerical staff. The Ya-Na's tribunal was established (or, more correctly, 'confirmed') in 1933: its members were the king himself and seven of the elders of Yendi (only four of them members of the traditional Council of Elders).[63] The remaining divisional tribunals followed in 1934 and 1935, and in each case the Ya-Na had to approve the list of proposed members.

Under the Ordinance eligibility for appointment was not confined to chiefs and elders, although in practice no effort was made to appoint commoners, educated or otherwise, until well after the Second World War. However, the king did insist that 'personal qualifications' would be 'the only real criteria' governing selection, and a number of elders were dropped from tribunals on grounds of idleness or incompetence.[64] A comparison of the tribunal members listed in an appendix to the 1930 constitution with the members of Native Courts chosen in 1934/5 shows little correlation between the two: in one case (Tolon) the divisional chief himself did not appear in the 1935 panel. Generally, however, the Native Courts contained a large proportion of court elders, usually headed by the *wulana* or *kpanalana* of the divisional chief.

In order to ensure that the Native Courts were obeyed, the administration set up a force of Native Authority police, at the behest of the king. (The Northern Territories Constabulary had been abolished in March 1929 and its members assimilated into the Gold Coast Police.)[65] The new force (whose number is not recorded) was created in 1932 under the direction of the king, to whom its members had to swear allegiance. The police were allotted to Subordinate Native Authorities, which had to contribute to their upkeep.[66]

The problem of clerical staff was a persistent difficulty: the administration insisted that only northerners should be used as court clerks and the Ya-Na was unwilling to employ mallams for this purpose, as Duncan-Johnstone suggested. Indeed, the Provincial Commissioner hoped to have *ajami* script (Arabic modified for use in Hausa) adopted by the Native Authorities and Courts, and the D.C.s were instructed to take lessons in Hausa, but Yendi was suspicious of innovations which might increase the power of the mallams.[67]

The government did establish a 'State Council book', in which 'all laws, native customs and decisions of the Ya-Na's council' were to be recorded. In 1936 Blair started a comprehensive survey of customary law, the results of which were to be approved by a conference of chiefs and elders. But when the D.C. asked the chiefs at a conference in March 1937 to 'consider on their own the question of codifying Native Custom', he met a rather apathetic response. He commented: 'They do not seem very keen except to lay it down that it is a heinous offence to ravish a chief's wife. A chief though may apparently do what he likes.'[68]

Yet the administration was fairly satisfied with the working of the Native Courts. While there were criticisms of the court elders, on grounds of incompetence and senility, the government argued that statistics showed that the courts were popular. In 1936/7, the Native Courts of the N.T. heard all together over 1,000 criminal cases, only eighteen of which led to appeals. In Dagomba the number of cases, in all categories, dealt with by Native Courts went up from 1,221 (in 1934/5) to 2,178 (in 1937/8): in the latter year only four appeals were lodged.[69]

Despite their success, the administration was reluctant to relax its tutelage over the courts and it still refused to allow lawyers to appear in them. The fear behind this refusal was no doubt that expressed by Blair's colleague Captain Cockey, in a letter to the Chief Commissioner written in 1936:

> The more one sees of Dagomba Native Custom the more one realizes how essential it is that we should get their courts established on a firm footing and do everything possible to protect their Customs and Courts from disruption by the introduction of Foreign Law and Procedure. As was written in a recent book, a great deal of our time must be taken up in protecting the Native from the evils of civilization which we represent.[70]

TREASURIES AND TAXATION

The government considered the successful introduction of direct taxation in the N.T. – preceding as it did the imposition of tax in the south – to be the major achievement of indirect rule. Again, the legislative basis was provided by an ordinance, the Native Treasuries Ordinance of 30 July 1932; but the new 'tribute tax' was not introduced until 1936.

The title of the 1932 Ordinance was misleading, since it did not in fact provide for the establishment of treasuries controlled by Native Authorities: four had already been set up when the Ordinance was enacted, and legislation was not required for this purpose. The idea of local treasuries to manage the proceeds of taxation had been advanced by Cardinall in 1928, and in 1931 a state treasury was established at Yendi. Divisional treasuries were subsequently organised at Tamale (for the Gulkpeogu division), Savelugu, and Kumbungu.[71]

But, without rates or local taxation, the income of these native treasuries was meagre. The Yendi treasury had a revenue of £149 in 1930/1 and by 1933 it had only risen to £593. In that year, indeed, the total receipts of all four treasuries were only £1,672: they depended on court fines and on fees charged for the use of cattle kraals, markets, ferries, and caravanserais. During the first four years the Native Authorities were able to contribute very little to local development schemes: their major item of expenditure was, in fact, the payment of small salaries to the chiefs and elders serving on the judicial tribunals. Thus in 1934 the Ya-Na drew an annual salary of £180, while the Gulkpe-Na, Yo-Na, and Kumbung-Na took £80 each, and five Yendi elders got all together £66.[72]

The administration regarded the main function of these treasuries as an educative one, preparing the Native Authorities for the day when direct taxation was imposed. It certainly did not divest itself of revenue for the benefit of the treasuries, a fact to which the Ya-Na drew attention at a conference at Yendi in 1932. On this occasion, Abudulai asked that he should be relieved of much of the development work he had undertaken in Yendi, since he was obtaining no reimbursement for his efforts, while the government was appropriating all local revenues. The king concluded: 'Even the best horse will not go unless he is fed.'[73]

The troubles of the Yendi treasury were not, however, limited to the admitted inadequacy of the king's revenue. A major problem encountered by Blair arose from the paramount's reluctance to assign to the treasury money which he received from 'customary sources' (notably money paid by candidates seeking chiefly offices). Blair remarked that it was impossible to keep an accurate account of the king's revenue because he gave away much of what he received as presents to retainers and visitors to the court: 'He feels that if he put the whole amount in the cash book he would not have the right to dash it to his people and naturally he does not like to lose the pleasure and conceit of distributing largesse.'[74]

But the ratification of the Geneva convention on forced labour and the continuing effects of the Slump made the development of local revenue-collection an urgent matter. The 1932 Ordinance was a product of this concern. It was intended to enable Native Authorities 'to manage their own finances' and to provide for 'the better control and regulation of Native Treasuries'. Under the Ordinance, the C.C.N.T. was empowered to make, subject to the Governor's approval, regulations 'declaring and defining the sources of revenue which may be paid into a Native Treasury . . . providing for the raising of revenue by means of levies and other specified forms of taxation and fixing the amount that may be raised by means of such levies and taxation'.[75] The government was also to prescribe the method of collection, the mode of payment, and the purposes to which revenue might be put (including 'the amount that may be allocated to any of such purposes'). There was provision, too, for control of accounting and supervision of the preparation of estimates.

Yet it was four years before any tax was collected in Dagomba. The delay was due not to legal difficulties, but to problems about the form, level, and handling of taxation, as well as to a certain political nervousness.[76] For the launching of direct taxation was, politically, quite distinct from other reforms entailed by indirect rule. It involved an assertion of sovereignty over the people as a whole, whereas the others involved, in reality, not much more than a reallocation of responsibilities between the government and the chiefs. This political factor underlay all discussions of taxation and it explains the manner in which it was presented.

The first problem which the administration tackled was that of the type of tax to be levied, and this led to a consideration of the forms of payment to be accepted. The officials were unanimous that, whatever kind of tax was adopted, the rate should be low, assessment should be lenient, and the amount should be kept stable for at least five years. With respect to the form of taxation, the choice was seen as one between a flat-rate poll tax and some type of graduated tax, proportionate to income. Graduated taxation was rejected, because it was felt that, in view of the general poverty of the north, the returns from such a tax would not compensate for the substantial administrative costs involved in assessment.[77] Nevertheless, several officers regretted that this choice had been forced upon them. Jones, notably, argued that not only was a flat rate tax unprogressive (in the sense that it would forever be tied to what a poor person could afford), but it also lacked the essential educational function provided by graduated taxation. For it would deprive the Native Authorities of the important experience of assessing liability without which they would, in his words, 'never acquire that sense of responsibility and fairness which it is essential that they should possess if they are to develop into true rulers of their people'.[78]

Political education was, then, one of the intended by-products of taxation. Another, as the debate about forms of payment revealed, was development of the local economy and in particular of trade. At least three D.C.s argued that, given the lack of cash in circulation in the N.T., it would be necessary to accept payment in kind (such as farm produce, animals, or even labour) at least for the first few years. Cockey further said that the government had already promised that it would not insist on payment in cash and that to do so would be a breach of faith. To the objection that payment in kind would involve the administration in the troublesome and doubtfully profitable business of selling produce, Blair replied that even if only 25 per cent of the value accrued to the treasuries, this was unimportant since, he said, 'the mere fact of the tax being brought in at all [would] have had the required educative effect'.[79]

Again, the main dissenter was Jones (the Chief Commissioner). While accepting that payment in kind might be inevitable during a transitional period, he felt that it was quite contrary to the objectives which taxation was meant to serve. Taxation, Jones argued, should be a stimulus to development, gently pushing the natives into paid employment or, at least, into commerce, so as to raise the cash required by the government (the classical colonial justification for taxes). Jones continued:

My fear is that so long as payment is accepted in kind, so long will the initiative to trade be lacking ... our aim should be to develop the Protectorate's resources so that with an increase in wealth the individual will be able, and rightly expected, to increase his contribution to the maintenance and extension of social services in his division.[80]

Eventually it was agreed that payment should be made in cash, although D.C.s were authorised to accept cattle or produce in lieu of money if there was no alternative. In practice, the administration seems to have had little difficulty on this score when collection began in 1936 and, once taxation was established, the bulk of payment was in cash.

Apart from political education and the development of the cash economy, taxation was intended as an assertion of sovereignty, not just by the British administration, but by the Ya-Na in relation to his divisional chiefs. This aspect of taxation emerged clearly in the process of establishing the basis and character of the new levy. As early as 1931, Miller (D.C., Western Dagomba) had suggested that by associating the proposed tax with the tribute paid to chiefs in earlier times, the tax would acquire some of the legitimacy attaching to custom and would therefore be more acceptable than a levy imposed merely as an arbitrary exaction of the colonial government.[81] Ingenious though it was, this formula presented difficulties. One was that it might be seen as confirming the assumption by chiefs of 'inherent rights': it was therefore open to the objection raised in respect of both Native Authorities and Native Courts – that it detracted from the sovereignty of the Crown.[82] The issue, nevertheless, came up again, in relation to the collection of taxes and the allocation of revenue, as we shall see.

Indeed, the notion of presenting the new tax as a commuted form of customary tribute did appeal to many administrators. The problem was to know if in reality tribute had been sufficiently regular or standard to provide a suitable basis for commutation. Cockey reported that the king had always received presents from his subordinates, but these, he thought, could not be regarded as amounting to 'tax or tribute, for there is no penalty for non-payment. There has never been any form of taxation.' The same applied to labour provided by the villages:

each village is responsible for a certain piece of work . . . and is called upon when work is necessary . . . Otherwise there seems to be no rule. But if the Na calls on any village to work, e.g. the Nasia road, the work has to be done . . . In fact it seems that Dagomba has practised quite successfully a rather fatalistic 'muddle through' policy.[83]

Despite these uncertainties, the government finally decided to use the 'tribute' formula, and it went to great lengths to persuade subjects that the new tax was a replacement for the offerings previously made to chiefs. In this respect, it showed more concern for traditional forms than it did with the Native Authorities and Native Courts.

After a visit to Tamale by the Governor in February 1934, it was decided to begin the process of introducing direct taxation and intensive enquiries were started into the nature and scale of customary tribute.[84] It was hoped that, with the resulting information, it would be possible to calculate a reasonable cash equivalent which might be demanded as tax.

Following investigations by the D.C., the administration identified three categories of dues paid to chiefs.[85] The first were religious dues (typically a fixed proportion of the harvest) paid to *tindamba* or chiefs, as well as offerings made in thanksgiving or in time of disaster. The D.C. remarked that every male adult paid some such tribute fairly regularly, but a very small proportion reached the king. The C.C.N.T. was flatly against tampering with dues in this category: they represented, he said, 'too integral a part of the religious life of the people to permit of this being done'.

Secondly, there were occasional gifts – those presented at the time of festivals or in homage to a new chief. Such donations were obviously inappropriate for purposes of taxation.

Lastly, there were dues which could be classified as 'feudal': 'payments by the conquered to the conquerors or by the protected to the protectors'. In this connection, evidence was more hopeful. The D.C. found (as we noted in Chapter 2) that there had been 'a well defined system of tribute' in pre-colonial Dagomba and that under this system some part of the tribute was appropriated at each level, the king taking the residue. In addition, subjects had provided labour service for agriculture and building.

The administration estimated that the tribute in produce represented a cash value of 2s 0d per annum: to it could be added 6d as the commuted value of labour service. Thus, Jones wrote, 'a tax of two shillings and sixpence a year would ... represent in Dagomba a fair commutation of the customary dues'.[86] After discussion with the Ya-Na, it was decided that the 'tribute tax' should be fixed at a level of 2s 0d for each adult male in the Dagomba area and at 1s 0d in the poorer, Konkomba divisions. Such a tax was thought to represent 1.5 per cent of the average income in the kingdom and could be expected to yield between £5,000 and £6,000 annually.[87] The tax was approved by the Secretary of State in September 1935 and promulgated on 2 April 1936: authorisation for the collection of this and similar levies elsewhere in the N.T. was issued on 24 June 1936.[88]

The issue of sovereignty came up as soon as the officials began considering the problems of collection. Some officers thought that the divisional treasuries should (like the divisional chiefs before the occupation) collect the tax and pass a defined proportion (say, 50 per cent) on to Yendi.[89] This would, they said, be in accordance with tradition and it would also provide the training in financial responsibility without which, as Jones had declared, indirect rule could not really succeed. On this point, however, Jones himself demurred. He insisted that, whatever resources might be allocated to the divisions, the tax itself must be administered directly by Yendi in the name of the Ya-Na. There was a basic principle at stake: 'the right to exact tribute flows from the right to exercise control over the disposal or allocation of the land owned by a community ... the right to levy taxation is an attribution of independence and thus of the paramount power'.[90] Now, according to the 1930 constitution, the Ya-Na 'owned all the land and all land cases were tried by him'.[91] It followed that tax should be levied in his name and, further, that he should have the prerogative of distributing the proceeds. The role of divisional treasuries should be merely that of accounting for revenue collected in the divisions and of spending such funds as Yendi saw fit to grant to them.

Any other course, Jones warned, might have serious political consequences. To allow the divisions to retain a substantial part of the tax revenue as of right would, he thought, lead to the disruption of kingdoms which had only recently been reunited. He continued:

The subordinate authorities will soon contend that the tribute is levied in their names and that the [proposed] ten per cent remitted to the head chief is an annual customary present ... The subordinate native authorities will struggle each for their own ends and an unhealthy disruptive spirit will rapidly permeate and pervade the body politic.[92]

96

In the desire to achieve dramatic results, he concluded, it was vital not to allow a strengthening of the Subordinate Authorities 'to the detriment and eventual destruction of the paramount authority'.

In the event, proceeds from the new tax were sent to the central treasury at Yendi. The village headmen were given responsibility for collection, though not without some trepidation on the part of officials and, indeed, on the part of the chiefs themselves. In return for their trouble, the headmen were to receive a rebate of 10 per cent on money gathered during the first month of collection and 5 per cent thereafter.[93]

The establishment of the new system was laced with administrative difficulties, not the least being the scarcity of educated northerners to act as treasury clerks. The N.T. officers conducted an elaborate and meticulous propaganda campaign throughout the early months of 1936 to explain the nature and the benefits of direct taxation. Given this effort, and the tensions created, it is not surprising that Jones reacted with irritation when, at the last moment, Accra expressed its apprehension 'lest the progress forecasted should prove too rapid in respect of the less advanced divisions'. In obvious annoyance, Jones replied:

Every step possible has been taken to make the object of direct taxation known to the people, as distinct from the chiefs ... Tribute in kind which they now pay to their chiefs is a far greater burden on them than the tax will be. This they have been told and assured that with the introduction of the latter the former will be abolished ... I am really at a loss to know what further action the Administrative Officers can possibly take in the matter.[94]

In fact, he had taken one other step which made his defence almost impregnable. On 19 August 1936, when the first collection of the tax had just got under way, he wrote to his D.C.s suggesting that while government officials were exempt from contributing to the cost of local services, they should nevertheless consider making a voluntary contribution. He proposed that all officers should pay into the Yendi treasury an amount equivalent to 0.5 per cent of their salaries (which, in his own case, meant £8 per annum).[95] Whether his colleagues agreed or not is not recorded. The only opposition to taxation in the N.T.s in fact came from southern civil servants at Navrongo – an opposition which was, as Jones cryptically noted, 'short-lived'.

The first exercise in direct taxation succeeded beyond even the Chief Commissioner's expectations. By the end of 1936, the Native Authorities in the N.T. had collected £19,114, compared to the target of £10,941 cautiously set by the administration. The Dagomba Native Authority collected £4,200 and during the next two years proceeds from the tribute tax (all of which went to the Native Authority) rose to £4,700. With the addition of market fees and other revenues handed over by the government, court revenue, and grants-in-aid, the total income of the central treasury in 1936/7 was £8,200.[96] As the C.C.N.T. pointed out to a Dagomba conference in March 1937, this meant that 'in five years ... the Dagomba Native Authority [had] multiplied its cash revenue 50 times'.[97]

Between March 1937 and March 1941 the government provided grants-in-aid totalling £13,634 and the Native Authority itself raised between £8,419 and £9,140 annually. The annual estimates meetings, which had been started in 1934, were turned over almost entirely to the chiefs and Native Authority staff, although the administration prepared and approved the estimates. In terms of the objectives of indirect rule, direct taxation was an undoubted success, providing a substantial injection of money for Native Authorities and replenishing the strength of Dagomba chieftaincy, with all the implications this bore for politics later on.

EDUCATION AND EMPLOYMENT

The problems which arose in implementing indirect rule were, in many respects, a function of the comprehensive nature of the policy: the success of each element depended on success in other spheres. In this sense, it was a development strategy. Duncan-Johnstone described quite succinctly the major strategic problem involved: 'the Native Administrations cannot function satisfactorily without revenue, sufficient revenue cannot be raised without taxation, and taxes cannot be gathered without an organisation, which means a certain amount of delay until we have trained the Native officials'.[98] So, although education was not a specific object of legislation under indirect rule, the government recognised that the achievement of its aims depended on a sound educational policy. 'Soundness' had both positive and negative connotations. Positively, the educational system should produce educated commoners for employment by the Native Authorities and should train the younger members of the ruling class in the skills of modern administration. Negatively, it should prevent both the subversion of the traditional culture by alien ideas and values and the formation of a group of 'Europeanised' commoners who, for reasons of numbers or attitudes, could not be accommodated within the structure of indirect rule. These negative concerns were, it should be said, at least as apparent in official statements as the positive ones, and often more so. They were accompanied by a somewhat fretful insistence that education must be supervised and regulated by the political service and an almost obsessive fear of the development of independent (especially mission-run) schools.

Under indirect rule, northern educational policy maintained, indeed strengthened, the commitment to a vocational, non-literary type of curriculum which had been adopted under Guggisberg. There was, however, some expansion of schooling, mainly through the creation of 'Native Authority schools'. By 1938 there were 91 pupils in the Dagomba Native Authority school, opened at Yendi in the previous year: in addition, there were 124 pupils at the Tamale central school (compared with 122 in 1929).[99] Native Authorities were responsible for building and maintaining schools (that at Yendi cost £1,000 to construct) and they also provided scholarships for post-primary education, on condition that those benefiting committed themselves to service with a Native Authority. In 1938 the Yendi treasury spent some £600 on education, a substantial part of which went to the maintenance of 37 scholarship-holders at various institutions, including Achimota, near Accra. The administration, for its part, was responsible for the training and payment of teachers, as well as for the provision of books and equipment.[100]

As regards the education of the aristocracy, Duncan-Johnstone had proposed in 1930 the creation of a special section at the Tamale government school where 'the future governing class' could be trained for the responsibilities of native administration.[101] The curriculum was to include administrative studies, local history, English, animal health, and road maintenance – a broad education by anybody's standards – and the D.C.s were urged to persuade the chiefs to send their sons in for training. The hope was that from this school would emerge the nucleus of a 'progressive' chieftaincy. Duncan-Johnstone reflected:

If they [the chiefs] do not rise to the intellectual level of the other members of the community, sooner or later the educated class will break down the traditional authority ... [But] if it is possible to turn out twenty to thirty literate Chiefs at the end of ten years it will revolutionise Native Administration in this province.[102]

The course for chiefs' sons does not, however, seem to have established itself and, in general, indirect rule did not produce any dramatic change in either the availability or the character of education in Dagomba. The administration was haunted by the fear of a repetition of events in the south, where, it thought, the authorities had 'allowed education to outstrip native administration in the race of progress'.[103] It therefore used its influence to restrict the number of pupils passing into post-Standard III schooling to the number which, in its estimation, could be employed by the Native Authorities. Thus in the N.T. only the Tamale school (with European staff and under the direct supervision of the Inspector of Schools) was permitted to take pupils to the level of Standard VII. During the early thirties it was expected that the number of northern boys reaching Standard VII would 'not exceed five per annum': in three later years (1936, 1937, and 1938) the number of pupils graduating annually with Standard VII was eleven, twelve, and fifteen respectively.[104] These pupils, it should be repeated, were drawn from all over the north (indeed, in earlier years a high proportion were southerners). With one exception, all the Tamale graduates were taken directly into Native Authority employment or went on to teacher-training, which eventually would take them into a Native Authority school.

Despite the shortage of teachers in the north, the administration's fear of 'alien influences' was such that in 1938 it resolved to send no more teacher-trainees to Achimota, the famous secondary school on the coast. Experience of life in the south produced, it was thought, an 'unsettled state of mind', expressed by the 'air of superiority', 'aloofness', and 'contempt for native custom' which some of the pupils manifested on their return. The Provincial Inspector of Schools demanded the withdrawal of pupils from Achimota and the establishment of a teacher-training college in Tamale. He declared:

The teachers must be men of sterling character, proud of their race, loyal to their chiefs, courteous always and in complete accord with the Policy of Native Administration. There must be no malcontents, no disturbing influences in any of the schools. The staffs are small, their responsibilities great and a single discontented teacher in a school can be its ruination.[105]

As for missionaries, the N.T. political conference in 1933 endorsed the Education Department's concern at the way in which Catholic mission schools seemed to be 'springing up in such a way as to be entirely beyond control'. The C.C.N.T. feared that mission schools would have a 'disintegrating effect' on the social system which the government was trying to build up and he observed (strangely, for the son of a Welsh Anglican minister): 'Christianity makes but little headway among a native community which has developed a sound social system of its own.'[106]

The indirect rulers' concern for the preservation of traditional forms was pervasive, passionate, and, at times, bizarre. They expressed great admiration for traditional Dagomba education and emphasised that they wanted the new schools to reinforce the values which it imparted, namely, 'respect, honour and obedience to parents and those in authority, loyalty to the clan, family, or tribe, and though them to the ruler, realization of the dignity of labour and the responsibility of every member of the family to pull his weight'.[107] The schools at Tamale and Yendi were deliberately organised as microcosms of native society under indirect rule. As Candler, the Superintendent of Education for the N.T. in the late twenties, reported,

The primary schools ... are organised on dual lines of Government by chiefs and administrative officers ... each house has its elder, each compound its Chief and each school its Paramount Chief, the Teachers, Masters and the Superintendent of Education, N.T.s, reproducing the Commissioner grades, so that the system in its own way does reproduce the dual lines of civil Government.[108]

When the Yendi school was opened, in February 1937, four of the Ya-Na's elders were deputed to act as wardens of dormitories named after four sections of the town, and the Mion-lana was given overall responsibility. The C.C.N.T. wrote:

In effect the Chief of Mion who lives within seven miles of the school and whose duties demand his frequent appearance in Yendi holds the chair of Native History and Folklore and delivers lectures regularly to the school on the ancient Dagomba traditions ... soon after the school opened [he] took it upon himself to address the boys on the subject of obedience to authority.[109]

Reverence for tradition was not reserved for the schools and, indeed, it took its more extreme forms in relation to local culture. The administration took a very strong line against the 'Tarbushi' clubs (associations for young people which started to appear in the late thirties). It was alleged that their members 'spent most of the night singing and dancing and so took little interest in the day's work' and they were also thought to be 'undermining the authority of the elders'.[110] Many D.C.s objected to Africans wearing European clothes. Indeed, at least one objected to them wearing any clothes at all.

The D.C., Dagomba, noted in his diary on 14 November 1939 (inaccurately, as it happens) that Ya-Na Andani had 'introduced clothes to the Dagomba (and in my opinion did his country a great disservice thereby)'.[111]

ADMINISTRATION UNDER INDIRECT RULE

The 'indirect rule team' never expressed (at least on paper) any serious doubts about the value or practicality of its policies. The Chief Commissioner believed that indirect rule had produced 'greater efficiency in administration' as well as 'greater contentment among the people'.[112] In principle, it should have eased the burden on the D.C., compensating for the reduction in staff by effecting a substantial transfer of responsibilities to the Native Authorities.

In fact, there is no evidence that the colonial administrator had an easier life under indirect rule than before. The reduction of resources following the Depression was partly to blame. The N.T. administration was trimmed from two provinces and eleven districts down to six districts. In the case of Dagomba, this meant that the D.C. and his assistant at Tamale had to govern an area of 9,696 square miles, containing 181,710 people. The transfer of district headquarters to Yendi, though consistent with the principles of indirect rule, had substantial administrative costs, isolating the D.C. from his superiors and from the technical services in Tamale.

The combination of economic austerity and a policy of indirect rule created further problems. D.C.s lost their allowances (including their travelling allowances) but, at the same time, they were exhorted to spend more time on trek, in accordance with the spirit of indirect rule. Duncan-Johnstone ordered his subordinates to spend at least ten days of every month on trek. In the *Standing Orders*, he declared: 'It is on foot in the bush, regardless of mileage and car allowances, moving amongst the people at their own pace in an atmosphere of calm unhaste that the most valuable work is done.'[113] In reality, administrative life seems to have been conducted more than ever in an atmosphere of frenzied bustle, for indirect rule brought with it a large increment of supervisory and propaganda work, on top of the perpetually increasing pressure of office work. In 1938 the C.C.N.T. reported that the D.C. at Tamale 'is unable to be absent from Tamale for more than two or three nights consecutively with the result that his tours of inspection are invariably hurried and, therefore, not as thorough as they should be for effective administration'.[114] Yet in 1940 Jones blandly told a new appointee to the post: 'I attach far more importance to maintaining contact with the people than I do to the running of an office.'[115]

In one respect, indirect rule did make for smoother administration. Under the new regime it was policy to give each district a fairly permanent staff of its own, on the principle that indirect rule required of officers a detailed knowledge of local languages and customs. Once 'worked in', therefore, the D.C. was assured of a reasonably long tenure in a familiar setting. Certainly, there was greater continuity of service than under direct rule. By 1937 all districts in the N.T. (except Krachi) had been under the same officers for between four and seven years. But the value of continuity depended, of course, on the value of the officer, and its attractions to him depended on the attractions of the district. Moreover, remarked Cockey, it was just such permanence of tenure which had produced the 'die-hardism' of the Walker-Leigh regime. Even with the transfusion of younger staff in the early thirties, the N.T. only gradually lost their long-established reputation as a dumping-ground for inferior officers.

The progress of native administration in Dagomba was monitored through a series of native conferences held each year (except 1933) until the outbreak of the Second World War. The reports on these conferences were occasions for celebrating the increasing self-confidence of the chiefs, the development of a willingness to speak out on the part of subordinates, and the general growth of 'a corporate spirit'. In 1934 the Chief Commissioner allowed himself a moderate degree of self-satisfaction over the fact that the chiefs had shown a better grasp 'than might be expected of a people who have only recently had real power conferred on them'.[116] And again, in 1935, Jones remarked on 'the success achieved in the education of the Dagomba Native Authorities to take a real interest in, and a reasonable share of, the management of local affairs. The Ya-Na is to be congratulated on displaying a power of decision which does him great credit and augurs well for his future administration.'[117] The Dagomba, noted the D.C., were 'at last' showing 'an interest in their country'. At the 1935 conference, the acting Chief Commissioner, Rake, urged the chiefs on to greater things, saying: 'Dagomba was now united and running its own show. They must not think they had reached the end of the race. It was not nearly time to pull up their horses.'[118] Reading such remarks, it is difficult to suppress a feeling of irony and bafflement that they should have been made by, of all people, men who so prided themselves on a knowledge of local history and culture. Considering the kingdom's three or four hundred years of turbulent court politics, it was, a reader might think, all rather as if fifteenth-century Florence had been taken over by a prep school headmaster.

CHAPTER 6

DAGOMBA POLITICS UNDER INDIRECT RULE, 1932–1947

> The Mion dancers have a wonderful medicine which they take, which makes them able to lay eggs, bear children, and turn into elephants. I must regard it as a merciful intervention of Providence which prevented them taking this medicine before dancing before the Acting Governor, who would have been at least surprised at the last item and deeply shocked by the first two.[1]

> I explained . . . what was 'going on' from the white man's point of view in Kumbungu – water supply, missionaries, fly-proof meat stalls . . .[2]

In this chapter I shall examine the working of indirect rule in Dagomba, the reasons for the disillusionment of administrative officers with the Native Authority system, and the effects of that system on the distribution and exercise of power in the kingdom. In so doing, I shall suggest, tentatively, the outlines of an interpretation which might be applied to the Yendi crisis and the events preceding it.[3] This interpretation will be developed further in the last three chapters.

The late thirties and the early forties represent a period of transition in Dagomba state politics and also in colonial thinking. Because colonial philosophy underwent a sea-change during this period, it is important to take account of the new official mood when we try to assess the successes and failures of indirect rule. For, if we say that indirect rule was a 'failure', we should add that this was as much because standards had changed as because institutions and policies proved inadequate to their purpose. The Dagomba Native Authorities did, indeed, fail to achieve much that the 'indirect rule team' had hoped for. The impatience and the dissatisfaction of officials during and after the war arose, nevertheless, at least partly from a rethinking of their own ideas and aims – a rethinking which made what had seemed in the thirties a bold vision of self-government look inadequate and a little futile.

Joyce Cary made just this point in *The Case for African Freedom*. He suggested there that indirect rule was founded on a notion of freedom inherited from nineteenth-century liberalism. This conception was essentially negative (and, we might add, 'protective' – the word so beloved of administrators in the thirties): it was, writes Cary, 'rooted first in legal security against violence, then in the old idea of liberty as an absence of restraint, and finally in self-development within local resources'. During the thirties and forties, a more dynamic concept gained currency, one which demanded active social and economic development, initiated and conducted by the state. As Cary remarks, the change in mood was accompanied by a change in standards: 'Critics no longer ask of a government, "Have you protected the religious liberty and respected the native institutions, as far as possible, of your dependent peoples?" but "What have you done to raise the standard of living, of health and education in your colonies?" '[4] In brief, smells, which had been facts, became problems.

In terms of 'positive freedom', indirect rule was thought by many people to have been a failure. In the Dagomba area this sense of dissatisfaction became more vocal during the war, as a result of an accumulation of disappointments and frustrations. We shall summarise the course of this disenchantment here and return to the details later in the chapter.

The immediate effect of indirect rule in Dagomba was to re-establish the authority of the paramount and his court over the subordinate, divisional chiefs. The effect was, of course, intended, and everything the government had done under indirect rule was meant to achieve this end. Apart from moving district headquarters to Yendi, recognising the Ya-Na as Native Authority, making his tribunal the senior court in the kingdom, and setting his treasury over all others, the administration got declarations of allegiance from the divisional chiefs and constantly encouraged the king to assert himself in public.

The problem about indirect rule was that whether or not the aims of the British were achieved depended, in the last resort, on the pursuit of these aims being compatible with the interests of the Dagomba chiefs and elders. It also depended on their administrative abilities. In fact, by emphasising the sovereignty of Yendi, the administration had wagered heavily on the political capacity of the king and his elders and it had assumed a proportionate risk to the reputation of the new policy. In a moral sense, the N.T. administration let itself be made a hostage to the processes, crises, and defects of Dagomba royal government.

Officials always recognised the problems which might occur and in particular they recognised the danger of gerontocracy presented by the Dagomba promotional system. As a rule, chiefs were fairly old by the time they achieved high office; but, no matter how senile they became, custom forbade dethronement or abdication. As early as April 1930 one N.T. official wondered aloud if the native administration system could actually be

made proof against the deficiencies in personnel. It is possible to envisage a situation where the younger literate Africans in Native Administration have become impatient at the incapacity or reactionary views of a chief thrown up by the gate system, and form a sort of 'Cave of Adullam'; or again where a chief proved unacceptable to the European, but was not unpopular with his people . . . if this danger is guarded against by dispersing the chief's powers among his elders and sub-chiefs, will there be a big enough binding force to hold the structure together?[5]

'Deficiencies in personnel' became apparent during the thirties, but the most notorious case was not among the chiefs but within the group of court elders at Yendi. It arose during the last years of Ya-Na Abudulai II and led in 1938 to a crisis known to the government as 'the Mbadugu affair'. This incident exposed a great deal of activity which officials regarded as corrupt and it confirmed suspicions that the elders were appropriating power to the detriment of the royal family. Some D.C.s therefore started to advocate greater participation in government by the royal princes (*nabihe*): in time this idea developed further, to an advocacy of real decentralisation within the kingdom.

The Second World War, however, exposed deficiencies in native administration itself: these deficiencies were not limited to Yendi and they were therefore not curable by devolution alone. They were, indeed, quite fundamental and concerned the very foundations of Dagomba government. Many D.C.s came to the conclusion that the chiefs had not, on the whole, assimilated the higher ideals of 'service' and 'progress' put before them by Jones and Duncan-Johnstone; instead, they were still happily absorbed in the traditional leisured pursuits of dynastic intrigue, womanising, and drinking. As this realisation dawned, officials grasped, a little desperately, for the political weapon of the moment, namely, democracy: they began casting around for ways of 'democratising' native administration.

This development was important because it coincided with the growth of a complementary pressure for wider participation by members of the royal family itself. In certain respects, the policy of indirect rule was a cause of the pressure. First, by emphasising the sovereignty of Yendi, it maintained and even increased the attraction of the royal skin as a prize in dynastic politics. The king got a substantial increment of political, financial, and judicial power from the administration. He had his own police force; he had a 'special relationship' with the D.C.; and he could deploy his much increased patronage with the assurance of government backing. As the power of the monarchy increased, so in time did the number of people claiming a right to appointment. Candidates who in the past would, strictly speaking, have been considered ineligible began to press their claims. Grandsons began to clamour for recognition as candidates for Yendi; in 1938 an attempt was made to get the office of regent (*gbonlana*) recognised as a gate skin (irrespective of whether or not the regent also occupied one of the three standard gate skins).

Secondly, although Yendi's power was consolidated by the indirect rule legislation, the same provisions did invest the divisional chieftaincies with courts, treasuries, and administrative functions. In this respect, indirect rule helped to perpetuate the old tensions between centre and periphery in the kingdom. To a certain extent, it also brought about a redistribution of power. In the general bureaucratisation of chieftaincy, the royal dukedoms were put on a par with the other divisions. The 1930 constitution accorded them precedence in the 'traditional' hierarchy, but subsequent legislation reduced them to the status of ordinary Subordinate Native

Authorities. In itself, this change did not greatly affect the balance of power in the kingdom since, as we noted in Chapter 2, the dukedoms had always been rather ineffectual, though commanding high status as gateways to Yendi.

The establishment of taxation and treasuries had a much more important effect, since it brought out the factor of inequality between eastern and western Dagomba. The main axis of communications ran through western Dagomba: Tamale had grown substantially as an administrative and commercial centre, and surrounding towns, especially Savelugu, had benefited from the same process of development.[6] The decision to set up the earliest treasuries in Tamale (for the Gulkpeogu division), Savelugu, and Kumbungu was an acknowledgement of the economic status of these towns; conversely, by the end of the war the only treasury in eastern Dagomba was that in Yendi.

The benefits of social and economic development were quite unequally distributed between the two parts of the kingdom. For example, the 1948 census recorded that, of 761 persons in Dagomba with education above the level of Standard III, 668 were resident in the west.[7] The western divisions yielded a larger revenue than the east and to a great extent this revenue was returned directly to them by the Yendi treasury.

We thus have the greatest degree of social change occurring in the part of the kingdom most distant from the traditional capital. We also find that schooling affected not the senior echelons of the royal family but the humbler cadet branches and the sons of the elders. Although the government set out to educate the chiefs' sons, it was the junior branches which took advantage of the opportunities for education: some of the dukes' sons went to school, but at Yendi there was considerable resistance to senior royals (that is, the *na-bihe*) receiving European education.

These facts are, I would argue, crucial to an understanding of political change in Dagomba. They produced a random distribution of merit, in the sense that those most qualified for office by 'traditional' criteria (age and seniority) generally were least qualified by 'modern' criteria (education, adaptability). Predictably, this tension led to demands for changes in the rules of office-holding. We find the junior royals (grandsons) demanding a greater share in the running of the kingdom or, at least, the right to be considered for appointment to the Yendi skin; we find the wealthier, younger, or better-educated chiefs demanding a larger part in the control of the state. In sum, the result was a challenge to the 'traditional constitution' on three vital matters: who was qualified to become king; who was responsible for selecting the king; and how power was distributed within the kingdom.

THE MBADUGU AFFAIR

Ya-Na Abudulai was not a young man when he succeeded in 1920 and by the early thirties it was clear that his health was failing. Moreover, while the government did all it could to back him up, the administration's private opinion of his abilities was not high, though it was softened by respect and affection. Parker, a temporary D.C. at Yendi in 1924, commented, as a newcomer to the kingdom: 'The chief of Yendi is not much use. He is a greatly overrated personage – and beside chiefs like Nandom, Jirapa and the late chief of Wungu he is a small boy.'[8] In the early years of indirect rule, matters moved smoothly enough and the Chief Commissioner remarked on a 'commendable eagerness' in the king's attitude to native administration. The high point of his activity came in February 1932 when he visited Tamale and addressed a durbar attended by all the Western Dagomba chiefs and some 2,000 of their subjects. It was on this occasion that the Ya-Na imposed a settlement of a dispute which had troubled the Gulkpeogu division (in which Tamale lay) since before the First World War. We noted in Chapter 4 how the *dakpema* (headman) of Tamale had exploited the absence of the divisional chief, the Gulkpe-Na, to represent himself to the government as the chief of the Tamale district. In the course of his enquiries preceding the 1930 conference, Blair unearthed the full story of the *dakpema*'s usurpation and he suggested that the Gulkpe-Na be asked to return to Tamale and reassert his authority as divisional chief. At the 1930 conference the *dakpema* acknowledged the rights of the Gulkpe-Na, and the Ya-Na, under some pressure from the administration, advised the divisional chief to take up residence in the west, at least for several months annually.[9]

Yet even before the Ya-Na suffered a stroke in 1933, the administration was worried by the indolence of the king and his councillors. The king was observed to be drinking heavily and in May 1932 Blair reported that he had 'talked seriously to the Na about his "line of least resistance" policy and showed him how difficult he was making it for us to help him by sheer supineness'.[10] Cockey also believed that it would 'be difficult to get a move on' under Abudulai's regime, since the king seemed to be satisfied with his 'happy go lucky, contented . . . life'.[11]

A much more serious situation developed with the king's illness. By December 1934 his faculties had returned, but he remained paralysed on one side and, despite occasional moments of self-assertion, he gradually grew weaker and eventually lost even the ability to speak. As Jones commented: 'For the two years preceding his death [in 1938], he was merely a figure-head, unable to reply to and, it is thought, even to understand what was said to him.' And he added: 'Such a situation generally presents a forceful and unscrupulous subordinate with an opportunity to usurp power to his own enrichment. The Ya-Na's illness proved to be no exception.'[12] With rather cruel irony, the subordinate in this case was the official mouthpiece of the paramount, the Mbadugu, a court elder. Much of the Mbadugu's power, like that of all Yendi elders, was based on the requirement that chiefs should approach the king through a court official. Mbadugu was not, in fact, one of the administrative elders of the Ya-Na, but he had the special privilege of acting as an intermediary between the king and all visitors to the court.[13]

The government became concerned about the power of the Mbadugu as early as 1933, although officers disagreed about whether it was being exercised benevolently or otherwise. Blair described Mbadugu as 'the backbone of the Native Authority', but Miller and Cockey were disturbed by the extent of usurpation and the Chief Commissioner remarked: 'The mouthpiece of a potentate, especially one so old and decrepit as the Ya-Na, generally becomes a person of considerable importance. Mbadugu should be watched but I do not advise snubbing him unless he is found to be acting against the interests of the people and the Ya-Na.'[14]

In August 1934 an incident came to light which seemed to fall into this category. A police corporal and several accomplices had seized cattle, sheep, and other property from a Konkomba village and they delivered their booty to the Mbadugu, Sheini, who, they alleged, had ordered the raid. It was never clearly established whether the Mbadugu had in fact been responsible, but the D.C. remarked that he had 'nothing to be proud of' in respect of the incident.[15]

During the last years of Abudulai's reign, factionalism thrived at the court and there were frequent accusations of corruption and partiality in the making of appointments. Mbadugu Sheini led one faction and was opposed by the Zohe-Na and Karaga-Na Ziblim.[16] Thus when the Governor visited the north in February 1934, it was rumoured that Zohe-Na had told Ziblim (for whom he was court 'father') that the government intended to depose the king and that he should be ready to take power. The Yo-Na also had a faction at Yendi preparing his succession and the D.C. found that it was almost impossible to stop the manipulation in which, it seemed, all the senior elders were engaged.[17]

The trouble came to a head shortly before Abudulai's death when a number of chiefs complained about the part taken by Mbadugu in the appointment of a new Kumbung-Na. The Karaga-Na, in particular, protested to the D.C. about the running of the kingdom. Armstrong wrote: 'He tells me Mbadugu and Kum-lana [another Yendi elder] are trying to run everything by themselves ... the *na-bihe* are not consulted over anything.'[18] The administration (which had discovered that Mbadugu Sheini was making substantial profits from a messing contract for the Yendi prison) agreed to hold a meeting and on 19 January 1938 the C.C.N.T. (Jones) and Armstrong conducted a full enquiry into the Kumbungu selection. Sheini had, in fact, died in the interim, but the story which emerged did not please officials who had looked to the chiefs and elders for disinterested and selfless leadership.

The Kumbungu chiefship was an 'elder' divisional skin and not therefore one which royals would seek. (The Karaga-Na's interest arose from the fact that, under Sheini's regime, his own son had been rejected for the *na-bihe* skin of Tong.) There had been twelve applicants for the post: the most prominent were the Tali-Na and the Gbulun-Na, junior elder chiefs in Tolon and Kumbungu divisions respectively. The Tali-Na claimed that the Kumbungu skin should be his because his father had occupied it, but also because he had paid Mbadugu a large sum of money for the use of his influence.

It transpired that, using the Bamvim-lana as an intermediary, Tali-Na had originally paid £5 to Mbadugu. But Sheini's reaction had been non-committal: 'When people go to Sheini', said Tali-Na, 'and ask him anything about Chieftainship, the only thing he would say always is "God is there."'[19] The Bamvim-lana had returned to Yendi with another £15, of which £5 was intended for the Ya-Na as 'information money'. The Mbadugu was told that Tali-Na would pay £50 for the skin, but Sheini replied 'that the Ya-Na would not agree so, and said to Bamvim-lana that if he really wanted Kumbungu Chieftainship, he must buy it for £100'.[20] Tali-Na dispatched the sum required, commenting that 'if a man is selling something and he prices it higher, one must buy it provided he likes it'. But the price then moved up to £150 and Sheini's successor refused to reduce it: he claimed that the money would be equally divided between the Ya-Na, the Native Authority treasury, and himself. Tali-Na then came to Yendi in person and handed the money over, along with a bangle for the king. The latter, who was present, 'said very good by way of a humming sound'. But shortly afterwards Mbadugu took the Gbulun-Na to the District Commissioner and introduced him as the new chief of Kumbungu.

What shocked Jones was not so much the story itself as the reaction to it of the other courtiers. The elders admitted that Mbadugu had usurped power, but they justified their silence by saying that if they had complained, Sheini would have told the king that they were plotting with the *na-bihe* to kill him. As for the ethics of payment, they felt that it was quite proper for candidates to give money in order to obtain offices; there was, however, some disagreement about whether Mbadugu was the proper person to take it and also about whether such payment was contingent on the candidate getting the skin he wanted.[21]

Jones was apparently outraged by what he regarded as the easy virtue of the Yendi court. He announced that Mbadugu would be required to resume his former low-ranking position and he pointed out that the usurpation had been achieved at the expense of the elders and the royal family. But, he said, the elders were themselves to blame for the situation. The Chief Commissioner declared:

I very much regret to realise that there is such an amount of corruption in Dagomba. It is a very unsatisfactory state of affairs that a man should have to buy his way to a post ... Whereas what you do want are men of ability and strength of character and honesty, and if you are going to allow what has been happening in the past to continue it will mean that the best men will not come to the top.

After questioning the source of the Tali-Na's funds, the C.C.N.T. concluded sternly:

Now we have a law which governs this question. All chiefs today ... are Public Officers. The Ya-Na and his Councillors are Public Officers. Now it is an offence under our law for anybody to try and corrupt a Public Officer. A person who is found guilty of trying to corrupt a Public Officer may be sentenced to two years imprisonment.[22]

In future (he said) the only payments to be made were those customarily given (he thought) after an appointment had been announced.[23]

The meeting also considered the constitutional issues arising from the paramount's illness. It made specific provision for a regency, under which the elders of Yendi and the four senior *na-bihe* (Karaga-Na, Yo-Na, Mion-lana, and Kworli-Na) were to form a council to administer the state. Although this decision seems to have been meant to apply only to the immediate situation in Yendi, Jones, interestingly, took it as marking a permanent and fundamental change in the Dagomba 'constitution' – a change, moreover, in the direction of 'democratisation':

Formerly decisions on questions affecting the whole of Dagomba were taken by the Ya-Na and his local council without consulting the five [sic] chiefs in charge of subdivisions. The law now is that the *na-bihe* [i.e. the principal subordinate chiefs], as well as the *kpamba* [the Yendi elders] must be invited to take part in the discussion of matters affecting the whole of Dagomba before a decision is reached ... This alteration widens the basis of control; it marks a movement towards a more democratic form of government.[24]

Thus we find the government inserting a wedge into the constitution drawn up, at its instigation, in 1930. From other directions, similar pressures were at work, as the king's death revealed.

REGENTS AND GRANDSONS

The 1930 'constitution' had clearly laid down that only chiefs holding the skins of Karaga, Mion, and Savelugu could be considered eligible for promotion to Yendi. It had also reaffirmed the old and more general rule, that no man could rise higher than his father. The Ya-Na himself went out of his way on at least one occasion to confirm publicly his attachment to the 'constitution'. The occasion was the selection of a new duke for Savelugu in 1935, and Abudulai declared that he would consider only sons of Ya-Nas for this post. For, as he told his listeners, 'at the Dagomba Conference they had informed Government that a grandson could not and never had succeeded to Yendi'.[25] But the very fact that he had to make such a declaration was indicative that pressure was being applied to change the rules. So, indeed, the D.C. remarked. While approving of the stand taken by the king, he remarked that it had undoubtedly 'caused some consternation by dishing the ambitions of many ... There is no doubt that among the grandsons strenuous efforts are being made to remove this Tabu.'[26]

The next opportunity to advance the cause came with the death of Abudulai in February 1938. The funeral ceremony and the selection of a new king were delayed: some of the elders apparently feared that a new Ya-Na would dismiss them because of the corruption which had been revealed at the enquiry into the Kumbungu appointment.[27] The actual selection process was only begun after the D.C. had ordered the regent to make the arrangements for the burial of his father.

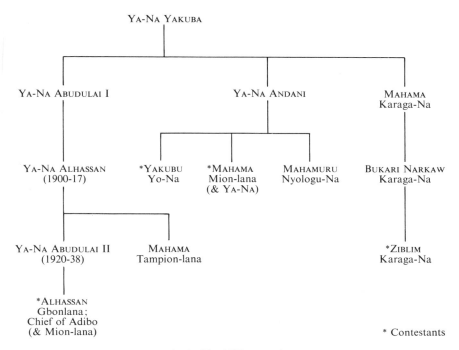

Fig. 3. The 1938 succession

There were four candidates for the skin (see Fig. 3). Two were from the Andani gate: Yakubu, the ninth son of Na Andani and, since 1935, Yo-Na; and Mahama, Andani's tenth son, and, since 1931, Mion-lana (the Mion-lana who lectured the pupils of Yendi on Dagomba history). The only candidate from the Abudu gate was Ya-Na Abudulai's son, the regent Alhassan. Now Alhassan was his father's eldest son but his only title, other than *gbonlana*, was that of chief of the village of Adibo: he did not occupy one of the three gate skins. Nevertheless, he put in a claim. The fourth candidate was also, theoretically, a non-starter: the Karaga-Na, Ziblim, the tenant of a gate skin but one who was only the son of a grandson of a para-mount.

Given the recent history of the court, it was hardly surprising that the selection of a new king was accompanied by confusion and intrigue. Thus, on 21 September, Zohe-Na appeared in the D.C.'s office to announce that his colleagues had chosen the Karaga-Na to be the new paramount. Armstrong was suspicious of the news, in view of the well-established alliance between Zohe-Na and the duke. After a few questions, he decided that the elder was lying.[28] However, since by this time a rumour was cir-culating that he had appointed Ziblim to be king, the D.C. felt that he

111

must call a meeting in order to point out to the chiefs and elders that 'Government did not intend to interfere in the matter unless a completely ineligible candidate was chosen.'[29] To show that he was in earnest, Armstrong told the meeting that he would leave Yendi for Chereponi, some fifty-five miles away, and would expect them to have reached a conclusion by the time he returned.

When the D.C. came back to Yendi, on 23 September, he found that the selectors had still not nominated a new king and it was only that evening that they finally plumped for the Mion-lana, Mahama. But at this moment Armstrong received a report

that the Gbonlana was trying to interfere with the new Na ... and [to] prevent him entering into his house. I, therefore, [Armstrong wrote] sent a message to the effect that if the Gbonlana did not at once desist I would come down and personally escort the new Na to the house and the Gbonlana to the guardroom. This had the desired effect and the Na was installed.[30]

The importance of the occasion was that, for the first time since 1899, the Andani gate had secured the paramountcy for one of its members. The thwarted regent, Alhassan, was immediately appointed Mion-lana by Ya-Na Mahama but he did not live to make another attempt at Yendi.[31]

The campaign to have grandsons accepted as candidates for kingship did not cease with the failure of Karaga-Na Ziblim. It tended to surface every time a vacancy occurred in a major office. In July 1941, for example, the Yo-Na, Yakubu, died. The new king chose his own brother, Mahamuru (Andani's twelfth son), to succeed to the Savelugu skin, but a number of chiefs complained. They said that the appointee was blind and 'bush' (Mahamuru had previously held only a minor village chieftaincy, that of Nyologu, and in their view was for that reason unfitted to run a division as big and important as Savelugu).[32] Moreover, they argued, 'the ... appointment should be made from the "Abudulai" side in order that that side of the family should have a candidate for the next Ya-Naship'.[33] Grandsons, they said, were eligible for gate skins, but in this case, they alleged, the grandsons had been told not to apply.

In reply, the D.C. pointed out that the Abudu gate already had a candidate on a gate skin (Alhassan, the Mion-lana). In any case, he remarked, even if a grandson did obtain the Savelugu post, he could not be considered for Yendi.[34] The complaints were rejected.

But the matter came up yet again, in 1944, when the Kworli-Na (a grandson of Na Abudulai I and leader of the campaign against Mahamuru) asked the Dagomba State Council for a ruling to clarify the standing of grandsons. At the insistence of the D.C., Ya-Na Mahama called a meeting and it was agreed at the meeting that while, as Kworli-Na claimed, grandsons were entitled to apply for the skins occupied by their fathers, they 'should not aspire to Yendi'.[35] Thus a grandson might become a duke; but he could never become king. Nevertheless, the clamour for a widening of the category of persons eligible to succeed to Yendi continued and grew louder in the postwar years.

D.C.s AND DIVISIONAL CHIEFS

Although they had moments of optimism, from the very beginning the experience of daily contact with native administration made most D.C.s sceptical of the willingness or the ability of chiefs to absorb the 'progressive' ideals of indirect rule. The assimilation of such ideals was, they felt, vitiated by the working of the promotional system, which generally led to the most important posts being held by men nearing senility. It was also obstructed by the acquired habit of relying on the government, a habit which enabled chiefs to avoid the responsibility (and unpopularity) of particular decisions or policies.[36] Although indirect rule, in theory, created the opportunity for taking initiative, it did not force chiefs to use it. Indeed, given the realities of colonial government, even under indirect rule, it was not surprising that they behaved with prudence and even timidity. Further, none of the chiefs was faced with the challenge of unaccustomed crisis or unamenable opposition: there was no movement on the part of 'youngmen' to reduce the powers of traditional rulers. The main, in fact the only, stimulus to the Native Authorities came from the government, as before: and, as before, that stimulus triggered the well-trained reflexes of avoidance, compliance, and straightforward abdication.

In the thirties and forties there were many cases of Native Authorities incapacitated by ageing chiefs. Yendi was, of course, the major case. Savelugu was another, and one not much less important since the division concerned was the most populous in the kingdom. Yo-Na Bukari Boforo was a particular embarrassment to the British administration. In August 1930, he was fined £10 by the Ya-Na, 'for disgracing Dagomba chiefs in general before the Acting Governor, for setting a bad example to his people in the matter of treating wives, and for general discourtesy towards whitemen [sic]'.[37] He drank heavily and both he and his elders were remarkably impervious to the theory of indirect rule. On 28 June 1932, Miller, the Assistant D.C., wrote despairingly: 'Had a long talk with the Savelugu-Na ... I am more than ever decided that he is not fit to be a Chief but should be in a lunatic asylum. The old man's head cannot hold a single thought that has the slightest intelligence.'[38] In his progress report on the development of native administration, Miller concluded about Savelugu:

This Native Administration suffers from one thing, the age and senility of its Chief. It is a Chiefdom which as far as I can see will never go ahead at all as successive Chiefs have all been so decrepit ... It is hampered also by the most aged *kpamba*. The *wulana* is very old and not capable of much understanding. The *kpanalana* has been an invalid for some time. The *gundona* is an ancient. The *kambong-na* is exceedingly old and decrepit and just manages to shuffle about. As a result the Native Authority is nothing more than a figure head administered by the District Commissioner.[39]

Under Yo-Na Yakubu there was some improvement, although he showed little interest in economic development. Indeed, when the Yo-Na declined to take over a demonstration farm formerly run by the Native Authority,

113

the D.C. remarked: 'He spends too much money on his 40 wives, guests, and horses.'[40] The 'bush' Yo-Na, Mahamuru, seems, ironically, to have been one of the more hard-working and successful of the Savelugu chiefs.

The problem of senility was recognised by the Dagomba system, insofar as it provided for the informal creation of regency councils. Such a body was, as we have seen, set up at the end of Ya-Na Abudulai's reign; another was established at Savelugu when Bukari Boforo became incapable of governing. But the difficulty was to find chiefs and elders who were less afflicted by old age than the title-holder. Blair came across a particularly inextricable case in December 1935. In the village in question, the heir to the chief was himself blind and bedridden. As Blair reported, the *wulana* to the divisional chief therefore

suggested that the 'young brother' should be the power behind the throne; 'young brother' then appeared white-bearded and hobbling on two sticks. I suggested that eldest son should be the power behind the power behind the throne, but was told that eldest son was crippled and couldn't leave compound. Called for second son as Assistant Deputy Power behind throne, and a wild youth of 17 appeared.[41]

The habit of casting responsibility for decisions on the administration survived and, indeed, flourished under indirect rule. Even Jones admitted that the chiefs were 'sometimes inclined to lean too heavily on the Administrative Officers for support': D.C.s were continually engaged in checking on treasury accounts, tax-collection, and the whole range of projects and services which, officially, came under the authority of 'native administration'. Administrative officers also found it very difficult to get the chiefs to tour their divisions: such touring, said the Assistant D.C., was 'a thing which these Chiefs will not do'. They would, he felt, 'rather leave it to the D.C.'[42]

The most common form of political abdication was, of course, that which concerned the appointment of chiefs. This, too, persisted under the new regime, despite repeated affirmations of neutrality by government officials. Thus in 1934 the acting C.C.N.T. minuted: 'Government refuses ABSOLUTELY to interfere in these elections to chieftainships . . . I have impressed on the Na that in considering candidates he must not imagine that by electing Ex-Government people he will cause satisfaction or remorse to Government.'[43] The selections of a Yo-Na in 1935 and again in 1941 were the occasions for similar denials. In 1935 the D.C. felt obliged to protest impartiality after a rumour began to circulate that the government had appointed the Vo-Na (an ex-interpreter) to the Savelugu skin. His statement did not stop candidates visiting him clandestinely to seek his support.[44] In 1941, when the complaints about Mahamuru, the 'bush' Yo-Na, were presented, the D.C., Armstrong, told the chiefs, as he recorded, 'that he had nothing whatsoever to do with the appointment or otherwise of the Dagomba chiefs. If he had, several of the assembled Chiefs would not be in the position they were.'[45] Armstrong's candour seems to have been infectious, for at the same meeting the ageing Nanton-Na got up and made a 'rambling complaint' about the lack of consideration accorded to his claims. In Armstrong's words, 'he was informed that, Nanton being a "dead end" as far as Dagomba Chieftainships were concerned, he could not succeed to any other stool [sic]. He admitted this but said that he had not realised that this fact was known to the District Officer.'[46]

As regards the Yendi succession in 1938, it is true that the 'drum history' records that 'the white man handed Yendi to Mahama' (just as it, correctly, put the responsibility for appointing Abudulai II in 1920 on the then C.C.N.T., Armitage).[47] It is, in fact, also true that in 1938 the C.C.N.T. said afterwards that Karaga-Na Ziblim 'would not have been a success' as Ya-Na. Further, the Mion-lana, Mahama, was undoubtedly well regarded by the government for his contributions to the Yendi school and to other projects.[48] These sentiments may have been communicated to the elders responsible for selection. But I have found no evidence in the archives to support Phyllis Ferguson's contention that 'the Administration stepped in and ... made Mion-Lana Muhammad Ya-Na'.[49] Indeed, whereas in 1920 Armitage had intervened openly and unapologetically, in 1938 the D.C. went out of his way to assert his neutrality, to the point of actually leaving Yendi for Chereponi. Influence may have been used privately, but the internal communications of the government provide no evidence of preferences, let alone of active interference.

THE SECOND WORLD WAR

The Second World War forced the British to practise the purest form of indirect rule. Trekking by D.C.s was cut down and staff was reduced; the officers who remained were given heavier responsibilities and smaller resources to depend on.[50] The result was to accelerate the process of disenchantment with indirect rule which had begun before 1939.

To start with, the early months of the war shook official assumptions about the unquestioning loyalty of natives to the colonial government. In October 1939, the D. C. reported that in some divisions it was commonly believed that the outbreak of the war meant an imminent end to European occupation.[51] Four months later the D.C. visited Nanton and noted: 'The general opinion is that there is no need to pay tax as the Germans are coming. Squashed that idea.'[52] Relations between the administration and the chiefs progressively lost that veneer of contrived geniality which had been so characteristic of the high period of indirect rule. Senior chiefs, such as Tolon-Na and Nanton-Na, were fined or reprimanded for 'inefficiency' and 'laziness'. Several chiefs were called to Yendi on the instructions of the Chief Commissioner, who commented: 'we must in some way or another indicate to the Chiefs our disapproval of their indifference to their duties'.[53] Yet throughout the war there were gloomy reports about the state of the Native Authorities. Thus at Kasuri and Lungbunga the D.C. found that 'no one seemed to know anything about Native Administration nor the reason why they paid tax'. At Karaga the tax returns were bad and the Karaga-Na (in the D.C.'s words) 'did not seem enthusiastic about stirring things up himself, as he said that he did not want people to think he was being hard on them'.[54] The authority of even the divisional chiefs seemed to be generally fragile. The D.C. reported that the Tolon-Na, for example, gave the impression of being 'terrified of his subjects': the Nanton-Na complained that he had 'no authority' and nobody obeyed him.[55]

The appointment in 1944 of a new D.C. led to a thorough exposure of the condition of chiefly government. The new D.C., Kerr, found at Yendi that it was impossible to discover the financial position of the Dagomba Native Authority for lack of reliable records; the court records were 'pretty poor' and the clerks displayed an 'amazing' ignorance of the relevant legislation.[56] Touring the divisions, Kerr formed a similar impression of indifference and apathy: 'at present', he wrote, 'these people seem to have no master but the D.C.' The Kumbung-Na seemed 'to depend mostly on what the D.C. did for him', while the Tolon-Na had appointed himself as 'his own treasurer and principal public works contractor'. The Gulkpeogu divisional administration was, Kerr found, blighted by 'ignorance, indifference, and incompetence' on the part of all concerned, the Gulkpe-Na included.[57] In eastern Dagomba, the poorer part of the kingdom, everything was run from Yendi. The Gushie-Na seemed, as a result, to be unable to distinguish decisions of the Native Authority from those of the government, an understandable failing.

At this point indirect rule had reached its lowest ebb, a matter of grave concern to the administration, if to nobody else. The state of affairs was, indeed, neatly epitomised by a sight which Kerr encountered on one of his tours of eastern Dagomba. Turning a corner in the road, he suddenly came across Ya-Na Mahama, stranded in the Native Authority lorry,

his conveyance belching forth smoke and stench and giving the appearance of imminent explosion. The Ya-Na, however, was completely unperturbed and was sitting in the front seat in rather a fetching travelling coat and a sort of super straw boater, waiting for the *deus ex machina* to arrive. There were quite thirty retainers in the back, men, women, and children in an apparently inextricable mass.[58]

The D.C., it seems, drove on.

CHAPTER 7

VOTIBU

South Birim East

> Frederick Nmesiansa LUGARD (C.P.P.)   . . . . . 1,395 Elected
> George Edward KWATENG (IND.)   . . . . 1,217[1]

Between 1946 and 1960 the politics of the Dagomba kingdom became increasingly entangled with national and regional politics. This involvement developed slowly and it was regarded with great misgiving by many politicians in the Northern Territories. For the first eight years, the north lay on the periphery of national politics, reacting to changes produced by the confrontation between nationalism and colonial government in southern Ghana. During this phase, the changes which occurred in the north were strictly local in character: they concerned the reform of local government, adjustments to traditional structures, and the establishment of a regional council. It was only in the mid-fifties, with the introduction of universal suffrage and the granting of full parliamentary representation, that the region became actively involved in national politics, and the national government and political parties became involved in local affairs. From this entanglement developed the complex of political interests engaged in the struggle which became known, in the late sixties, as 'the Yendi skin dispute'.

GOVERNMENT AND THE CHIEFS, 1946–51

Because of the absence of party politics from the north, the colonial administration had a relatively free hand in deciding how to rid local government of the faults which were evident in the old Native Authority structure. However, the strategy of reform which it adopted in the first instance was one based on the norms and assumptions of indirect rule: it envisaged alterations to the structure of native administration such as would minimise the costs of a gerontocratic system.

For, by this time, officials recognised that the weaknesses of indirect rule were not just due to the weakness of individual chiefs or to a lack of supervision by the government. They were, rather, directly related to the character of Dagomba traditional government itself. The main fault of the Dagomba constitution, as officials saw it, was excessive rigidity – a criticism made in successive annual reports. The rule that no son could rise higher than his father was (argued the D.C. at Yendi) obstructive, since it excluded able people from achieving high office. The promotional system, in addition, meant that few people, able or not, achieved high office until they were well past their prime. Thus, the D.C. reported,

with perhaps two exceptions, every one of the twenty or so powerful chiefs of Dagomba is an old man, full of years and wisdom admittedly, but incapable of touring his sub-division thoroughly or of easily assimilating new ideas. Inflexibility is also produced by the infrangible rule that a chief, even the smallest, is chief until he dies.[2]

It might be, thought some officials, that the present system was really 'a corruption of a once more efficient system', one which in its heyday had used the talents of younger men more effectively. In this respect, Dagomba had suffered a severe deterioration:

Today it seldoms happens that a major chiefdom is held by a man of even middle age. The pattern of simple seniority is repeated in the organisation of the extended family so that the young members lend their support to the senior man of their line though he is rarely the most able; a young man has neither the wealth nor the prestige to command respect or buy favour. Dagomba [the D.C. concluded] is a Gerontocracy.[3]

Serious administrative deficiencies resulted from this pattern of clientage: it made for both corruption and overcentralisation. The Yendi elders still ran the Native Authority, through its Finance Committee, and, as the D.C. commented, 'the high-handed and bureaucratic methods which were used ... caused much ill-feeling in the subdivisions ... subdivisional initiative has been frustrated'.[4] Even so, the administration saw little hope of change coming about through popular pressure, given the apparent passivity of the commoner class. The Dagomba, intoned one annual report,

has little initiative of his own. He is not a fighting man, in spite of his love of horses, guns and military trappings ... He is not gifted with trading acumen and as a farmer he is not forced, by poor soil and limited land, to work harder than is absolutely necessary. If he is in need of help he turns instinctively to his chief – with a present in his hand.'[5]

Several reforms were considered. One D.C., Kerr, proposed decentralisation, giving more scope to divisional chiefs and increasing the number of divisional treasuries. Furthermore, he suggested the transfer of authority from elders to chiefs at both state and divisional levels.[6] To generate interest in development and financial matters, he organised a conference for the western Dagomba chiefs in October 1946.

The results of these initiatives were, however, disappointing. The chiefs, Kerr found, 'were all against partaking in the Dagomba Court and Administration' and even in western Dagomba they showed little interest in plans for development: 'One would like to hear some criticisms and suggestions from the chiefs but one gets little enough of either from either Savelugu or Kumbungu, even interest in the Treasuries is very limited.'[7]

In the face of such failures (compounded, as it happened, by one or two particularly glaring cases of extortion),[8] officials concluded that the only real hope of improvement lay in the emergence of a class of younger, educated chiefs – the hope expressed back in 1930 by Duncan-Johnstone. But, in this respect at least, there were signs of progress. For in 1946 there were four fully literate chiefs in western Dagomba and by 1948 there were at least eleven literate chiefs throughout the kingdom (Pisigu-lana, Tampion-lana, Vo-Na, Sanerigu-Na, Bamvim-lana, Lamashe-Na, Nyankpala-Na, and Tali-Na in the west; Sunson-Na, Mang-Na, and Sang-lana in the east). In addition, by the end of the war there was in the N.T. a sizeable body of educated commoners (and chiefs' sons), many holding posts in native administration.[9] The Chief Commissioner pointed out at a conference in 1945 how much this body had grown since the early days of indirect rule. 'Today,' he said, 'there are close on 200 clerks, teachers, etc., the majority of whom are not below Standard VI and whose aggregate annual salaries amount to nearly £5,000.'[10]

In 1946 the administration created a Territorial Council in the N.T., at least partly with the aim of providing a vehicle for the advancement of educated chiefs and commoners. The Territorial Council was a non-statutory body and its role was consultative. In principle, it consisted of the heads of the Native Authorities, with an additional member for western Dagomba, but the Native Authorities could delegate other chiefs or commoners and were expected to bring with them their principal advisers. On the working of the Council, Lord Hailey remarked: 'A good deal of consultation is noticeable among the younger members of the delegations, who are often literate minor chiefs ... This is strengthened by the growing practice of appointing literate representatives.'[11] At the first session of the Council, Dagomba was represented by the Nyankpala-Na (a former government agricultural officer), the *wulana* of Savelugu, and the Sunson-Na (a younger brother of Karaga-Na Ziblim). Subsequently, the delegation was headed by two men who later became the leading Dagomba figures in national politics: J. H. Allassani; and Alhaji Yakubu Tali, Tali-Na, and, from 1953, Tolon-Na.

Allassani was a commoner from a village near Tamale. Born in 1906, he had entered the government primary school at Tamale in 1914, at the same time as J. S. Kaleem, later the headmaster of the Yendi Native Authority school and, after independence, Principal Education Officer for the Northern Region. Completing his schooling in the south, Allassani became a teacher at St Peter's Roman Catholic School in Kumasi in 1927 and stayed in Kumasi until 1949, when he gave up a headmastership to become State Secretary to the Dagomba Native Authority.[12] He was offered this post on the recommendation of Ya-Na Mahama and his friend Kaleem. Though Allassani remained a Dagomba representative on the Territorial Council until 1954, he gave up the Native Authority post in 1951 to become a member of the new Legislative Assembly in Accra and was appointed a Ministerial Secretary in Dr Nkrumah's first government. Throughout the subsequent troubles in Dagomba, Allassani and Kaleem were the most vocal supporters of the Andani gate, to which Ya-Na Mahama belonged and of which his son was the leading representative.

Yakubu Tali was born in 1916 and educated at the Tamale government school and Achimota. On leaving Achimota, he returned to the north as a teacher. He was employed in a Native Authority school at Sandema, near Bolgatanga, when in July 1946, with the death of his father, the skin of Tali became vacant.[13] Over the opposition of the then Tolon-Na (who had a right of nomination to the post), Yakubu Tali obtained the skin. This caused the D.C. some alarm, since he found Yakubu Tali 'over-ambitious', but the Chief Commissioner was enthusiastic about the appointment, remarking: 'It is in the appointment of young, literate and forward-looking chiefs such as this that the salvation of the Dagomba chieftainate probably lies.'[14] In 1948 Yakubu Tali was appointed to the Territorial Council and in 1950 he became an extraordinary member of the Legislative Council, at the time of the debates on the Coussey Committee's constitutional proposals. Like Allassani, he was elected to the new Legislative Assembly in 1951 and kept his post as M.P. thereafter, becoming President of the N.T. Council and Tolon-Na in 1953.[15]

The rise of men like Allassani and Yakubu Tali was the result both of administrative encouragement and of pressure from below. Such pressure, deriving mainly from a 'chiefly intelligentsia', was typified by a letter which the C.C.N.T. received in 1945 when the Nanton divisional chieftaincy became vacant. The writer, an ex-schoolteacher and a younger brother of the deceased chief, declared: 'It is now time that we Educated Princes should hold important posts in the Native Administration for the betterment of the country. If I am appointed I will set better and model Native Administration for the rest to follow.'[16] Encouraged, perhaps, by such gestures of support, the administration took the opportunity of Ya-Na Mahama's death in 1948 to launch a set of reforms which, though partially abortive, had a considerable impact on dynastic politics.

THE 1948 SUCCESSION

Ya-Na Mahama II, who had been appointed in 1938, died on 6 February 1948. His tenure of the Yendi skin had revived the prospects of the Andani gate: his younger brother Mahamuru was appointed Yo-Na in 1941, and by 1947 his eldest surviving son, Andani, had reached Sanerigu, a gate to Savelugu. However, Mion was occupied by a son of Ya-Na Alhassan, Mahama, who had been appointed after the death of Abudulai II's son Alhassan; and Karaga was held by Ziblim, a member of the so-called 'Kworli gate' and a great-grandson of Na Yakuba.

When Karaga-Na Ziblim died in May 1947, the Ya-Na (by then over eighty) seized the chance to elevate his own son, Andani, to the gate skin. This action, taken apparently without consulting the elders of Yendi, provoked strong opposition. The D.C. reported that 'the people of Karaga stated firmly that they would not have [Andani] as their Na and expressed a desire for another to be appointed'.[17] Ziblim's younger brother, Sunson-Na Adam, defied the paramount and moved into Karaga before Andani could occupy the skin.[18] The Ya-Na considered reversing his decision, but was obstructed by Abudulai, Bamvim-lana, whom he had appointed to succeed Andani at Sanerigu. Quite naturally, Abudulai was reluctant to move down a rung once more. Eventually, the D.C., Talbot, intervened and suspended the appointment of a Karaga-Na. The Ya-Na, allegedly, committed suicide, because of the shame brought upon him by this episode.[19]

Shortly before the Ya-Na died, the Chief Commissioner was sent an anonymous petition, signed 'an unknown Dagomba citizen'. The burden of the petition was a request for changes to the Dagomba constitution so as to give more scope to educated royals, and particularly to royal grandsons (*yanse*). The petitioner declared that Dagomba was suffering from the incompetence of its senior chiefs, a condition made worse, he said, by Ya-Na Mahama's tendency to appoint only members of the Andani gate. More efficient government required that grandsons should be allowed to occupy the gate skins to Yendi (though not necessarily the paramountcy itself). Therefore, the petition continued,

if the leaders really have it as their aim to have this land delivered from the rule of illiterates, a list should be prepared of literate sons of the chiefs, and there is no doubt that the list will shew names of mostly grandchildren of Ya-Nas, well trained in literatecy [sic]: and if their fathers are debarred from reaching the skins of Mion, Karaga and Savelugu, how on earth can we have literates in the administration of Dagbon [?][20]

In earlier times, it had been possible to get rid of bad chiefs by warfare, but under colonial government this had been stopped. Nevertheless, the petitioner warned,

for our present generation we as Dagombas, are not going to be silent to be ruled by unable princes, if there happens to be a sensible and able grandson ... Therefore an agreed arrangement should be made, ignoring the former constitution written down when Dagomba was still very dark, and when poor interpreters were a cause to some mistakes.

The British did, indeed, sponsor changes in the constitution, though it is not clear from what level in government the initiative came. In any event, the annual report for 1947/8 records that in the period following the death of Mahama II,

the proposal that Sub-Divisional Chiefs should be *elected* was introduced. There was at first considerable opposition especially from those who visualized what they had believed to be a 'safe skin' slipping from their grasp, but eventually the force of the ideal that the people should have an opportunity of selecting their own masters prevailed. A State Council (composed of all the Sub-Divisional Chiefs) was called and on 2 March 1948 it was agreed unanimously that all eligible candidates should stand for election, and the Yidana or head of each family compound, paying head tax, should cast a vote in a Secret Ballot.[21]

This was, indeed, democratisation with a vengeance, taking away from Yendi the right to appoint senior chiefs and handing over that right to the mass of subjects. The D.C. realised the implications:

This departure from old established custom constitutes a very considerable advance and clears the way for the election of many younger and more active men to these skins ... It is not unreasonable to hope that before many years have passed there will be literates in the three gates to Yendi and when that occurs the eventual selection of a literate Ya-Na will be assured.[22]

The administration went much further and sponsored a change in the mode of selection of the king himself. In so doing, it clearly had the support of a number of divisional chiefs who, under this reform, seized the critical right of nomination from the elders of Yendi. According to the minutes of a meeting of the Dagomba State Council held on 12 May 1948,[23] the State Council decided that

the following chiefs and elders [should be] responsible for the election and appointment of the chief to the Nam of Yendi, and if a unanimous decision cannot be reached, it shall be decided by means of a secret Ballot and a majority vote.

Divisional chiefs	Elders
Gushie-Na	Kuga-Na
Yelzori-lana	Zohe-Na
Nanton-Na	Tuguri-nam
Gulkpe-Na	Gagbindana
Sunson-Na	
Tolon-Na	
Kumbung-Na	

At one stroke, therefore, the State Council seemed to have abolished a major rule of the Dagomba constitution, at least as recorded in 1930: the rule that kings were chosen, after divination, by a small committee of elders.

This decision became an object of controversy in later years and several of the issues raised may be noted here. The Andani gate have said that the decision was legally doubtful, because the only valid meetings of the State Council were those presided over by the king. On this occasion, the king being dead, the regent had chaired the meeting. This contention is dismissed by the Andanis' opponents. Another suggestion (made by S. M. Sibidow, a protagonist of the Andanis) is that the decision was accomplished by deceiving the elders.[24] They, it is alleged, were allowed by 'the educated people' to believe that they would continue to perform the main rituals of selection and that the only function of the new body would be advisory. This deception was, supposedly, facilitated by including four elders in the new committee; the minutes were signed by (among others) eight elders, which seems to indicate consent.[25] The actual text is clear enough; but there could be conflicting interpretations of 'responsibility' and, given the differences in literacy among those present, it is easy to imagine how misunderstanding might arise or be contrived.

Another point, made by Abudu supporters, is that the 1948 decision merely formalised the business of consulting senior chiefs which had in the past taken place privately.[26] It is fairly clear that such consultation, however unofficial, did take place before the partition: it was, indeed, necessary to the peace of the kingdom that it should. For the Abudus, then, the 1948 resolution amplified rather than abrogated the provisions of the 1930 constitution. To those on the Andani side who contend that it did infringe custom, the Abudus reply that the State Council possessed sovereign authority to change custom in accordance with changing circumstances and that it had exercised this right constitutionally in 1948. And, they point out, the meeting in question was chaired by the senior member of the Andani gate, the regent Andani.

Four candidates laid claim to the monarchy (see Fig. 4). Two were from the Andani gate: the Yo-Na Mahamuru, a younger brother of the deceased Ya-Na; and the regent Andani, who, as we have seen, was hovering between the skins of Sanerigu and Karaga. A third candidate was the other claimant on Karaga, Sunson-Na Adam. Lastly, there was the Abudu candidate, Ya-Na Abudulai II's younger brother, Mion-lana Mahama. Of the four, Sunson-Na Adam was a great-grandson and therefore not strictly eligible, while only the Yo-Na and the Mion-lana were actually occupying gate skins.

The selection process had several interesting features. First, it did not, oddly enough, involve the newly enlarged selection committee: it was the old king-making elders who made the nomination. The reasons for the failure of the new procedure to take effect are not clear: those hostile to the innovation argue that the educated chiefs and their advisers were content to see it lapse on this occasion, once they were sure that the elders intended anyway to pick the candidate they favoured.[27] According to this view, there was a good reason for not convening the new committee if at all possible, namely, that the elders might discover that they had been misled about its functions.

Secondly, there was a dispute between the regent and the Mion-lana over the question of who had the right to perform the funeral ceremony of the king – a right which, some people considered, carried with it a presumptive right to succeed to Yendi. On this matter, at least, the State Council gave an unequivocal ruling, resolving at its meeting on 24 March 1948 that 'according to Dagomba custom it is the Mion-lana who performs the Ya-Na's funeral ... and that the present Mion-lana is responsible for the performance of Mahama II's funeral custom'.[28] The State Council did not, however, say that performance of the funeral gave a presumptive right to the Yendi skin.

Thirdly, the selection process raised again the question, implicit in the funeral dispute, of whether or not the regency could be considered as a fourth gate to Yendi. The State Council did not rule on this point and the question therefore remained open. But the regent did apply, and he apparently did so on the strength of that title and being the king's eldest son: he had not been accepted or recognised as Karaga-Na.

The selection of the Ya-Na was accompanied by considerable tension,

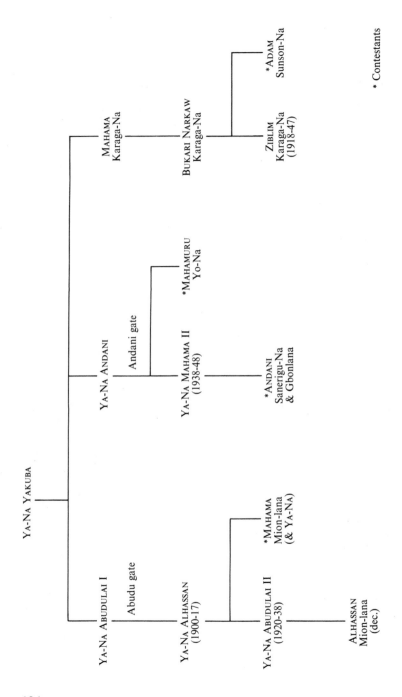

124

Fig. 4. The 1948 succession

* Contestants

notably between the supporters of the regent and those of the Mion-lana. Finally, the selectors announced the nomination of the Mion-lana as the new king, with the title 'Mahama III'. As he moved to Yendi, the regent moved to the vacated skin at Mion and Sunson-Na Adam was confirmed as Karaga-Na.

The 1948 succession was critical for Dagomba politics in two respects. First, it was associated with a radical and controversial alteration in the constitution, even if that alteration did not immediately take effect. Secondly, it saw a reversion of the Yendi skin back once more to the Abudu gate. By the time the new Ya-Na died, the Abudus would have occupied the royal palace for forty-three of the preceding fifty-three years. For the Andanis, it was becoming increasingly necessary that they secure the skin before long, since without such replenishment the line's title to kingship could die out in the next generation.

Although the evidence is not conclusive, it does seem that the alteration of the rules about royal selection was only one facet of a more general campaign to 'democratise' chieftaincy, sponsored by the government and supported by the more educated chiefs and their literate advisers. But if the intention of the administration was indeed to bring about a democratic revolution, then it failed. For by 1951 the scheme for the election of divisional chiefs by household heads had been quietly abandoned. Thus in January 1950 a questioner in the Territorial Council asked whether the administration 'intended to continue its recently introduced policy of encouraging the election of people to fill vacancies for Chieftainships in the N.T.s rather than observe the custom by which such appointments [were] made by Head and other chiefs'.[29] To this, the Assistant Chief Commissioner replied: 'Beyond ensuring that Chiefs are acceptable to the majority of their people this Administration is not greatly concerned with their appointment and is quite prepared to leave this to be done in the customary way.' In 1951 the D.C., Dagomba, admitted (in connection with a dispute over the Gushiegu divisional chieftaincy) that 'the Dagomba Council's resolution of May [sic] 1948 that all subdivisional chiefs should henceforth be selected by majority votes of the people of their subdivisions is no longer favoured, and neither in the Gushiegu case nor before has it been put into effect except once'.[30]

In truth, the British had by this time lost interest in 'reforming chieftaincy', since, following the Coussey Report of 1949, the major functions of native authorities were to be transferred to largely elected local government councils. Of the broader strategy for 'improving' the traditional constitution, the only item to survive was the eleven-man selection committee for choosing the king, and that not because of its 'democratic' connotations, but because it was useful to a group of dynastic politicians. The campaign to institutionalise democracy in traditional government thus failed: it was followed by a resounding success: that of the chiefs in taking over popular democracy.

INDIRECT LOCAL GOVERNMENT

As in the early thirties, political change in the N.T. in the late forties was imposed from outside and in the face of local resistance. The north was scarcely touched by the events which brought Kwame Nkrumah to power as Leader of Government Business in February 1951, but it was affected by the constitutional reforms (proposed by the Coussey Committee) which led to Dr Nkrumah's assuming office.[31] Coussey's scheme (as adopted by the colonial government) concerned both national and local government. At national level, it envisaged the creation of an executive council (with a majority of 'representative' ministers) answerable to a legislative assembly, the members of which were to be variously chosen by popular direct election, indirect election, and nomination. Of the 84 members, 19 were to represent the N.T. and were to be elected by a specially constituted Northern Electoral College, comprising the 16 members of the Territorial Council and 104 delegates of District Councils formed from the existing Native Authorities. On local government, Coussey proposed the replacement of the old Native Authorities by a three-tier system of local government, consisting of councils with up to two-thirds of their members directly elected.[32]

The N.T. Territorial Council accepted the Coussey proposals, although considerable disquiet was expressed about the prospects of the north under a southern-led and almost certainly C.P.P.-dominated government. Yakubu Tali asked in January 1950 for assurances from the British government that it would not annul its treaties of protection concluded with N.T. rulers, until the northerners themselves had indicated a desire to relinquish the status of protected persons.[33] Both he and Allassani advocated caution in the acceptance of self-government for the Gold Coast. 'A person who wishes to become a driver,' said Yakubu Tali, 'must begin first as a driver's mate.' Allassani likewise urged that progress should be gradual: 'It will be a tragedy to attempt to jump all at once from the ground to the top. We have to start from the bottom and climb step by step to the top.'[34] The philosophy of indirect rule had, indeed, won its champions.

The difference between northern and coastal thinking was clearly revealed by a report of the Territorial Council's committee on local government reform. The committee, chaired by the C.C.N.T., was set up in January 1950 to examine the Coussey proposals, but its conclusions diverged substantially from them in spirit and in detail.[35] Coussey had been critical of the Native Authorities, pointing out their inflexibility, clumsiness, and domination by illiterate or 'semi-educated' members: it had suggested that all 'local government' functions should be taken away from the traditional bodies and vested in 'entirely new councils more democratic in composition'.[36]

The N.T. committee, while denying that northern leaders were 'reactionary', concluded that there were special circumstances in the north which (in its view) made 'any rapid or revolutionary change' impracticable. Among them were 'the absence of an educated class', the fear that rapid change would involve a 'large influx' of southern officials, and the fear that southern-based parties would come in to exploit 'the ignorance, inexperience, and apathy of the Northerner' (arguments which, by a strange paradox, echoed at almost every point those advanced by Walker-Leigh and his colleagues in the late twenties). In addition (like Messrs Gilbert and Rutherford), the committee pointed out that northern government had a distinctive feature, namely:

the reliance on, and satisfaction with, a traditional form of government in which the authority of the Chief is respected and his person is inviolable. His rule is patriarchal and is suited to a people whose needs are simple and who have never felt an urge for the acquisition of wealth, social prestige or political power.[37]

The recommendations of the committee were completely against the spirit of the Coussey proposals.[38] The committee wanted the elevation of the Territorial Council to the status of 'a Provincial Legislative Assembly' (to be entitled 'the Regional Council'): the executive committee of this assembly would 'establish, manage, and control all local authorities within its sphere of administration'. It also suggested the creation of six District Councils, formed from, and bearing the titles of, existing 'Native States'; under them there would be subordinate local authorities, enjoying only delegated powers. While accepting that head chiefs should not be eligible for membership of the new councils, the committee agreed with Coussey that at least one-third of the members should be nominated by traditional authorities and, indeed, it went on to suggest that the remainder should be 'partly nominated by Chiefs and Councillors' (i.e. elders) and partly elected. The D.C.s, it believed, should be *ex officio* chairmen of the Administrative and Financial Committees of the new District Councils and they should have 'at all times . . . a right of audience at any meeting of a District Council and of a Committee of a District Council'.[39]

The government did not accept the recommendations of the Territorial Council, but they are nevertheless interesting for what they reveal of the character and outlook of the postwar N.T. elite. Both may aptly be des-cribed as 'neo-traditional'. For, while anxious to enhance the status of those with education and administrative responsibility, this elite could hardly be termed 'meritocratic' in outlook: it was not at all opposed to traditional forms of government and, indeed, many of its members had a chiefly back-ground. The consensus in this group was undoubtedly expressed by a Gonja representative in the Territorial Council when he said, 'Local government is just a nominal change with slight variations.'[40] And this in turn echoed the consensus of an earlier age: 'Local government is but another term for indirect rule' – the words of the Chief Commissioner in 1937.

The government rejected the specific scheme put forward by the N.T. Council, and the 1951 Local Government Ordinance did not give the Coun-cil any right to oversee the work of the new local authorities. Even so, the Ordinance did enable both the chiefs and the administration to exert a strong influence on these bodies. It established 37 District Councils, 230 Local

Councils, and 11 Urban Councils, all under the control of a Ministry of Local Government in Accra. For Dagomba, it provided a District Council and twelve Local Councils, plus a Tamale Urban Council. In all these bodies, one-third of the members were to be nominated by the relevant 'traditional' authorities (in the case of the District Council, which was indirectly elected, the 'traditional' members were nominated from among the 'traditional' members of the Local Councils).[41]

Further, the new structure of council areas followed closely the lines of the old Native Authority structure. The Chief Regional Officer (the successor to the C.C.N.T.) wrote that, in order to ease the transition from one system to another, 'district council areas were made to conform with the areas of native authorities, and local council areas in general to those of subordinate native authorities which had been based on traditional political allegiance'.[42] Thus the Dagomba District Council covered the same area as the old Native Authority and each of the Local Councils had an area corresponding to that of a Subordinate Native Authority (see Table 7).[43] Also, the divisional chief (at Yendi, the Ya-Na) was to become president of the new Local Council: the presidency was an honorific position, but it symbolised the continuing authority of chieftaincy.

Indeed, the elections held for the new councils in 1952 demonstrated how strong that authority was, since a substantial number of chiefs and elders were returned for 'representative' seats, to join those appointed as 'traditional' members. The elections were not fought on party lines and only 9 of the 100 seats were contested. At least 35 chiefs and elders took 'representative' seats and there may well have been more among the remaining 65: the records are incomplete and they do not, in any case, document family background.[44] Since another 51 seats were reserved for 'traditional' members, it is clear that the chiefly estate was still firmly in control of local government, especially in the non-Konkomba divisions of western and central Dagomba.[45] Several of the new councils were, Tait reports, 'dominated by chiefly chairmen' and many of the council clerks were literates from cadet branches of the royal family or commoners holding minor elder chieftaincies.[46]

Continuity with indirect rule was also evident in the role of the administrator in the local government organisation. The Chief Regional Officer (C.R.O.) enjoyed substantial powers of supervision and rights of access, most of which he could delegate to the Government Agents (replacing the District Commissioners). Central control passed to the African Minister of Local Government, but, locally, administrative officers continued to draw up estimates and supervise the treasuries as they had done under indirect rule.

The new authorities were, in fact, more obviously dependent on central government support than their predecessors, largely because they were expected to offer a wider range of services without being given sufficient means to do so.[47] The matching of council boundaries with those of the defunct Native Authorities led to the establishment of councils which were

TABLE 7   *Dagomba District and Local Councils, 1952[a]*

Unit	Previous Unit	Head-quarters	Population (1954)	Council membership Elected:	Traditional:	President
DAGOMBA District Council	Dagomba Native Authority	Yendi		16[b]	8	Ya-Na
TAMALE Urban Council	Gulkpeogu Subordinate N.A.	Tamale	30,502	14	7	Gulkpe-Na
CHEREPONI Local Council	Chereponi Subordinate N.A.	Chereponi	13,349	6	3	Chereponi-fame
GUSHIEGU Local Council	Gushiegu Subordinate N.A.	Gushiegu	10,558	6	3	Gushie-Na
KARAGA Local Council	Karaga Subordinate N.A.	Karaga	13,290	6	3	Karaga-Na
KUMBUNGU Local Council	Kumbungu Subordinate N.A.	Kumbungu	9,681	6	3	Kumbung-Na
KWORLI Local Council	Kworli Subordinate N.A.	Nakpali	3,905	6	3	Kworli-Na
MION Local Council	Mion Subordinate N.A.	Sambu	13,120	6	3	Mion-lana
NANTON Local Council	Nanton Subordinate N.A.	Nanton	7,568	6	3	Nanton-Na
SAVELUGU Local Council	Savelugu Subordinate N.A.	Savelugu	42,279	16	8	Yo-Na
SUNSON Local Council	Sunson Subordinate N.A.	Sunson	8,847	6	3	Sunson-Na
TOLON Local Council	Tolon Subordinate N.A.	Tolon	13,143	6	3	Tolon-Na
YELZORI Local Council	Yelzori Subordinate N.A.	Zabzugu	8,496	6	3	Yelzori-lana
YENDI Local Council	Dagomba Native Authority minus other council areas	Yendi	29,397	12	6	Ya-Na

[a]As established by Instruments dated 28 Feb. 1952 (*Gold Coast Gazette*, 21 March 1952).
[b]Delegated by the Local Councils (traditional members nominated by the Ya-Na and the Council of Elders).

too small to be financially viable. Five of the new councils served populations of less than 10,000 and one (Kworli) served only 3,905. In these circumstances, as the C.R.O. reported,

there was no possibility of the councils concerned demonstrating their local government function of raising revenue in order to provide services for the ratepayers ... in some cases their sources of revenue were too small to cover more than the payment of their administrative staff, and complete reliance had to be placed on Government grants to keep councils of this nature alive.[48]

The dependence of some Dagomba councils on central government was marked, as Table 8 shows: in 1955/6 only three councils were getting even half of their revenue from local sources. The scope for increasing the yield from such sources was, of course, restricted by the low level of income in the area and the lack of rateable property. In the late fifties the government tried to rationalise the local government structure, drastically reducing the number of units and abolishing the District Councils. Subsequently, however, the C.P.P. allowed local authorities to multiply once again, using the local government structure as a means to reward areas and individuals loyal to the party.[49] Few councils were able to contribute much to local development and credit for improvements usually went to central government, in particular to the community development organisation.

The reform of local government did not, then, produce a redistribution of power between centre and periphery. It did, however, entail some redistribution in local politics, since the reform established a distinction between 'traditional' functions and 'local government' functions – a distinction which was absolutely contrary to the principles of indirect rule.[50] The chiefs, of course, had their representatives in the councils, and could (with certain exceptions) stand for election to office both locally and nationally.[51] Yet the role allotted to 'traditional authorities' in representative bodies was progressively reduced during the fifties: 'territorial' members disappeared from the Legislative Assembly in 1954 and 'traditional' representation in Local Councils was abolished in 1959, a year after the Northern Territories Council (another stronghold of the chiefly interest) was disbanded.[52]

The paradox of chieftaincy has been that successive governments have, while assaulting the political power of chiefs, affirmed an almost sacred reverence for the institution itself.[53] There have been numerous attempts to define and protect chieftaincy by legislative action. The State Councils (Northern Territories) Ordinance of 1952 was enacted to define the rights of traditional authorities. It was followed by the Head Chiefs (Recognition) Instrument, which provided that the holders of specified titles should be recognised as the head chiefs of particular areas (called, with a surrealist touch, 'traditional areas'). The State Councils were made responsible for enquiring into and determining 'any matter of a constitutional nature arising within the areas of their authority'. In Dagomba, the Ya-Na was recognised as a head chief and the State Council assumed the powers laid down by the 1952 Ordinance. Later, a House of Chiefs was established in each region

TABLE 8 *Revenue and expenditure, Dagomba local authorities, 1955/6*

	Revenue			Expenditure
	% from rates and fees	% from central government (grants/reimbursements)[a]	Total (£)	% spent on council administration, treasury and police
DAGOMBA District Council	31.1	66.4	(112,681)	13.6
TAMALE Urban Council	68.6	28.4	(16,528)	25.9
CHEREPONI Local Council	69.6	30.4	(1,428)	58.7
GUSHIEGU Local Council	50.1	48.2	(2,344)	19.1
KARAGA Local Council	10.7	89.2	(9,515)	30.6
KUMBUNGU Local Council	49.5	49.9	(6,298)	18.7
KWORLI Local Council	8.1	91.9	(4,013)	36.0
MION Local Council	20.6	77.7	(2,393)	24.3
NANTON Local Council	47.3	52.5	(6,035)	3.2
SAVELUGU Local Council	24.9	74.8	(20,562)	9.9
SUNSON Local Council	17.3	82.7	(7,460)	36.1
TOLON Local Council	24.4	75.6	(13,464)	19.1
YELZORI Local Council	30.4	69.4	(5,968)	11.0
YENDI Local Council	49.8	43.6	(8,125)	17.6

[a]In certain cases, small amounts of revenue were provided by court fines and 'miscellaneous' sources. These have been excluded from calculation.

SOURCE: Gold Coast (1955).

to advise the government on 'traditional matters', and post-independence governments continued the payment of salaries to chiefs, through local authorities.[54]

The fact was that the proliferation of government measures defining, regulating, and protecting chieftaincy signified a further degradation of the political status of the institution. Its formal status was preserved as its major functions were removed.[55] 'Traditionality' was interpreted in terms, not of political authority, but of constitutional form. For when governments declared that chieftaincy matters 'should be kept outside the realm of politics', they were in effect disenfranchising the chiefs. What was perhaps more dangerous was that in disenfranchising the chiefs, no government ever destroyed the actual power they still exercised in rural communities. Moreover, the state did not completely disengage itself from chieftaincy matters: it kept the ultimate prerogative of arbitrating in disputes, receiving appeals, appointing commissions of enquiry, and withdrawing recognition.[56] The formal relationship between the state and the chiefs was not very different after independence from that which had obtained under indirect rule, although there was a real change in social relations between the actors involved.[57] Confusion, ambiguity, and inconsistency permeated the relationship between 'modern' and 'traditional' authorities at every level and were amply apparent in the gathering dispute over the Dagomba kingship.[58] With the roles and jurisdictions of 'traditional' and 'non-traditional' office-holders so incoherently defined, there was every opportunity for 'neo-traditional' politics to flourish, and flourish they did, the weeds in a political no-man's-land.

CHAPTER 8

PARTY POLITICS

If you make friends with a monkey, you will follow him into the
tree.[1]

The year 1948 was a watershed in Dagomba and Ghanaian politics. It was
the year in which a major reform occurred in the political structure of the
Dagomba kingdom and that in which, through the accession of another
Abudu gate Ya-Na, the prospects of the Andani gate began to seem in
jeopardy. It was also the year in which Nkrumah and his followers began
their rapid rise to power.

In Dagomba history the twenty years which followed can be seen as a
distinct period, a period characterised by a developing conflict over particular issues and a period having its own *dramatis personae*. In national
terms, it was the period in which the Gold Coast became independent and
in which Nkrumah's one-party regime rose and fell.

Taking national and local politics together, it is possible to discern three
quite self-contained phases between 1948 and 1968. The first opened with
the death of Na Mahama III in 1953 and closed in August 1960. It saw the
accession of yet another Abudu gate paramount, the launching of a lengthy
campaign to have him deposed, and the imposition, in August 1960, of a
settlement by Dr Nkrumah and the C.P.P. government.

The second phase lasted from 1960 until the overthrow of the Nkrumah
government in February 1966. Nationally, it was a period of one-party
government, under which the formula imposed on Dagomba in 1960 was
maintained, with the acquiescence, if not the support, of both sides of the
royal family. The third phase opened with the seizure of power by the
military National Liberation Council in 1966 and ended, with a return to
civilian rule and the shootings at Yendi, in September 1969. It saw the death
of the Abudu gate paramount installed in 1954 and an extended struggle
between his regent and the Mion-lana Andani, the latter fighting for the
survival of his gate as claimants to the Yendi skin. In the course of this
struggle, the formula devised by Nkrumah was abandoned and a major
enquiry was made into the Dagomba constitution, following the abortive
selection of a Ya-Na in November 1968. The return to civilian government
brought with it a fresh involvement of party politics in chieftaincy affairs,
enlarging and further complicating the troubles in Dagomba. The announcement of a decision by the committee of enquiry favouring the Abudu gate
set the conflict alight once more, and led to a direct confrontation between
government forces and Andani gate supporters. In this chapter we shall

133

examine the events leading up to the 1960 settlement; the second and third phases form the subject-matter of Chapter 9.

The death of Ya-Na Mahama III focussed attention once more on the two major issues in Dagomba politics. The first was the constitutional issue: who was eligible for the paramountcy and who was responsible for selecting the paramount. The second was the dynastic issue: whether the Andani gate could wrest the skin from the Abudus. Mahama II's son, Andani, now Mion-lana, had tried and failed in 1948; his uncle, Yo-Na Mahamuru, was well over eighty and therefore unlikely to reach the paramountcy. Ya-Na Mahama III, on the other hand, had a son in his twenties and if he succeeded, it might be forty years before the kingship became vacant. Everything, therefore, depended on the Mion-lana, and he was already in his fifties.

In September 1953 the Mion-lana announced his candidature. With it he claimed, for the first time, the existence of a rule of rotation in occupancy of the Yendi skin which, he asserted, gave him the right to succeed.[2] Three other candidates entered the ring: the Yo-Na, Mahamuru; Mahama III's eldest son, the regent Abudulai; and Karaga-Na Adam. The regent did not hold even a village chieftaincy, while Adam was only a great-grandson of a paramount.

The succession was initially confused by a dispute over the regency. Mahama III had (allegedly) declared that his son should not be the regent because the young man was physically defective.[3] In order to comply with Mahama's wishes, the Abudu family suggested that Mahama's brother, the Kpating-lana, should become co-regent with Abudulai and should perform the king's funeral. The Andanis objected to this arrangement on the grounds that the king's death-bed statement had not been made in the presence of the senior elders and that, in any case, sons had a prior right to the honour of acting as regent. They were supported by J. H. Allassani, an M.P. and, by this time, a Ministerial Secretary in Nkrumah's government.[4] The outcome of this peculiar dispute was that, though Abudulai was permitted to act as regent, his uncle, the Kpating-lana, decided that he, too, should put his name forward on the pretext that Kpatinga had once been a gate to Yendi.[5]

The State Council met on 11 December 1953 to decide on this claim and to clarify other constitutional matters. It began by rejecting the Kpating-lana's claim and decided that 'there should be no addition to the three existing gates to the Skin of Yendi'.[6] Even more significantly, the meeting confirmed the resolution of May 1948 setting up the eleven-man selection committee for the paramountcy. The Council did, however, delete the provision originally made for a secret ballot, replacing it with one stating that 'where a unanimous decision could not be reached, election should be by majority vote'.[7] It is important to note, in view of subsequent events, that both the Mion-lana and the Kuga-Na were present at this meeting and that the

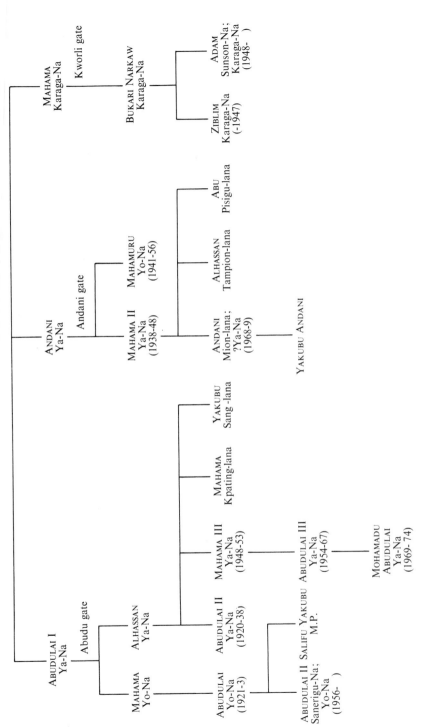

Fig. 5. Abudu versus Andani, 1954–69

Mion-lana confirmed the minutes afterwards.[8] These minutes do not record a decision which Tait asserts was made on this occasion, namely, a decision to recognise the regency as a gate skin to Yendi.[9]

The rulings of the State Council did not discourage the Kpating-lana from pressing his suit and they certainly did not prevent tension rising in Yendi itself. According to Tait, throughout January and February 1954 the town was crowded with hundreds of chiefs and commoners: 'The three bars with refrigerators did such a trade that beer was sold before it had time to cool; the price of a small leg of mutton rose from about five shillings to over fifteen shillings; the price of firewood trebled.'[10] The excitement was all the greater since political parties were forming or becoming active in the area, although at this point they were not involved at all deeply in dynastic affairs. Allassani was perhaps the exception in that he emerged as a partisan of the Andani gate (an alliance he maintained for the next sixteen years), but the C.P.P. was not committed as a party to the Mion-lana. Rumours of affiliation went round Yendi, one linking the new Moslem Association Party with the Mion-lana, but it is clear that all the parties were preoccupied with the general elections arranged for June 1954.[11] As for wider followings, Tait thought that 'among the peasant farmers and the educated classes alike, the strongest current was for the Chief of Mion with the Chief of Karaga a little behind him'.[12] But Karaga was just a great-grand-son, though a man of substantial wealth and ambition. Andani's problem was that it was believed by some members of the court that he had poisoned the king. As Tait points out, the chiefs of Mion had the reputation of being sorcerers, a reputation, he considered, which was 'no more than an expression of the structural opposition between the ruling paramount and his probable successor. But the accusation provided an excuse for supporters of other claimants to damage the reputation of the Chief of Mion.'[13] He was, indeed, stopped from performing the king's funeral as a result of this story.

The enlarged selection committee met for the first time on 10 March 1954, and again on 19 March. It is still not clear what passed at these meetings, except that a majority of the members finally voted for the regent Abudulai as Ya-Na, with perhaps two members voting for the Mion-lana.[14] It was alleged later that the final selection was rushed through while the soothsayers were still divining for a successor; but two of the king-making elders (Kuga-Na and Tuguri-nam) were apparently present when the selection was made.[15]

In any event, the Andani gate reacted sharply and immediately to the decision. The aged Yo-Na was seen 'walking about shaking and speechless with rage' and the Andanis straightaway accused the selection committee of partiality. This charge has, indeed, been repeated many times since and it deserves consideration. The argument runs that most of the members of the committee were indebted to the Abudu gate for promotion which they had received under Abudulai II and Mahama III. Thus Sibidow, the main publicist in the Andani cause, declares that the 1954 selection made it crystally clear that the committee system was adopted not just to protect the interest of the Abdu [sic] Gate but ultimately to eliminate the Andani Gate from the contest. Since most of the members of the committee owed their position to Abdu Gate it did not need any other evidence to justify that the loyalty of most of them lay with the Abdu Gate.[16]

Given that there had been an Andani paramount for only nine of the preceding fifty-three years, it was of course inevitable that any senior chief or elder would have received promotion at some stage from an Abudu gate king. Four of the seven divisional chiefs on the selection committee had in fact been appointed by Mahama III, including the Gushie-Na, who chaired the committee, and the new Tolon-Na (Yakubu Tali), who was, indeed, connected by marriage to the Abudu family.

The Andanis, of course, also had personal objections to the new Ya-Na, Abudulai III. He was, they felt, too young; he was said to be physically flawed; he did not hold one of the gate chieftaincies; and he had neither education nor experience of office. The appointment seemed to go against the ruling made by the State Council only three months earlier and it caused outrage among the supporters of all three royal dukes. There were, indeed, moves to install the Mion-lana in Yendi by force, but they came to nothing. The situation of the Andani gate was, nonetheless, dire; and at just this point the political parties arrived in search of votes.

PARTY POLITICS, 1951–7

Between 1951 and 1954 the N. T. were represented in the Legislative Assembly by 19 members, elected indirectly, and by a college consisting of the 16 members of the Territorial Council and 104 district delegates.[17] In effect, it was the elite of chiefs, educated royals, commoner clerks, and teachers which dominated the 1951 elections, as it dominated the Native Authorities and the new local authorities. Under these arrangements, the Dagomba–Nanumba district was allocated twenty-five delegates and four of them emerged in February 1951 as members of the Legislative Assembly. Yakubu Tali came top of the poll with 73 votes; Allassani came next with 56; lower in the poll came J. B. Harruna, Bogundo-Na, and Alhaju Osumanu, a government pensioner and farmer from Tamale.[18]

An interesting feature of this and later elections was that, on the whole, the senior divisional chiefs did not put themselves forward as candidates. The rather large exception was Yakubu Tali, Tolon-Na; but the only other Dagomba divisional chief ever to become a member of an elected assembly was Demon-Na Mahama Bukari, who was elected in a by-election in May 1953 and retired in 1954.[19] Junior royals were, as we shall see, quite another matter and, indeed, the senior chiefs were very ready to nominate and sponsor candidates (in the 1951 election, six of the eight delegates sponsoring the successful Dagomba candidates were senior chiefs or elders).[20]

In 1954, the government introduced direct election throughout the Gold Coast and at the same time established universal suffrage for national

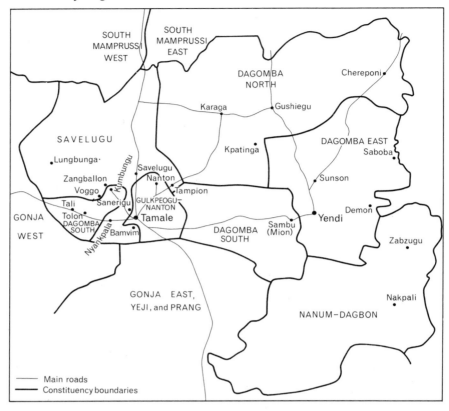

Map 3. Electoral constituencies, 1954 and 1956

elections. The north was divided into twenty-six Rural Electoral Districts (single-member constituencies), six of which were created in Dagomba (Gulkpeogu–Nanton, Savelugu, Dagomba South, Dagomba East, Dagomba North, and Nanum–Dagbon).[21] The new constituencies (subsequently increased to nine) were based on Local Council areas.[22] The traditional authorities ceased to enjoy special representation either through an electoral college or through reserved seats in the assembly.[23] Instead, from 1954 onwards, there was a complete structure of elective representation, existing alongside, and in some respects over, the existing traditional and bureaucratic structures. Thereafter local politics involved a complicated set of relations between chiefs, civil servants, M.P.s, ministers, local councillors, party officials, and latterly even officers of the police and the army. Politics, in the fullest sense, had therefore arrived.

It had, in fact, arrived slightly before the C.P.P. was ready for it. Throughout the Gold Coast the C.P.P. was in difficulties, for not only was it faced by regional parties in the north and in Togoland, but the cohesion of the party itself was threatened by a massive scramble for nominations, the result of which was an embarrassing profusion of disgruntled 'independent' or un-official C.P.P. candidates.

In the N.T. the government party's position was especially weak, given its lack of experience and the fear and resentment directed at southern poli-ticians. Whereas in the south the C.P.P. had already won a great victory, in the north it had to fight its first elections against a new regional party, the Northern People's Party, which had the support of many of the members of the N.T. Council as well as a large number of the educated commoners and junior royals controlling the local government structure.[24] The N.P.P. had been formed between February and April 1954 by a group of northern leaders, among whom the Tolon-Na was prominent. Also in process of formation was the Moslem Association Party, a body concerned particularly with the defence of Muslim immigrants in the towns.

The C.P.P.'s organisation in the north was rudimentary. In 1950 it claimed to have 3,000 members in Tamale but in fact its support scarcely extended beyond the town.[25] Even in Tamale the party was divided by a running battle between two factions, one headed by R. S. Iddrissu, a transport owner and relative of the chief of Lungbunga, the other by Ebenezer Adam, an Achimota-trained teacher and chairman of Tamale Urban Council.[26] Even Allassani's conversion to the C.P.P. (which followed his appointment to the government) was a mixed blessing: he was felt to have ignored his con-stituency since becoming a Ministerial Secretary and his support of the Mion-lana had not endeared him to the Yendi court.

In January 1954 the C.P.P.'s paper, the *Evening News*, reported that Ebenezer Adam had predicted a great C.P.P. victory in the north: '"We are definitely sweeping all the 26 seats with surprising easiness," he affirmed loudly.'[27] Loudly, but perhaps not very confidently. For, given the continu-ing rise of the N.P.P., it was essential that the C.P.P. should go out and draw some chiefs on to its side if the government was to have, if not a victory, at least a chance of an honourable defeat in the north. Back in 1951, Nkrumah had, in a speech to the Territorial Council, gone out of his way to disavow any hostility to the traditional rulers:

I want to make it plain that the policy of the Convention People's Party ... is not against chieftaincy in this country ... chieftaincy is the fabric upon which the institutions of this country rest ... with the advent of democracy we feel, even then, that we cannot leave out our chiefs in the administration of the country.[28]

The same theme was taken up by Imoru Ayarna at a 'supermonster' rally in Tamale on 5 February 1954, when he declared that

the C.P.P. was not formed to destroy chieftaincy but rather to fight against Imperialism for the chiefs and peoples of the Gold Coast ... Some few years ago when the Chiefs were coming to Tamale from their various stations to the N. T. Council, they were all packed on their district lorries, but now, nearly all the big chiefs are possessing cars.[29]

In April 1954 Nkrumah visited the north and called on the new Ya-Na, hoping to obtain his endorsement for the election. Abudulai, however, replied in the oblique, allegorical manner beloved of the Dagomba courts. The king asked what would happen if three women, respectively nine months', five months', and three months' pregnant, were required to give birth simultaneously, the meaning of which was (as the N.P.P. continually said) that the north was not yet ready to move into national politics as an equal partner. The most that the C.P.P. could get from the king was a declaration of neutrality and this declaration was broadcast over the radio in Tamale and Yendi. This annoyed the N.P.P. which claimed that the failure of the king to come out openly for the northern party had lost it the election in the Dagomba East constituency.[30] But the paramount equally refused his support to Allassani, the C.P.P. candidate in Dagomba East.[31]

In the event, the C.P.P. won only two of the five truly Dagomba seats (see Table 9). Allassani himself only scraped in with a majority of 295 over his N.P.P. rival and, allegedly, only after he had sent 'educated followers' round the villages to spread a rumour that the elections had been postponed.[32] The elections of 1956 (the last before independence) followed much the same pattern. Throughout the north the C.P.P. did manage to improve its position and in Dagomba it got three of the five seats: Dagomba North (S. I. Iddrissu, without a contest); Dagomba East (Allassani); and Gulkpeogu–Nanton (R. S. Iddrissu, who had for the time being resolved his feud with Adam). But the N.P.P. was still taking nearly 40 per cent of the vote and it controlled Savelugu, the most populous constituency.[33] In the east, too, Allassani only got in on a minority vote. The only loss was that of Gulkpeogu–Nanton by its associate, the M.A.P.

After 1954, the C.P.P. became more intolerant of its opponents and attacked both the N.T. Council and colonial officials for associating with the N.P.P.[34] Even so, it was unable to dispense with chiefly support and, in reality, there was not much difference between the C.P.P. and the N.P.P. in respect of the candidates they chose and the tactics they used. Nkrumah's men sought chiefly patronage as avidly as their rivals, for, as Austin remarks,

the radicalism and 'verandah boy' appeal of the C.P.P., that often held the party steady in the south, were a disadvantage in the north where the common man was still firmly under the authority of the chief. It was only by competing with the N.P.P. on its own terms, and by asserting its authority as a government to back its appeal as a party, that the C.P.P. later succeeded in splintering – and eventually breaking – the N.P.P.[35]

Indeed, it was as a government rather than as a party of the commoners that the C.P.P. ultimately brought the Dagomba chiefs into line. In the early years it had to find candidates with an aristocratic background or chiefly support and it had to dabble in local disputes. Thus in Dagomba South, faced by the Tolon-Na (Independent–N.P.P.), the C.P.P. exploited fears that an N.P.P. victory would lead to the abolition of the separate Kumbungu council. In choosing a candidate, it began with R. I. Alhassan, the educated son of a Kumbung-Na, and eventually adopted

S. D. Abudulai, the grandson of another Kumbung-Na. As a result of these tactics, the Tolon-Na got an official majority of only ten votes.[36]

In Gulkpeogu–Nanton, the Gulkpe-Na supported R. S. Iddrissu, because of his connections and his deference towards chiefs, but Nanton-Na Sulemana (who died in 1954) was a firm supporter of the M.A.P. and it was largely through the accession of Nanton votes that Osumanu defeated Iddrissu.[37] Both parties adopted members of the royal family as candidates for Savelugu. Indeed, three candidates (Sumani Bukari, J. B. Harruna, and Salifu Yakubu) were sons of former Yo-Nas, while the Tampion-lana Alhassan (who stood in 1954 as an independent) was a younger brother of Mion-lana Andani. The C.P.P.'s insistence on parachuting Ebenezer Adam (a commoner from Tamale) into this constituency in 1954 had disastrous consequences, since, facing three candidates related to the royal house, Adam ended up in third place.[38] Conversely, Salifu Yakubu, the N.P.P. candidate for Savelugu in 1956, was sponsored by his elder brother, Abudulai, Sanerigu-Na (after the election, Yo-Na), by the Nyankpala-Na, and by a senior elder of Savelugu, the Bilisi-Na. With this support, Yakubu was able to unseat the sitting member, Sumani Bukari.

Despite Adam's failure in 1954, the C.P.P. sponsored him again in 1956, this time for Dagomba South. Again he lost, not because he was a bad candidate but because he could not conceivably muster the local influence needed to beat the Tolon-Na in his own division. Outside Tamale, the only M.P. who had any reputation for seeking commoner support without the use of chiefly intermediaries was S. I. Iddrissu and he, once elected, became a vocal defender of chieftaincy.[39] Thus in Dagomba, as elsewhere in Ghana, the C.P.P. tended to take on the colour of its surroundings, involving itself in local disputes and picking up supporters on the rebound from the opposition.[40] Having become thus entangled, the party found it scarcely possible to avoid involvement in the biggest conflict of all, that between the two branches of the Dagomba royal house.

We have seen that Ya-Na Abudulai did not publicly attack the C.P.P. He would, indeed, have been foolish to commit himself openly for or against any political party, given the widely held prejudice against chiefs becoming involved in politics. But to many C.P.P. leaders a declaration of neutrality was tantamount to a declaration of war, and, in Abudulai's case, this reflex was strengthened by the king's known connections with the Tolon-Na, the effective leader of the N.P.P. in Dagomba. His refusal to see representatives of the Ashanti-based N.L.M. (an ally of the N.P.P.) did not save him from the charge of partiality.[41] Indeed, S. I. Iddrissu alleged that the king (in association with the Tolon-Na and Salifu Yakubu) had in 1956 'forced the Northerners much against their will to vote for the N.P.P.'[42] In any case, no matter how neutral he might wish to be, Abudulai was the object of the relentless hostility of the Andani gate, and the Andani gate had the backing of J. H. Allassani, by this time Minister of Education under Nkrumah. It was, in fact, alleged that in 1954 the C.P.P. 'went and gave the Mion-lana the assurance that if he was able to persuade his people to support them and they came into power they would make him the Ya-Na'.[43]

TABLE 9 *Election results, 1954 and 1956, Dagomba constituencies*

Constituency	Component council areas	Population	Candidate	Party	Votes	Comment
			1954			
DAGOMBA EAST	Yendi, Sunson L.C.s	38,244	J. H. Allassani	C.P.P.	2,766	Secretary of N.T. Youth Association:
			Z. A. Eddy-Cockra	N.P.P.	2,471	ex-C.P.P. 'letter-writer and politician'; grandson of Nanton-Na
				Total	5,237	
DAGOMBA NORTH	Chereponi, Gushiegu, Karaga L.C.s	37,227	S. I. Iddrissu	C.P.P.	6,880	Teacher; son of Yendi mallam; related to Abudu gate through mother Opposed by Karaga-Na
			A. M. Osumanu	N.P.P.	3,465	Son of Zongo chief, Yendi; teacher; 'Gushiegu' candidate
				Total	10,345	
DAGOMBA SOUTH	Mion, Tolon, Kumbungu L.C.s	35,944	Yakubu Tali	Ind.-N.P.P.	3,838	Tolon-Na
			S. D. Abudulai	C.P.P.	3,828	Grandson of former Kumbung-Na; council clerk; 'Kumbungu' candidate
				Total	7,666	
GULKPEOGU–NANTON	Tamale Urban Council;	38,070	Alhaji Osumanu	M.A.P.	2,238	Ex-M.L.A. farmer and pensioner
	Nanton L.C.		R. S. Iddrissu	C.P.P.	1,468	Transport owner; son of Lungbung-Na
				Total	3,706	
SAVELUGU	Savelugu L.C.	42,279	Sumani Bukari	Ind.	1,755	Son of Yo-Na Bukari (1910–21); council clerk; originally C.P.P. candidate
			J. B. Harruna	Ind.	938	Bogundo-Na; ex-M.L.A.; son of a Yo-Na
			E. Adam	C.P.P.	751	Chairman, Tamale U.C.
			A. Mahama	Ind.	675	Tampion-lana; son of Ya-Na Mahama II
				Total	4,119	

1956

Constituency	Electorate	Candidate	Party	Votes	Notes
DAGOMBA EAST	Yendi, Sunson L.C.s 38,244	J. H. Allassani	C.P.P.	2,576	
		I. B. Bukari	Ind.	2,256	Teacher from Saboba; large Konkomba vote
		Al-H. Braimah	Ind.	752	Nanumba council clerk
		Z. A. Eddy-Cockra	N.P.P.	200	
			Total	5,784	
DAGOMBA NORTH	Chereponi, Gushiegu, Karaga L.C.s 37,227	S. I. Iddrissu	C.P.P.	unopp.	
		(Mahama Bukari)	Ind.		Demon-Na)[a]
DAGOMBA SOUTH	Mion, Tolon, Kumbungu L.C.s 35,944	Yakubu Tali	Ind.-N.P.P.	4,205	Tolon-Na
		E. Adam	C.P.P.	2,191	Chairman, Tamale U.C.
			Total	6,396	
GULKPEOGU–NANTON	Tamale Urban Council; Nanton L.C. 38,070	R. S. Iddrissu	C.P.P.	2,830	
		Alhaji Osumanu	M.A.P.	1,732	
		N. B. Alhassan	Ind.	248	Contractor and farmer
			Total	4,810	
SAVELUGU	Savelugu L.C. 42,279	S. Yakubu	N.P.P.	2,323	Son of Yo-Na Abudulai (1921–3); brother of Sanerigu-Na; police sergeant
		Sumani Bukari	C.P.P.	2,248	
			Total	4,571	

[a] The Demon-Na's candidature appeared in *Gold Coast Gazette*, 27 June 1956, but was withdrawn before the election.

On 6 March 1957 Ghana became independent, under a C.P.P. government, in which J. H. Allassani, sometime enemy of Nkrumaism, was Minister of Health. Within eighteen months the campaign to depose Abudulai was under way.

In the attack on the Ya-Na, Allassani took the lead, even, it is said, making a public speech in Yendi on market day announcing that the government would depose Abudulai.[44] A petition demanding the deskinment of the Ya-Na was organised and signed by fifty-two local notables. The majority of the signatories were C.P.P. activists and local government councillors (including four members of Tamale Urban Council and ten members of the new Western Dagomba Local Council). Heading the list were three M.P.s (Allassani; R. S. Iddrissu; and Salifu Yakubu, who, as we shall see, had joined the C.P.P.) and four chiefs (those of Bamvim, Nyankpala, Lamashegu, and Kudani).[45] By no means all of the C.P.P. leaders in Dagomba supported Allassani in the campaign: S. I. Iddrissu, Ebenezer Adam, and Yahaya Iddi gave their support to the Ya-Na.[46]

The petitioners argued that Abudulai had been improperly selected, that he was deformed, and that he was a tyrant. These charges were considered and rejected by the State Council at a meeting on 20 September 1958: Abudulai, it concluded, had been 'customarily and properly enskinned with the approval of the Selection Committee and the then Government'.[47] The Andani gate and its supporters (now including two of the king-making elders, Tuguri-nam and Gomli) then decided to appeal to the government and a further petition was lodged on 4 May 1959.[48] The signatories complained that the State Council had refused to hear them, that the Council's decision was contrary to custom, and that it was biassed in favour of the Abudus. The government's response was to appoint a committee of enquiry under a barrister, S. D. Opoku-Afari. The Afari Committee's report was never published, but it is generally accepted that it came down against the Ya-Na and recommended that he be deposed.[49]

Interestingly, the C.P.P. government hesitated at this point. According to Allassani, when the report came before the Cabinet the Minister of Justice, Ofori Atta, said: 'I suggest that the verdict should be reversed. For if it is carried our party will suffer severe set-backs in the whole north.' Allassani's account continues: 'When he concluded, the Prime Minister [Nkrumah], without allowing anyone else to speak said "Yes I agree with the Minister. I declare the verdict reversed. And I take responsibility for this upon myself."'[50] Shortly afterwards, the government invited a number of chiefs to Accra. A witness later described their meeting with Nkrumah:

[Nyankpala-Na] spoke a lot on behalf of the ... Mion-lana and the question he put to the then government was, 'Was this the agreement we had in 1956? Were you not the person who gave us the assurance that you would destool this chief [i.e. the Ya-Na]?' Then the President squeezed his face and denied and said that he had never seen the man during his election campaign.[51]

144

To understand why Nkrumah, slightly miscast, was behaving in this Peter-like way, it is helpful to look at certain political developments in the north. The principal development was that, with the devastating pragmatism of its kind, the aristocracy of Dagomba had abandoned the N.P.P. and joined forces with the government party.

The first of the local N.P.P. leaders to make his peace with Nkrumah was Salifu Yakubu, M.P. for Savelugu. Yakubu's political career had only begun in 1956 and once in Parliament he quickly developed friendships with C.P.P. members.[52] On 14 March 1958 he rose to announce that his career had indeed been 'misdirected by joining hands with the Opposition', which, he said, had 'diabolical plans' to sabotage Ghana. Yakubu then declared that, 'with the consent of' his 'constituency', he was going to cross the carpet to the government's side. He concluded: 'I do hope the indomitable leader, Dr Kwame Nkrumah, will receive me into his fold as I am determined to pay obeisance to his leadership till the end of time.'[53] Soon afterwards Yakubu joined Allassani in attacking the Ya-Na (though both he and his brother, Yo-Na Abudulai II, were of the Abudu gate). On 2 July he delivered a eulogy of Nkrumah, whom he described as 'our great and dynamic leader', 'the Star of Africa', and 'the liberator and founder of Ghana'.

Yakubu claimed that he had been asked by the chiefs of Savelugu to change sides.[54] In the case of the Tolon-Na, who moved across to the C.P.P. in December 1958, the actual letter of instruction, from the Secretary to the Dagomba State Council, was read out in Parliament. This letter told Yakubu Tali that the Ya-Na and all the divisional chiefs had decided that he 'should resign from the United Party' (the opposition alliance, including the N.P.P.). The letter continued:

2. You are expected to do so within this session of the National Assembly.
3. *It is a fervent desire by all the chiefs to you to do this*, for you are representing the Chiefs and people of the Dagomba State. So you may respectfully accept the advice of your fellow *Head Chiefs* in the Dagomba State in the interest of all.
4. They have all stressed that since they support the C.P.P. Government without you in the C.P.P. Party, it means they are nowhere, since you are a prominent figure in the Dagomba State.[55]

Tolon-Na hastened to correct the anomaly and both he and Yakubu were well rewarded by Nkrumah. In July 1960 the Tolon-Na was appointed deputy speaker of the National Assembly and he subsequently became High Commissioner to Nigeria. Salifu Yakubu, for his part, was made Resident Minister in Mali, a post which he kept until the 1966 *coup*.[56]

Thus, from Nkrumah's point of view, the situation in the north had changed by the time the Afari report was presented. Yendi had previously been an N.P.P. stronghold, whereas now the paramount was seeking Nkrumah's approval. Clearly, Nkrumah was not willing to reject the Ya-Na's cooperation simply to satisfy Allassani and the Andani gate. Further, Nkrumah had been warned by several northern M.P.s (among them S. I. Iddrissu) that if he followed Allassani's advice and deposed the Ya-Na, not only would this be quite contrary to custom but it would create a precedent, encouraging similar campaigns elsewhere in the north.[57] The result might well be political trouble; and at the least the government would have made itself unpopular with the chiefs.

Allassani thus found himself neatly outflanked by the Yendi court. His career never recovered from the defeat. In July 1959 he was removed from the Cabinet and sent to Guinea as Resident Minister. He kept this post for only eleven months before being made deputy chairman of the State Housing Corporation. In January 1965 he became chairman of the State Paints Corporation, an appointment which symbolised in a grotesque manner the personal tragedy he had suffered. For, though he continued to enjoy a large income (legitimately and otherwise), his political career effectively came to an end in July 1959 and largely as a result of his attempt to get Ya-Na Abudulai deposed.[58]

In Dagomba itself, the effect of the State Council's conversion to the C.P.P. was to create a division within the party between the earlier 'militants' and the new converts. Allassani later described bitterly how in Yendi the Ya-Na

became the Chairman of the Convention People's Party which he designated 'NEW C.P.P.' We were the old C.P.P. He sent messages to all the chiefs asking them to recognise the New C.P.P. and to see to it that at all party ward and district elections the candidates of the New C.P.P. won, with the result that from that time up to the day of the Coup no old party member held any party official post in the area.[59]

THE 1960 SETTLEMENT

The alliance between Allassani and the Andanis survived their defeat in 1959 and, indeed, it secured a compromise which was more than satisfactory to the Mion-lana and his followers.

After the decision not to depose Abudulai, the Mion-lana sent a letter (drafted by Allassani) to Nkrumah. He said that he accepted the government's decision and understood the political arguments behind it, but he asked the Prime Minister to understand that if he died without reaching Yendi, his children and their descendants would be excluded from the skin for ever. The Mion-lana asked Nkrumah to be 'gracious enough to do something to save [them] from this tragedy'.[60] The government decided, after further consultation, to impose upon the Dagomba kingdom a settlement which, it was hoped, would end the dispute between the Abudus and Andanis by prescribing the succession to Yendi automatically and in perpetuity. Its formula for the settlement was embodied in Legislative Instrument No. 59, issued on 25 August 1960.[61]

L.I.59 was a courageous blow at the Gordian knot of 'tradition'. Instead of exploring the detailed precedents regarding eligibility and selection, the government simply laid down, in L.I.59, an order of succession to the Yendi skin and provided mechanisms for its continuation.

The Instrument reaffirmed that only sons of Ya-Nas occupying the skins

of Mion, Savelugu, and Karaga were eligible for Yendi. But it also specifically recognised the existence of the two royal gates, Andani and Abudulai,
and stated that occupation of the skin should 'be in rotation among the . . .
ruling families'. To ensure such alternation, it provided that when Abudulai
died, the Mion-lana would succeed him. If (as seemed very likely) Andani
died before the paramount, another member of the Andani gate would
occupy Mion and would move to Yendi when it eventually became vacant.
Further, the Instrument declared that all Andani's sons should be regarded
as sons of a paramount, irrespective of whether or not their father had
actually become Ya-Na before his death.

Having thus primed the mechanism of rotation, L.I.59 went on to provide
that, following Abudulai's death, the Andani family should successively
provide two paramounts: 'thenceforth the customary law of succession by
rotation shall proceed in the normal way: that is to say from the Abudulai
family and thence from the Andani family'.[62] In order to make the rotation
work properly, it laid down that there should always be at least one member
of either family on a gate skin. If (as was probable) there were two members
of one family on gate skins when the paramountcy became vacant, the
member who had first moved to a gate skin was to have priority in the
succession to Yendi.

As a solution to the dispute, L.I.59 had real merits, both political and
technical. Its provisions represented an attempt at equity, giving, in the long
run, equal access as of right to the two gates. The government had also
tried to cover every eventuality, insofar as it was possible to do so by
administrative ordinance. The measure was, of course, open to the criticism
that it severely undermined the 'traditional' constitution. For whereas the
1930 codification (and the decisions of 1948 and 1953) merely laid down
rules of procedure, specifying who was eligible and who was to choose,
L.I.59 effectively denied officials in the kingdom itself any part in appointing
a Ya-Na.

The provision that the Andanis should occupy the skin twice in succession
was also open to question, for it created a danger to the Abudu gate. If
the first Andani paramount succeeded at 25 and lived until he was 70, to
be followed by a 45-year-old son, then some ninety years would have elapsed
before an Abudu son was due to succeed. By that time there might be no
surviving paramounts' sons on the Abudu side.[63] In this respect, L.I.59
perhaps overcompensated the Andanis for the exclusion they had suffered.
However, since Abudulai was still under 40, it seemed that they might have
to wait until 1990 before entering Yendi.

In fact, the arrangement was necessarily vulnerable at many points to
accidents of birth and death. It was also based on the dubious assumption
that rotation was the normal mode of succession. Nevertheless, it was an
impressively comprehensive attempt at solving the dispute and one which
gave to both sides of the royal family the promise of survival.

CHAPTER 9

THE YENDI TRAGEDY

The 1960 legislation, whatever its faults, gave the Dagomba kingdom six years of peace, though during this period the regime which was responsible grew corrupt and finally collapsed, on the morning of 24 February 1966. While it lasted, the C.P.P. regime expanded its patronage continually.[1] In 1962 a whole new set of Local Councils came into existence and were filled by party nominees; by 1965, Dagomba had nine M.P.s; schools, roads, and welfare facilities developed in the north as never before, bringing with them new opportunities for the young, as well as jobs and contracts for their elders.

As long as the C.P.P. remained in power, the two branches of the royal dynasty accepted Legislative Instrument No. 59. The only disturbance of the truce was caused by an attempt on the part of the Abudus to win favour among the grandsons (a category which included both the Yo-Na and the Karaga-Na) and, in effect, to undermine the settlement. In 1961 some members of the State Council produced a document which, ignoring the provisions of L.I.59, defiantly re-stated the rules of succession adopted in 1953. The Ya-Na claimed that this document had been approved unanimously by the State Council, but the Mion-lana said that it had not even been discussed: the signatures on the document had (he alleged) been obtained by misrepresentation of its contents.[2]

Apart from listing the members of the selection committee, the document contained a remarkable paragraph on eligibility for the skin:

Persons who are eligible to occupy the Yendi Skin shall be the occupants at the time of the Karaga Skin, Savelugu Skin, Mion Skin and the reigning Gbong-Lana, i.e. Regent of a deceased Ya-Na on the Yendi Skin after the death of the father. These three Dukedoms i.e. Karaga, Savelugu and Mion, may be filled either by *direct sons of deceased or former Ya-Nas, or their grandsons*. The Grandsons of the Ya-Nas are now eligible for the Skin of Yendi, but formerly they were not.[3]

Several other assertions followed: that the regent was eligible to apply regardless of whether or not he held any skin; that the identity of a Ya-Na could not be known before his predecessor's death; and that the dukes were ranked in an order of precedence, with Karaga top, Savelugu second, Mion third, and the regent last.[4] The document emphasised that the elders traditionally used as kingmakers and responsible for the enskinment had 'no power to choose or appoint a Ya-Na', and it denied that there was any custom of rotation.[5]

This curious 'statement of custom' was not subsequently referred to by the government, nor indeed by the committee of enquiry in 1969; it was not even approved by the regional House of Chiefs. The statement seems to have been produced as an attempt to reassert the authority of the State Council and, perhaps, to smuggle into government files a version of custom which might with profit be invoked by the Abudus at a suitable moment, that is, when the political climate had changed. If adopted, it would, of course, have enabled Karaga-Na Adam and Yo-Na Abudulai II to succeed to Yendi and presumably the Abudus of Yendi felt that there was no harm in securing their goodwill against future troubles. The two dukes were certainly aware of the document, as we shall see.

THE REVOCATION OF L.I.59

The abolition of L.I.59 was brought about, first, by the *coup* of February 1966, and, secondly, by the unexpectedly early death of Abudulai III, on 14 September 1967.

Even before the Ya-Na died, there were moves to get L.I.59 revoked. On 25 May 1967 'the Electoral Committee of the Dagomba State Council' submitted a petition to the military government in which it argued that the Instrument violated 'the norm of Dagomba Custom that no successor to any skin is known or should be determined during the reign of its incumbent'.[6] The petitioners ridiculed the notion that rotation between the royal gates was customary: they further argued (contrary to the 1961 statement) that the regent had 'equal powers with the occupant skins [sic] of Mion, Savelugu, and Karaga in contesting for the Yendi Skin'.

These assertions naturally upset all the royal dukes. The Mion-lana said that it was wrong to regard L.I.59 as one of the 'crimes' of Nkrumah, for (he said) it was 'an instrument merely accepting the recommendations of the Northern Regional House of Chiefs': it had been approved by the King and by the three dukes as members of that body.[7] Andani further attacked the '1948' selection committee for having 'usurped the functions of the kingmakers'. The Yo-Na and Karaga-Na were upset by the promotion of the regent to parity with themselves. The Yo-Na further believed that the king wanted to have him excluded from the House of Chiefs and on this account he boycotted a meeting at Tamale for the inauguration of Dr Busia's Centre for Civic Education – a meeting which, as it happened, was broken up by a large swarm of bees, 'believed to have been invoked on the other chiefs by the Savelugu-Na'.[8]

The government took no action on the petition: the Secretary to the National Liberation Council referred it back, on the grounds that it had not been discussed by the House of Chiefs in Tamale. Within five months, however, the issue was revived by the death of Ya-Na Abudulai.[9] Abudulai left a son, Mohamadu Abudulai, who at the time of his father's death was nineteen years old and a pupil at the Government Secondary School at Tamale. Like his father, Mohamadu Abudulai did not hold even a village chieftaincy when he became regent.

On 21 October 1967 the Dagomba State Council discussed Abudulai's funeral and the question of L.I.59. Mohamadu Abudulai announced that, as regent, he wished Karaga-Na Adam to carry out the funeral and suggested that it be postponed until October 1968.[10] The Mion-lana naturally protested that his office entitled him to the honour and referred to the Council's own ruling in 1948. But, though the Yelzori-lana and Kuga-Na supported Andani, the majority was against him (indeed, he was unable to get the royal family even to accept the 'burial kit' usually presented by claimants to the skin).[11] The Council decided to postpone the funeral as suggested and, meanwhile, to demand again the annulment of L.I.59. When the House of Chiefs rejected its petition, advising the government to apply the provisions of the Instrument and make Andani the new Ya-Na, the State Council returned to the charge, protesting that custom had been 'seriously undermined by politics' and that L.I.59 was the work of Nkrumah, Allassani, and the C.P.P.[12] It warned the N.L.C. that the Mion-lana himself and Wahabu (Allassani's political agent in Yendi) 'were former advocates of the C.P.P., the spirit of which still [remained] inherent in them. Such persons as Wahabu need be checked immediately, else they stir up the minds of the innocent against our new found freedom'.[13]

While the Mion-lana and the Abudu supporters in the State Council petitioned the authorities against each other, the Yo-Na and Karaga-Na were caught between the two. Karaga had been swayed towards the Abudus by their decision to let him perform Abudulai's funeral, but he and the Yo-Na were anxious about the Council's neglect of the 1961 document entitling them to claim the paramountcy. They became more worried when, in searching for the precious statement of 'custom', they found that (in their own words) 'the original copy and even the whole minutes book of the traditional council meetings [had] mysteriously vanished from the office of the traditional council'.[14] They appealed to the Chairman of the Regional Committee of Administration 'to recover the minutes book' and told him that grandsons of paramounts had been 'from time immemorial qualified to the Yendi skin'.[15]

The most interesting feature of the period between October 1967 and November 1968 was the emergence (or re-emergence) of patrons in Accra – highly placed officials sponsoring in private the interests of one or other gate. Both the Yo-Na and the Andanis became particularly suspicious of the activities of one member of the N.L.C., B. A. Yakubu, Deputy Commissioner of Police. Yakubu came from Gushiegu and was the son of a Gushie-Na.[16] His elder brother, Sugri Issa Yakubu, had been appointed Gushie-Na by Abudulai III and the Abudu gate had also appointed his father to the post.[17] Although B. A. Yakubu had been absent on police service for over twenty years, he showed an active interest in Dagomba affairs and it was assumed that his interest inclined towards Mohamadu Abudulai, the regent, although he always denied any partisanship.[18]

In May 1968 J. H. Allassani reappeared in Dagomba politics, after serving a term in jail for perjury committed while he was under investigation for corruption.[19] Allassani wrote to the traditional kingmakers, informing them that they were 'the only constitutionally authorised persons' who could select a paramount and, for his pains, was thoroughly abused by the other elders of Yendi as 'a veritable hooligan' who concealed within him 'the spirit of the disbanded C.P.P.'[20] The ex-Minister also attacked his old rival, the Tolon-Na, along with B. A. Yakubu, for intriguing with the Abudus to get L.I.59 revoked.[21]

Several members of the government other than Yakubu were also suspected of taking sides in the Yendi struggle. Brigadier Afrifa, an Ashanti and the leader of the *coup*, was believed to favour the regent (Afrifa had been ceremonially adopted as a son by Abudulai III in recognition of his role in the overthrow of Nkrumah). Ankrah, the chairman of the N.L.C., was widely thought to support the Andani gate (supposedly because he was gathering political followers in the hope of obtaining high office in a future civilian government).[22] The Andanis, however, found their main spokesman in Ibrahim Mahama, a civilian Commissioner under the N.L.C.[23] Mahama, a lawyer, had graduated from the University of Ghana in 1966 and was a leading light in the newly formed Northern Youth Association.[24]

Thus, even before Abudulai III's funeral, the ramifications of the Yendi dispute had spread into national politics. The result was to confuse even more the issue of succession. On the particular question of L.I.59, the Northern Region House of Chiefs, meeting on 17 March 1968, refused a second time to recommend the annulment of the 1960 settlement. The paramount chiefs of Gonja and Mamprussi argued that L.I.59 represented the only formula that could ensure peace in Dagomba. They were criticised by Karaga-Na Adam, who remarked that 'most of the Legislative Instruments Nkrumah enacted throughout the country were being revoked, there was no reason why this L.I.59 of 1960 should be made to hold only in Dagbon'.[25] The State Council was equally immovable. When it met in July, only the Kumbung-Na and Kuga-Na showed any sympathy for either L.I.59 or the Mion-lana. Five of the Yendi elders, plus the Karaga-Na and Sunson-Na, backed the regent in denying Andani any right to carry out the deceased paramount's funeral (a right he was still claiming despite earlier rejections).[26]

As the time for the funeral drew near, the government added to the confusion. It first issued (but did not publish) an instrument (L.I.596) revoking L.I.59 (the revoking instrument bore the same number as an instrument of 30 September 1968, concerned with the state Cocoa Marketing Board). On 17 September the government reversed its decision: by N.L.C. Decree No. 281, it declared that L.I.59 should continue in force. On 15 October yet another decree (N.L.C.D.296) revoked its predecessor and once more declared L.I.59 abolished.[27] This final decree was issued after a committee of enquiry, led by Mr Justice Siriboe, had been appointed and had reported, with considerable speed, in favour of revoking the 1960 instrument. The Siriboe Committee apparently concluded that L.I.59 was technically defective, since, whatever the Mion-lana had claimed, the regional House of Chiefs had not in fact specifically recommended its adoption.[28] Having thus demonstrated its powers of decision, the N.L.C. rather lamely instructed the Dagomba State Council to proceed with the funeral and 'to select their Ya-Na in accordance with Dagomba custom'.

The funeral of Abudulai III took place on 7 November 1968. The selection of a new king was, however, unsuccessful, because the king-making elders and the members of the 1948 selection committee met separately and nominated different candidates.

By the time of the funeral, there were four contenders for the skin: the regent, Mion-lana Andani, Karaga-Na Adam, and Yo-Na Abudulai II. Only the first two were royal sons. On 5 November the District Administrative Officer, Nsaful, received a letter purporting to come from Kuga-Na, Tugurinam, Gomli, and Kpati-Na (a village chief involved in enskinment). This letter announced that, after consulting soothsayers, the elders had concluded that 'the Mion-lana [Na Andani] should be installed as the Ya-Na according to custom'.[29] It transpired that neither of those who signed as 'Gomli' and 'Kpati-Na' in fact held the office claimed.[30] But it seems that, whatever the authenticity or otherwise of the letter, Kuga-Na and Tugurinam had at about this time consulted the oracles and had decided that the Mion-lana should be nominated as king. In token of this decision, Kuga-Na sent kola nuts to Andani, and the Gushie-Na was summoned so that he could carry out the ceremony of presenting a straw from the palace roof to the nominee.[31]

Meanwhile, three members of the government (B. A. Yakubu, Brigadier Afrifa, and Ibrahim Mahama) had arrived in Yendi for the king's funeral.[32] On the morning of 7 November, Mr Yakubu's brother, the Gushie-Na, entered Yendi but, having ceremonially 'seized' the palace, he withdrew, without nominating a new king. Contrary to custom, he spent the night in the royal capital and was reported to have dispatched the piece of straw back to Gushiegu.[33]

On the day after the funeral (8 November), Yendi was to all appearances dead. Iddi noted: 'There is no drumming of any sort in Yendi. Dead silence. The market is empty. Only small groups of people can be seen in front of the houses of the contestants they support.'[34] But in reality there was great activity among the chiefs and officials. During the morning the 1948 selection committee met, under the chairmanship of the Gushie-Na, who had convened the meeting. Five divisional chiefs and two elders (Zohe-Na and Gagbindana) were present: Kuga-Na, Tuguri-nam, and the divisional chief of Kumbungu refused to attend. According to the minutes, the Yelzori-lana nominated Mohamadu Abudulai as the new Ya-Na and was supported by Zohe-Na, Gagbindana, and two divisional chiefs (Gulkpe-Na and Nanton-Na), with Sunson-Na abstaining. At this point the Tolon-Na said that, as there was a majority for the regent, he would add his vote to it. The Gushie-Na remarked that it was his duty to accept the committee's decision and he asked the Secretary to the State Council to inform the authorities of what had been decided.[35]

The administration, represented by Nsaful, had wisely decided to put an armed guard on the *katini duu*, the hut in which the rituals of enskinment take place. During the day both the Mion-lana and the regent were led to the *katini duu* by their supporters and both in turn were refused entry by the police. Nsaful himself was besieged by complaining chiefs and elders. The three royal dukes arrived in the morning after hearing of the selection committee's decision and declared that they opposed the choice of the regent: the Yo-Na and Karaga-Na said that they would accept Andani as paramount rather than Mohamadu Abudulai.[36] Later, after the regent had been turned away from the *katini duu*, members of the selection committee came to demand that the D.A.O. allow them to enskin their nominee. But Nsaful, having consulted the police and probably also his superiors in Tamale (by radio), ordered that the installation of a king should be suspended. The Mion-lana, meanwhile, had been taken to another hut and invested with some of the regalia of kingship by his followers.[37]

Matters rested there until 5.45 next morning, when listeners to Radio Ghana's Dagbane service were informed that the Mion-lana had been appointed Ya-Na and that the regent had been given the Mion skin. At the same time, the Accra *Daily Graphic* appeared, with a photograph of Brigadier Afrifa dancing at the funeral, followed by a statement, attributed to the regional administrative office in Tamale, to the effect that the Mion-lana had been 'nominated by the kingmakers of the Dagomba Traditional Area'. It was later alleged that Ibrahim Mahama (at the time Commissioner for Information) had used his position to get the announcement of Andani's selection broadcast and, indeed, that the announcer in question was actually a tenant in Mr Mahama's house.[38]

For the next nine days there was stalemate. The Karaga-Na and Yo-Na wrote to General Ankrah complaining that Yakubu had 'informed all the skinmakers to vote for the regent' and on 14 November a statement appeared, signed by the three dukes, objecting to the selection of the regent, on the grounds that he was too young and inexperienced.[39] The petitioners demanded that diviners be used to choose the new king. Meanwhile, the Regional Committee of Administration in Tamale called for a report from Nsaful for submission to the N.L.C.

Nsaful's lengthy memorandum pointed out the confusion surrounding the issue of selection procedure. The D.A.O. concluded that the Kuga-Na's version (that selection was carried out by him and other elders in consultation with soothsayers) was 'more in line with tradition and reason' and he commented: 'In the present dispute the Kuga-Na had followed tradition up to the time the installation was suspended. The general impression is that the elders are shutting their eyes deliberately for unknown reasons to what they know is the truth.'[40]

On 18 November Nsaful was informed that the Regional Committee of Administration had decided that the Mion-lana had been properly selected and he was instructed 'to inform the Dagomba Traditional Council that they may proceed with the installation of the Mion-lana as the Ya-Na'. It is not clear if authorisation for this order had been obtained from Accra.[41]

During the evening of 21 November, the Mion-lana was escorted to the *katini duu*. The ceremony there was abbreviated and most of the divisional chiefs and elders (including Zohe-Na and Kpati-Na) absented themselves in protest. Later in the evening supporters of the regent began to demonstrate and were dispersed with tear-gas. On 25 November, after a brief stay in the houses of Zohe-Na and Mbadugu, Andani received homage at court from his supporters (as well as from the D.A.O. and two police inspectors). The palace was filled by members of the Andani family, the men in richly coloured smocks, the women in blue and white cotton cloth and adorned with gold necklaces and bangles. On the same day, at Gushiegu, B. A. Yakubu's brother, the Gushie-Na Sugre, died. To the victorious Andanis, his death was a punishment inflicted by the royal spirits for the several infringements of custom he had committed on 7 and 8 November.[42]

THE ANDANIS IN POWER

Andani lived for only four months after his enskinment and by the time of his death a counter-attack by the Abudu gate was under way. The government nevertheless continued to recognise him until his death. An official notice of recognition was published in the *Local Government Bulletin* of 14 December 1968 and several members of the Regional Committee of Administration visited Yendi on 28 November to pay their respects to him.[43]

But, within three days of his entry into the *katini duu*, the dissident divisional chiefs and elders had drawn up a petition to the N.L.C., declaring that Andani had not been properly selected or enskinned. Both Gomli and Kpati-Na protested that they had not taken part in the alleged consultation with soothsayers. The petitioners also said that several important rituals of enskinment had been omitted.[44] Two delegations were sent to Accra to complain about government interference in the dispute and on 13 December a group of Abudu supporters attacked the police station in Yendi, compelling the government to send reinforcements to the town.

The government's response to this campaign was to establish another committee of enquiry, headed by Nene Azzu Mate Kole, a southern chief, vice-chairman of the government's Chieftaincy Secretariat, and an old enemy of the C.P.P. The other members of the committee were Nana Obiri Yeboah, a lawyer and also a southern chief, and Jatoe Kaleo, ex-M.P. for Wala North and at one time a member of the executive of the N.P.P.[45] The committee's terms of reference were as follows:

(a) To ascertain the custom and customary procedure for the nomination and/or selection of the new Ya-Na.
(b) Whether the new Ya-Na was properly nominated and enskinned in accordance with the said Dagomba Traditional Custom.
(c) Whether or not the said installation was unduly influenced by the presence of

armed soldiers and policemen and of the District Administrative Officer in the area.[46]

The Mate Kole Committee took eight months to carry out its work and it received a considerable volume of evidence from counsel and witnesses for both gates and for neither. By the time it reported, on 8 August 1969, the political context had changed radically.[47] Andani had died in March: his son, Yakubu Andani, a 25-year-old schoolteacher, had become regent and the Andani family stayed in the palace in Yendi, determined that they would have Andani buried, as a king, in the royal compound. Otherwise, dynastic struggle was suspended: the chieftaincies of Mion and Gushiegu remained vacant, since the Mate Kole Committee had asked Andani not to make new appointments while its enquiries were taking place. Relations between the gates remained tense: in disturbances following Andani's death, one man was shot dead and five others were seriously wounded. The Andanis were convinced that the appointment of the Mate Kole Committee had been arranged by B. A. Yakubu and the Tolon-Na to prepare the way for the installation of the regent as Ya-Na (and of B. A. Yakubu as Gushie-Na, to succeed his brother). According to Sibidow, Yakubu had remarked that the purpose of the committee was 'to establish and confirm the truth that Mion-lana is not a Ya-Na and that Mohamadu [the regent] is the only one properly selected Ya-Na and should be recognised as such'.[48]

THE GENERAL ELECTIONS OF 1969

The direction of national politics increased the anxieties of the Andani gate. In April 1969 General Ankrah resigned (or was pushed) from the chairmanship of the N.L.C. and was replaced by Afrifa. Soon afterwards Ibrahim Mahama was removed from his post of Commissioner, largely (it is said) because of his disagreement with Afrifa and Yakubu over the Yendi dispute.[49] The loss of these allies was all the more worrying to the Andanis since it was clear that Afrifa wanted a quick return to civilian government and hoped to see the establishment of an administration headed by Dr K. A. Busia, Nkrumah's principal opponent and leader of the United Party until his exile in 1959.[50]

On 1 May 1969 the ban placed on political parties by the N.L.C. was lifted and on 29 August elections for a new National Assembly took place.[51] The principal contestants were the Progress Party (P.P.), led by Dr Busia, and the National Alliance of Liberals (N.A.L.), led by K. A. Gbedemah, at one time Nkrumah's Minister of Finance. Not surprisingly, the P.P. was seen as a revival of the old United Party, while the genteel-sounding N.A.L. was regarded as a C.P.P. front organisation.

Dagomba was divided into seven single-member constituencies, for a registered electorate of 110,304.[52] The registration of voters was poor in some areas: in Savelugu only 24.4 per cent of the population were registered as voters and there were also low rates of registration in Tolon, Gushiegu, and Mion–Nanton.[53] The turnout was also poor: the highest turnout was in Savelugu (60.4 per cent), the lowest in Mion–Nanton (32.8 per cent), and the overall turnout was only 48.4 per cent.[54]

The election was characterised by a direct confrontation between the two major (and southern-based) parties.[55] Indeed, one of the most interesting features of the campaign was the non-appearance of a 'northern' party. The basis of such a grouping seemed to exist within the Northern Youth Association, but its unity was broken by revelations that several leaders, notably Ibrahim Mahama, had committed themselves to the N.A.L. Indeed, during the elections the N.Y.A. was generally seen as an affiliate of Gbedemah's party.[56]

The contest was further polarised by a clear identification of each party with one of the royal gates – the P.P. with the Abudus and the N.A.L. with the Andanis. Sibidow remarked that

during the general elections Dagombas voted according to where the principal figures in Dagbon were inclined to. Since Ibrahim Mahama [was] the General Secretary of the National Alliance of Liberals people in the Andani Gate automatically voted for N.A.L. On the other side people who were identified with the Abudu Gate automatically decided to vote for the Progress Party.[57]

The skin dispute dominated the elections at all levels. It provided another element of division within the Northern Youth Association. When a delegation, including members of the Association, went to Tamale airport to meet Gbedemah, those affiliated with the Abudu gate noticed a large contingent of Andanis awaiting the N.A.L. leader. Deducing that there was a pact between that party and their opponents, they moved *en bloc* into the Busia camp.

The same alignment appeared in the constituencies. A correspondent of *West Africa* reported that voters in Yendi had

definitely identified Mr Mahama Saibu, the N.A.L. man, with the Andani family claimant to the Skin and Mr Shanni Mahama, the P.P. man, with the Abudulai family claimant. In this constituency and in the neighbouring one of Mion–Nanton you can see that villages are wholeheartedly for one party or the other ... the great issue in the Tolon constituency, as in all Dagomba constituencies, was the Yendi skin.[58]

The cleavage was deepened by a conflict within the Dagomba Muslim community which had begun at least as early as 1958, when Malam Ajura, of the Bolgatanga Road mosque in Tamale, and Malam Wahabu of Yendi (Allassani's friend), both C.P.P. supporters, had signed the petition demanding the removal of Abudulai III. In July 1968, when the conflict over L.I.59 was at its height, there had been fighting in the Yendi mosque between supporters of the two gates, while in Tamale Malam Ajura's followers had ceased attending Friday prayers at the central mosque.[59]

One important qualification to this neat symmetry of interests should be mentioned, namely, that in the context of 1969 'ex-C.P.P.' did not necessarily mean 'N.A.L.', nor was 'ex-U.P.' automatically equivalent to 'Progress Party'. True, most of the old United Party politicians rallied behind Busia, though often grudgingly, and this was apparent locally – the Tolon-Na and his family being the obvious examples. But there were several factors preventing an equal resurgence of the old C.P.P., not the least being the disqualification of so many of its leaders from holding public office. Further, the C.P.P. was not monolithic: some activists were personally devoted to Nkrumah and were not enthusiastic about Gbedemah as a leader.[60] The attachment of others to the party had been quite instrumental (or, to put it less politely, opportunistic): at least two prominent Tamale C.P.P. leaders moved over to Busia's party, in one case even before it had been officially launched.[61]

In the Dagomba area very few of the old politicians in fact put themselves up for election in 1969. Only one candidate from an earlier election stood again (S. D. Abudulai, who had stood unsuccessfully for Dagomba South in 1954). But an examination of the list of candidates reveals a deeper continuity with the pre-*coup* period: for, as in 1954 and 1956, many of them had chiefly connections (see Table 10). There were, indeed, more titled candidates than before.[62] Of the twelve people nominated by the two main parties in the six predominantly Dagomba constituencies, eleven had a chiefly background. Five were royals on their fathers' side. Abudulai Yakubu (Zangballon-Na) and Yisifu Yinusah were Andanis (and N.A.L. candidates); Abudulai Iddrissu and Allassan Yakubu were Abudus (and P.P. candidates); Ziblim Adam was a son of Karaga-Na Adam. Ibrahim Mahama (N.A.L., Tamale) and Shanni Mahama (P.P., Yendi) both had maternal connections with the royal family, while another four candidates were related to elder divisional chiefs: Yakubu Tali, Tali-Na (P.P., Tolon) as brother to the Tolon-Na; Mumuni (P.P., Gushiegu) as son of a Gushie-Na; M. S. Mahama (N.A.L., Yendi) and S. D. Abudulai (N.A.L., Tolon) as relatives of chiefs of Kumbungu.

The extent of royal affiliation can be seen from Fig. 6, which shows what, in eighteenth-century phraseology, might be called 'Savelugu's connection'. The Yo-Na, Abudulai II, was engaged in some very intricate political manoeuvres during this campaign. Two of his sons were candidates, one sponsored by the People's Action Party in Tolon, the other (Abudulai Iddrissu) by the P.P. in Savelugu itself. The Yo-Na, a member of the Abudu gate, supported Dr Busia, allegedly in the hope that, if the regent became paramount in the wake of the Mate Kole Committee's report, his eldest son (an illiterate who was not standing in the election) would eventually be allowed to succeed his father at Savelugu. The three principal rivals to this son were all Andanis (the Vo-Na, a diplomat; Sanerigu-Na, a doctor in Kumasi; and Zangballon-Na, the N.A.L. candidate in Savelugu). Unfortunately for the Yo-Na, his other sons disliked his scheme and set to work helping the N.A.L. candidate.[63]

In the Mion–Nanton constituency there was a rather simpler confrontation between the two royal gates: a grandson of Na Andani II was N.A.L. candidate, opposing a grandson of Na Abudulai I (backed by the Nanton-Na). The Mion section of the constituency naturally voted heavily for the

157

TABLE 10 *Election results, 1969, Dagomba constituencies*

Constituency	Composition	Population (approx.)	Voters eligible	Candidates	Party[a]	Votes	Comment
TAMALE	Tamale Municipal Council area, minus two wards	60,000	30,541	Ibrahim Mahama	N.A.L.	7,649	General Secretary, N.A.L.; grandson of Mion-lana (Ya-Na) Andani through mother
				I. M. Braimah	P.P.	6,159	Regional chairman, P.P.; son of chief driver in Tamale; not a royal
				Iddrissu Abu	P.A.P.	408	Son of R. S. Iddrissu, M.P. for Gulkpeogu–Nanton, 1956–60
				Mahama Sulemana	U.N.P.	179	Member of early educated elite; typist and clerk
					Total	14,395	
TOLON	Tolon Local Council area, minus Kumbungu	40,072	11,941	Ben A. Yakubu Tali	P.P.	3,137	Brother of Tolon-Na; teacher; Tali-Na
				S. D. Abudulai	N.A.L.	2,190	C.P.P. candidate in 1954; clerk; grandson of former Kumbung-Na
				E. A. Alhassan	P.A.P.	481	Tampie-Kukuo-Na; son of Yo-Na Abudulai II; ex-veterinary officer
					Total	5,808	
SAVELUGU	Savelugu Local Council area, plus Kumbungu	41,573	10,145	Abudulai Yakubu	N.A.L.	3,141	Zangballon-Na; son of Yo-Na Yakubu (1935–41) (Andani gate)

Constituency	Electorate	Candidate	Party	Votes	Notes
		Abudulai Iddrissu	P.P.	2,446	Son of Yo-Na Abudulai II; teacher
		M. I. Mahama	A.P.R.P.	300	---
		Imorow Sumani	U.N.P.	246	---
			Total	6,133	
MION–NANTON	41,110	Nanton Local Council area, plus wards from Yendi and Tamale council areas (including Sambu and Mion province)[b]		14,154	
		Yisifu Yinusah	N.A.L.	2,799	Son of Zangballon-Na Sitobu and grandson of Na Andani II (Andani gate)
		Allassan Yakubu	P.P.	1,601	Son of Kpating-lana Allassan and grandson of Na Abudulai I (Abudu gate)
		Sumani Yakubu	U.N.P.	245	---
			Total	4,645	
YENDI	41,152	Parts of Yendi and Zabzugu Local Council areas		17,552	
		Shanni Mahama	P.P.	3,987	Son of Mahama, Botin-Na, and grandson of Karaga-Na Adam through mother; teacher; manager of Naa Gbewa football team
		M. S. Mahama	N.A.L.	3,343	Ex-employee of Ministry of Information; lay magistrate; member of Constituent Assembly, 1969; related to Kumbungu chiefly family
		Mahama Abubakari	A.P.R.P.	362	Not seen during campaign
		Andani Bukari	U.N.P.	343	---
			Total	8,055	

159

TABLE 10 (cont'd.)

Constituency	Composition	Population (approx.)	Voters eligible	Candidates	Party[a]	Votes	Comment
GUSHIEGU	Gushiegu Local Council area, plus part of Yendi Local Council area (including Karaga)	40,000	12,761	Z. S. Adam	N.A.L.	3,629	Son of Karaga-Na Adam
				M. A. Mumuni	P.P.	2,712	Lele-lana; son of a Gushie-Na and cousin of B. A. Yakubu; teacher and clerk
					Total	6,341	
CHEREPONI–SABOBA	Chereponi and Saboba Local Council areas, plus parts of Zabzugu Local Council area	40,243	13,210	E. S. Yarney	P.P.	4,464	Ex-C.P.P. councillor
				Johnson Blido	N.A.L.	3,560	– – –
					Total	8,024	

[a]A.P.R.P. – All People's Republican Party.
N.A.L. – National Alliance of Liberals.
P.A.P. – People's Action Party.
P.P. – Progress Party.
U.N.P. – United Nationalist Party.
[b]Mion Local Council disappeared in 1958 and, like Karaga, Kumbungu, Kworli and Yelzori, was not re-established in 1962.
Eligible voters recording votes: 53,401 of 110,304 or 48.4%.
% of recorded votes for N.A.L.: 26,311 of 53,401 or 49.2%.
% of recorded votes for P.P.: 24,506 of 53,401 or 45.8%.
% of recorded votes for all third parties: 2,584 of 53,401 or 5.0%.

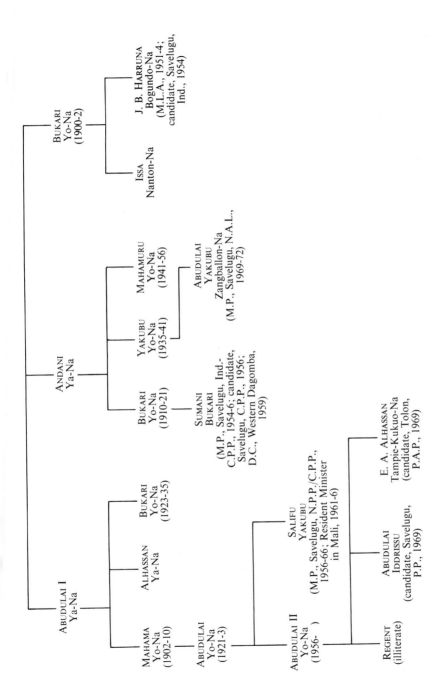

Fig. 6. Chiefs and politicians, Savelugu division

161

party associated with the family of their ex-duke. The contest in Gushiegu was in some ways the most interesting of all, since it involved a battle for influence between Karaga-Na Adam and B. A. Yakubu, who had persuaded a cousin, the Lele-lana, to stand against the duke's son, Ziblim. By this time, the Karaga-Na was on very bad terms with the Yendi court. He felt that he had been cheated by the regent, Mohamadu Abudulai, in 1968 and he was particularly hostile to Yakubu, whom he regarded as responsible for the establishment of the Mate Kole enquiry and other acts favourable to the regent. Instructions therefore went out to the villages under Karaga to turn out for the N.A.L. and the duke's son – which they did, with humiliating consequences for Yakubu.

Indeed, the results in general were disappointing for the P.P. and the Abudu gate. The P.P. obtained only 45.8 per cent of votes cast in the Dagomba area, as against 49.2 per cent for the N.A.L. Three P.P. members were returned (for Tolon, Yendi, and Chereponi–Saboba), while the N.A.L. took Tamale, Savelugu, Mion–Nanton, and Gushiegu.[64] Such results were all the more annoying to Busia's party and the Abudus, since, outside Dagomba, the P.P. had taken 22 of the 27 seats in the Northern and Upper regions, and throughout the country had won 105 of the 140 seats in the new assembly.

THE YENDI SHOOTINGS

As in November 1968, the Andanis' victory was short-lived. On 3 September Dr Busia became Prime Minister and the next day the new government released the findings of the Mate Kole Committee. The principal findings of the committee – all sustaining the Abudu case – were as follows:

(a) that 'those eligible [for the paramountcy] are the occupants of the skins of Karaga, Savelugu, or Mion if they are sons of a Ya-Na and the Gbong-lana of Yendi[;] these are the four persons from among whom a Ya-Na could be selected'.

(b) 'that the body traditionally authorised to select a Ya-Na is the body agreed upon by the Dagomba State Council in 1948 and accepted by Government'.

(c) 'that the Mion-lana was not selected by the recognised body of Selection Committee, his alleged selection by soothsayers consisted of [sic] Kuga-Na, Tuguri-nam, Amadu Gomle and Mahama Kpatia is not the custom as at present recognised'.

(d) that the Mion-lana's 'alleged installation on 21 September [sic], 1968 was not performed by the Gomli, Malle, Kpahigu, Gagbindana, the Kpati-Na and the Gulkpe-Na. He did not undergo ceremonies at Zohe-Na's house, Mba Buga's house or Mbadugu's house'.

(e) that 'the Bolon or Gbewa ceremony was not performed on him. His alleged enskinment cannot therefore be in accordance with Dagomba Traditional custom and procedure'.[65]

The committee also decided that the D.A.O. and the Superintendent of Police at Yendi had interfered quite improperly with the selection process, by preventing the regent from entering the *katini duu* on 8 November. By taking Andani into the *katini duu* on 21 November, the two officials had (in the view of the committee) been guilty of 'unduly influencing the installation on that day'.[66]

In support of its conclusions, the committee declared that the constitution of 1930 'was not a formulation of customary law but a factual record of the customary law as [it] existed at that time and agreed to as such by the King and his Council'.[67] It argued that those provisions of the 1930 constitution dealing with selection procedure had been legitimately superseded by the 1948 resolution and asserted that 'selection of a Ya-Na only by means of consulting an oracle' had been discarded at the time of Na Gungobili (at the end of the eighteenth century).[68] The committee pointed out that the Mion-lana and the Kuga-Na had both accepted the alteration of procedure at the time and that Kuga-Na and Tuguri-nam had taken part in the selection committee's proceedings in 1954.

On the question of the eligibility of the regent, the committee found 'overwhelming evidence' that the rule limiting eligibility to Karaga-Na, Mion-lana, and Yo-Na was 'subject to the right that sons are eligible to the Skin of Yendi'.[69] The regent was therefore (in its view) entitled to apply for the skin, once he had been created Bolon-lana (an honorific title bestowed before the regency was assumed). The committee accepted that various elders, including all the traditional kingmakers (except Kuga-Na), had functions to perform during the actual enskinment but denied that any of them had exclusive rights to select a paramount. It also dismissed the contention of the Andanis that there was a rule of rotation between the royal gates in occupying the Yendi skin.[70] Concerning the events of November 1968, the committee declared that both the regional and district authorities had exceeded their legal powers in directing that Andani should be installed, since by law only Traditional Councils or committees specifically appointed by the government were entitled to arbitrate in chieftaincy disputes.[71]

In a White Paper also issued on 4 September, the government announced its acceptance of the Mate Kole Committee's findings and declared that 'the alleged enskinment of Mion-lana was repugnant to Dagomba custom and . . . therefore . . . null and void'. The White Paper 'deplored' the role played by the local administration in the events of November 1968 and concluded: 'Government accepts the finding of the Committee that the Gbon Lana Mohamadu Abudulai was properly selected and directs that the ceremony of installation as Ya-Na should now be performed on the Gbon Lana as soon as possible.'[72]

Even as the White Paper was being issued in Accra, a force of sixty armed police was on its way to Yendi, because of minor disturbances in the town. Following further trouble, in the course of which the regent's grandmother was shot dead and five people were seriously wounded, the government

163

increased its forces in the town, until there were two hundred riot police and soldiers on patrol as well as guarding the royal palace. On 6 September a dusk-to-dawn curfew was imposed on Yendi and troops began to search for and confiscate arms. Meanwhile, officials of the Regional Committee of Administration travelled to Yendi and on 8 September met Mohamadu Abudulai (for the Abudu gate) and the Karaga-Na, Yo-Na, and Yakubu Andani, the Kampakuya-Na (representing the dissidents). It was agreed 'to guard all the rivals so as to avoid any attack on them by rival supporters'. On the same day, Ibrahim Mahama issued a statement calling on the government to rescind its decision on the Mate Kole report and to find a compromise solution.[73]

During these events the relatives of Andani were still living in the palace and were intent on staying there until the funeral of their Ya-Na could be performed.[74] It was at the palace on the morning of 9 September that the shootings occurred. In the nature of such incidents, there are conflicting and mutually exclusive accounts of what happened. Indeed, the government's own version changed somewhat in succeeding days.

Its initial statement, issued on 10 September, said that while searching for arms, a force of soldiers and police had been attacked 'by a mob of about 2,000 led by the Karaga-Na': 'In spite of warning shots fired by the army and the police, the crowd did not disperse but rather persisted and intensified their attack on the army and the police with such lethal weapons as cutlasses, cudgels, sticks and stones.'[75] The troops had therefore been 'compelled to fire, resulting in the death of five men and two women'. A rather different account was provided on the same day by the chairman of the Regional Committee of Administration, Mr Nuamah, who said that fighting had broken out when the soldiers and police had tried to eject the occupants of the palace.[76] The government subsequently accepted that the incidents had occurred in the vicinity of the palace but asserted that they had taken place during an arms search. According to the Attorney-General, when the soldiers and police arrived at the palace 'to do their official duties', they found that

supporters of two factions, one for the Mion-lana, the other for [the Abudus], had massed themselves up within close range of each other in front of the palace. . .at 7.45 a.m. the same day, war drums were beaten from the direction of the palace. . . When the Police tried to get in, they were faced with bows and arrows and even shot-guns. . .the supporters of the Mion-lana openly defied the Police and resisted their entry into the palace to do their official duties.[77]

The shooting had started, the Attorney-General said, when a man ran forward threatening the senior police officer with a dagger. According to yet another statement, the troops 'fired in self-defence on inmates of the Ya-Na's palace for firing on them during a search for offensive weapons'.[78]

The account put forward by the Andani gate and its allies was that the government's overriding concern had been to remove the Andani family from the palace in anticipation of the installation of Mohamadu Abudulai. Ibrahim Mahama alleged that the Abudus had been given advance information about the Mate Kole report and the government's decision on it. There had, he pointed out, been no attempt on the part of the government to consult the various factional leaders (as had been done in 1960).[79] Troops had been dispatched even before the announcement had been made and the government had 'immediately asked members of the royal family [i.e. the Andanis] to quit the palace'. On 8 September the Andanis had petitioned the Regional Committee of Administration for permission to perform their chief's funeral before leaving the palace. But during the evening of that day, machine guns had been mounted in front of the palace, which had been surrounded throughout the night:

Early in the morning when the inmates were busily taking their breakfast and others were coming to pay homage, soldiers and policemen were led to the palace to join those who had already surrounded the palace. And, to the shock of every person the police started firing at the inmates of the Ya-Na's palace. ... and within a very short time, 18 of them had been shot dead.[80]

Perhaps the most important allegation made by the opposition (specifically by Mahama and by J. H. Allassani, in a letter to Busia) concerned a transfer of command on 8 November. Allassani said that the Deputy Superintendent of Police, Yendi, had been in Accra on 4 September but had not been informed of the government's decision on the Yendi skin.[81] On 8 September it was rumoured in Yendi that 'the Government had intended earlier on to open fire on those inhabitants [of the palace] but that those in command of the army and the police thought this was an unwise step'.[82] Mahama remarked that in fact the officers in command were asked to leave Yendi on 8 September and 'new officers were brought in'.[83] Allassani claimed that it was the newly appointed police superintendent, Allassan, who had brought up the reinforcements on the morning of 9 September. One of Allassani's friends in Yendi, Dawuda Yahaya, had been present and gave the following description of Allassan's actions:

When he came within about 30 yards of us he halted. Then he posted his men at distances to our right and left. The man who carried what was called bren gun was posted facing us. We never suspected any evil. We knew that soldiers always carry their guns wherever they went, and the leader showing them where to stand was a normal practice with them. When he had finished posting his men we thought he was now going to come to us to tell us what message he brought for us. But to our surprise he did not come forward. He stood where he halted and raising the pistol he held he shouted, 'Clear them off,' and fired the first shot sending Zagyuri Na to the ground. Then the soldiers opened fire and men fell and reeled over on the ground. There was a great commotion as we tried to run for shelter which was not available. It was some of the soldiers who had been with us for some time who shouted to us that we should fall to the ground and not try to run ... When Allassan saw many of us lying dead and wounded, he shouted 'Cease fire.'[84]

The Andani supporters pointed out that there had been no casualties among the troops on the morning of the shooting and that most of those killed had been shot in the back.[85]

It is very difficult to assess these accounts in retrospect and in a sense it is not important who fired first and why, given the long history of tension and ill-feeling which led up to this incident. The only undisputed facts are the tragic ones of death and injury: twenty-three people were killed and at least forty were injured.[86] In addition, some seven hundred people were arrested, and government forces confiscated large quantities of arms, among them forty-four flint-lock guns and a revolver. The Karaga-Na and Yo-Na were brought before a court and bound over to keep the peace for twelve months, and they, along with Andani's brothers, the Tampion-lana and Pisigu-lana, were banned from Yendi.

On the night of 12/13 September, Mohamadu Abudulai was escorted to the *katini duu* and finally installed as paramount of Dagomba. A heavy military guard was provided and during the preceding day a helicopter was used to keep watch on the movement of crowds. There was no trouble, however, and following the enskinment the government gradually relaxed its control of the town. Following protests from the N.A.L. (which demanded an enquiry into the shootings) and an appeal from the Northern Region House of Chiefs, Dr Busia invited the four banned chiefs to Accra.[87]

Although the Yo-Na and Karaga-Na seemed content with the results of their meeting with Busia, the two Andani chiefs were not. At a press conference given in the house of an opposition M.P., they denounced the enskinment of Mohamadu as Ya-Na. In consultation with Ibrahim Mahama, they petitioned the government for a referendum in Dagomba on the succession and repeated the opposition's demand for an enquiry. The two chiefs declared: 'We and our people who constitute more than half of the population of Dagbon should not be exchanged for Mohamadu, Tolon-Na, and Mr B. A. Yakubu, who have no following in Dagbon, and who want to reverse the course of history.'[88]

The government refused to order an enquiry, although it did agree to a debate in the National Assembly on its handling of the Yendi crisis. During this debate, members on both sides blamed the troubles on interference by 'politicians' in chieftaincy matters. Daniel Bayensi, a northern P.P. member, declared: 'Some misguided politicians have sought to make themselves chieftaincy contractors...it is imperative that the institution of chieftaincy should be raised above party politics and not left to the whims and caprices of misguided politicians who masquerade as princes.'[89] In the same vein, Abudulai Yakubu, Zangballon-Na and N.A.L. member for Savelugu, remarked: 'I really regret that the custom of the Dagombas has been mingled with politics.'[90] At the end of the debate, the Assembly accepted a motion which, while conveying its sympathies to the wounded and its condolences to the bereaved, nevertheless commended the government for 'the prompt and efficient manner in which it handled the Yendi Affairs'.

THE KINGDOM SINCE 1969

By the end of the year most of the government troops had left Yendi and a rather fragile peace descended on the town and the provinces of Dagomba.

There have, however, been certain developments since December 1969, some of which suggest the possibility of further conflict in the kingdom.

Apart from Mohamadu Abudulai, the most immediate beneficiary of the new regime was the policeman B. A. Yakubu. On 27 September 1969 Yakubu was appointed Inspector-General of Police and held this post until June 1971. In February 1971 he was nominated as Gushie-Na by the new king and, on retiring from the police in June, he moved up to Gushiegu.[91] Thus, after twenty-five years' absence, Yakubu returned to his home town as a senior divisional chief and took the skin which his brother had vacated. He immediately set to work building a large new palace, with the proceeds from the generous pension awarded to him as a former member of the N.L.C. Among the buildings under construction in 1971 were an assembly hall to seat a thousand people and stables to hold two horses and three cars, including a Pontiac and a Mercedes-Benz.

The Tolon-Na, Yakubu Tali, also flourished. He was relatively untouched by the purges conducted against C.P.P. activists and, after a period in retirement from public life, he resumed his career as a diplomat and in 1972 became High Commissioner to Sierra Leone and (from 1973) Ambassador to Guinea.[92] Salifu Yakubu was detained by the N.L.C. and subsequently investigated for corruption. Though required to repay a substantial amount of money thought to have been improperly obtained, he had by 1971 become a prosperous farmer at Savelugu with an impressive quantity of mechanical equipment and a large acreage under cash-crops.

Allassani, disgraced after the 1966 *coup*, was much less fortunate. He found himself evicted from his house and, as he told Busia, he and his family 'constructed a shed with old aluminium sheets' which some friends had provided. 'So,' he said, 'Yakubu and his people had achieved their goal. I was now a homeless pauper. God's open sky was now the roof over our heads.'[93]

In Dagomba itself, the king and his supporters used their victory to reward friends and punish enemies. The Ya-Na became a member of the Council of State of Ghana in September 1969 and in May 1970 he was elected president of the Northern Region House of Chiefs. With his assent, the Kuga-Na, Karaga-Na Adam, and Kumbung-Na Osumanu were excluded from the Dagomba State Council for failure to attend its meetings: as a consequence of this exclusion, the two divisional chiefs were expelled from the Northern Region House of Chiefs. In this way, Mohamadu Abudulai punished those who had opposed his selection in November 1968. The Yo-Na, however, made his peace with the king, swearing allegiance to him in June 1970.[94]

Andani's son, Yakubu Andani, who had been injured during the shootings of September 1969, was also excluded from power. The Abudus demanded that his father's body should be exhumed from its grave in the palace at Yendi and taken back to Mion. Although orders to this effect were apparently given by B. A. Yakubu on 14 September 1969, it seems that, fearing further disturbances, the authorities resisted the pressure for a reburial. Nevertheless, instead of appointing Yakubu Andani to his father's skin, the

Ya-Na promoted his great-uncle, the Sang-lana, to Mion, thus blocking any promotion for his rival's son.[95]

However, further consolidation by the Abudus was stopped by the *coup* of 13 January 1972, which brought to power Colonel I. K. Acheampong and his National Redemption Council. Busia, deposed (according to modern custom) while out of the country, went into exile in Oxford and a large number of Progress Party members (including Shanni Mahama, M.P. for Yendi and a Ministerial Secretary in Busia's government) were taken into detention.

Meanwhile, Colonel Amadu Iddissah, a member of the Regional Committee of Administration in 1968, returned to power as Regional Commissioner in Tamale.[96] Three days after the coup Iddissah announced at Yendi that the National Redemption Council was 'not out to enskin or dis-enskin chiefs', adding that such matters were the sole concern of traditional authorities. On 20 January 1972 he felt compelled to make a further statement, in which he remarked that his Yendi speech had

apparently been misconstrued in certain quarters to mean that the N.R.C. was giving formal recognition to the Ya-Na. I would like to state that this is not the time for the N.R.C. to get itself involved in chieftaincy disputes. . .the N.R.C. will not interfere in traditional matters.[97]

Nevertheless, it was noticed that the administration had a way of seating Yakubu Andani next to the Ya-Na on public occasions and of introducing him to visiting dignitaries. It was assumed by many people that, given the close connection between the Abudus and Dr Busia's regime, the accession to power of the new military government would inevitably lead to a re-examination of the decisions taken in 1969. The Andanis, indeed, immediately began to petition for posthumous recognition of Andani as paramount.

Given the humiliation suffered by the Andani gate and its allies under Busia, attempts at mediation by army officers had small hope of success, especially since Ibrahim Mahama, a major opponent of Busia, had renewed his demands for a fresh examination of the Yendi dispute. In the summer of 1972 the N.R.C. was persuaded to establish yet another committee of enquiry into Yendi affairs, this time under the chairmanship of Mr Justice N. A. Ollennu, former Speaker of the National Assembly and a highly respected member of the Ghanaian elite.

So once more lawyers were hired, evidence was collected, and money was gathered from the chiefs and commoners of Dagomba, to present once again the cases of the two royal gates. The cycle of pseudo-traditional dispute had started all over again, each side passionately invoking the support of custom, each indignantly attacking the political involvements of its rival, and each assiduously courting the leaders of national government. Beneath their passions, complaints, and contradictions, the two sides were united by an untarnished devotion to the status and authority of chieftaincy, the pursuit of which still seemed to be the consuming preoccupation of all Dagombas of appropriate age and rank.

CHAPTER 10

CONCLUSIONS

> Insofar as the past has been transmitted as tradition, it possesses
> authority; insofar as authority presents itself historically, it
> becomes tradition.[1]

Any study of social behaviour, if conducted with at least minimal realism, ends up facing certain irreducible ambiguities of individual behaviour. The exercise is, nevertheless, worth undertaking, because on the way we should acquire a clearer definition of the problems and choices before the participants and an enhanced ability to conceptualise other, comparable situations. This, as I understand it, is the justification of comparative politics; it is also the point of this book.

It remains, therefore, to extract from the preceding account an assessment which must include two elements: an assessment of the case itself and an assessment of its significance within the wider field of comparative studies. The first is the more delicate evaluation of the two, for it necessarily prompts questions of personal responsibility and judgement. These questions are especially pointed in the present case, for the reason that the denouement involved death or serious injury for over sixty men, women, and children. It would be as naïve to conclude that this tragedy was the abstract responsibility of impersonal forces as it would be to suppose that it could be blamed on one or two individuals. An observer, certainly one having the privileged immunity – and inadequate knowledge – of an outsider in transit, should, nevertheless, not presume to allot responsibility. I have, in any case, tried to show that responsibility in the Yendi dispute is diffuse (though, again, not insignificant) and, in my view, it certainly extends further back in time than most participants seem to believe.[2] As for individual cases, I leave these to the reader to judge.

The case-study itself illuminates several major themes in colonial and post-colonial politics. Perhaps the most striking feature of Dagomba political history has been the resilience and adaptability of the chiefly class. I have tried to contrast the turbid atmosphere of intrigue which surrounded pre-colonial state politics with the air of aseptic improvement which flowed around the office of the District Commissioner. The contrast may be overstated, but it is quite clear that there was a pronounced discrepancy between the values, goals, and assumptions of the Dagomba ruling class and those of British officials. Moreover, this discrepancy was emphasised rather than eroded by indirect rule. Without disparaging the sincerity or the benevolent intentions of the officers concerned, it is evident that indirect rule was ambiguous as a formula of self-government and ineffectual as a strategy for change. It did not really alter the distribution of power within the colony and it did not lead to the development of a new and more integrated political structure.

For, despite its philosophical ramifications, indirect rule was essentially an administrative strategy, designed (like other forms of native administration) to maximise the assimilation of indigenous structures to the bureaucratic principles of colonial government. Like other policies, it was concerned with establishing clear, authoritative hierarchies, a fixed and explicit allocation of functions, and reliable, impersonal procedures for the transfer of office. In this context, the conventional distinctions between different schools or traditions of native administration must seem both formal and superficial. As Klein rightly remarks, 'Both the French and the British governed indirectly inasmuch as they remained outside the societies they ruled, operating through and dependent on the chiefs. But both governed directly insofar as they kept real power in their own hands.'[3] The inherently administrative character of indirect rule produced the paradox, noted in a recent study of north-west Tanzania, that assertions of commitment to local self-rule were accompanied by continued devaluation of the political mechanisms which had ensured the dynamism of traditional government. In Ralph Austen's formulation: 'The more colonial native policy, the less African tribal politics.'[4]

The desire to depoliticise indigenous government did not, in fact, eliminate the competition for office and its attached benefits which had marked politics in the pre-colonial kingdom. To a certain extent, it may actually have increased competition, since under indirect rule the authority of the chiefs was actively sustained by the government and was protected against challenge by the Native Authority Ordinance. The authority of the monarchy in particular was entrenched and the elders of Yendi took command of the administration of the Dagomba Native Authority.

The natural consequence of this trend was, in the sphere of dynastic politics, to encourage the attempt, underlying the current dispute, to establish primogeniture in succession to the Yendi skin. The possibility of such a development was always present in the Dagomba system. Its emergence was dependent on one line within the royal family acquiring sufficient power and wealth to exclude its rivals from office until, by the operation of the established rules governing eligibility, they no longer had the right to compete. It is arguable that indirect rule, by enhancing the power of Yendi, gave the Abudulai gate, which controlled the kingdom for eighteen years between the wars, the vital advantage over its main competitor.

It has consolidated this advantage ever since, notably by effecting constitutional changes which allowed the regent to succeed directly to the royal skin and which widened the group of selectors to include divisional chiefs. The latter could reasonably be expected to support the innovation concerning the selection committee, since it increased their status and diminished the power of the (illiterate) Yendi elders. Moreover, the change had a (spurious) 'democratic' quality which appealed not only to the British administration but also to the more educated junior members of the royal family (many of them members of the Abudu gate), as well as to their commoner allies and clients. Politically, the change in selection procedure could fairly be expected to work to the advantage of the Abudu gate, for most of those co-opted into the new committee were, through the normal operation of royal patronage over many years, either members or clients of the ruling line.

In a wider context, the movement towards primogeniture was also congruent with the general trend towards removing chieftaincy from the arena of 'politics', insofar as it would reduce the scope for 'disputes' and related 'agitation'. However, it is clear that no such neat outcome has occurred and, indeed, it would be opposed by those who favour the regulation of succession by democratic and other competitive means. The present state of relations between central government and 'traditional' authorities is, therefore, confused and ambiguous.

Indirect rule enabled chieftaincy to survive into the period when, through the advent of elective assemblies and political parties, the local arena became a crucial focus of conflict and ambition in national politics. The pattern of relationships involved in local politics, and in communication between centre and periphery, became as a result more complex. Intricate networks of alliance were formed between patrons and clients at national and local levels to exploit the opportunities for advancement and exchange presented by a political structure of singular incoherence. Parochial matters surfaced in the agenda of civilian cabinets and military councils, while the fortunes of national governments could affect the most mundane issues in local politics. Thus the N.L.C. became riven by a dispute over procedure governing the selection of a northern chief, while the fall of Nkrumah led, directly and explicitly, to a re-allocation of butchering days between two Muslim butchers in Yendi.[5]

At first glance, such incidents might seem to indicate a quite phenomenal degree of political integration, but the impression is deceptive. Indeed, not only are linkages of this kind intermittent but they in fact reveal the lack of stable institutional arrangements. In part, this lack expresses persistent discontinuity between national and local politics, a discontinuity which is itself a product of uneven development and internal inequalities. Ghana, like Uganda, is 'a nation of competing sub-systems'.[6] In this competition, Dagomba has, in the final analysis (an analysis made, no doubt with relentless frequency), relatively little leverage where the time and money of central government are concerned. Admittedly, under civilian government the kingdom represented a substantial reservoir of votes for party politicians. But if it seems brutal to suggest that the concern shown by Nkrumah, Busia, and Gbedemah for Dagomba affairs stemmed only from electoral considerations, how much more brutal was the subsequent military intervention of September 1969 as a revelation of the inferior consideration accorded to the north. Dependence may be a fact of life for local politicians throughout Ghana, but some areas are undoubtedly more persuasive and successful mendicants than others.

Also, into the general throng, some can dispatch more delegates than others. Dagomba has a meagre stock of potential 'brokers', bearing with them a fairly humble range of wares (the most valued of which seems to be their skill in making the inside pages of *Le Monde Diplomatique*). Brokers are, in fact, the main beneficiaries of the cultural gap which exists between the world of Dagomba village and court life and the world of Ministries and committees in Accra. The latter is still regarded by Dagomba parochialists with some unease and, as under colonial administration, the government is seen as a beast of uncertain temper, best approached at an oblique angle and then only by persons suitably equipped for the task. Where possible, the creature is to be given space to reflect and ruminate and it should always be addressed in the manner to which it is accustomed: hence the use of emissaries and the incessant dispatch of letters and petitions. Above all, it must not be gratuitously ill-treated: the Dagomba royals have made it clear to the M.P.s whom they regard as their delegates that wilful opposition to 'the government of the day' is short-sighted folly. (Only in such a culture would it be possible to head a letter 'Crossing the carpet', as if to indicate the operation of a routine administrative procedure.)

The prominence and power of unofficial brokers thus reflects the absence of a stable and clearly articulated political structure in Ghana. The instability of national governments has tended to weaken even the structure which exists, since it has aggravated the propensity of competing interests to attempt conclusive and annihilating pre-emptive strikes against their opponents while fortune, plus a few battalions, is on their side.

The incoherence of centre–periphery relations is matched by a confusion regarding the functions and boundaries of different institutional hierarchies. As Kilson writes:

In Ghana and elsewhere in Africa no small part of the problem of the institutionalization of political order is a 'boundary problem' ... the sacred or non-secular constituents of sociopolitical relations are poorly distinguished, functionally speaking, from the secular. Above all, the political uses of sacred constituents of group interaction are ill-defined; there are few rules, norms, and habits in regard to what mixture of secular and sacred constituents of group interaction is allowed.[7]

A particularly interesting way of approaching this 'boundary problem' consists, I believe, in examining the vocabulary used by participants when describing relations between the relevant structures and when justifying their own actions and preferences. I shall end this study by considering two terms which have dominated arguments about Dagomba affairs from the 1920s until the present day. The first is 'politics'; the second is 'tradition'.

'Politics', as we have seen, is used in a restricted, pejorative, and rather formalistic sense, to mean competitive manoeuvres and processes properly taking place outside the realm of 'traditional' government and therefore, by implication, originating outside the local arena altogether (since Ghana is, after all, an amalgam of 'traditional areas'). It is not seen as a natural or permanent phenomenon, but as an occasional, unsought, and even un-controllable occurrence, rather like the insurance companies' 'Acts of God' or an attack of flu. This idiosyncratic usage is not unique to Dagomba or Ghana.[8] For example, current writing on Nigeria frequently refers to some-thing called 'the return to politics' and in the Ivory Coast informants re-counting to me the glories of activism against the French often identified a particular incident with the remark, 'Ça, c'était pendant le temps de politi-que' (that was long ago).

This usage occurred frequently in the Parliamentary debate on Yendi affairs in December 1969. A typical case appears in a speech by a northern P.P. member, Adam Amandi: 'The unfortunate new phase of this problem is that the unscrupulous and uninformed politician has stepped in and he is usually out for an ill-conceived advantage ... certain politicians unwisely and incautiously interfered with the performance of these duties' (i.e. the duties of selecting a Ya-Na).[9] It is obvious that the analysis of such speeches should proceed with wise and cautious regard to context: that is, the voca-bulary used by politicians, like Mr Amandi, should be seen as an instrument of persuasion, and its significance arises from the purposes, and the audience, envisaged by the speaker.

For many of those who attack 'politics' and 'politicians' can be shown to have themselves engaged in manoeuvres of a 'political' kind in relation to chieftaincy: such, indeed, constitute a major focus of factional and (when appropriate) party activity at local level throughout West Africa. The in-teresting point is that such manoeuvres come within the 'pragmatic' rather than the 'normative' sphere of political competition: many people practise 'meddling in chieftaincy affairs', but none (to my knowledge) actually preaches it. For the normative (or jural) rule is that chieftaincy is a matter for 'traditional authorities' and 'administration'.[10] But because in reality chiefs still have authority and exercise power (i.e. are, in the wider sense, 'political' figures), the formal separation of 'traditional' and 'political' spheres has to a great extent been disregarded by chiefs and politicians alike. The distinction is, in short, usually invoked only when it is to some-body's advantage (and somebody else's disadvantage) to do so: it is rarely observed, even (or least of all) by those who proclaim it most loudly. His-torically, the distinction is a legacy from the days of indirect rule: that it is still an effective weapon in the rhetorical armoury of Ghanaian politicians is further evidence of the uncertainty and ambiguity which have charac-terised more recent attempts to define central–local relations and the res-pective spheres of 'traditional' and 'political' institutions.

The current status of the term 'tradition' is implied in the preceding analysis. 'Tradition' is a publicly acknowledged value: everybody holds that it is a Good Thing. But in the Dagomba case it is virtually impossible to obtain a generally acceptable account of its content (it may, indeed, be naïve to try). Neither side in the Yendi dispute could really claim to have 'tradition' unequivocally on its side. The Abudu gate's case rested on con-stitutional innovations made under colonial government: these are said to be 'traditional' either because they were a formalisation of earlier practice (which is doubtful) or because they were approved by a 'traditional' body, the Dagomba State Council. Neither argument carries the moral force which an appeal to 'tradition' generally bestows. The Andanis had a stronger 'traditional' case in arguing that selection by the elders and soothsayers was the norm; but, then, this practice was abolished by the official 'traditional' authority in 1948. In what sense, therefore, was it still 'traditional' thereafter? Further, they claimed as 'traditional' the rule of rotation between the gates. But 'gates' are temporary phenomena, created by the development of the royal dynasty; and the rule limiting eligibility to the royal dukes did not imply a rule of circulating succession, with each duke succeeding in turn to the royal skin. Nor was it clear that occupation of a particular gate skin conferred a right of precedence over occupants of the other two gate skins.

To point out such discrepancies is not, of course, to suggest that 'tradition' is either a mirage or a fraud. It is, however, to suggest that it lacks the permanence, clarity, and immutability intrinsic to objects of sacred devotion. The point, indeed, is so obvious that it would scarcely be worth making, were it not that 'tradition' has figured so prominently in African politics and, in the Dagomba case, has been a matter of such bitter and enduring dispute. It is, therefore, necessary to distinguish again between the normative and the pragmatic: between traditionalism as a formal, public value and pseudo-traditionalism as a rhetorical device and a technique of political manipulation.

The recasting and selective use of tradition (or myth) is not a new phenomenon in West Africa. Nadel, for example, commented that the Nupe (another people under royal government) used 'objective' history in an 'ideological' form: that is, like any other people, they developed an official history which, to an observer, embodied 'a system of accepted beliefs and traditions influencing social behaviour in the group'.[11] Whether such history is 'true' or 'false' is, for sociological (and indeed political) purposes, rather beside the point: it is an ideological construct, moulded by the imperatives of legitimising and protecting the state and its supporting social order. The 'drum history' of Dagomba – a state originating in conquest and incorporating distinct and alien social strata – could be interpreted in a similar manner. We have noted, for instance, how its accounts of royal succession in this century attribute responsibility for selecting Ya-Nas to the colonial administration. Such attribution may have been 'objectively' false, but 'ideologically' it served the function of minimising tension within the Dagomba ruling class.

Pseudo-traditionalism is not, therefore, a new phenomenon. Tradition has always been made to serve 'political' ends, and politics has always been intrinsic to 'traditional' government. What is new is the context and the complexity of pseudo-traditionalism as practised under colonial and post-colonial governments. It involves manipulation of a diverse, unfamiliar, and unstable set of interests and connections, often by indirect and unreliable means, in a setting which is wide and, at its limits, remote. Such a process is both more complicated in character and less predictable in its outcome than a superficial analysis in terms of 'tradition versus modernity' might suggest. It does not necessarily either serve or subvert goals of 'political integration', 'nation-building', or 'development'. It merely serves, as it is intended to, the interests of some participants in Dagomba politics, and undermines the interests of others. It also demonstrates the resilience and vitality of chieftaincy and politics in contemporary Ghana, as well as the support which chiefs and politicians mutually provide. The Lions of Dagbon are not dead yet; and they certainly have not been put in a reserve.

POSTSCRIPT

As is the way with such books, this study became out of date within five days of the final dispatch of the manuscript. On 23 April 1974 the government of Ghana published a White Paper based on the report of the Ollennu Committee (a report which was not itself published). In accordance with the committee's findings, the government stated that Mohamadu Abudulai had not been correctly selected or enskinned and that, as a result, his appointment was null and void. Conversely, the government acknowledged that Andani had been duly chosen as Ya-Na in 1968. It further accepted the committee's view that the proper method of selection for the Yendi skin was that involving the use of soothsayers, and it affirmed the existence of a rule of rotation between the gates in occupation of the skin. The '1948 selection committee' was declared invalid.

The White Paper prescribed that the funeral of Andani should be carried out at Yendi at the end of May and that a new paramount should then be selected from the Andani side of the royal family. It laid down that, meanwhile, the order banning certain members of the Andani gate from access to the capital should be revoked. The Gushie-Na, B. A. Yakubu, and the Gulkpe-Na, Alhassan Iddi, were simultaneously removed from office and the government took charge of property attaching to the two skins.

During May funerals were held for the deceased Kuga-Na and Zohe-Na and new elders appointed in anticipation of the selection of a new Ya-Na, to take place on 31 May. Strict security measures were imposed in Yendi, though on this occasion the government took a number of precautions before announcing its decisions. Colonel Acheampong saw both Mohamadu Abudulai and the Gushie-Na to inform them of the contents of the White Paper, and the deposed king was persuaded to remain in Accra until the installation of his successor was completed. In Yendi the police stopped a victory march through the town by supporters of the Andani gate.

The funeral of Andani began with the arrival of Kumbung-Na Sumani Issa in Yendi after a seventy-mile journey on horseback. According to *West Africa*, the Kumbung-Na, 'in war dress and wearing many talismans, was accompanied by his traditional army, some with bows and arrows, some with guns . . . The regalia he carried to Yendi included the legendary bees used by the Dagomba to fight past wars, and the historical giant bow and quiver of arrows.'

Following Andani's funeral, the Kuga-Na and the other 'traditional king-makers' met and consulted diviners. They then announced that the new Ya-Na was to be Andani's son, Yakubu Andani, then Kampakuya-Na. The 30-year-old king, who took the title 'Yakuba II', was escorted to the *katini duu* and enskinned, to cries of 'Hail the Lion' and 'Ruler of Grasses and Trees'. A young Andani gate regent was thus established in place of a young Abudulai gate regent and, once more, by virtue of central government inter-vention.

APPENDIXES

APPENDIXES

1. SELECTION PROCEDURE FOR YENDI: THE 1930 CONSTITUTION

No grandsons of a Na have ever yet succeeded to the Nam of Yendi.

10. The Paramount Chief of Yendi, i.e. of Dagbon, is chosen from the holder of the Chieftainship of

KARAGA
MION
SAVELUGU

METHOD OF ELECTION

The Gushie-Na, the Kuga-Na, the Tuguri-Nam and the Gomli form the committee of selection. All these candidates present themselves for selection and recourse is made to the spirits of the dead Chiefs, the cult of whom is controlled by the Gulkpe-Na, Baghali-Na and the Kuga-Na and, from the results of a sacrifice, it is decided which of the candidates is the possessor of a 'good head', i.e., the man whom the spirits desire. Having been selected the candidate is taken into a dark room by the Zohe-Na where he is made to choose one of a number of staves which he cannot see. These staves are believed to be imbued with the souls of the dead Chiefs and according to the stave chosen so does the soul of the respective dead Chief enter into the body of the new Na. He, the Na elected, remains in this dark room for some days, during which time the actual investiture takes place. The object primarily conferring the power on the newly-elected Na is the 'Bolon' [,] a lump of wood which is kept by the Chief of Kpatia and which is brought from there to Yendi for the investiture by the Togasi-Nam [sic] and the Gomli who are the only other persons who may touch or ever see this highly sacred object. When seated upon the 'Bolon', the Na is stripped of all his clothes, and washed, from which moment he becomes a Bumbiogo (an object of Tabu).

He is then invested with the beads and the hat in which the secondary power lies.

SOURCE: Duncan-Johnstone and Blair (1932), pp. 29, 31–2.

2. SPEECH BY SIR ARNOLD HODSON (GOVERNOR OF THE GOLD COAST)
AT DURBAR, NAVRONGO, NORTHERN TERRITORIES, 16 MAY 1940
(extracts)

[The Governor began by thanking the people of the N.T. for their contributions to the war effort.]

I must also thank you for the splendid response you have made to our war Charity Fund. As you know, you will soon have your own ambulances in France and these will be marked with your own names so that the people who are fighting in France will remember you for the good you have done.

[The Governor went on to provide an account of the historical background of the war.]

I want to try ... to convey to you a picture of what is happening in the world. In the last war, as you all remember, England and France beat the Germans. And they had the Germans at their mercy. They could have killed all the men and swept all the cities away, but the English and the French people are very merciful, so they met at a place called Versailles and at that place a solemn treaty was drawn up. The Germans swore by their fetish and their great Oath that they will abide by the treaty; so when the Germans have sworn that Oath the English and French did not kill them or destroy their cities but they said you are not to rearm; you are not to build canoes that shoot or the ships that fly in the air and kill, but we will give you money and you can trade and you can go to other parts of the world and trade as our own subjects. The piece of country called the Rhineland you must not fortify because it is on the borders of the French line.

As you all know, the English and French do not like war; so when this treaty was signed they said now we will go back and plant our yams and be with our wives. We will break up a lot of our war canoes and we will go back to our planting and doing good. We made a great mistake in believing the Germans. Seven years went by and we heard whispers that the Germans were rearming. People said they had great factories where they were building war canoes and arms and that they were making ships in the air which kill and they are doing very bad things.

[The Germans then moved into the Rhineland.] So the French chiefs and the British chiefs went to Hitler and they said why have you broken the great Oath sworn on the fetish. Hitler said that I am not going to break any more oaths so let me stay where I am and I will do nothing more. The English and French believed him and we went on with our farming and trade.

[Hitler then moved into Austria.] The poor little boys in the schools and the Girl Guides were shot down because they did not like the Germans in their country ... The girls and boys were killed because they said down with Hitler ... Again France and England went to Hitler and said, What have you done again; why have you broken the great oath on the fetish.

[Hitler met Chamberlain at Munich and said] I swear again on the great fetish that I will not take any part of the world and this time he actually wrote it on a piece of paper and gave one to the French and one to the English.

[Hitler took Czechoslovakia.] After this England and France started to rearm really. The English people were called from their yam fields and from their families. They stopped playing golf, cricket, football and they worked night and day.

SOURCE: On file, N.A.G.T., ADM. 2/29; uncorrected.

3. PETITION FROM UNKNOWN DAGOMBA CITIZEN TO C.C.N.T.

YENDI N.T.

24 December 1947

This petition lies from an unknown Dagomba citizen to His Honour the Chief Commissioner, Northern Territories.

1. Your humble petitioner begs to state, with an undaunting trust, that though he chooses to conceal his name, you will take his plain facts, which a white man can never know among Africans, as a guide to the management of native affairs within Dagbon: –

2. That if the leaders really have it as their aim to have this land delivered from the rule of illiterates, a list should be prepared of literate sons of the chiefs, and there is no doubt the list will shew names of mostly grandchildren of Ya-Nas, well trained in literatecy [sic]: and if their fathers are debarred from reaching the skins of Mion, Karaga, and Savelugu how on earth can we have literates in the administration of Dagbon.

3. That if the Dagomba history of the enquiry into the Dagomba constitution states that no grand son of Ya Na has ever aspired to the skin of Yendi it does not follow, that they do not go as far up to the three main heads of Karaga, Mion, and Savelugu. There are instances when grandsons have been – e.g., Allassani, Bukari, and Zibilim Karaga chiefs. Mahama alias Piage, Abudulai and even Pusamli who was a contender for Savelugu.

4. That formerly, when a chief died, the Ya-Na watched and listened to his elders, before choosing a suitable prince to a vacant skin, but now he chooses either his sons or his relatives irrespective of ableness, simply because he wants after his death to have the whole of Dagbon ruled by his sons and relatives. If a review is made, of the rule of Ya-Na Abudulai II, it will reveal a fact that he appointed the present Ya-Na to Mion and his brother Yakubu to Savelugu, though he had brothers and sons of equal right to rule at those places.

5. That the present Ya-Na, wholes [holds] it, that references to the two main ruling branches the Abudulai side ruled for forty years and likewise Andani's side should do the same. That period of course was God's wish and should not be a rule. This is the main reason why at this present reign he appoints to the present vacant skin of Karaga his own first son; with the view that after his death when he becomes Gbong-lana he will automatically become a Ya-Na in his stead, whether he is suitable or not.

6. Ya-Na Allassani put the late Na Abudulai to Mion, when he was still alive, and when he died he became Gbong-lana and remained in the skin. This is a wrong conception – for after the death of Mion-lana Kalim, the Dagbomba land was divided into two by the two powers of English and German. There was not an eligible prince near by, so Na Abudulai was appointed Mion-lana. After the death of Na Allassani the land was still under the division, so Na Abudulai remained Gbong-lana for many years until after the 1914 war when Dagbon came under the rule of the English. At the meeting with the Chief Commissioner and the Dagomba chiefs, Na Abudulai as Gbong-lana declared, that he was keeping the skin of Yendi for his father Bukari Yo-Na, the brother of the present Ya-Na to come for his inheritance. He refused it on the grounds, that he was old and that there was no use uprooting an old tree and emplanting same in its stead.

7. That if the white man stand out and say we are left to our custom many of us are suffering a great deal within the British rule, a thing of course unknown to the British blood. What was formerly known in Dagbon was that when a Ya-Na chose a village needing a chief and stayed in the chief house waiting for the Ya-Na to bring his favourite – the result was war. But during this time such cannot be. Therefore an agreed arrangement should be made, ignoring the former constitution written down, when Dagomba was still very dark, and when poor interpreters were a cause to some mistakes. When Na Yakubu chose Sunson-Na Yahaya (Kundawumda) for Karaga, Adama seized the chieftainship of Karaga from him after a war.

8. That for the fact, that no grandson has ever aspired to Yendi skin does not mean it does harm to the state or the people, but no chance has yet fallen again after the reign of one grandson. For our present generation we as Dagombas, are not

going to be silent to be ruled by unable princes, if there happens to be a sensible and able grandson. History tells us that Nanumbas, Mamprusis and Dagombas come from the same Na Gbewa. Well, in the case of Nanumbas there has been a period of not less than fifty years when grandsons have been ruling without any harm. This is the reason why the Dagomba paramount chiefs fear to appoint grandsons to higher chieftainships to eliminate the happening in Nanumba. This of course is mere selfishness; and the selfishness will certainly retard our progress on the principle of modern civilisation.

9. I hope after reading this petition His Honour the Chief Commissioner and the District Commissioner will on due consideration investigate and put things right at their earliest convenience expedient before worse comes to worst.

> I have the honour to be, Sir,
> Your humble petitioner,
> AN UNKNOWN DAGOMBA CITIZEN

SOURCE: N.A.G.T., ADM. 1/382; uncorrected.

4. THE DECLARATION OF CUSTOMARY LAW (DAGOMBA STATE) ORDER, 1960 (LEGISLATIVE INSTRUMENT 59, 25 AUGUST 1960)

Whereas the Northern Region House of Chiefs, acting under the provisions of section 17 of the House of Chiefs Act, 1958, (No. 20), has made recommendations to the Minister for the Modification of the customary law relating to succession to the Yendi Paramount skin in the Northern Region;

And whereas the Minister is satisfied that the declaration of the customary law as contained in the said recommendations is not repugnant to the laws of Ghana as being contrary to natural justice, equity and good conscience;

Now therefore in exercise of the powers conferred upon the Minister of Justice by section 44 of the House of Chiefs Act, 1958, it is hereby directed with effect from the date hereof that:

1: Succession to the Yendi skin shall be in rotation among the Abudulai and the Andani ruling families.

2: Persons who are eligible to occupy the Skin shall be the sons of deceased or former Ya-Nas and who occupy one of the Skins of the towns of Mion, Savelugu, and Karaga; and accordingly sons of deceased or former Ya-Nas occupying skins other than those specified in this paragraph shall not be eligible for appointment to the Yendi Skin.

3: Whenever the present occupant of the Yendi Skin ceases to occupy the skin by reason of his death or any other customary cause, the person holding the title of Mion Lana at the date of this Order and who hails from the Andani family shall be the next Ya-Na. In the event of the present Mion Lana predeceasing the present Ya-Na, the next Mion Lana who shall be from the Andani family shall occupy the Ya-Na Skin.

4: Whenever the present Mion Lana dies his sons shall be regarded as the sons of a former or deceased Ya-Na and thereby qualified for the Ya-Na Skin in terms of paragraph (2) herein irrespective of whether or not he occupied the Ya-Na Skin before his death.

5: Candidates from the Abudulai family having twice in succession occupied the Ya-Na Skin, candidates from the Andani family shall occupy the skin twice in succession beginning with the death of Ya-Na Abudulai III and thenceforth the

181

customary law of succession by rotation shall proceed in the normal way: that is to say from the Abudulai family and thence from the Andani family.

6: In order to facilitate the application of the rule of alternation between the two ruling families of Abudulai and Andani there shall at any one time be at least one member from either family on one or other of the three skins of Mion, Savelugu and Karaga.

Whenever two candidates from either family become eligible simultaneously for appointment to the Yendi Skin, the senior one (i.e., the one who first occupied the skin of a 'Gate') shall be nominated for the skin.

> Made at Accra this 25th day of
> August 1960.

> A. E. A. OFORI-ATTA
> Minister of Justice

5. DOCUMENTS RELATING TO 'MODIFICATION OF CUSTOM', MAY 1961

(a) *Covering letter from Ya-Na to Clerk to Northern Region House of Chiefs*
My Ref. No. B6/88.

> State Council Office,
> Dagomba-State,
> Post Office Box 2,
> Yendi – N.G.
> 14 June 1961

ANTIQUATED CONSTITUTIONS, CUSTOMS
PROCEDURES IN TRADITIONAL AREAS

With reference to item 12/61 Minutes of the Dagomba State Council of 30 May 1961, I forward herewith a certified true copy of the succession to Yendi Skin (Paramountcy) vide letter No. 4900/56/128 of 8 July, 1960, from the Ministry of Local Government on the above subject, for your necessary action please.
This was unanimously approved by the State Council.

2. Three copies of the above are being sent to the Regional Commissioner – Tamale and the Minister of Local Government – Accra.

> I am,
> Yours faithfully,

> (Sgd.)   ABUDULAI III
>   YA-NA, PRESIDENT
>   DAGOMBA STATE COUNCIL

The Clerk to the Northern Region House
of Chiefs – *Tamale.*

cc. The Regional Commissioner – Tamale.
 The Minister of Local Gov't – Accra.
 To all State Council Members – Dagomba State.
 The District Commissioner – Yendi.
 The District Commissioner – Saboba.

The District Commissioner – Tamale.
The District Commissioner – Savelugu.

(b) *Statement of Custom, 30 May 1961*

SUCCESSION TO YENDI SKIN (PARAMOUNTCY)

Succession to Yendi Skin should not be in *rotation of any type* but by majority decision of the Selection Committee of the Dagomba State Council legally formed by the State Council in 1953, namely: –

The Gushiegu-Na	Divisional Chief
The Yelzori-Lana	" "
The Gulkpe-Na	" "
The Tolon-Na	" "
The Kumbungu-Na	" "
The Nanton-Na	" "
The Sunson-Na	" "
The Kuga-Na	Ya-Na's Elder
The Zohe-Na	" "
The Gagbin-dana	" "
The Tuguri-nam	Kuga-Na's Elder

The Selection should always be secret and properly recorded by the Selection Committee of the State Council. The choice or selection may be based on the candidates' Merit, Ability, and his respect for all. In addition, the candidate should have wide knowledge, and experience and should be ready to support the Government of the day. Lastly, the candidate should have 'GoodHead' which is well known to the Selection Committee *only*. (Seniority in age is not a criterion.)

2. Persons who are eligible to occupy the Yendi Skin shall be the occupants at the time of the Karaga Skin, Savelugu Skin, Mion Skin and the reigning Gbong-Lana, i.e. Regent of a deceased Ya-Na on the Yendi Skin after the death of the father. These three Dukedoms i.e. Karaga, Savelugu and Mion, may be filled either by *direct sons of deceased or former Ya-Nas, or their grandsons.* The Grandsons of the Ya-Nas are now eligible for the Skin of Yendi, but formerly they were not. By custom the Gbong-Lana of the deceased Ya-Na (whose father's vacant post is being contested) has the right to apply for his father's post (this has happened many times before in the history of the Dagomba Kingdom) regardless of whether he is a chief or Regent (Prince at the time).

3. It is important to note that there will not be any type of Gate system at all in Dagbon because all the Chiefs, princes, and princesses are from one Great Grand Father – Na Yakubu. It is worth noting also that a Ya-Na is never known before hand until after the death of a reigning Ya-Na. If one is not a *born Ya-Na* one can never become a Ya-Na. It is God's creation. It is generally believed that if one is not loyal to a reigning Ya-Na and faithful to the people of the Dagomba State one can never become a Ya-Na. It is a 'Taboo' to know who the next Ya-Na or the Ya-Na's deputy is going to be when there is a reigning Ya-Na.

(b) ORDER OF PRECEDENCE OF DUKEDOMS TO YENDI SKIN ARE AS FOLLOWS:

1. Karaga-Na
2. Savelugu-Na

   3. Mion-Lana

   4. Gbong-Lana (Reigning Regent of a deceased Ya-Na)

4. If the Reigning Regent (Gbong-Lana) loses his candidature he automatically occupies the Skin made vacant by the success of any of the three Dukes of Karaga, Savelugu or Mion. (That is to say supposing a Karaga-Na becomes the Ya-Na after the funeral of a Ya-Na has been performed, the Gbong-Lana (Regent) automatically succeeds the Karaga Skin by custom).

5.
SELECTION COMMITTEE

As soon as the Selection Committee appoints one of the four candidates i.e. the Karaga-Na, Savelugu-Na, Mion-Lana or the Reigning Regent (Gbong-Lana) he automatically becomes the Legal Ya-Na as from the date and time of his appointment. The successful candidate is informed officially by letter from the State Council, and by the Gushiegu-Na, Yelzori-Lana and Kuga-Na customarily.

6. A report is then sent to the Government through the District Commissioner, or any Government Representative holding such posts at the time of the appointment.

CUSTODIANS TO THE NAM OF YENDI

7. The necessary customary performances will then be done. But whether all performances are done or not the Selection Committee's appointment is final and the appointee becomes the recognised Ya-Na as from the date of the appointment.

   The most important custodians or King makers are the Tuguri-nam, Malle, Gulkpe-Na, Gagbindana, Kpati-Na, Gomli, Namo-Na, Akarima, Zohe-Na, Chong-Na, Mbadugu and Kikaa who should be present at the installation ceremony, when everybody is indoors at mid-night.

   These custodians or King makers can be represented in the performance of their customary duties and can be present themselves. In the absence of any of the above custodians at the installation ceremony the installation is still valid. The absentee can be asked to perform his duties at a later date, by the successful candidate who is the newly installed Ya-Na.

   It is here emphasised that these King Makers have no power to choose or appoint a Ya-Na. They are bound by custom to attend and perform their customary rites to the candidate at the installation ceremony. The Selection Committee's decision appointing the Ya-Na is what makes one the Ya-Na.

8. Destoolment of a properly appointed Ya-Na is a taboo in the Dagomba constitution. He is only said to be deposed when death takes him away. He cannot also abdicate.

9. There is no such thing as an election by the people themselves to Yendi Skin or any Dagomba Chieftainship. It is only by appointment either by the Ya-Na, Divisional Chiefs, or the Selection Committee, in the case of the Ya-Na.

LIST OF PERSONS WHO CAN ASPIRE TO KARAGA, SAVELUGU, MION MAINLY FROM
THE ROYAL BLOOD

1. Ya-Na Yakubu's	Grandsons	
2. Ya-Na Abudulai I's	"	
3. Ya-Na Andani's	Sons and grandsons	
4. Ya-Na Allassan's	"	"

5. Ya-Na Abudulai II's	Sons and grandsons
6. Ya-Na Mahama II's	" "
7. Ya-Na Mahama III's	" "
8. Ya-Na Abudulai III's	" "

And any other subsequent Ya-Nas.

10. All sons of former Chiefs of Karaga, Savelugu and Mion are also eligible to their father's posts. The appointment of the above is the responsibility of the reigning Ya-Na. There is no force that a particular candidate should be appointed. Priority is given to any obedient royalist or candidate who always serves the Na customarily and who respects the old and young in the Dagomba State. Efficiency, obedience, experience, and education is also taken into account, by the Ya-Na.

(Sgd.)   ABUDULAI III

YA-NA PRESIDENT OF
DAGOMBA STATE COUNCIL

SOURCE: Filed at Northern Region
House of Chiefs.

NOTES

---

1 The people refer to themselves as Dagbamba (sing. Dagbana) and to their kingdom as Dagbon; their language is Dagbane.

2 On the Konkomba, see Tait (1953), Tait (1958), and Tait (1961) (a full bibliography of Tait's writings on the Konkomba appears in the last work).

3 On the Chokosi, see Manoukian (1952), p. 55; Tait (1961), pp. 4, 8; Cornevin (1962), pp. 41, 131.

4 In 1960 the Dagomba represented 3.2 per cent of the population of Ghana (Ghana (1964), *Special Report 'E'*, *Tribes in Ghana*, pp. xxxiv, 5).

5 Gold Coast (1932), pp. 204, 220; Manoukian (1952), pp. 11–12; Hailey (1951), p. 261; Ghana (1967a), p. 124. The six constituencies were Tamale, Tolon, Savelugu, Mion–Nanton, Gushiegu, and Yendi; the latter two have a substantial Konkomba population.

6 After independence Tamale (previously the headquarters of the Northern Territories administration) became the capital of the Northern Region, governed by a Regional Commissioner. It is the major centre of communications for the north – on the main road from Kumasi to Bolgatanga (capital of the Upper Region) and served by shipping services on Lake Volta through the port of Yapei. On the present structure of Tamale, see Kumasi University of Science and Technology (1969).

7 In 1970 Tamale had, by contrast, five secondary institutions as well as two teacher training colleges (Bening (1971), p. 42).

8 Based on figures in Ghana (1967a), p. 124. In 1948 overall population density in the Dagomba District was 23.4 per square mile (18 per square mile in Eastern Dagomba, 36 per square mile in Western Dagomba).

9 Oppong (1965), p. 9; appendices, p. 5. Only nine villages in Dr Oppong's sample had populations of between 1,000 and 9,000.

10 Ghana (1964), *Special Report 'E'*, *Tribes in Ghana*, pp. 108, 112.

11 Average annual rainfall at Tamale is 43 inches (Ghana (1967b), p. 2). The dry season is from November until June and the rainy season, with breaks, from June until October. See Prussin (1969), p. 25.

12 Levtzion (1968), p. xii. Cf. Bourret (1949), p. 69.

13 Ghana (1964), *Special Report 'E'*, p. 90. Christine Oppong remarks, however, that during the early sixties an exodus of young men from the land was becoming apparent: 'The lure of wage labour has led many young men to the towns down south "SAAFA" to earn money to buy the luxuries they cannot get at home such as spring mattresses, radios, lamps, clothes, etc. Thus the agricultural force is depleted of those on whom it most depends' (Oppong (1965), p. 16). In 1960, there were 18,490 Dagombas resident in Ashanti and Brong–Ahafo, the main cocoa-growing areas of Ghana (Ghana (1964), *Special Report 'E'*, p. 5).

14 Ghana (1964), *Special Report 'E'*, p. 90.

15 *Ibid*, p. 60.

16 The main sources of Dagomba history are Tamakloe (1931); Rattray (1932) (especially vol. 2); Duncan-Johnstone and Blair (1932). Other sources dealing with the process and chronology of Dagomba settlement are Eyre-Smith (1933), p. 7; Fage (1964); Ferguson (1973), pp. 18–33; and Wilks (1971), pp. 348–9.

17 Levtzion (1968), p. xii. The singular is *tindana*.

18 Court history ('drum history') was collected by Tait, whose transcripts are held by

the Institute of African Studies, University of Ghana. One collection (referred to subsequently as 'Tait "A"') contains manuscripts entitled 'Na Gbewa Bihe' (the sons of Na Gbewa) and 'History of Ya Nanima Ya-Na Zirile to Ya-Na Mahamabila'. The other (cited subsequently as 'Tait "B"') is a manuscript entitled 'Dagomba Kings from Na Zajili to Na Al-Hassan'.

19 Fage (1964), pp. 177ff; Duncan-Johnstone and Blair (1932), p. 5; Cardinall (1925), pp. 3–4; Wilks (1971), pp. 347ff; Ferguson (1973), pp. 29–31. It was once suggested that the Dagomba were related to Egyptian Coptic exiles who had, supposedly, arrived in the area at some date before the fourteenth century (Tranakides (1953), pp. 34–44). This theory was rejected by Tait and there seems to be no empirical evidence for it (Tait and Strevens (1955), p. 195). Some administrators were attracted to the notion of an eastern origin (see, e.g., Eyre-Smith (1933), p. 6).

20 Fage (1964), pp. 177–8; Ferguson (1973), pp. 20, 30–1; Fage (1959), p. 22; Wilks (1971), p. 348. According to Cardinall, the migration was caused by famine in the north (Cardinall (1925), p. 3).

21 Ferguson (1973), pp. 21–8. There is disagreement between the sources on the number, sex, and order of Na Gbewa's children: see Manoukian (1952), p. 14; Rattray (1932), vol. 2, p. 562; Fage (1964), p. 184; Hilton (1962), pp. 80–1; Tait 'A'. On Yendi Dabari, see Shinnie and Ozanne (1962).

22 Ferguson (1973), pp. 22–7; Tait 'A'; Duncan-Johnstone and Blair (1932), p. 7; Tamakloe (1931), p. 16; Rattray (1932), vol. 2, p. 563.

23 Cardinall (1925), p. 16; Eyre-Smith (1933), p. 25. Cardinall also held that the Ya-Na would prostrate himself before the local *tindana* and would visit him dressed as a pauper – a view rejected by at least one of Cardinall's successors.

24 Ferguson suggests that the eastward movement began quite early, after the reign of Nyagse's grandson Datorli (Ferguson (1973), p. 34). Cf. Duncan-Johnstone and Blair (1932), p. 7; Tait (1961), p. 4.

25 Tait (1961), pp. 4, 8–10. On Konkomba origins in western Dagomba, see Tait and Strevens (1955), p. 206; on the military failure of Konkomba, see Tait (1953), pp. 220–1. Some Dagomba penetrated into Bassari country, where they acquired the chieftaincy of two cantons: later expeditions allegedly reached into the area now northern Dahomey (Cornevin (1962), pp. 41–2; Ferguson (1973), p. 34).

26 On Jakpa and Gonja, see Jones (1962); Wilks (1966); Goody (1967); El-Wakkad (1961–2).

27 Jones (1962), pp. 18–19; Wilks (1971), pp. 357, 362; Tamakloe (1931), pp. 19ff; Fage (1964), p. 180; Ferguson (1973), pp. 37–8; Manoukian (1952), pp. 14–15.

28 Ferguson (1973), pp. 38–9.

29 Wilks (1961); Wilks (1962); Goody (1964), pp. 201, 204; Goody (1966a). The Dagomba were active militarily in north-western Ghana before the Gonja invasion and it has been suggested that this activity was directed at control of trade and of gold-fields (Goody (1964), p. 201; Wilks (1971), pp. 351, 354).

30 Tait 'A'; Tamakloe (1931), pp. 18, 27; Rattray (1932), vol. 2, p. 564; Shinnie and Ozanne (1962), p. 88 (where 1650 is suggested as 'a likely date' for the abandonment of Yendi Dabari). Ferguson believes that the court finally settled at Yendi in the reign of Andani Sigili (in the first half of the eighteenth century) (Ferguson (1973), p. 192).

31 Tamakloe (1931), p. 27.

32 Duncan-Johnstone and Blair (1932), p. 10; Wilks (1971), p. 381; Gill (n.d.), p. 5; Tamakloe (1931), pp. 30–1.

33 Ferguson (1973), pp. 3, 87, 89–90; Wilks (1965); Wilks (1971), p. 384; Tamakloe (1931), p. 30; Oppong (1965), pp. 3–4.

34 Northcott (1899), p. 18. On the role of Muslim officials at court, see Ferguson (1973), pp. 192ff; Wilks (1971), p. 383.

35 Tait 'A'. Wilks points out a number of Muslim features of Dagomba culture, including use of the Muslim calendar, Muslim names, and Muslim forms of circumcision and burial. Muslim festivals have also been adopted, though in many instances they bear Dagbane names (Wilks (1965), p. 87).

36 Fage (1964), p. 180.
37 Duncan-Johnstone and Blair (1932), pp. 10–11; Tamakloe (1931), pp. 32–3; Wilks (1971), p. 377; Ferguson (1973), pp. 40, 216ff. There is little doubt that the invasion occurred in 1744–5, *pace* Tamakloe who suggests that it took place between 1697 and 1731.
38 For different accounts of the quantity of tribute, see Wilks (1961), p. 14; Rattray (1932), vol. 2, p. 564; Tamakloe (1931), pp. 32–3; Iliasu (1971), p. 56; Tait 'A' and 'B'.
39 Wilks (1961), p. 14; Wilks (1971), p. 377; Fage (1964), p. 180; Tamakloe (1931), p. 33. Cf. Ferguson (1973), p. 40, where it is argued that the Dagomba rulers 'in some sense accepted protectorate status'.
40 Tait 'A'.
41 Duncan-Johnstone and Blair (1932), p. 11.
42 Iliasu (1971), pp. 54, 58. Ferguson remarks that the 'commercial pre-eminence' of Dagomba dated from the reign of Gariba and was due to the links which he forged between Yendi and Kumasi. She also considers that 'Asante control over Dagomba affairs was of an indirect nature' (Ferguson (1973), pp. 225–6, 40–1).
43 Dupuis (1824), pt II, p. xxxix.
44 Bowdich (1819), p. 178.
45 *Ibid*, p. 235.
46 The Ya-Na is entitled to sit on a lion skin, whereas other chiefs sit on a heap of cows' skins: 'skin' is used figuratively, like 'throne', to refer to the office itself. Both Rattray and Tait emphasise the quantity of borrowing from Akan in Dagomba military usage (Rattray (1932), vol. 2, pp. 565–9; Tait and Strevens (1955), p. 195). Cf. Fage (1964), p. 180; Manoukian (1952), p. 58; Ferguson (1973), pp. 224–5.
47 Iliasu (1971), p. 58.
48 According to Tait, the brothers of Na Yakuba went to Kumasi and asked the Asantehene to insist on payment of tribute by their nephew, Ya-Na Abudulai. They hoped by embarrassing Abudulai to revenge themselves for his seizure of the skin (Tait 'A').
49 Ferguson and Wilks (1970), p. 343.
50 Binger (1892), vol. 1, p. 481. Cf. Ferguson (1973), p. 43.
51 Ferguson and Wilks (1970), p. 343.
52 On this period, see Tamakloe (1931), pp. 33–44; Gill (n.d.), pp. 6–10; Duncan-Johnstone and Blair (1932), p. 11; Fage (1964), p. 180.
53 Ferguson and Wilks (1970), pp. 326–7. In her thesis, Phyllis Ferguson argues that the increased power of the Ya-Na (symbolised by the growth of the bureaucracy) was a result of the move to Yendi, giving the paramount greater independence of the western Dagomba princes (Ferguson (1973), p. 39). She and Ivor Wilks also maintain that the monarchy was strengthened by the Ashanti connection (Ferguson and Wilks (1970), p. 342).
54 Ya-Na Sumani Zoli was killed by Yakuba, who became king in his place.
55 On the Zabarima, the best source is Holden (1965). Holden says that the Zabarima originally came from the area south-east of Niamey. It is not clear whether they came to Dagomba as mercenaries or came as traders and later became auxiliaries of the Dagomba army. Cf. Cardinall (1925), p. 9, and Tamakloe (1931), pp. 45–9.
56 Cardinall (1925), p. 10. Holden considers, however, that it was Dagomba rulers who invited the Zabarima to fight with them (Holden (1965), pp. 64–6).
57 Cardinall (1925), p. 9.
58 Tamakloe (1931), p. 42. 'The Dagbambas were killed in great numbers: heaps of dead bodies were to be found in all directions, with horses that fell under their riders' (*ibid*, pp. 42–3). Cf. Ferguson (1973), p. 44.
59 This section is largely based on the documents and commentaries in Metcalfe (1964) and on Cornevin (1969).
60 Metcalfe (1964), p. 433; Cornevin (1969), pp. 139, 151, 154.
61 Metcalfe (1964), p. 466.
62 *Ibid*, p. 466.
63 Cornevin (1969), pp. 148, 149.
64 Metcalfe (1964), pp. 471, 479–80, 487; Cornevin (1969), pp. 139, 151, 154.

65 Metcalfe (1964), pp. 487, 491–3; Cornevin (1969), pp. 149–52; Tamakloe (1931), pp. 42–3; Ferguson (1973), pp. 44–5.
66 Holden (1965), pp. 82–5; Ferguson and Wilks (1970), p. 344; Ferguson (1973), pp. 41, 45; Tamakloe (1931), pp. 54–5; Duncan-Johnstone and Blair (1932), p. 11.
67 Tamakloe (1931), p. 55.
68 Cited in Metcalfe (1964), p. 505.
69 Cornevin (1969), p. 155.
70 Cited in Metcalfe (1964), p. 504.
71 N. T. Administrative Ordinance, 1902; Hailey (1951), pt III, p. 256; Metcalfe (1964), pp. 523–4.

CHAPTER 2 DAGBON

1 Tamakloe (1931), p. 64.
2 Lloyd (1965), p. 63.
3 Maquet (1971), p. 86.
4 Cf. Maquet (1971), pp. 94, 99; Kabery (1957), p. 233; Balandier (1972), pp. 22–49 especially.
5 Maquet (1971), p. 88: 'Legitimacy seems to us to be a secondary phenomenon on the level of the collective representations that a society projects of itself ... Legitimacy, even when understood as consensus, cannot be usefully incorporated into the definition of political relations.'
6 I adopt here the criteria listed by Nadel (1942), p. 69. Nadel asserts that states are, virtually by definition, 'inter-tribal' or 'inter-racial': I would argue that this is commonly but not necessarily the case and that the characteristics of political and administrative structure provide a sufficient definition. Maquet defines the state empirically as 'a complex institution of government endowed with sovereignty ... a permanent organisation of rulers' (Maquet (1971), pp. 104–5). Cf. Krader (1968), p. 13; Mair (1962), p. 125.
7 Vansina (1962), p. 325. Maquet provides a similar distinction: 'Where the number of subjects and density of population allowed the monarch to rule directly, we call the political unit a chiefdom. It is called a kingdom when the sovereign has to delegate his power to officials who exercise it in his name' (Maquet (1971), p. 90).
8 Manoukian writes that the patrilineal line 'confers jural status, rights of inheritance and succession to property and offices, ritual privileges and obligations, and determines political allegiance, while the patrilineage is the basis of social organisation' (Manoukian (1952), p. 25).
9 *Ibid*, pp. 32–3.
10 *Ibid*, p. 26.
11 Although succession and inheritance largely take place through the male line, ties of confidence and affection exist between children of the same mother and persist beyond childhood. In commoner lineages, there are 'brother' segments, each comprising the children of one mother in a polygamous household (Oppong (1965), p. 41; Manoukian (1952). p. 26).
12 Manoukian (1952), p. 28; Oppong (1965), pp. 36–8.
13 On the concept of a 'global society', see Maquet (1971), p. 14. The essential feature of such a society is that it is self-sufficient and self-perpetuating: as Maquet puts it, 'One can grow up, marry, work and grow old without even having to "step outside" one's global society.'
14 Manoukian (1952), pp. 16–20; Oppong (1965), p. 12.
15 Monoukian (1952), pp. 60, 84–6; Eyre-Smith (1933), pp. 17, 18, 25, 27. The *tindana* was a votary rather than a soothsayer: the latter role was taken by the *baga*.
16 Eyre-Smith (1933), p. 18.
17 Assistant D.C., Dagomba, to D.C., Dagomba, 13 Aug. 1936 (N.A.G.T., ADM. 2/15); Eyre-Smith (1933), pp. 23, 26, 27.
18 Assistant D.C., Dagomba, to D.C., Dagomba, 13 Aug. 1936 (N.A.G.T., ADM. 2/15). In March 1939 one of Blair's successors persuaded the Tampion-lana (a senior royal

chief) to accompany him on a visit to the local *tindana*. The D. C. noticed that the chief was uneasy about the idea and reported: 'Apparently Na and Tendana don't sit down and chat together, they merely give each other periodical salutations' (Assistant D.C., Dagomba, *Informal Diary*, 16 March 1939 (N.A.G.T., ADM. 1/304)). Eyre-Smith likewise suggests that the relationship was generally distant and wary, but both he and Manoukian note that under colonial government chiefs sometimes usurped the power of the *tindana* (Eyre-Smith (1933), pp. 25, 27; Manoukian (1952), p. 60).

19 'The rules of succession are backed by the most powerful sanctions of the ancestor cult' (Manoukian (1952), p. 27).

20 Ghana (1964), *Special Report 'E'*, p. lxxxi. Only 0.5 per cent were enumerated as Christians.

21 For example, the story of Ya-Na Zagale who was required by a fetish to sacrifice his first son and first daughter. The king refused, on the grounds that the sacrifice would destroy his line, and declared: 'The fetish be damned. Because the fetishes had been taken into consideration in the past they have become impudent.' Next day Zagale had the fetish destroyed. The 'drum history', which records this story, does not suggest that the Ya-Na was punished, or, indeed, that he deserved to be punished (Tait 'B').

22 'There are no rights of succession, but there may be good grounds on which to base a claim ... Grounds for succession to big chiefdoms must be patrilineal, though a maternal nephew of a very big Chief may make that his ground of claim to a small chiefdom' (Assistant D.C., Dagomba, to D.C., Dagomba, 13 Aug. 1936 (N.A.G.T., ADM. 2/15)).

23 See Tamakloe (1931); Tait 'A'; Tait 'B'; Duncan-Johnstone and Blair (1932), Rattray (1932), vol. 2, p. 564; Wilks (1965), pp. 96–7.

24 Using Tamakloe's list, one obtains an average of 17 years. Fage corrected Tamakloe's chronology, correlating incidents in Dagomba history with incidents elsewhere for which quite firm dates are known (Fage (1964), pp. 177–81). Tait apparently considered 10 years to be a reasonable average (cited in Manoukian (1952), p. 14).

25 Cf. Wilks (1971), p. 350; Manoukian (1952), p. 28; Goody (1966), p. 37.

26 Thirteen younger brothers, if we include Darimani at the end of the nineteenth century.

27 It is difficult to say how often eldest sons who did not directly succeed their fathers have been usurped by their younger brothers. The genealogies are incomplete or contradictory and it is often impossible to say at a given point of succession how many sons were still alive.

28 As Goody remarks, 'each method of perpetuating an office and its associated organization has its own implications and concomitants; each system solves certain problems and produces its own particular dilemmas ... No system of succession is completely automatic, even setting on one side the recurrent possibility of dethronement, abdication or usurpation' (Goody (1966b), pp. 2, 13). Cf. Gluckman (1963), p. 131: 'rarely in Africa do we find clear and simple rules indicating a single prince as the true heir. Frequently the rules of succession are in themselves contradictory in that they support different heirs (e. g. Bemba) and more often still they operate uncertainly in practice (e.g. Swazi and Zulu). Almost every succession may raise rival claimants.'

29 Cf. Wilks (1971), pp. 350–1.

30 Goody (1966b), pp. 30–1.

31 Duncan-Johnstone and Blair (1932), p. 10. According to Ferguson, there had been disagreement between the diviners and the elders over the appointment of Gungobile: after his death, the *na-bihe* and the elders opposed consultation of the diviners (Ferguson (1973), pp. 90–1).

32 Tamakloe (1931), p. 27. The incident is also recorded in Duncan-Johnstone and Blair (1932), p. 49; Tait 'B'; and Ferguson and Wilks (1970), p. 341.

33 Ferguson (1973), p. 93. Tamakloe suggests that the other candidates actually borrowed money from Zangina for the purpose of bribing the Na-yiri. Zangina, however, secretly sent 40,000 cowries, a bangle, and a gown to the king: Tamakloe implies that these gifts were decisive (Tamakloe (1931), p. 27).

34 Wilks (1971), p. 351; Manoukian (1952), p. 55; Tait (1961), p. 6; Duncan–Johnstone and Blair (1932), pp. 10, 58.

35 Manoukian (1952), p. 55. In an unpublished paper, Tait points out that whereas under Savelugu and Karaga there are chiefdoms for the sons, grandsons, and other relatives of the royal dukes, 'there are no such chiefdoms for the descendants of Chiefs of Mion: the reason given is, of course, that the Chief of Mion always goes on to the paramountcy'.

36 Iddi (1968), vol. 1, pp. 53, 72.

37 *Ibid*, p. 72. Cf. Northcott (1899), pp. 15–16: 'The Kingdoms of Pigu (i.e. Mion), Karaga, and Savelugu are allowed a certain amount of independence, and the heir to the throne is generally put on the stool of the first.'

38 Iddi (1968), vol 1, pp. 72, 78.

39 *Ibid*, p. 40. Rattray wrote that the royal dukes were 'equal in rank, with Karaga as a kind of *primus inter pares*' (Rattray (1932), vol. 2, p. 575). In 1914 the acting Provincial Commissioner, Southern Province, informed his superior: 'The Chief of Karaga is next for the stool of Yendi, he is in turn succeeded by that of Savelugu and then by Miong. These are the only three stools that succeed in rotation to that of Yendi' (Acting P.C., Southern Province, to C.C.N.T., 26 Feb. 1914 (N.A.G.A., ADM 56/1/189)). This statement should be read in the context of the state of Dagomba at the time – partitioned, with Karaga and Savelugu on the British side of the border and Mion on the German side. The question of 'rotation' is taken up in Chs. 8 and 9.

40 Indeed, it is certainly naïve to accept at face value the formal simplicity of procedure in earlier days as presented in 'traditionalist' accounts. Nevertheless, there is substantial agreement on the 'received version' and that is what I recount here.

41 Oppong (1965), p. 19; Iddi (1968), vol. 1. p. 4. Cf. Maquet: 'Interregna were periods of a type of crisis which was institutionalised (in the sense that provision was made for disorders that were expected and followed a predictable course) but which was nonetheless fraught with anxiety. Only when a new monarch had been installed could nature and man's life resume its course again' (Maquet (1971), p. 103). On ritualised disorder, see also Goody (1966b), pp. 10–12.

42 Iddi (1968), vol. 1, p. 6; vol. 2, p. 20; Tamakloe (1931), pp. 71–2; Cardinall (1921).

43 Rattray says that the name *gbonlana* must not be mentioned in the king's presence and he adds: 'Every man has a Gbonlana – his eldest son, who on his father's death is going to take charge of his funeral customs' (Rattray (1932), vol. 2, pp. 573–4). The Mionlana looked after the relatives of the paramount until the regent took over (Iddi (1968), vol. 1, p. 53).

44 Manoukian (1952), p. 55; Iddi (1968), vol. 1, p. 46; vol. 2, pp. 18–19, 36; Duncan-Johnstone and Blair (1932), p. 31. Blair writes of the Gushie-Na: 'In position he is the greatest chief under Yendi, although he cannot succeed to Yendi ... being technically senior to Yendi.' Blair asserts that originally 'Gushiegu had the nomination of the Na of Yendi' and that it was his failure to nominate on the death of Gungobile which led to the Na-yiri's arbitration. But, he adds, 'the Gushie-Na does still play the largest part in the nomination of a succeeding Chief of Yendi. He is advised by and generally follows the advice of certain councillors who are *ipso facto* on the electing committee' (D.C., Eastern Dagomba, *Informal Diary*, 31 May 1930, 20 June 1930, 25 June 1930 (N.A.G.T., ADM. 1/131; ADM. 1/132)).

45 Iddi (1968), vol. 1, p. 47; vol. 2, pp. 35–68. Tamakloe observes that, during the period of divination, 'bribes are heaped upon the diverse elders in secret by the chiefs or the candidates concerned, who again spend large sums of money on the mallams who used to make for them charms and kindred necromantic and magical amulets to be buried on the graves of some notable men, and on the various roads leading into the town from without; these things are of course done during the night when all is silent' (Tamakloe (1931), p. 67). Iddi, while accepting that divisional and village chieftaincies may be bought, argues that the paramountcy cannot be purchased (Iddi (1968), vol. 1, p. 78).

46 Iddi (1968), vol. 1, pp. 52–3.

47 Iddi remarks that it is customary for the Mion-lana to present his 'burial kit' first and implies that this is further evidence of the precedence of the Mion-lana over the other dukes in consideration for Yendi (*ibid*, p. 78).

48 The cow was slaughtered and certain parts of it were eaten: the remainder was cut up and

dropped in wells and ponds throughout the kingdom. It was believed that water infected by this meat would kill anybody who had slept with a wife of the king.

49 Based on Tamakloe (1931), pp. 67–8; Manoukian (1952), p. 55; Rattray (1932), vol. 2, pp. 580–1, 583–4, Iddi (1968). vol. 1, pp. 45, 48–51; vol. 2, pp. 18–19, 36, 57; vol. 3, pp. 5, 11, 14; Tait 'A'.

50 Iddi (1968), vol. 1, p. 68; vol. 2, p. 58; Tamakloe (1931), pp. 69–71; Rattray (1932), vol. 2, pp. 585–6.

51 Cf. Balandier on the Kongo kingdom: 'The king, the provincial chiefs and those of the vassal territories are placed, each at his respective level, in an identical situation and the political arrangement has a repetitive air: the chiefs resemble the sovereign, the small capitals resemble San Salvador, where the king resides' (Balandier (1972), p. 138).

52 Tamakloe (1931), p. 58.

53 Mion was also known as 'Pigu' and 'Sambu' (the capital of the province).

54 Members of the royal patriclan had certain ritual observances in common, particularly taboos on eating the flesh of animals regarded as sacred (for example, lions and monkeys) (Oppong (1965), p. 39).

55 Manoukian (1952), p. 36; Oppong (1965), p. 20.

56 Tait (1961), p. 6.

57 Duncan-Johnstone and Blair (1932), p. 59. Cf. Manoukian (1952), p. 55.

58 Tait 'A'; Tamakloe (1931), p. 11. Kpatuya is a quarter of Yendi: another quarter, Kulogo, also had a chieftainess. There was also provision for chiefdoms to be given to the sons of women of the royal house (e.g. sons of the paramount's sisters). Such skins were known as *paga-bihe-nama*; but Manoukian, citing Blair, states that there were no regular offices of this kind (Rattary (1932), vol. 2, p. 576; Iddi (1968), vol. 2, pp. 14–15; Manoukian (1952), p. 56).

59 Manoukian says that Gulkpeogu was also reserved for 'patrilineal descendants of the original holders of the post' (Manoukian (1952), p. 56). This conflicts with Tait's view, that Gulkpeogu is a normal promotion for Mbadugu (an elder) (Tait 'A'). The two versions are hardly more compatible if we allow for the fact that Mbadugu, as a eunuch, would have no heirs. Tamakloe asserts that both Gulkpe-Na and Gushie-Na were originally fetish priests, though not, apparently, *tindama* (Tamakloe (1931), p. 9).

60 For most elder chiefdoms, the drum history records first appointments in the reigns of Nyagse, Datorli, and Zoligu, though three posts were established in the eighteenth century. In nearly all cases they replaced murdered *tindamba* (Tait 'A'; Iddi (1968), vol. 2, p. 64).

61 Tait 'A'. The 1930 'constitution' gave a different order of precedence, viz., Gushiegu, Yelzori, Gulkpeogu, Nanton, Sunson, Tolon, and Kumbungu: other sources accord Tolon the highest place (Duncan-Johnstone and Blair (1932), p. 63; Tait (1961), pp. 7, 8; Oppong (1965), p. 17).

62 Cf. Fallers (1956), pp. 230–1, and criticisms in Goody (1966b), pp. 25–6. On the separation of the king and the lineage, Lloyd notes: 'The installation ceremonies of the African king usually symbolize his withdrawal from active participation in the affairs of his own lineage: he assumes an office in which he reigns impartially over all his people' (Lloyd (1965), p. 87).

63 Ferguson and Wilks (1970), p. 326. I have avoided using the word 'bureaucracy' here because certain features of ideal-typical bureaucracy were absent (notably the existence of a free contractual relationship).

64 According to Manoukian, the elders 'were originally eunuchs who had been captives in war, slaves, children of slaves, or sons of women found guilty of witchcraft' (Manoukian (1952), p. 67). Examples are given in Tait 'A' and Tamakloe (1931), p. 76.

65 Tamakloe (1931), pp. 15, 62; Tait 'A'; Rattray (1932), vol. 2, p. 562. The royal antecedents of Kuga-Na are recognised in the way he is greeted by the king, namely as '*yaba*' ('ancestor' or 'grandfather').

66 Wilks (1971), p. 351.

67 'Holders of the newer (achieved) offices ... derived their authority by direct mandate from the king, and were in a real sense his servants' (Ferguson and Wilks (1970), p. 326).

68 Rattray (1932), vol. 2, pp. 572, 573; Oppong (1965), p. 90.

69 The officials were Kuga-Na, Zohe-Na, Kum-lana, Balo-Na, Mba Malle, Bunga, Gagbin-dana, Kpahigu, and Gullana.

70 Manoukian (1952), pp. 55, 59; Duncan-Johnstone and Blair (1932), p. 65; D.C., Eastern Dagomba, *Notes on the Dagomba Constitution and Native Administration*, n.d. (N.A.G.T.). The power of the elders over the king is freely acknowledged in Dagomba: 'the Ya-Na doesn't do anything; everything is done for him . . . he is like an egg, he needs protecting, and it is the *Kpamba* [elders] who do this; one cannot bypass them. Ya-Na does not own anything except the name Ya-Na. All the land in Dagbon is owned by other people . . . Whenever anything is done in Dagbon, it is always said that Ya-Na has done it, but in point of fact, this is not so; everything is done by others – the *Kpamba*' (Ferguson (1972), pp. 15–16).

71 Manoukian (1952), p. 55; Duncan-Johnstone and Blair (1932), pp. 56–7. Cardinall described the elders as 'a small body of men who actually ruled the kingdom and who were so highly held in esteem that they could contradict the Na, differ from his views and even abuse him' (Cardinall (1927), p. 115).

72 Tamakloe (1931), p. 60. Cf. Manoukian (1952), p. 57; Rattray (1932), vol. 2, p. 574.

73 According to Rattray, the fee generally consisted of 12,000 cowries and a sheep. The sheep was slaughtered as a sacrifice and the money was divided between the elders and the royal treasury (Rattray (1932), vol. 2, pp. 574–5).

74 In the case of Bagele (the village housing the shrine of the royal family) the customary *nam ligidi* was (in the 1920s) £15. In 1911 the administration noted that sums as high as £17 had been paid to the Yo-Na by candidates seeking appointment as divisional chief (Kumbung-Na). (*Note re Case of Complaints of Sub-Chiefs of Kumbungu re installation of new Chief of Kumbungu* (N.A.G.A., ADM. 56/1/252)). In 1938 a fee of £150 was charged for Kumbungu chiefship (and that to an unsuccessful candidate).

75 Rattray (1932), vol. 2, pp. 575–6; Northcott (1899), p. 18; Tait (1961), p. 7; Iddi (1968), vol. 1, pp. 67, 69.

76 Tait 'A'; D.C., Eastern Dagomba, *Notes on the Dagomba Constitution and Native Administration*, n.d., (N.A.G.T.).

77 Oppong (1965), pp. 29–30. Tait writes: 'The term *wulana* is reserved for that elder who is closest to his chief and in all cases . . . a *wulana* lives near by the chief' (Tait (1961), p. 7). The main exception, as Tait notes, is the Tolon-Na who is *wulana* to the king and lives in Western Dagomba, near Tamale.

78 D.C., Eastern Dagomba, *Notes on the Dagomba Constitution and Native Administration*, n.d. (N.A.G.T.).

79 Oppong (1965), pp. 27–8.

80 Tait 'A'; Iddi (1968), vol. 1, p. 65. I have not dealt with Islam in detail, both because I am not sufficiently informed about the background and because the subject has been so well covered by Phyllis Ferguson (Ferguson (1973)).

81 Iddi (1968), vol. 1, p. 68; vol. 2, p. 30. On Muslim offices at Yendi, see Ferguson (1973), pp. 192–204.

82 The first seems to be the official referred to by Ferguson as Zemole (Ferguson (1973), pp. 192–4). Ferguson lists Mba Malle as another important Muslim official.

83 On which see Ferguson (1972). The head of the community was known as Yidan Baba, who was head butcher to the Ya-Na. The cattle trade was (and is) a major source of wealth in Dagomba and the Muslims are dominant in this sector. Tait writes that butchers 'are the wealthiest class in Dagomba. They are far wealthier than the chiefs. Further, they invest money, not so much in other trading ventures, but in house property. It is they, for example, who build the stores found around Dagomba markets which are rented out to southern store-keepers' (Tait (1961), p. 27). In 1960, some 56 per cent of the butchers in Ghana were Dagomba (Ghana (1964), *Special Report 'E'*, Appendix C, pp. C34–49). Polly Hill has recently published a very interesting account of the cattle trade in this area (Hill (1970), Ch. 5, 'The Northern Ghanaian cattle trade').

84 Wilks (1971), p. 384.

85 Tamakloe (1931), p. 64.

86 A useful discussion of this question is to be found in Goody (1971), pp. 39–56. Goody's main point is that the variety of political systems in West Africa 'correlated not so much with differences in the ownership of the means of production (nor yet in the objects of production themselves) but rather in the ownership of the means of destruction and in the nature of those means' (*ibid*, p. 43).

87 Wilks (1971), p. 345.

88 Rattray (1932), vol. 2, pp. 565–7; Tait (1961), p. 7; Oppong (1965), pp. 4–5.

89 Rattray (1932), vol. 2, p. 569. Rattray's work as a government anthropologist was regarded sceptically by some of his colleagues and superiors in the administration. Given his subsequent reputation, it is sometimes rather startling to come across such comments as the following: 'The opinions of Captain Rattray who has only spent a day or two in Dagomba, and does not speak its language, should be disregarded' (Acting C.C.N.T. to Colonial Secretary, Accra, 4 March 1931 (N.A.G.T., ADM. 1/196)).

90 Tait and Strevens (1955), p. 195; Rattray (1932), vol. 2, pp. 565–6; Tamakloe (1931), p. 64.

91 Rattray (1932), vol. 2, pp. 567–8; Manoukian (1952), p. 58. The head of the spearmen was called *tob-wubega* (literally 'war hawk').

92 Cf. Goody (1971), pp. 29–30. Maquet remarks: 'Two conditions are necessary for the emergence of a chiefdom or kingdom: first, all the families, or at least most of them, must produce more than they consume; secondly, all or at least the greater part of this surplus must be concentrated in the hands of one man. For this single reason he is chief or king' (Maquet (1971), p. 99).

93 Goody (1971), p. 29.

94 'If you have landlords, you can also have tenants and serfs; unfree tenancies mean little unless land is highly valued and your peasantry has nowhere else to go' (*ibid*, p. 31).

95 Gluckman (1960), p. 166. Dagomba was richer than Zululand but qualitatively not much different.

96 Eyre-Smith (1933), pp. 32, 26.

97 C.C.N.T., memorandum, 6 Nov. 1934 (N.A.G.T., ADM. 1/32).

98 Phyllis Ferguson cites some remarkable contemporary accounts of the wealth of the Yendi area. She also points out (following Wilks) that Dagomba's affluence coincided with the decline of the Atlantic slave trade and the reactivation of the inland trade in kola nuts (Ferguson (1973), pp. 216–34).

99 Ferguson and Wilks remark: 'The economic deterioration of Dagomba in the last three decades of the nineteenth century was matched by a decline in the power of the centre – of the king in Yendi – in relationship to the divisions' (Ferguson and Wilks (1970), p. 343).

100 Cf. Ferguson (1973), p. 43.

101 Northcott (1899), p. 13.

102 Macaulay (1906), vol. 1, pp. 34–5. Cf. Gluckman (1956b), pp. 163–4.

103 As Maquet writes: 'In small chiefdoms and kingdoms, the equilibrium point of the forces of coercion and resistance was fairly low: pressure from all sides was weak. Rulers could not lay their hands on very much (in view of the level of production and the number of subjects); subjects did not have to put much energy into resistance (they were protected by the kinship network, and the necessarily direct relationship they maintained with rulers)' (Maquet (1971), p. 127).

104 'Being part of the system of domination, being essential to the maintenance of the position of the monarchy, the ruling estate were in a position to make demands as well as give support; the one entailed the other' (Goody (1971), p. 49). Goody compares the consequences of dependence on horsemen with those of dependence on firearms: 'with the horse one required a mass dynasty, with the gun one could dispense with all except a stem dynasty' (*ibid*, p. 51).

105 Southall (1956), pp. 248ff. Concerning this model, Phyllis Kaberry remarks ((1957), p. 233): 'We should ... restrict the category of segmentary political states to those in which ... continuously segmenting unilineal or quasi-unilineal groups are vested with political functions': in other words, distinguish between states in which there are self-

sufficient components which may break away and others in which the central government is merely less effective on its periphery. I think that there was sufficient replication
of structures within Dagbon to justify using the label 'segmentary state', though admittedly there was no actual disintegration, even in the nineteenth century.

106 Rattray (1932), vol. 2, p. 565.
107 Eyre-Smith (1933), p. 26.
108 Manoukian (1952), p. 58.
109 Goody (1966b), p. 13.
110 Tait 'A'; Tait 'B'; Tamakloe (1931), pp. 33–44; Gill (n.d.), pp.5–10, 12–15; Fage (1964),
    p. 181. On the structural determinants of competition, see Ferguson and Wilks (1970),
    pp. 347–8.
111 See Gluckman (1963), pp. 86–7; Gluckman (1965a), p. 28; Gluckman (1965b), pp. 164–5.
112 Cf. Audrey Richards on the Citimukulu, paramount of the Bemba: 'the belief in his
    power, both political and religious, is the main source of tribal cohesion throughout
    this scarcely populated area' (Richards (1959), p. 168).
113 Maquet (1971), p. 99. Cf. Balandier (1972), p. 39: 'power must justify itself by main-
    taining a state of collective security and prosperity. This is the price to be paid by those
    who hold it – a price that is never wholly paid.'

CHAPTER 3 COLONIAL RULE, 1899–1930

 1 The men of Gambaga to the Dagomba, at the time of the Gonja wars (citied in Gill (n.d.),
   p. 4).
 2 D. P. O., Yendi, *Informal Diary*, 11 Aug. 1920 (N.A.G.A., ADM 56/1/259).
 3 Northern Territories Order-in-Council, 26 Sept. 1901, reprinted in Metcalfe (1964), p. 523;
   see also Kimble (1963), p. 324. For the earlier treaties, see Metcalfe (1964), pp. 505, 445.
 4 Kimble (1963), pp. 533–4.
 5 *Ibid*, pp. 325, 431; Hailey (1951), p. 256.
 6 Bourret (1949), p. 40; Kimble (1963), p. 536.
 7 Kimble (1963), p. 536.
 8 *Ibid*, p. 535; see also *ibid*, p. 325.
 9 The Northern Territories Administrative Ordinance, No. 1 of 1902.
10 Order No. 8 of 15 Oct. 1925; Order No. 9 of 15 Oct. 1925; correspondence on file,
   N.A.G.A., ADM. 56/1/274.
11 Until 1926 there was no Public Works Department in the north.
12 E.g., issuing building permits, regulating markets, enforcing public health and sanitary
   regulations. The original instructions to D.C.s stated: 'Officers in charge of Districts will
   be directly responsible to the Commissioners and Commandant for the efficient
   administration of their Districts and for the Discipline and Training of the Gold Coast
   Constabulary placed under their orders ... they must clearly understand that it is their
   duty to keep the Commissioner constantly informed of the condition and progress of
   their commands ... especially it is desired that suggestions should be made with a view to
   the development of trade' (*Instructions to Officers in Charge of Districts Re Administration of
   the Northern Territories*, 9 March 1899 (N.A.G.A., ADM. 56/1/35)).
13 Heussler makes the cautionary point (which I completely accept) that 'the reality of the
   power structure is not conveyed in most official documents, which, indeed, tend to obscure and confuse it. In the papers of administration, especially annual reports, gazettes,
   and minutes of official conferences, one finds exaggerated deference ... allowing an
   impression of strict adherence to the wishes of higher authority. From the start the very
   regularity and official character of reports made them stereotyped and pretentious' (Heussler (1968), p. 85). But he goes on to note a tendency in colonial administration 'to
   assign so much integrity of position to a particular office as virtually to depersonalize its
   human occupant' and he gives some remarkable examples of 'the rigid formality of the
   Colonial Service' (p. 89). Canon Blair informs me that, as one might expect, social
   relations in the N.T. administration were rather less stiff than in Nigeria, though (as he
   amusingly demonstrates in his memoirs) visits by higher authority were somewhat fraught
   occasions.

14 *Instructions to Officers in Charge of Districts Re Administration of the Northern Territories* (N.A.G.A., ADM. 56/1/35).

15 D.C., Eastern Dagomba, *Informal Diary*, 5 Jan. 1926; 2–5 Dec. 1925. The Chief Commissioner was alarmed by these burnings. He wrote: 'Could you imagine headlines in papers at home if they heard of it?' The D.C. defended himself thus: 'I fail to see why the Government consider burning a bit of grass and a few sticks not "British Justice". It is far more effective than a collective punishment would be and far less hardship to the people' (N.A.G.T., ADM. 1/126).

16 *Instructions to Officers in Charge of Districts Re Administration of the Northern Territories* (N.A.G.A., ADM. 56/1/35).

17 Kimble (1963), pp. 533–4.

18 *Ibid*, p. 534. On the outbreak of the First World War, the Colonial Secretary in Accra told the C.C.N.T.: 'the object of government in the immediate future must be to reduce not to increase expenditure especially in the Northern Territories' (*ibid*).

19 Cited in *ibid*, p. 326. Cf. Ferguson and Wilks (1970), pp. 333–4.

20 Kimble (1963), p. 327.

21 The principal source was ferry tolls (which in 1924–5 provided 67.6 per cent of the total revenue of the N.T.): other sources included court fees and fines, firearms taxes, market fees, rents for building plots, and sales of postage stamps.

22 Of those recruited in 1909, 1,216 were used as bearers and 1,764 were employed for 'station work and the agricultural garden'; of those recruited in 1912, 3,366 were used as bearers (*Annual Report, Tamale District, 1909* (N.A.G.A., ADM. 56/1/433); *Annual Report on the Southern Province for the Year 1910* (N.A.G.A., ADM. 56/1/446); *Annual Report on the Southern Province for the Year 1912* (N.A.G.A., ADM. 56/1/466)).

23 *Yendi Information Book 1916–30* (N.A.G.A., ADM. 67/5/1); Ferguson and Wilks (1970), p. 334.

24 *Annual Report on the Southern Province for the Year 1910* (N.A.G.A., ADM. 56/1/446).

25 *Annual Report on the Southern Province for the Year 1914* (N.A.G.A., ADM. 56/1/470).

26 *Quarterly Report, Southern Province*, first quarter, 1920 (N.A.G.A., ADM. 56/1/487).

27 *Annual Report of the Northern Territories for 1925–26* (N.A.G.T., ADM. 1/97). In 1924 some 643 carriers had been recruited in Western Dagomba and by 1926–7 the figure was down to 415 (*Western Dagomba, Report for Year Ending 31 March 1924*, 11 April 1924 (N.A.G.A., ADM. 56/1/506); *Annual Report on the Western Dagomba District for the Year Ending 31 March 1927*, 19 April 1927 (N.A.G.A., ADM. 56/1/506)).

28 Calculated from *The Gold Coast Civil Service List*, 1908–25.

29 Bourret (1949), p. 40.

30 Gold Coast (1930); Gold Coast (1931). In 1913 the total police strength of the Southern Province was 63 (*Quarterly Report, Southern Province*, first quarter, 1913, (N.A.G.A., ADM. 56/1/469)). The police force was increased after the occupation of Eastern Dagomba where the British inherited the problem of feuding between Konkomba villages.

31 Many were, of course, the same officers, resuming duty after leave. There were several D.C.s who became particularly associated with Dagomba through long periods of service there (for example, Armstrong, Blair, and Gilbert).

32 Captain Armstrong served for four years (from September 1937 to December 1941) with only one six-month break; Gilbert, in the twenties, did two stretches of eighteen months and one of seventeen.

33 The C.C.N.T. remarked in 1926: 'Since the advent of motor cars, Political Officers find that they can see a great deal more of their Chiefs and people than formerly, and Chiefs are frequently taken round in the Commissioner's car for various reasons. A tour taking ten days with carriers, can now be done easily in a day' (*Annual Report of the Northern Territories for 1925–26* (N.A.G.T., ADM. 1/97)). Major Walker-Leigh went on to report that he had personally 'been to every station and through all the Districts of the country, in some cases three or four times during the year' (*ibid*).

34 C.C.N.T. to acting D.P.O., Yendi, 23 Oct. 1916 (N.A.G.A., ADM.56/1/211).

35 In one year (from June 1916 to July 1917) the D.P.O. (Evered Poole and Cardinall successively) spent 191 days on trek, visiting 247 villages (*Yendi Information Book 1916–30* (N.A.G.A., ADM. 67/5/1)).

36 D.P.O., Yendi, to C.C.N.T., 6 Jan. 1921 (N.A.G.A., ADM. 56/1/287).
37 *Quarterly Report, Southern Province*, third quarter, 1921 (N.A.G.A., ADM. 65/1/487).
38 *Annual Report on the Western Dagomba District for the Year Ending 31 March 1928*, 25 April 1928 (N.A.G.A., ADM. 56/1/506)).
39 Some officers had unusual qualifications: one had been 'mentioned in Foreign Office Despatches in 1910 and thanked for services rendered in translating the Saxon Birth Statistics'; Rutherford had commanded a night-fighter squadron; and Duncan-Johnstone was for some time 'attached to the Great Central Railway' (which I take to mean 'employed by').
40 In one epidemic, in 1937–8, five Europeans died (Gold Coast (1938)).
41 D.P.O., Yendi, *Informal Diary*, 25 May 1920 (N.A.G.A., ADM. 56/1/259).
42 *Informal Diary of the Commissioner, Southern Province*, 20 Sept. 1929, 27 Sept. 1929 (N.A.G.T., ADM. 1/126). On Duncan-Johnstone's Highland entertainments, see Boyle (1968), pp. 124, 133.
43 Visitors provided an occasion for shooting parties and (in Eastern Dagomba) they could be offered fishing in the Daka or Oti rivers.
44 *Yendi Information Book 1916–1930* (N.A.G.A., ADM. 67/5/1). The *Informal Diaries* present a remarkable picture of frenetic activity on a multitude of greater or lesser projects. Sometimes, too, they report setbacks, such as the poignant entry in the Yendi diary: 'November 23rd: The government bull died' (D.C., Eastern Dagomba, *Informal Diary*, 23 November 1922 (N.A.G.A., ADM. 67/5/4)).
45 Kimble (1963), p. 535.
46 *Ibid.*
47 Acting Commandant, N.T.C., to C.C.N.T., 22 Aug. 1911 (N.A.G.A., ADM. 56/1/67).
48 P.C., Southern Province, *Informal Diary*, 6 Oct. 1913 (N.A.G.A., ADM. 65/5/1). There were about 50 Twi-speakers in Tamale, as well as a significant number of Nigerian traders, Hausa and Yoruba: the administration reported incidents between the latter and local people in the markets (*Annual Report on the Southern Province for the Year 1908*, 27 Feb. 1909 (N.A.G.A., ADM. 56/1/431); D.C., Western Dagomba, *Informal Diary*, 27 Aug. 1928 (N.A.G.T., ADM. 1/126)).
49 Cf. Kimble (1963), p. 535; Ferguson (1973), p. 1.
50 *Instructions to Officers in Charge of Districts Re Administration of the Northern Territories* (N.A.G.A., ADM. 56/1/35).
51 *Annual Report on the Southern Province for the Year 1910* (N.A.G.A., ADM. 56/1/446); *Quarterly Report, Southern Province*, fourth quarter, 1914 (N.A.G.A., ADM. 56/1/474). The conquest of Eastern Dagomba brought into the British sector a flourishing caravan trade through Yendi down to Kete-Krachi and Kumasi. The Administration was, however, unhappy about the role of southern merchants in the north. The P.C., Southern Province, wrote: 'From the point of view of the Protectorate as an entity the very worst class of trader stalks the land, i.e. the man who brings goods up for sale from Coomassie etc. and returns with cash, and then repeats the process. In this way most of the cash finds its way back to the coast again.' He also (heretically) thought that the 'transit trade' did not bring 'any benefit at all to the N.T.s' (*Annual Report on the Southern Province for 1914* (N.A.G.A., ADM. 56/1/470)).
52 *Annual Report on the Southern Province for the Year 1908*, 27 Feb. 1909 (N.A.G.A., ADM. 56/1/431); *Annual Report, Tamale District, 1909* (N.A.G.A., ADM. 56/1/433); *Annual Report on the Southern Province for the Year 1912* (N.A.G.A., ADM. 56/1/466).
53 *Annual Report on the Southern Province for the Year 1910* (N.A.G.A., ADM. 56/1/446).
54 In 1929 the D.C., Western Dagomba, remarked that famine was unknown to the people of his area (this was not, in fact, true) and he observed: 'With regard to their own crops we have nothing to teach and much to learn. Their farming, especially in congested areas, is wonderful' (D.C., Western Dagomba, *Native Administration – Development Programme*, 30 Dec. 1929 (N.A.G.T., ADM. 2/18)).
55 *Annual Report, Tamale District, 1909* (N.A.G.A., ADM. 56/1/433).
56 P.C., Southern Province, *Informal Diary*, 3 Jan. 1915 (N.A.G.A., ADM. 65/5/1).
57 *Minutes of Conference at Tamale, 11 March 1921* (N.A.G.A., ADM. 56/1/258). Guggisberg, as we shall see, was in favour of reinforcing the pre-colonial states and his concern with

these entities had an economic aspect. At this conference, he noted, with misgiving, 'a tendency for the bigger states to break up to the detriment of development and trade' (*ibid*).

58 C.C.N.T., *Informal Diary*, 14 July 1928, 24 Aug. 1928 (N.A.G.T., ADM. 1/8).
59 Marginal comments on *ibid*.
60 This is, for reasons of space, a highly compressed account. A useful discussion of labour recruitment in the north is Thomas (1973). Other material is to be found in Hailey (1938), pp. 607, 620, 642–3; Kimble (1963), pp. 41–3; and in the Ghana archives (N.A.G.A., reports: ADM. 56/1/204, ADM. 56/1/211, ADM. 56/1/258, ADM. 56/1/487; diaries: ADM. 56/1/259, ADM. 56/1/276, ADM. 67/5/4).
61 Kimble (1963), p. 43.
62 Bourret (1949), p. 105.
63 *Annual Report on the Southern Province for the Year 1910* (N.A.G.A., ADM. 56/1/446); *Handing-over Report, Southern Province*, 15 April 1919 (N.A.G.A., ADM. 56/1/92); *Annual Report on the Western Dagomba District, Southern Province, N.T.s for the Year Ending 31 March 1926* (N.A.G.A., ADM. 56/1/506); *Annual Report on the Southern Province for the Year Ending 31 March 1926* (N.A.G.A., ADM 56/1/501); Superintendent of Education, Northern Territories, to Director of Education, Accra, 19 April 1929 (N.A.G.T., ADM. 1/7); Oppong (1965), Appendix. The Tamale school originated in the organisation of policemen's sons for drilling by one of their number; the C.C.N.T. ordered a literate constable to teach the boys reading and arithmetic and in 1909 a Hausa-speaking schoolmaster was appointed to establish a proper school.
64 *Annual Report. Tamale District, 1909* (N.A.G.A., ADM. 56/1/433); Bening (1971), p. 24.
65 Bening (1971), p. 23. Cf. Oppong (1965), pp. 115ff.
66 Programme on file; acting C.C.N.T. to Director of Education, Accra, 19 Aug. 1915, and notes on file (N.A.G.A., ADM. 56/1/88). On the prevailing educational system, a subsequent Inspector of Schools commented: 'The curriculum was that of the Colony as interpreted by second-rate teachers ... It had no relation to local life or to general development, and was presumably meant to be nothing more than clerk-producing' (Gold Coast (1938), section by M. F. G. Wentworth, Provincial Inspector of Schools, p. 51).
67 *Palaver Held at Yendi with the King of Yendi, 8 March 1921* (N.A.G.A., ADM 56/1/258).
68 Gold Coast (1938), pp. 53ff.
69 Guggisberg hoped that this would be set up within ten years: in reality it was not established until after World War II.
70 Previously education in the N.T. had been supervised, most ineffectually, by the Provincial Inspector for Ashanti.
71 Gold Coast (1938), p. 55. Bening, in his valuable article on education in the N.T., remarks on this bias against missionaries: 'The disparity in educational development between northern and southern Ghana is due less to the late start of schools in the Protectorate than to the peculiarly restrictive policy pursued by the British administration in the matter of missionary education' (Bening (1971), p. 40). The administration apparently feared that the missionaries would offend the Muslims and introduce ideas subversive of authority, old and new. Cf. Heussler (1968), pp. 116, 122, 171; Nicolson (1969), pp. 74, 242–3.
72 Gold Coast (1938), pp. 55–6; Bening (1971), pp. 26, 27, 31; Oppong (1965), p. 112.
73 Gold Coast (1938), p. 56.

CHAPTER 4 DAGOMBA DIVIDED AND UNITED, 1899–1930

1 Cited in Kimble (1963), p. 323.
2 'In both Wa and Dagomba the British regarded their position as legitimated by the treaties of the 1890's but also saw their authority as in some way following on from that of earlier local rulers' (Ferguson and Wilks (1970), p. 330).
3 *Ibid*. In 1917 the acting C.C.N.T. wrote: 'On the Boundary being made the Chief of Karaga was recognised by our Government as the Paramount Chief of English Dagomba and as such for all purposes of our administration had nothing whatever to do with the

King of Yendi and was in no way subservient to him; he was moreover informed that he should for the future have no dealings with the King of Yendi' (acting C.C.N.T. to D.P.O., Yendi, 9 July 1917 (N.A.G.A., ADM. 56/1/211)). Cf. Duncan-Johnstone and Blair (1932), pp. 11–12.

4 For example, a document entitled 'Laws and custom N.T.', dated 1914, states: 'As in Mamprussi all the Chiefs in Dagomba hold their positions by hereditary right, subject to the approval of the Government.' It concludes with the (sadly inaccurate) comment: 'The Dagombas and Gonjas have always been on friendly terms with each other' (N.A.G.A., ADM. 56/1/91). Officials with intellectual ability were not always regarded as good administrators. This was particularly the case with Rattray, for whom the post of Government Anthropologist was created in compensation for his being 'unacceptable as a Deputy Provincial Commissioner or senior Secretariat Officer' (Wraith (1967), p. 206).

5 Hailey (1951), p. 262.

6 *Instructions to Officers in Charge of Districts Re Administration of the Northern Territories*, 9 March 1899 (N.A.G.A., ADM. 56/1/35).

7 P.C., Southern Province, *Handing-over Report, Southern Province, Northern Territories*, March 1909 (N.A.G.A., ADM. 56/1/92). Irvine recommended that matrimonial, land, and farm disputes, as well as petty assault cases, should be judged in the first instance by the chiefs, with provision for appeal to the commissioners' courts if necessary.

8 P.C., Southern Province, *Informal Diary*, 9 Oct. 1914 (N.A.G.A., ADM. 65/5/1).

9 *General Instructions Issued by His Excellency to the Officer Commanding Field Force Togoland*, in *Yendi Information Book 1916–1930* (N.A.G.A., ADM. 67/5/1).

10 *Minutes of Conference at Tamale, 11 March 1921* (N.A.G.A., ADM. 56/1/258). On this occasion, an interestingly ambiguous exchange took place: '*His Excellency*: "[Since 1897] we have been trying to restore the power of the chiefs. I would like to know how far the power of the Chiefs has been advanced towards what it should be." *Deputy C.C.N.T.*: "It has advanced considerably. Native rule and customs are greatly improved."'

11 The D.C. normally informed the Provincial Commissioner of the nomination and eventually a letter was issued, the following being typical:

"No. 297/8/1927   27 March 1928

The Chief Commissioner of the Northern Territories approves of the appointment of Buguli Dagomba, Wulana of Tamale, to the vacant stool of Wulshie, on the usual year's probation.

The District Commissioner,   E. O. Rake,
Western Dagomba, Tamale.   Ag. Commissioner S.P."

(On file, N.A.G.T., ADM. 1/186). The southern term 'stool' was used by administrators until well into the thirties, despite disapproval by the indirect rule purists.

12 Ferguson and Wilks (1970), p. 334.

13 P.C., Southern Province, *Informal Diary*, 7 Oct. 1913, 16 May 1916 (N.A.G.A., ADM. 65/5/1); *Yendi Information Book 1916–1930* (N.A.G.A., ADM. 67/5/1). In 1919 a ward chief from Yendi was imprisoned and in 1921 two village chiefs from Karaga were fined for failure to provide labourers.

14 P.C., Southern Province, *Informal Diary*, 15 Aug. 1923 (N.A.G.A., ADM. 56/1/276).

15 *Handing-over Notes, Western Dagomba District*, 13 Aug. 1924 (N.A.G.A., ADM. 56/1/362). Why the Karaga-Na might seem to have 'got above himself' may be clear from the later parts of the chapter.

16 The background to these cases is discussed below.

17 P.C., Southern Province, to C.C.N. T., 22 Sept. 1917 (N.A.G.A., ADM. 56/1/67). Hobart, the earlier P.C., had laid down a scale of 'seduction fines': £12 for the seduction of a paramount chief's wife, £6 for that of an ordinary chief's, and £2 for that of a commoner's wife. This was a matter of great concern to the chiefs, since it was quite common for a young girl, married to a chief by her father, to desert her husband in favour of a younger man: the chiefs were anxious both to discourage desertion and to squeeze financial consolation out of the seducer if they failed.

18 C.C.N.T. to P.C.s, 20 Sept. 1918 (N.A.G.A., ADM. 56/1/67).

19 Both quotations from acting Commissioner, Southern Province, *Report on Native Administration in the Northern Territories*, 20 July 1928 (N.A.G.T., ADM. 1/7).

20 *Yendi Information Book 1916–1930* (N.A.G.A., ADM. 67/5/1). The Karaga-Na seems also to have made very heavy demands for labour on his sub-chiefs, whom he got fined by the D.C. when they resisted (P.C., Southern Province, *Informal Diary*, 21 March 1921, 19 April 1921 (N.A.G.A., ADM. 56/1/276)).

21 Eyre-Smith (1933), pp. 38–40. He noticed that chiefs were using mallams to help in the intimidation of their subjects. For similar comments on the manipulation of spiritual power, see Hailey (1951), p. 262, and Manoukian (1952), p. 64.

22 Cornevin (1969), p. 171. During this period, the Ya-Na was referred to by the British as 'the chief' or 'the King' of 'Yendi'. I regret that I have been unable to provide an account of changes on the German side of the frontier through an examination of German colonial records.

23 Duncan-Johnstone and Blair (1932), p. 12. As Cardinall later reported, Karaga was the dominant power in the west (acting Commissioner, Southern Province, *Report on Native Administration in the Northern Territories*, 20 July 1928 (N.A.G.T., ADM. 1/7)).

24 Blair, *Notes on the Dagomba Constitution*, 1930 (N.A.G.T., ADM. 1/480).

25 *Note re Case of Complaints of Sub-Chiefs of Kumbungu re Installation of New Chief of Kumbungu by Chief of Savelugu*, 19 Feb. 1911 (N.A.G.A., ADM. 56/1/252). The phrase about consulting the Commissioner was symptomatic of a trend towards tactical abdication from decisions which is discussed later in the chapter.

26 Duncan-Johnstone and Blair (1932), p. 12.

27 Acting Commissioner, Southern Province, *Report on Native Administration in the Northern Territories*, 20 July 1928 (N.A.G.T. ADM. 1/7).

28 Ferguson and Wilks (1970), p. 345.

29 *Ibid*; Tait 'A'. This is not to suggest that competition for the skin was seen exclusively in terms of Abudu versus Andani. The various uncles (younger brothers of Abudulai and Andani) also represented potential gates – a potential realised if and when they actually reached Yendi. The Abudu/Andani contest only took the centre of the political stage after the partition was ended and only became acute when the stock of Andani candidates eligible for Yendi became perilously small.

30 Ferguson and Wilks (1970), pp. 344–5; Holden (1965), p. 85; Ferguson (1973), p. 45; Tait 'B'.

31 Tamakloe (1931), p. 44.

32 *Handing-over Report, Southern Province, Northern Territories*, March 1909 (N.A.G.A., ADM. 56/1/92).

33 The only real exception was the skin of Bamvim, held by Abudulai, son of the deposed Yo-Na, Mahama. Bamvim and Sanerigu were generally regarded as gates to Savelugu.

34 C.C.N.T. to Colonial Secretary, Accra, 21 Aug. 1927 (N.A.G.A., ADM. 11/1275); *Handing-over Report, Southern Province, Northern Territories*, March 1909 (N.A.G.A., ADM. 56/1/92); acting C.C.N.T. to D.P.O., Yendi, 9 July 1917 (N.A.G.A., ADM. 56/1/211).

35 C.C.N.T. to D.P.O., Yendi, 31 Aug. 1917; A. W. Cardinall, notes on 'Dagomba constitution' (N.A.G.A., ADM. 56/1/211); *Yendi Information Book 1916–1930* (N.A.G.A., ADM. 67/5/1).

36 Cornevin (1969), p. 209. An account of the campaign appears in Lucas (1920).

37 D.P.O., Yendi, to C.C.N.T., 7 Nov. 1920 (N.A.G.A., ADM. 56/1/258). On this period, see Metcalfe (1964), pp. 549–51; Ferguson and Wilks (1970), p. 346. The British were very impressed by Yendi. Duncan-Johnstone, on his first visit to the town, wrote: 'In Yendi with its shady walks, its picturesque market, one has the curious impression of being in a French Sudan station, except of course everything is much cleaner' (*Informal Diary of the Commissioner, Southern Province*, Sept. 1929 (N.A.G.T., ADM. 1/126)).

38 Metcalfe (1964), p. 551. On the agreement between France and Britain, see Cornevin (1969), p. 212, and Bourret (1949), p. 95. Instructions for the administration of the British sector were given in a letter from the Colonial Secretary, Accra, to the C.C.N.T., 24 Sept. 1914 (*Yendi Information Book 1916–1930* (N.A.G.A., ADM. 67/5/1)).

39 Sir Hugh Clifford to Sir Lewis Harcourt, 14 Sept. 1914 (reprinted in Metcalfe (1964), pp. 549–50).

40 Colonial Secretary, Accra, to C.C.N.T., 24 Sept. 1914 (*Yendi Information Book 1916–1930* (N.A.G.A., ADM. 67/5/1)).

41 Thus when Alhassan's nephew, the Bamvim-lana Abudulai, asked if he might send a present to the Ya-Na, he was told that 'he might send some tobacco but that there was to be no interference on the part of Yendi with the Chiefs of Dagomba' (P.C., Southern Province, *Informal Diary*, 31 Oct. 1914 (N.A.G.A., ADM. 65/5/1)). Similarly, the D.P.O., Yendi, warned his successor that the Ya-Na was 'not permitted to interfere in any way with the Dagombas in the Northern Territories Protectorate' (*Handing-over Report, Yendi District*, 16 Dec. 1915 (N.A.G.A., ADM. 56/1/204)).

42 Speech on file, N.A.G.A., ADM. 56/1/211.

43 C.C.N.T. to acting D.P.O., Yendi, 23 Oct. 1916 (N.A.G.A., ADM. 56/1/211).

44 Acting C.C.N.T. to D.P.O., Yendi, 27 May 1917 (N.A.G.A., ADM. 56/1/252).

45 Memorandum in *Yendi Information Book 1916–1930* (N.A.G.A., ADM. 67/5/1). Both the Yo-Na and Abudulai of Kpabia were sons of Ya-Na Andani.

46 D.P.O., Yendi, to C.C.N.T., 23 July 1917 (N.A.G.A., ADM. 56/1/211).

47 C.C.N.T. to D.P.O., Yendi, 17 Aug. 1917 (N.A.G.A., ADM. 56/1/211).

48 Enclosed with letter from D.P.O., Yendi, to C.C.N.T., 23 Aug. 1917 (N.A.G.A., ADM. 56/1/211). The petition was signed by Zohe-Na, Kum-lana, Balo-Na, Mbadugu, and Kuga-Na.

49 D.P.O., Yendi, to C.C.N.T., 24 Aug. 1917 (N.A.G.A., ADM. 56/1/211).

50 C.C.N.T. to D.P.O., Yendi, 31 Aug. 1917 (N.A.G.A., ADM. 56/1/211). Armitage was infuriated by Poole's suggestion, in his letter of 23 August, that the Chief Commissioner was being misled by his interpreters and retorted: 'My decision was arrived at without their assistance, and solely through the knowledge of the natives concerned that I venture to think that I possess' (*ibid*).

51 C.C.N.T. to D.P.O., Yendi, 31 Aug. 1917 (second letter) (N.A.G.A., ADM. 56/1/211). This was a shrewd thrust, since Poole's assessment of the Dagomba was generally unflattering. In his handing-over report of October 1916, he said that they had sunk from being 'a masterful and warlike tribe' to become 'lazy, effete, passive resisters of the worst description, and in my opinion gradually dying out'. To which he added: 'If any race required the German method of coercion the Dagombas do.' The Konkombas, on the other hand, were 'industrious, merry, and prolific' (sic) (*Handing-over Report, Yendi*, 25 Oct. 1916 (N.A.G.A. ADM. 56/1/204)).

52 D.P.O., Yendi, *Informal Diary*, 4 Oct. 1917 (N.A.G.A., ADM. 11/1375).

53 C.C.N.T. to D.P.O., Yendi, 25 Oct. 1917. Armitage wrote: 'I distinctly laid down that he was to be known by no more resounding title than that of "Chief of Yendi"' (*ibid*).

54 All quotations from: P.C., Southern Province, to C.C.N.T., 31 Aug. 1917 (N.A.G.A., ADM. 56/1/252). The matter was apparently settled by the Chief Commissioner: I have found no other reference to it in the archives.

55 The Tamale administration wanted a reconciliation but insisted that the regent and his elders should recognise that Bukari's disregard of Yendi during the partition was 'due *not to any individual action of the Chief of Karaga but to the orders that he was given by this Government*' (acting C.C.N.T. to D.P.O., Yendi, 9 July 1917 (N.A.G.A., ADM. 56/1/211; emphasis in original)). Bukari's son alleged that the regent had been plotting to poison his father so as to stop him from achieving the paramountcy: Abudulai swore on his fetish that he had not been involved in such a plot (C.C.N.T. to P.C., Southern Province, 17 Nov. 1917; D.P.O., Yendi, to C.C.N.T., 3 March 1917 (N.A.G.A., ADM. 56/1/211)).

56 Three noble families, if the family of the deceased Karaga-Na is included.

57 Note on 'Karaga succession', 24 April 1918 (N.A.G.A., ADM. 56/1/252). At this point, Andani's second son, Bukari, was at Savelugu; his third son was at Kpabia (i.e. the 'British' Mion-lana); his fourth was at San; his fifth at Sanerigu; his ninth at Kpatinga; and his tenth at Tampion (Mahama, a future king). Others were in less important royal chiefdoms in western Dagomba. The Abudus controlled Yendi, Bamvim, and Voggo.

58 P.C., Southern Province, to C.C.N.T., 13 May 1918 (N.A.G.A., ADM. 56/1/252).

59 C.C.N.T., *Informal Diary*, 15 May 1918 (N.A.G.A., ADM. 56/1/252).
60 *Ibid.*
61 D.P.O., Yendi, *Informal Diary*, 13 Aug. 1920 (N.A.G.A., ADM. 56/1/259). Other material from: D.P.O., Yendi, to C.C.N.T., 5 July 1920 (N.A.G.A., ADM. 56/1/258); *Handing-over Report, Yendi*, July 1920 (N.A.G.A., ADM. 56/1/204); D.P.O., Yendi, *Informal Diary*, 26 July 1920 (N.A.G.A., ADM. 56/1/259).
62 Cornevin (1969), pp. 215, 218; Bourret (1949), p. 96; Metcalfe (1964), pp. 590–2.
63 Metcalfe (1964), p. 592.
64 Togoland under British Mandate Order-in-Council, para. 4 (Metcalfe (1964), pp. 592–3).
65 Sir Hugh Clifford to W. H. Long, 29 April 1918 (reprinted in Metcalfe (1964), pp. 567–9). After the armistice further pressure was applied. In June 1919, Armitage sent a telegram to Accra asking that the petition presented earlier by the Togoland Dagomba chiefs 'in favour of being united once more to their people of the N.T.s ... may be brought again to the notice of Secretary of State for Colonies as former were cut off by Eastern Boundary arbitrarily made without reference to and without consent to Dagomba Tribe' (C.C.N.T. to Officer-in-charge, Tamale (for transmission), 8 June 1919 (N.A.G.A., ADM. 56/1/211)).
66 Armitage was to become Governor of the Gambia. There is a suggestion in Poole's letter that he felt the election was being hurried so as to provide a suitable climax to Armitage's career in the N.T.
67 D.P.O., Yendi, to C.C.N.T., 7 Nov. 1920 (N.A.G.A., ADM. 56/1/258). Abudulai had also won favour by his handling of the dispute with Karaga-Na Bukari Narkaw. As the P.C. later remarked: 'Had he not exercised his influence the cavalry of Miong would certainly have gone out to meet the mounted men of Karaga.' The P.C. also noted that in 1917 Abudulai had offered 75 men as recruits for the Gold Coast Regiment (P.C., Southern Province, to C.C.N.T., ? July 1928 (N.A.G.A., ADM. 56/1/300)).
68 C.C.N.T. to Colonial Secretary. Accra, 24 Nov. 1920 (N.A.G.T., ADM 2/18).
69 *Ibid.*
70 *Ibid.* The 'drum history' provides an interesting account of these events. It relates how Abudulai went to Tamale and handed over 'the walking stick of the chieftainship' to Yo-Na Bukari; how Bukari gave it back on account of his age and blindness; and how 'on the following morning the Chief Commissioner asked Na Abudulai to hand over to him the walking stick. The Chief Commissioner took the walking stick, called Na Abudulai and Ziblim, chief of Karaga, studied them closely and handed back the walking stick to Na Abudulai' (Tait 'A'). Ferguson and Wilks print an almost identical version, apparently based on the Tait transcripts (Ferguson and Wilks (1970), p. 346).
71 C.C.N.T. to Colonial Secretary, Accra, 24 Nov. 1920 (N.A.G.T., ADM. 2/18).
72 *Handing-over Notes, Eastern Dagomba District*, 14 May 1924 (N.A.G.A., ADM. 56/1/362). Mbadugu, the Ya-Na's linguist, acted as go-between.
73 Acting P.C., Southern Province, to D. C., Western Dagomba, 16 Feb. 1927 (N.A.G.T., ADM. 1/186).
74 P.C., Southern Province, to C.C.N.T., ? July 1928 (N.A.G.A., ADM. 56/1/300).
75 *Minutes of Conference at Tamale 11 March 1921* (N.A.G.A., ADM. 56/1/258).
76 P. C., Southern Province, *Informal Diary*, 24 April 1921 (N.A.G.A., ADM. 56/1/276).
77 Letter to Guggisberg on file, N.A.G.A., ADM. 11/1377.
78 Cf. Balandier (1972), p. 160.
79 Whitaker (1967).
80 *Ibid*, pp. 216–17.

CHAPTER 5 THE BATTLE OF WATHERSTON ROAD

1 P.C., Southern Province, *Memorandum on the Introduction and Development of Native Administration*, 14 April 1930 (N.A.G.T., ADM 1/145).
2 C.C.N.T., memorandum of 28 Dec. 1928 (N.A.G.T., ADM. 1/7).
3 Acting C.C.N.T., *Memorandum on Native Administration in the Northern Territories*, 18 March 1931 (N.A.G.T., ADM. 1/153).

4 Wraith (1967), p. 265.

5 *Ibid*, p. 266.

6 Cf. Hailey (1938), pp. 628–9.

7 Cited in letter from C.C.N.T. to P.C., Northern Province, 20 Jan. 1931 (N.A.G.T., ADM. 1/155).

8 See Gailey (1971). The Aba troubles were invoked in the N.T. by those who wanted direct taxation to be preceded by a detailed survey of native social organisation.

9 The Cameron quotation is in Nicolson (1969), p. 244: 'Cameron seems quite deliberately to have rejected the "philosophy" of "indirect rule" as "a rather mysterious business", and to have insisted that, henceforward, it was simply "local native administration" or "local government".' The Chief Commissioner in the late thirties, W. J. A. Jones, remarked: 'local government is but another term for indirect rule' (C.C.N.T. to D.C.s, 5 April 1937 (N.A.G.T., ADM. 1/296)).

10 Minute of the acting Governor, 3 July 1928 (N.A.G.T., ADM. 1/7). Thomas had been appointed Colonial Secretary in 1927, having previously served in Nigeria. Slater, his superior, had been Colonial Secretary of the Gold Coast from 1914 to 1922 and Governor of Sierra Leone from 1922 until 1927.

11 Acting Colonial Secretary, Accra, to acting C.C.N.T., 1 Aug. 1928 (N.A.G.T., ADM. 1/7).

12 Acting P.C., Southern Province, to Colonial Secretary, Accra, 21 July 1928 (N.A.G.T., ADM. 1/7); acting P.C., Southern Province, to acting C.C.N.T., 17 Aug. 1928 (N.A.G.T., ADM. 1/145). Cardinall felt that because of the novelty of indirect rule, 'so delicate a political situation as would obtain during the first few years of the new regime could only be handled by officers most intimate with the existing state of affairs'.

13 D.C., Eastern Dagomba, to P.C., Southern Province, 8 Feb. 1930 (N.A.G.T., ADM. 1/145).

14 Leigh wrote: 'The power of the Chiefs has NOT been broken ... all our Public Works, Policing, Control of cattle routes, etc. are administered through the Chiefs ... Our system is now quasi indirect and at present we cannot go further until the people are better educated' (notes on *Political Conference Held at Tamale on Thursday 3 January 1929* (N.A.G.T., ADM. 1/7)). In 1928 he claimed: 'The general policy has been a system of indirect rule through the Chiefs' (Gold Coast (1928)).

15 D.C., Western Dagomba, *Native Administration – Development Programme*, 30 Dec. 1929 (N.A.G.T., ADM. 2/18). The Dagomba (said Rutherford in his report for 1929–30) 'is a great peace lover and unless disturbed remains quietly happy'. 'Like a yam', Duncan-Johnstone wrote in the margin (*Annual Report on the Western Dagomba District for the Year Ending 31 March 1930* (N.A.G.A., ADM. 56/1/506)).

16 Minute of acting Governor, 9 Sept. 1928 (N.A.G.T., ADM. 1/7).

17 Marginal comment, *ibid*; C.C.N.T., memorandum of 28 Dec. 1928 (N.A.G.T., ADM. 1/7).

18 Notes on *Political Conference Held at Tamale on Thursday 3 January 1929* (N.A.G.T., ADM. 1/7).

19 C.C.N.T., memorandum of 28 Dec. 1928 (N.A.G.T., ADM. 1/7).

20 *Ibid*. On the question of labour, Leigh remarked: 'the labour going to the Coast will cease and become paid labour up here ... we shall lose all communal labour and all the men who work 24 days per annum on the roads'. These objections became irrelevant with the adoption of the Geneva convention on forced labour.

21 Colonial Secretary, Accra, to C.C.N.T., 21 Oct. 1929 (N.A.G.T., ADM. 1/7).

22 *Ibid*.

23 D.C., Western Dagomba, to P.C., Southern Province, 28 Feb. 1930 (N.A.G.T., ADM. 1/145).

24 Duncan-Johnstone replied to Rutherford: 'You are against taxation and now against a subsidy being paid to the Chiefs. If you read [the Governor's] memorandum you will see that Chiefs will be an integral part of the Government machinery ... How are the wretched chiefs to live and pay the Native Officials?' (note on letter from D.C., Western Dagomba, to P.C., Southern Province, 28 Feb. 1930 (N.A.G.T., ADM.

1/145)). Cardinall argued that the payment of salaries would put a stop to extortion (acting P.C., Southern Province, to C.C.N.T., 17 Aug. 1928 (N.A.G.T., ADM. 1/145)).

25 P.C., Southern Province, *Informal Diary*, 9 Jan. 1930 (N.A.G.T., ADM. 1/132).

26 Although Walker-Leigh had been in the north for thirty years, he had not served as a D.C. since the beginning of World War I. Whittall believed that, as a result, Leigh did not 'realise that the people had advanced considerably' and to this he attributed Leigh's opposition to indirect rule (P.C., Northern Province, to C.C.N.T., 14 May 1931 (N.A.G.T., ADM. 1/155)).

27 *Annual Report on the Dagomba District for the Year, 1937–38* (N.A.G.T., ADM. 1/448).

28 Two Assistant Chief Commissioners replaced the Provincial Commissioners, abolished in 1937. I am most grateful to Mrs Elizabeth Hook and Canon H. A. Blair for background information on officers serving in this period.

29 It is probably significant that Jones and Duncan-Johnstone worked together in the Colony just before Duncan-Johnstone was posted to Tamale.

30 Duncan-Johnstone required complete obedience to the new regime: of his *Standing Orders*, issued in 1930, he wrote: 'it must be clearly understood that they contain the official policy of the Province and any critical discussion of them is an act of disloyalty and insubordination' (N.A.G.T., ADM. 1/195). His reaction to opposition was to demand the removal of doubters and the creation of a 'picked team of optimists'. He had a low opinion of his staff, writing in 1930: 'I can't think of a single man at present up here I would be prepared to hand over to ... Here we have to take what we are given and be truly thankful' (P.C., Southern Province, *Informal Diary*, 5 Jan. 1930, 7 Jan. 1930 (N.A.G.T., ADM. 1/132)).

31 *Informal Diary of the Commissioner, Southern Province*, 7 Sept. 1929, 22 Sept. 1929 (N.A.G.T., ADM. 1/126).

32 P.C., Southern Province, *Informal Diary*, 1 Jan. 1930 (N.A.G.T., ADM. 1/132).

33 P.C., Southern Province, *Notes on Policy and Standing Orders to Political Officers, Southern Province, Northern Territories*, 1930 (N.A.G.T., ADM. 1/195).

34 P.C., Southern Province, *Memorandum on the Introduction and Development of Native Administration in the Southern Province*, 14 April 1930 (N.A.G.T., ADM. 1/145). It was by such a process, Duncan-Johnstone believed, that 'the British became a nation'.

35 Gold Coast (1938), p. 18.

36 D.C., Dagomba, *Minutes of the Dagomba Conference Held at Yendi in March 1936* (N.A.G.T., ADM. 2/29). Jones also compared Dagomba government to a seedling, crushed by a stone (the Administration): 'The seedling cannot grow till the stone is lifted. Time has arrived to remove the stone and let Dagomba arise and manage its own affairs' (*ibid*).

37 P.C., Southern Province, *Memorandum on the Introduction and Development of Native Administration*, 14 April 1930 (N.A.G.T., ADM. 1/145).

38 Gold Coast (1937).

39 P.C., Southern Province, *Informal Diary*, 8 July 1930 (N.A.G.T., ADM. 1/132).

40 Marginal comment on acting P.C., Southern Province, *Report on Native Administration in the Northern Territories*, 20 July 1928 (N.A.G.T., ADM. 1/7).

41 H. A. Blair, *Notes on the Dagomba Constitution*, 1930 (N.A.G.T., ADM. 1/480).

42 D.C., Eastern Dagomba, *Informal Diary*, 2 Aug. 1930 (N.A.G.T., ADM. 1/132). This meeting was historic in that it was conducted entirely in Dagbane.

43 Address by acting C.C.N.T. at opening of Dagomba conference, 21 Nov. 1930 (N.A.G.T., ADM. 1/477).

44 Duncan-Johnstone and Blair (1932), p. 29.

45 *Ibid*, p. 31. For the selection procedure approved at the conference, see Appendix 1.

46 Duncan-Johnstone and Blair (1932), p. 33.

47 The Native Authority (Northern Territories) Ordinance No. 2 of 1932 (30 Jan. 1932), Cap. 84; Order No. 1 of 1933 (constituting Dagomba divisions as Subordinate Native Authorities); Order No. 2 of 1933 (constituting the Dagomba Kingdom as a Native Authority).

48 The Native Authority (Northern Territories) Ordinance, section 3.
49 *Ibid*, sections 12, 14.
50 *Ibid*, sections 4, 8, 17.
51 D.C., Western Dagomba, to acting P.C., Southern Province, 23 April 1931; acting P.C., Southern Province, to D.C., Western Dagomba, 29 April 1931 (N.A.G.T., ADM. 1/479).
52 Gold Coast (1938).
53 P.C., Southern Province, *Informal Diary*, 8 July 1930 (N.A.G.T., ADM. 1/132).
54 *Ibid*.
55 Austen (1968), p. 148. Elsewhere, Austen remarks: 'conscious expressions of dedication to Indirect Rule are consistently accompanied by the strengthening of a bureaucratic apparatus which denies the possibility of autonomous local development' (*ibid.*, p. 254).
56 Governor's Order No. 1 of 1932 (Togoland under British Mandate) and Northern Territories No. 5 of 1932. The Western Dagomba section was in fact incorporated into the Eastern Section. There was still a D.C. at Tamale, known as the Assistant D.C., Dagomba.
57 Acting P.C., Southern Province, to C.C.N.T., 17 Aug. 1928; P.C., Southern Province, *Memorandum on the Introduction and Development of Native Administration*, 14 April 1930 (N.A.G.T., ADM. 1/145).
58 Acting P.C., Southern Province, to C.C.N.T., 17 Aug. 1928 (N.A.G.T., ADM. 1/145).
59 Secretary for Native Affairs, *Informal Diary*, 21 March 1930 (extract on file, N.A.G.T., ADM. 1/196). Duncan-Johnstone had earlier written that one of the tasks facing the new regime was 'to frame a Native Administration Ordinance ... recognising that the chiefs have inherent jurisdiction' (*Memorandum on the Introduction and Development of Native Administration*, 14 April 1930 (N.A.G.T., ADM. 1/145)).
60 Gold Coast (1938).
61 Native Tribunals Ordinance No. 1 of 1932, amended by the Native Courts (Northern Territories) Ordinance, 1 July 1935. Cf. Bourret (1949), pp. 100–1; Hailey (1951), pp. 269–71.
62 Schedule to Native Courts (Northern Territories) Ordinance, 1 July 1935; Hailey (1951), p. 270. The Bimbilla-Na was the paramount chief of Nanumba, which lay within the Dagomba District, though traditionally it was independent of Yendi.
63 Order No. 3 of 1933: D.C., Dagomba, *Informal Diary*, 11 Dec. 1933 (N.A.G.T., ADM. 1/235); Assistant D.C., Dagomba, to D.C., Dagomba, 21 March 1935 (N.A.G.T., ADM. 2/29).
64 D.C., Dagomba, *Report of the Dagomba Conference at Yendi, 4 to 8 March 1935* (N.A.G.T., ADM. 2/29).
65 P.C., Southern Province, *Informal Diary*, 10 May 1929 (N.A.G.T., ADM. 1/126). The abolition of the N.T.C. was a matter of particular bitterness to Walker-Leigh.
66 Documents and correspondence, N.A.G.T., ADM. 1/232, ADM. 1/480, ADM. 2/18.
67 P.C., Southern Province, *Informal Diary*, 4 July 1930 (N.A.G.T., ADM. 1/132); acting D.C., Eastern Dagomba, to P.C., Southern Province, 16 July 1930; acting D.C., Eastern Dagomba, to P.C., Southern Province, 27 Aug. 1930 (N.A.G.T., ADM. 1/480). Cf. Ferguson and Wilks (1970), p. 337.
68 D.C., Dagomba, *Informal Diary*, 25 March 1937 (N.A.G.T., ADM. 1/271).
69 Gold Coast (1937); Gold Coast (1938); *Annual Report on the Dagomba District for the Year, 1937–38* (N.A.G.T., ADM. 1/448); *Dagomba District. Report for Togoland under British Mandate for the Year Ended 31 December 1934* (N.A.G.A., ADM. 11/1534); *Dagomba District. Report on Togoland under British Mandate for the Year Ended 31 December 1935* (N.A.G.A., ADM. 11/1534).
70 D.C., Dagomba, to C.C.N.T., 22 Oct. 1936 (N.A.G.T., ADM. 2/15). The book in question may have been Graham Greene's *Journey without Maps*, which was first published in 1936. Reflecting on the impact of colonialism on Sierra Leone, Greene wrote: 'The District Commissioner's work was to a great extent the protection of the native from the civilization he represented.' Greene went on to remark: 'The "noble savage" no longer exists; perhaps he never existed....' (Greene (1971), p. 61).
71 Acting P.C., Southern Province, to C.C.N.T., 17 Aug. 1928 (N.A.G.T., ADM. 1/145);

P.C., Southern Province, to C.C.N.T., 23 Jan. 1931 (N.A.G.T., ADM. 2/18).
72 P.C., Southern Province, to C.C.N.T., 23 Jan. 1931 (N.A.G.T., ADM. 2/18); Gold Coast (1931); acting P.C., Southern Province, to C.C.N.T., 22 Aug. 1931 (N.A.G.T., ADM. 1/477); D.C., Dagomba, *Informal Diary*, 5 March 1934 (N.A.G.T., ADM. 1/235); Assistant D.C., Dagomba, to D.C., Dagomba, 21 March 1935 (N.A.G.T., ADM. 2/29).
73 D.C., Western Dagomba, *Informal Diary*, 21 July 1932 (N.A.G.T., ADM. 1/232); *Minutes of the Dagomba Annual Conference Held at Yendi on 21 July 1932* (N.A.G.T., ADM. 1/519).
74 D.C., Dagomba, *Informal Diary*, 16 Oct. 1931 (N.A.G.T., ADM. 1/131).
75 Native Treasuries Ordinance No. 10 of 1932 (30 July 1932), Cap. 86, section 3.
76 As early as March 1932 Jackson (C.C.N.T.) had said that 'he was prepared to start collecting the tax in January 1933'; in December 1933 Jones (his successor) asked his colleagues 'whether the time had not arrived when direct taxation must be imposed [in the N.T.] independently of Ashanti and the Colony' (*Note of a Conference Held at Tamale on 27 March 1932* (N.A.G.T., ADM. 1/230); *Minutes of the Political Conference Held at Tamale upon the 2nd and 3rd of December 1933* (N.A.G.T., ADM. 1/206)).
77 Acting C.C.N.T. to D.C.s, 24 Dec. 1935 (N.A.G.T., ADM. 1/32); P.C., Southern Province, *Memorandum on the Introduction and Development of Native Administration*, 14 April 1930 (N.A.G.T., ADM. 1/145); C.C.N.T. to Colonial Secretary, Accra, 14 Sept. 1931 (N.A.G.T., ADM. 1/230); *Direct Taxation Propaganda Notes* with covering letter from P.C., Southern Province, to D.C., Western Dagomba, 6 Jan. 1932 (N.A.G.T., ADM. 2/18)).
78 C.C.N.T. to Colonial Secretary, Accra, 5 Nov. 1934 (N.A.G.T., ADM. 1/32).
79 D.C., Dagomba, to C.C.N.T., 6 April 1934 (N.A.G.T., ADM. 2/18).
80 C.C.N.T. to D.C., Dagomba, 12 Feb. 1935; C.C.N.T. to Colonial Secretary, Accra, 5 Nov. 1934 (N.A.G.T., ADM. 1/32).
81 D.C., Western Dagomba, to acting P.C., Southern Province, 14 Oct. 1931 (N.A.G.T., ADM. 1/480).
82 This may explain why the 1932 political conference resolved 'that Government should ignore the customary tribute to the chiefs, or rather not interfere with it' (*Notes of a Conference Held at Tamale on 27 March 1932* (N.A.G.T., ADM. 1/230)). The policy certainly changed totally once Jones became C.C.N.T.
83 D.C., Eastern Dagomba, to P.C., Southern Province, 29 Dec. 1931 (N.A.G.T., ADM. 2/18).
84 Notes on file (N.A.G.T., ADM. 1/32).
85 Based on: D.C., Dagomba, to C.C.N.T., 6 April 1934 (N.A.G.T., ADM. 2/18); C.C.N.T., memorandum of 6 Nov. 1934 (N.A.G.T., ADM. 1/32).
86 C.C.N.T., memorandum of 6 Nov. 1934 (N.A.G.T., ADM. 1/32).
87 *Minutes of the Third Dagomba Conference Held at Yendi on 3 January 1934* (N.A.G.T., ADM. 1/477); C.C.N.T. to Colonial Secretary, Accra, 26 May 1936, 5 Nov. 1934 (N.A.G.T., ADM. 1/32).
88 Colonial Secretary, Accra, to C.C.N.T., 24 June 1936 (N.A.G.T., ADM. 1/32); Gold Coast (1937).
89 The D.C., Dagomba, had suggested that divisional treasuries should pay half of their revenues into the Yendi treasury (D.C., Dagomba, *Informal Diary*, 22 July 1933 (N.A.G.T., ADM. 1/235)).
90 C.C.N.T. to Assistant D.C., Dagomba, 17 Oct. 1933 (N.A.G.T., ADM. 2/18).
91 Duncan-Johnstone and Blair (1932), p. 34. The rights of the *tindana* were also recognised.
92 C.C.N.T. to Assistant D.C., Dagomba, 17 Oct. 1933 (N.A.G.T., ADM. 2/18).
93 By the mid-forties the administration was using itinerant tax-collectors; but it is not clear from the archives when this practice began or whether it was general.
94 C.C.N.T. to Colonial Secretary, Accra, 26 May 1936 (N.A.G.T., ADM. 1/32).
95 C.C.N.T. to D.C.s, 19 Aug. 1936 (N.A.G.T., ADM. 1/32).
96 Gold Coast (1937); Gold Coast (1938); D.C., Dagomba, *Minutes of the Dagomba Annual Conference Held at Yendi in March 1937* (N.A.G.T., ADM. 2/29); Dagomba Native Authority estimates, 1938–9 (N.A.G.T., ADM. 1/30).

97 D.C., Dagomba, *Minutes of the Dagomba Annual Conference Held at Yendi in March 1937* (N.A.G.T., ADM. 2/29).
98 P.C., Southern Province, *Memorandum on the Introduction and Development of Native Administration*, 14 April 1930 (N.A.G.T., ADM. 1/145).
99 Superintendent of Education, N.T., to Director of Education, Accra, 19 April 1929 (N.A.G.T., ADM. 1/7); Provincial Inspector of Schools, N.T., *Annual Report on Education, Northern Territories, 1938–39* (N.A.G.T., ADM. 1/337).
100 Gold Coast (1938); *Annual Report on the Dagomba District for the Year, 1937–38* (N.A.G.T., ADM. 1/448); *Annual Report on the Dagomba District for the Year, 1938–39* (N.A.G.T., ADM. 1/449).
101 P.C., Southern Province, to acting C.C.N.T., 27 Jan. 1930 (N.A.G.T., ADM. 1/7); P.C., Southern Province, *Memorandum on the Introduction and Development of Native Administration*, 14 April 1930 (N.A.G.T., ADM. 1/145).
102 P.C., Southern Province, *Notes on Policy and Standing Orders*, 1930 (N.A.G.T., ADM. 1/195).
103 C.C.N.T. to Colonial Secretary, Accra, 5 Nov. 1934 (N.A.G.T., ADM. 1/32).
104 Superintendent of Education, N.T., to Director of Education, Accra, 19 April 1929 (N.A.G.T., ADM. 1/7); Gold Coast (1937); Gold Coast (1938); Provincial Inspector of Schools, N.T., *Annual Report on Education, Northern Territories, 1939–40* (N.A.G.T., ADM. 1/339).
105 Provincial Inspector of Schools, N.T., *Annual Report on Education, Northern Territories, 1938–39* (N.A.G.T., ADM. 1/337).
106 Gold Coast (1938); C.C.N.T. to Colonial Secretary, 5 Nov. 1934 (N.A.G.T., ADM. 1/32).
107 Gold Coast (1937).
108 Gold Coast (1930).
109 Gold Coast (1937).
110 Assistant D.C., Dagomba, *Informal Diary*, 2 Jan. 1939 (N.A.G.T., ADM. 1/304); D.C., Dagomba, *Informal Diary*, 9 June 1937, 10 June 1937 (N.A.G.T., ADM. 1/271).
111 D.C., Dagomba, *Informal Diary*, 14 Nov. 1939 (N.A.G.T., ADM. 1/299).
112 Gold Coast (1937).
113 *Notes on Policy and Standing Orders*, 1930 (N.A.G.T., ADM. 1/195).
114 Gold Coast (1938).
115 Marginal comment, Assistant D.C., Dagomba, *Informal Diary*, 7 March 1940 (N.A.G.T., ADM. 1/348). Such contempt for office work was not universal in colonial administration. For example, Colonel Casey, in Hanley's *The Consul at Sunset*, declared: 'It is the filing system which runs the country – indeed, the Empire. The Empire is a filing system' (Hanley (1952) p. 14).
116 C.C.N.T. to Colonial Secretary, Accra, 5 Nov. 1934 (N.A.G.T., ADM. 1/32).
117 C.C.N.T. to D.C., Dagomba, 27 March 1935 (N.A.G.T., ADM. 1/477).
118 D.C., Dagomba, *Report of the Dagomba Conference at Yendi, 4 to 8 March 1935* (N.A.G.T., ADM. 2/29).

CHAPTER 6 DAGOMBA POLITICS UNDER INDIRECT RULE, 1932–1947

1 D.C., Eastern Dagomba, *Informal Diary*, 24 Aug. 1930 (N.A.G.T., ADM. 1/131).
2 Assistant D.C., Dagomba, *Informal Diary*, 1 Feb. 1938 (N.A.G.T., ADM. 1/304).
3 I must emphasise that the hypotheses explored here and later are, necessarily, based on rather thin documentation. There are many gaps in the jigsaw and the links of causality are, in several cases, weak. When the archives for the later years are available, I hope that further research will be carried out; and such research will certainly invalidate some of my ideas.
4 Both quotations from Mahood (1964), p. 76. Miss Mahood's book gives a vivid picture of colonial society in the bush as well as a very interesting account of Cary's literary development.
5 'Some impressions and experiences of one's first tour of service', 1930, filed N.A.G.T.,

ADM. 1/206. It is unfortunate that this essay is anonymous, since it contains some of the most perceptive observations on indirect rule to be found in the archives..

6 In 1938 the Assistant D.C. remarked: 'Savelugu is getting bigger and bigger and . . . even the doubtful ladies of Tamale are following the stranger population to rent-free, rate-free, police-free Savelugu!' (Assistant D.C., Dagomba, *Informal Diary*, 29 Aug. 1938 (N.A.G.T., ADM. 1/304)).

7 Gold Coast (1950a), pp. 292–312. Of 393 with Standard VII or a higher qualification, 361 were living in the west – the great majority in the Tamale area.

8 D.C., Eastern Dagomba, *Informal Diary*, 25 July 1924 (N.A.G.A., ADM. 67/5/4). Nandom and Jirapa were in the Northern Province where Parker had served after entering the Gold Coast service in 1921.

9 The question was complicated by taboos on the Gulkpe-Na visiting Tamale more than three times during his lifetime. In April 1932 the Gulkpe-Na took courage, defied the taboos, and established his own court in Tamale. He lived there for at least another fifteen years, although there were periodically disputes between him and the *dakpema* (who became a member of the Gulkpeogu tribunal).

10 D.C., Eastern Dagomba, *Informal Diary*, 20 May 1932 (N.A.G.T., ADM. 1/235).

11 D.C., Eastern Dagomba, to P.C., Southern Province, 29 Dec. 1931 (N.A.G.T., ADM. 2/18).

12 Gold Coast (1938). The king attributed his illness to his having killed a snake whose parents in revenge had cast a spell on him.

13 Mbadugu was the elder responsible for the king's treasury and, under the Native Courts Ordinance, he was appointed a member of the Yendi native tribunal; he also sat in his own tribunal with the Damanko, a minor elder (D.C., Dagomba, *Informal Diary*, 12 July 1934 (N.A.G.T., ADM. 1/235)).

14 Marginal comment, D.C., Dagomba, *Informal Diary*, 1 May 1934 (N.A.G.T., ADM. 1/235). Miller remarked: 'It is very evident that Mbadugu is a gentleman who has usurped a lot of power he is not entitled to. He is definitely only the mouthpiece of the Ya-Na and only has power to say what he is told.'

15 D.C., Dagomba, *Informal Diary*, 24 Aug. 1934 (N.A.G.T., ADM. 1/235).

16 D.C., Dagomba, *Informal Diary*, 25 Jan. 1934 (N.A.G.T., ADM. 1/235). Cockey maintained that there was an 'anti-Mbadugu cabal' at Yendi.

17 Miller said: 'I only wish [the] elders would be more helpful especially Kuga-Na and Zohe-Na, the latter especially is making capital of being one of the usual channels to the Ya-Na and it will take a lot of stopping' (D.C., Dagomba, *Informal Diary*, 19 Feb. 1934 (N.A.G.T., ADM. 1/235)).

18 D.C., Dagomba, *Informal Diary*, 26 April 1937, 6 Dec. 1937 (N.A.G.T., ADM. 1/271).

19 Minutes, *Meeting Held before the Chief Commissioner, Northern Territories, on a Palaver Concerning the Election of Kumbungu Na for Dagomba, 19 January 1938* (N.A.G.T., ADM. 1/611). The Bamvim-lana, a member of the Abudu gate, was a former civil servant of some affluence; he had been jailed previously for petty embezzlement. Tait, in his unpublished account of the 1954 election, notes: 'Minor chiefs who felt pulled between loyalty to a kinsman or patron and their own chances of advancement would say, "Ah well! God will decide" or "God will show".' (I am most grateful to Mr Tia Sulemana of Tamale for lending this document to me.)

20 *Ibid.*

21 Asked by Jones whether it was proper for Mbadugu to take £50 from Tali-Na, Mba Malle said: 'Provided the Tali-Na is appointed, he is right to take the money for himself.' Zohe-Na said that all such money should go to the king, and the new Mbadugu, Sandow, said that Tali-Na was entitled to get it back in the event of somebody else being appointed (*ibid*).

22 Jones had remarked: 'a chief is not like a cow or a sheep – It is not a thing to be put on the market to be sold to the highest bidder.' He also suggested that Tali-Na had got his money by extortion but the Tali-Na said later that 'he had . . . been selling livestock – mostly pigs – for the past five years, and had also pawned four of his sons – since redeemed for £10 a time'. So Jones was wrong to think that offices were being sold like sheep

or cows; they were, in fact, being bought with pigs and pawn-tickets. The Bamvim-lana was, in later years, reprimanded for 'illicit fining'. The Assistant D.C. commented on this occasion: 'His attitude is "I paid £25 for the Bamvim-Na's skin and lost £50 trying to get Savelugu. I must get the money back somehow and most people agree to pay my fines"' (Assistant D.C., Dagomba, *Informal Diary*, 3 June 1946 (N.A.G.T., ADM. 1/348)).

23 The elimination of 'information payments' would, Jones thought, 'enable anybody, however poor he may be, to have his claim considered' (*Meeting Held before the Chief Commissioner . . . 19 January 1938* (N.A.G.T., ADM. 1/611)).

24 Gold Coast (1938).

25 D.C., Dagomba, to C.C.N.T., 11 Sept. 1935 (N.A.G.T., ADM. 1/611). In the event, it was Yakubu, Kpatinga-Na and a son of Na Andani, who was appointed.

26 D. C., Dagomba, *Informal Diary*, 30 Aug. 1935 (N.A.G.T., ADM. 1/271); D.C., Dagomba, to C.C.N.T., 11 Sept. 1935 (N.A.G.T., ADM. 1/611).

27 The D.C. commented: 'As to my mind, they are nearly all quite useless this might not be a bad thing' (D.C., Dagomba, *Informal Diary*, 22 March 1938 (N.A.G.T., ADM. 1/299)).

28 D.C., Dagomba, *Informal Diary*, 21 Sept. 1938 (N.A.G.T., ADM. 1/299). Zohe-Na was not, of course, one of the selection committee; he was the Karaga-Na's 'father' at court.

29 D.C., Dagomba, *Informal Diary*, 22 Sept. 1938 (N.A.G.T., ADM. 1/299).

30 D.C., Dagomba, *Informal Diary*, 23 Sept. 1938 (N.A.G.T., ADM. 1/299).

31 The Yo-Na, who had not pressed a claim, congratulated the D.C. 'for not forcing on the Dagombas the Karaga-Na who he said had absolutely no right by birth to be even [chief of Karaga]'. He added that there would have been a civil war if Karaga had been appointed (Assistant D.C., Dagomba, *Informal Diary*, 6 Oct. 1938, 9 Oct. 1938 (N.A.G.T., ADM. 1/304)).

32 Nyologu was a village with a population of 240 in Savelugu division. In 1948 the division itself had a population of 42,279.

33 *Report on a Meeting of Chiefs Held at Yendi on 1 October 1941* (N.A.G.T., ADM. 1/611). The previous holder of the skin had been from the Andani gate.

34 *Ibid.* At the same meeting, two of the sons of Yo-Na Bukari, who had withdrawn from the paramountcy in 1920, complained that, despite Armitage's promise, they were not being treated as sons of Ya-Na: this the D.C. denied. Both held *na-bihe* chieftaincies under Savelugu: one was chief of Voggo, the other Tibung-lana.

35 D.C., Dagomba, *Informal Diary*, 20 April 1944 (N.A.G.T., ADM. 1/347).

36 The colonial presence itself had strengthened the position of the older generation. The D.C. remarked, in connection with resistance by young Konkombas to taxation, that the Pax Britannica had 'both closed one outlet to youthful exuberance and increased the doddering section of the community' (D.C., Dagomba, *Informal Diary*, 16 June 1939 (N.A.G.T., ADM. 1/299)).

37 The second charge referred to the incident (mentioned in Chapter 5) of the young wife who had been beaten and put in irons; the first to the occasion in June 1930 when he had 'marred the proceedings by turning up very drunk and being violently sick before His Excellency's arrival'. The third charge seems to have been just a placatory gesture to the administration (P.C., Southern Province, *Informal Diary*, 3 July 1930 (N.A.G.T., ADM. 1/132); acting D.C., Eastern Dagomba, to D.C., Western Dagomba, 27 Aug. 1930 (N.A.G.T., ADM. 2/18)).

38 D.C., Western Dagomba, *Informal Diary*, 28 June 1932 (N.A.G.T., ADM. 1/232). In September 1933 Miller was still trying to explain the principles of indirect rule: 'This is about the twenty-fourth time they have been told of Native Administration and they still don't understand' (Assistant D.C., Dagomba, *Informal Diary*, 1 Sept. 1933 (N.A.G.T., ADM. 1/232)).

39 Assistant D.C., Dagomba, *Report on Native Administration of Dagomba Sub-District*, 27 Sept. 1933 (N.A.G.T., ADM. 2/16).

40 Savelugu continued to be troubled by domestic strife. The Assistant D.C. remarked on

this matter: 'The Savelugu-Na says the women in Dagombaland are "going to blazes", their men can't control them, he blames the white-man's laws' (Assistant D.C., Dagomba, *Informal Diary*, 15 Feb. 1938, 30 Dec. 1938, 8 Jan. 1939 (N.A.G.T., ADM. 1/304)).

41 D.C., Dagomba, *Informal Diary*, 10 Dec. 1935 (N.A.G.T., ADM. 1/271).

42 Assistant D.C., Dagomba, *Informal Diary*, 8 Nov. 1934, 9 Nov. 1934 (N.A.G.T., ADM. 1/232). These comments arose from an order which the D.C. had given to the Tampionlana, Mahama (a young brother of the Ya-Na), to tour the villages in his district.

43 Note on file (N.A.G.A., ADM. 56/1/300). In September 1931 the D.C., Western Dagomba, pointed out that a new appointee to the skin of Voggo had previously been a government interpreter and commented: 'He is the fifth interpreter, I believe, to become a chief. He has gone over several people to this Chieftainship. I hope it is on the Natives' appraisement of his merits and not done just to please Government' (D.C., Western Dagomba, *Informal Diary*, 9 Sept. 1931 (N.A.G.T., ADM. 1/132)).

44 D.C., Dagomba, to C.C.N.T., 11 Sept. 1935 (N.A.G.T., ADM. 1/611); D.C., Dagomba, *Informal Diary*, 28–9 Aug. 1935, 30 Aug. 1935 (N.A.G.T., ADM. 1/271).

45 *Report on a Meeting of Chiefs Held at Yendi on 1 October 1941* (N.A.G.T., ADM. 1/611). Interestingly, Armstrong also 'pointed out that the two Dagomba chiefs who had been appointed by the "Whiteman" were both wrong appointments'. It was not clear from the context which chiefs he was referring to.

46 *Ibid.*

47 Tait 'A'. The transcript describes how Mahama 'arrived in Yendi and stopped in the Kinkansi Na's house, seeking the chieftaincy. Ziblim, Chief of Karaga also arrived seeking the chieftaincy. Then the whiteman handed Yendi to Mahama.'

48 When Armstrong reported that Ziblim had left Yendi 'in a huff', Jones replied: 'He would not have been a success and we would have been blamed' (D.C., Dagomba, *Informal Diary*, 24 Sept. 1938, and marginal comment by C.C.N.T. (N.A.G.T., ADM. 1/299)). Some informants suggested to me that Mahama was chosen because he had ingratiated himself with Abudulai II.

49 Ferguson and Wilks (1970), p. 348. My purpose here is not to criticise Miss Ferguson's account (which is otherwise admirable) but rather to suggest an interesting contradiction between the administrative record of events and the 'official' Dagomba version, which, I think, is further evidence of the ruling class's tendency to cast responsibility on to the government or on to Providence – a reasonable stratagem in a society where political intrigue is conducted at close quarters over many years at a time. The use of poisoning, a particularly anonymous kind of weapon, is also intelligible in this context. The historical parallels in Elizabethan and Jacobean drama are interesting.

50 The D.C., Dagomba, was required to administer the Krachi district, as well as his own, with a reduced staff. One indication of the reduction in trekking is that Nanton, only sixteen miles from Tamale, was not visited by the Assistant D.C. for seven months at a time (C.C.N.T. to D.C., Dagomba, 12 March 1940 (N.A.G.T., ADM. 1/348)).

51 D.C., Dagomba, *Informal Diary*, 22 Oct. 1939 (N.A.G.T., ADM. 1/348).

52 Assistant D.C., Dagomba, *Informal Diary*, 16 Feb. 1940 (N.A.G.T., ADM. 1/348). In October over 300 recruits for the army were sent into Tamale by the divisional chiefs, 'in accordance with instructions issued by the Ya-Na'. A large number deserted within a few days and were pursued by troops of the Gold Coast Regiment: in the end only 52 of the recruits remained (Assistant D.C., Dagomba, *Informal Diary*, 9 Oct. 1939, 12 Oct. 1939 (N.A.G.T., ADM. 1/304); D.C., Dagomba, *Informal Diary*, 9 Oct. 1939 (N.A.G.T., ADM. 1/299)). A remarkable account of the origins of the war was provided for northern chiefs by the Governor in 1940 (see Appendix 2).

53 C.C.N.T. to D.C., Dagomba, 12 March 1940 (N.A.G.T., ADM. 1/348).

54 Assistant D.C., Dagomba, *Informal Diary*, 26–7 Jan. 1940, 21 Feb. 1940 (N.A.G.T., ADM. 1/348). In February 1940 the D.C. discovered that the Kumbung-Na had 'been helping himself' to amounts totalling £30 from the Native Treasury; the treasury clerk himself was subsequently jailed on (unrelated) charges of embezzlement. Several years

later the D.C. reported after an inspection of the Savelugu Native Authority: 'Yo-Na full of spirits, treasury clerk quietly drunk.' The Yo-Na had been bound over for a year in 1943 on a charge of theft (Assistant D.C., Dagomba, to D.C., Dagomba, 6 Feb. 1940 (N.A.G.T., ADM. 1/30); *Report on the Dagomba–Nanumba Native Treasury 1940–41* (N.A.G.T., ADM. 1/30); Assistant D.C., Dagomba, *Informal Diary*, 26 Jan. 1947, 11 Nov. 1943 (N.A.G.T., ADM. 1/348)).

55 Assistant D.C., Dagomba, *Informal Diary*, 7 March 1940, 16 Feb. 1940 (N.A.G.T., ADM. 1/348).

56 D.C., Dagomba, *Informal Diary*, 7 Sept. 1944 (N.A.G.T., ADM. 1/347); Assistant D.C., Dagomba, *Informal Diary*, 22–3 Feb. 1946 (N.A.G.T., ADM. 1/348). Kerr remarked: 'The slackness of the Dagomba Native Authority is unbelievable.'

57 D.C., Dagomba, *Informal Diary*, 25 Sept. 1944, 26 Sept. 1944 (N.A.G.T., ADM. 1/347). His verdict on Karaga was mournful: 'A desolate spot and a depressed ruler.' The trouble with Karaga was that it was isolated from the main axes of communication, as Kerr's successor pointed out: 'Karaga is alive with history and legend, but dead in all other respects and in a few more years, I fear, it will be but a hamlet' (D.C., Dagomba, *Informal Diary*, 12 Aug. 1946 (N.A.G.T., ADM. 1/347)).

58 D.C., Dagomba, *Informal Diary*, 19 July 1945 (N.A.G.T., ADM. 1/347).

CHAPTER 7 VOTIBU

1 Returns of election held for regional assemblies, *Ghana Gazette*, 27 October 1958. *Votibu* is the Dagbane term invented to refer to the British electoral process introduced after World War II.

2 *Annual Report, Dagomba District, 1946–1947* (N.A.G.T., ADM. 1/515). In 1948 the D.C. remarked: 'For years past the progress of Dagomba has been held up by old and illiterate men who have put obstructions in the way of anything that might possibly reduce their power' (*Annual Report, Dagomba District, 1947–1948* (N.A.G.T., ADM. 1/536)).

3 'Even now,' the D.C. thought, 'an able and incorruptible Chief could appoint sound men to the Chiefdoms which follow him. Perhaps during the days of Dagomba expansion the higher Chiefdoms were attained by younger and more vigorous men' (*Annual Report, Dagomba and Nanumba District, 1949–1950* (N.A.G.T., ADM. 1/514)).

4 *Ibid.* In 1950 the Finance Committee of the Native Authority still consisted 'almost entirely of residents of Yendi' and the D.C. commented: 'the administration is very much over-centralised in Yendi'.

5 The fault, said the D.C., 'may well lie with the Chiefs themselves, for the nature of their constitution and their chiefly progress is usually the result of individual efforts made to persuade and bribe the person within whose power it lies to award promotion' (*Annual Report, Dagomba District, 1946–1947* (N.A.G.T., ADM. 1/515); *Annual Report, Dagomba District, 1947–1948* (N.A.G.T., ADM. 1/536)).

6 Kerr proposed that at Yendi the divisional chiefs should replace the elders as members of the Native Authority bodies (principally the Ya-Na's council, his tribunal, and the Finance Committee). At divisional level the village chiefs should be brought in to replace the elders of the divisional chiefs. Kerr thought that the village chiefs should be given full responsibility for tax-gathering and he also wanted the creation of a separate municipal authority for Tamale (D.C., Dagomba, to acting C.C.N.T., 16 September 1944 (N.A.G.T., ADM. 1/347); D.C., Dagomba, to acting C.C.N.T., 22 September 1944 (N.A.G.T., ADM. 1/348)).

7 Assistant D.C., Dagomba, *Informal Diary*, 27 June 1946. Kerr endorsed the view of his superior that the reluctance of the chiefs to take a greater role in state administration was due to '25 per cent custom and 75 per cent laziness'. This seems a rather shallow observation: under his reforms the Ya-Na still exercised considerable patronage and could withdraw his favour (as could the elders) from aspirant chiefs who showed themselves eager to meddle in Yendi business. The chiefs, it will be noticed, did not object to greater decentralisation.

8 The major case of extortion in this period concerned the Demon-Na. In April 1944

he was fined £50 by the Ya-Na for plundering Konkomba villages and required to return his booty. In March 1945 the Konkombas in Demon revolted against the divisional chief and formed their own council of headmen. They continued to acknowledge the authority of Yendi and undertook their own tax collection. The Ya-Na proposed that he should personally rule the Demon Konkombas, but this was unacceptable to the D.C. Eventually, in November 1946, the Demon-Na was deposed. The D.C. remarked on this occasion that the Demon case exemplified the problems arising from the Dagomba taboo on deskinning chiefs: it had only been possible because 'it was discovered that the chief was an "ordinary man" and not . . . of the royal blood'. But, as he added, 'it was an expedient turning upon a very fine point' (D.C., Dagomba, *Informal Diary*, 15 April 1944, 17 March 1945, 24 March 1945, 2 June 1946, 24 Sept. 1946, (Assistant D.C., Yendi) 4 Nov. 1946 (N.A.G.T., ADM. 1/347); *Annual Report, Dagomba District, 1946–1947* (N.A.G.T., ADM. 1/515)). For other cases of extortion by Dagomba chiefs in the Konkomba area, see Tait (1961), pp. 9–10.

9 In 1950 the D.C. noted: 'A new commercial middle class is beginning to emerge. It is composed of storekeepers and lorry-load collectors. [Another] class which may be called an Intelligentsia is appearing. It is composed in the main of Teachers and Clerks. Many of these strengthen the District Councils and Committees which would otherwise comprise only Chiefs and their followers' (*Annual Report, Dagomba and Nanumba District, 1949–1950* (N.A.G.T., ADM. 1/514)).

10 *Minutes of a Conference of Officers in the Northern Territories Held at Tamale, 22 January to 27 January 1945* (N.A.G.T., ADM. 1/206). In 1936 recurrent expenditure by the government on education in the N.T. was £847: the estimate for 1945 was £8,210 (*ibid*). Yet in 1950 there were only 403 pupils at the nine Native Authority schools in Dagomba, plus another 388 at the two senior schools in Tamale (which, however, served all the N.T.). There were twelve Dagomba students at the new Government Teacher Training College in Tamale (*Annual Report, Dagomba and Nanumba District, 1949–1950* (N.A.G.T., ADM. 1/514)).

11 Hailey (1951), p. 262. The Council was empowered 'to discuss matters of common interest to the Native Authorities in the Northern Territories and to make recommendations thereon to the Chief Commissioner', and, further, 'to advise the Chief Commissioner as to the expenditure of the joint funds of the Native Authorities in the Northern Territories and as to the distribution of Government grants'. In 1950 it was given a statutory basis similar to that of the Joint Provincial, Asanteman, and Southern Togoland councils, its membership was increased from 15 to 22, and its title was changed to 'Northern Territories Council' (Gold Coast (1955), p. 19; Austin (1964), pp. 8, 185–6).

12 In 1930 Candler suggested inviting Allassani to take charge of the course for chiefs' sons which Duncan-Johnstone wanted to establish. A good summary of Allassani's career is given in Ghana (1968e), pt I, *Report on Mr. Joseph Henry Allassani*.

13 An account of Yakubu Tali's life appears in *West Africa*, no. 2083 (16 March 1957).

14 *Annual Report, Dagomba District, 1946–1947* (N.A.G.T., ADM. 1/515). The D.C. had written: 'This chief will need careful watching as, despite his obvious abilities, he is over-ambitious and no friend of his subdivisional chief' (Assistant D.C., Dagomba, *Informal Diary*, 21 Nov. 1946, 27 Dec. 1946 (N.A.G.T., ADM. 1/348)).

15 Yakubu Tali was also chairman of the new Dagomba District Council from 1952 to 1955.

16 The petitioner, J. B. Harruna, did not become Nanton-Na but was later elected to the Legislative Assembly and was given the minor office of Bogundo-Na. It should be said that his letter concluded: 'I am prepared to pay £40 for the vacant skinship of Nanton through the District Commissioner to Ya-Na' (J. B. Harruna to C.C.N.T., 16 March 1945 (N.A.G.T., ADM. 1/611)).

17 *Annual Report, Dagomba District, 1947–1948* (N.A.G.T., ADM. 1/536); Ferguson and Wilks (1970), p. 349.

18 Ferguson and Wilks (1970), p. 349; Iddi (1968), vol. 1, p. 38. Sunson was normally a 'terminus' for grandsons.

19 *Annual Report, Dagomba District, 1947–1948* (N.A.G.T., ADM. 1/536). Cf. Ferguson and Wilks (1970), p. 349; Ghana, *Parliamentary Debates*, Second Series, vol. 1 (11 Dec. 1969), col. 588. One informant suggested that the Ya-Na's decision to commit suicide (if such it was) may have had a tactical rationale in that he knew Mahama, the then Mion-lana, would succeed him and calculated that his own son Andani would then move to Mion (a better gate than Karaga, which in any case he would have to fight for). Indeed, this was exactly the sequence which occurred.

20 Petition from 'an unknown Dagomba citizen' to C.C.N.T., 24 Dec. 1947 (N.A.G.T., ADM. 1/382). The text of this petition is printed in Appendix 3.

21 *Annual Report, Dagomba District, 1947–1948* (N.A.G.T., ADM. 1/536; italics in original).

22 *Ibid.*

23 Ghana (1969), pp. 21, 26. Tait, in his untitled manuscript, remarks that the decision 'to introduce a system of popular election to the paramountcy' was taken by 'a senior administrator, against the advice of his District Commissioner'. However, the acting D.C., Bennett, witnessed and apparently approved the minutes of this meeting.

24 Sibidow writes that 'it was not until a few years later in 1954 that the Kuga-Na actually discovered that the Committee was meant to take over his traditional and customary duty in the making of a Ya-Na, but not merely [sic] a committee to help the soothsayers in choosing Ya-Na as the educated people had explained'. The elders, he says, 'were not told the truth about the committee's role, but were merely given a raw deal by the educated people who brought up the idea' (Sibidow (1969), p. 12).

25 The signatories included the regent, Andani, the Yo-Na, the Mion-lana, the *gbonlana* of Karaga, seven divisional chiefs, and eight Yendi elders.

26 One informant said to me that in 1969 the Yelzori-lana had told the Mate Kole Committee investigating the troubles at Yendi that the selection of Mahama II had been made jointly by the elders and the divisionals.

27 Tait, untitled manuscript; Sibidow (1969), pp. 12, 13.

28 Cited in undated letter from four divisional chiefs, Tali-Na, and five divisional chiefs' representatives to D.C., Dagomba (Iddi (1968), vol. 2, pp. 3–4). The chiefs added: 'Abudulai [II] the late Ya-Na who was then Mion-Lana performed the funeral custom and that was not the first time of our forefathers.'

29 Gold Coast (1950b).

30 *Annual Report of the Dagomba District, 1950–1951* (N.A.G.T., ADM. 1/550). The dispute involved a rejection by a large number of people in Gushiegu of the Gushie-Na chosen by the king, on the grounds that the nominee did not come from one of the three gate skins to Gushiegu. Cf. Tait (1961), p. 10.

31 At the time of the riots and boycott of European stores in Accra in February 1948, it was (according to the D.C.) 'clearly illustrated how far divorced the North [was] from the South'. He continued: 'In a town like Yendi, little if any comment was made and life went on much the same, except for certain shortages of goods, that normally come from Kumasi or Accra ... neither Dagomba nor Nanumba have been affected to an appreciable extent by the influences that are at work in the Colony and Ashanti' (*Annual Report, Dagomba District, 1947–1948* (N.A.G.T., ADM. 1/536). Six detained Convention People's Party leaders were, in fact, kept in detention in the N.T. (one, Akufo-Addo, later President of Ghana, was kept at Yendi).

32 See Austin (1964), pp. 85–6, 103; Apter (1955), pp. 170, 172–3, 180.

33 The Tali-Na further declared: 'I do not wish to recount the story of Ashanti exploitation in this country but thanks to the British those days are over. And can it not be said we have worked very amicably together?' (Gold Coast (1950b)).

34 Gold Coast (1950b). In October 1950 both Yakubu Tali and Allassani attended a meeting in Kumasi concerned with the establishment of a 'National Congress' of chiefs and moderate nationalists to oppose Nkrumah and the Convention People's Party. Ultimately, this idea was dropped and instead it was decided 'to oppose the C.P.P. where the party was thought to be most vulnerable, in the rural chiefdoms within each constituency' (Austin (1964), pp. 135–6).

35 Both Allassani and Yakubu Tali were members of the committee. The administration

evidently allowed its views to be known and sometimes did so a little clumsily. Thus when the C.C.N.T. opened the debate on Coussey by the Territorial Council, he put the question as whether the Council approved Coussey's proposals 'or whether you consider these reforms to be in conflict with the political aspirations of the Northern Territories at its present stage or not' (Gold Coast (1950b)).

36 On the development of local government following Coussey, see Nsarkoh (1964); Schiffer (1970); Centre for Civic Education (1971); Hannigan (1955); Journal of African Administration (1951), (1952); Apter (1955), pp. 193–6.

37 Gold Coast (1951b). In a debate on Coussey, the Tali-Na said: 'No chief in the Northern Territories objects to surrendering of part of his power to the common man; what I feel all chiefs in the Northern Territories object to is the surrendering of part of their power to the common man only for it to be snatched away from him by an outside agent whom they perceive is waiting cannibally by ... they are the only qualified persons to say whether the "baby" can now eat by itself or must still be fed in a way peculiar to him' (Gold Coast (1950c)). The parallel between the language of Tali-Na and that of Jones in the thirties is very striking: Jones, it will be recalled, had described the Dagomba as infants in political matters, needing to be fed, washed, and guided by a 'mother' government.

38 Gold Coast (1951b).

39 'During the transitional period while African Local Government is feeling its feet [sic] the leadership of the District Officers from within the system (as distinct from his criticism and advice from outside it) is of the greatest practical value, assuming, of course, that it is applied in a liberal and not an autocratic spirit' (Gold Coast (1951b)).

40 Gold Coast (1951a).

41 On the 1951 Ordinance, see Journal of African Administration (1952); Nsarkoh (1964), p. 10. The Dagomba councils were established by Instruments dated 28 February 1952 (*Gold Coast Gazette*, 21 March 1952). The first elections were held in May and June 1952.

42 Gold Coast (1955); cf. Nsarkoh (1964), p. 19.

43 The only exception was Demon division, which was put directly under the Yendi Local Council.

44 Based on election returns published in *Gold Coast Gazette*, 10 May 1952, 23 May 1952, 21 June 1952, 26 July 1952, 30 September 1952, 6 December 1952. Two chiefs were defeated in contests in the Gushiegu Local Council area. The only other notable to be defeated was an elder of Karaga, beaten by S. I. Iddrissu, later to become C.P.P. Member of Parliament for Dagomba North.

45 Of the 40 councillors elected for Savelugu, Tolon, Kumbungu, Mion, and Nanton councils, 24 were chiefs or elders.

46 Tait, untitled manuscript. Tait commented: 'a new class has appeared in Dagomba, an educated class that has been to a great extent excluded from traditional Dagomba politics. Even now, the new local councils are largely composed of chiefs and are usually dominated by chiefly chairmen.' He also made the point that, since the children of senior royals were generally given traditional forms of education, those educated in schools and employed by local authorities were usually 'the children of commoners and lesser chiefs'.

47 Cf. Schiffer (1970), pp. 59–60. A. S. Y. Andoh has pointed out that the ineffectiveness of councils perpetuated the habit, bred under 'D.C. rule', of looking to central government for development funds (Andoh (1967)).

48 Gold Coast (1955). Similar comments were made by A. F. Greenwood in his report of 1957 which led to the amalgamation of many councils (Ghana (1957)).

49 In 1958 the Dagomba councils were reduced to two, the Eastern Dagomba and Western Dagomba Local Councils; Tamale kept its separate Urban Council. At elections in 1961 all candidates were sponsored by the C.P.P. and all were returned unopposed (*Local Government Bulletin*, 9 June 1961). In 1962 nine Local Councils were set up in Dagomba (Kumbungu, Mion, Sunson, Karaga, and Kworli were not accorded the status of having seperate councils again). On the politics behind the multiplication of authorities, see S. N. Woode, 'The Old Structures of Local Government' in Centre for Civic Education (1971), p. 8; Schiffer (1970), p. 73; and Ghana (1968), p. 5.

50 Coussey stated: 'We recommend ... that a clear distinction should be made between the functions of State Councils and the new local authorities, and that all local government functions should be assigned to the local authorities' (Great Britain (Colonial Office) (1949), p. 26).

51 The Local Government Ordinance (s. 16) disqualified paramount chiefs and presidents of councils from standing for election to councils; the 1961 Local Government Act declared members of the regional Houses of Chiefs to be ineligible.

52 'Traditional' membership of Local Councils was abolished by the Local Government (Amendment) Act, (No. 14, 1959); the N.T. Council was disbanded under the Councils (Northern Territories and Trans-Volta/Togoland) Dissolution Bill of 1958. The C.P.P. held elections for new 'regional assemblies' in October 1958, but these bodies, too, were abolished, in March 1959 (see Austin (1964), p. 380).

53 On the position of chieftaincy in Ghana, see Mensah-Brown (1969); Rubin (1967); and Rubin and Murray (1961), pp. 190, 206, 210.

54 The regional houses were established by the Houses of Chiefs Act (No. 20, 1958). The Chieftaincy Act (No. 81, 1961) confirmed their position and laid down (s. 47) that 'traditional councils' (i.e. the old State Councils) must report decisions 'affecting chieftaincy' to their regional House of Chiefs which could make declarations of customary law and submit proposals to the government for the modification of custom. The Ya-Na, Karaga-Na, Mion-lana, Yo-Na, and Chereponi-fame were *ex officio* members of the Northern Region House of Chiefs, which sat in Tamale. In 1955/6 the Dagomba District Council spent £13,823 on payment of salaries to traditional authorities. By 1972 the salary of the Ya-Na was NC.240 per month (roughly £100); the three dukes each received between NC.50 and NC.100 monthly; and the Yendi elders got between NC.6 and NC.12 in salary. Village chiefs continued to receive a rebate on taxes and rates gathered by them (Gold Coast (1955), p. 92; Gold Coast (1956), p. 13).

55 Cf. Lloyd (1964), especially pp. 408–9; Owusu (1970), pp. 167–8.

56 Successive acts and ordinances allowed for the submission of appeals on chieftaincy matters to the government (latterly through the Houses of Chiefs) and for the appointment of committees of enquiry by the executive (the Governor or the President). The government also retained the right to withdraw recognition from chiefs and in the case of disputes concerning paramount chiefs, a judicial commissioner appointed by the government had 'original jurisdiction' to hear and determine matters in dispute (The State Councils (Northern Territories) Ordinance 1952; the Chiefs (Recognition) Act (No. 11, 1959); the Houses of Chiefs Act, 1958; the Chieftaincy Act, 1961; Rubin and Murray (1961), pp. 189, 190, 206; Gold Coast (1953a), p. 14; Gold Coast (1955), p. 8.

57 See Dunn and Robertson (1973), pp. 162–3, 196–201.

58 'Assuming even that there existed in the past known rules of constitutional law in matters of paramountcy, one can argue that since the colonial period the position of traditional rulers *vis-à-vis* the central government has reached a situation in which their constitutional structure under the customary law is in a state of confusion and uncertainty' (Mensah-Brown (1969), p. 59).

CHAPTER 8 PARTY POLITICS

1 Dagomba proverb, from list compiled by H. A. Blair and Phyllis Ferguson.

2 Mion-lana Andani to acting President, Dagomba State Council, 23 Sept. 1953 (reproduced in Ghana (1969a), p. 20). Andani said: 'election to the Nam of Yendi has normally been made from the two ruling houses of Andani and Abudulai respectively; this is an established and customary fact in the Dagbon State which history does prove since the death of Andani'.

3 Abudulai was said to have had very bad eyesight and six toes on one foot (Sibidow (1969), p. 13; Iddi (1968), vol. 1, p. 73).

4 Allassani acknowledges this support in a letter to Dr K. A. Busia of 10 Oct. 1970 (on file, Northern Region House of Chiefs, Tamale). Cf. Sibidow (1969), p. 13.

5 One informant said that Mahama III had actually promised the Kpating-lana that he would inherit the skin (the Kpating-lana was also, of course, a king's son). Cf. Ghana (1969a), pp. 23–4, 25; Iddi (1968), vol. 1, pp. 59, 73.

6 C.R.O. to G.A., Yendi, 10 Feb. 1954, citing minutes of State Council meeting of 11–12 Dec. 1953 (reprinted in Ghana (1969a), pp. 25–6).

7 C.R.O. to G.A., Yendi, 10 Feb. 1954 (Ghana (1969a), p. 26).

8 Mion-lana Andani to Secretary, Dagomba State Council, 22 Dec. 1953 (reprinted in Ghana (1969a), p. 22).

9 Tait, untitled manuscript. Tait writes: 'The Council decided that the regent was eligible. But the English word "eligible" is too sharp and legal a translation of a Dagomba phrase. A regent could and often did apply for the office he held temporarily but I know of no instance in which he got it.'

10 Tait, untitled manuscript. 'There was,' Tait wrote, 'the quite serious danger of brawls between the supporters of the regent and those of the Mion-lana.'

11 There was also in existence a Dagomba Youth Association which was, according to Tait, circulating leaflets supporting the Kpating-lana.

12 Tait, untitled manuscript. Tait, incidentally, believed the Mion-lana to be 'the probable and ... right successor' to Ya-Na Mahama III.

13 Tait, untitled manuscript. Cf. Iddi (1968), vol. 1, p. 59; Ferguson and Wiiks (1970), p. 349.

14 According to one account, the committee initially picked the Kpating-lana but abandoned him because it doubted if he would be acceptable. The actual vote seems to have been nine in favour of the regent, two in favour of the Mion-lana: Tait suggests that the Mion-lana got three votes. The Tolon-Na, reportedly, began by supporting the Kpating-lana, but when the latter had been dropped and the Yo-Na started pushing his claim, Tolon switched to the regent. See Ghana (1969a), p. 6.

15 Sibidow (1969), pp. 14–15; Tait, untitled manuscript; Ghana (1969a), pp. 4, 6. Both Phyllis Ferguson and Dassana Iddi claim that Abudulai was installed as a result of 'government intervention' (Ferguson and Wilks (1970), p. 349; Iddi (1968), vol. 1, pp. 59–60). There is no documentary evidence available to the writer on this point: it is not *prima facie* obvious why the government should take the regent's side, especially as the most influential member of the government in the area was Allassani, who backed the Andanis.

16 Sibidow (1969), p. 15. Sibidow claimed that the new selectors were able to dominate because 'the Andani gate had no influential literate to fight their case for them'. With the exception of Tolon-Na, the Abudus did not have many literates. Indeed, the junior branches of the Andani gate contained several chiefs with education and influence. The Andanis were certainly poorer. Allassani said later: 'as far as wealth is concerned the Andani family are no better than the church rat ... As for the Abudulai family money seems to be their god' (J. H. Allassani to Dr K. A. Busia, 10 Oct. 1970).

17 Cf. Austin (1964), pp. 147–8; Gold Coast (1950d), pp. 18ff; Gold Coast (1950). The 'district councils' selecting the delegates were transient bodies set up in 1950 without clearly defined powers; they were replaced in 1952 by the councils established under the 1951 Ordinance.

18 *Gold Coast Gazette*, 29 Jan. 1951, 14 Feb. 1951; Austin (1964), p. 148.

19 The Demon-Na's name appeared again, as a candidate for the Dagomba North constituency in the 1956 elections; but he apparently withdrew before polling day, since S. I. Iddrissu, his opponent, was recorded as having been returned unopposed.

20 *Gold Coast Gazette*, 29 Jan. 1951.

21 Gold Coast (1953b), p. 30; Gold Coast (1955), p. 22; Austin (1964), pp. 202–3.

22 In 1964 the number of seats in the National Assembly was increased from 104 to 198. The nine Dagomba constituencies coincided broadly with Local Council boundaries as established in 1962. The new seats were filled in the notorious 'one-party' election of June 1965 when, by presidential fiat, the C.P.P.'s nominees were returned unopposed (Ghana (1965), pp. vii, xiv; *Ghana Gazette*, 6 Nov. 1964).

23 Chiefs were not disqualified from standing for Parliament, though in 1953 a proposal to disqualify them was unsuccessfully introduced (Austin (1964), pp. 206–7).

24 Austin (1964), pp. 201–2, 209–25; Nkrumah (1959), pp. 172–3.

25 The claim to have 3,000 members in Tamale was quoted by the Tali-Na in the Territorial Council (Gold Coast (1950c)).

26 The history of Tamale politics is rather complicated and incidental to the main theme of this book. Indeed, the degree to which Tamale kept to itself politically is an interesting feature of northern politics. Briefly, the history of factionalism was as follows. Adam headed a 'youth' faction, including the contractor Yahaya Iddi (brother of Gulkpe-Na Iddi) and the journalist and C.P.P. branch secretary Tarponee Cobla. Iddrissu was the wealthier and better connected of the two and had the ear of C.P.P. leaders in Accra. He was therefore able to get Adam excluded from the party's slate in 1954, until protests from the 'youth' faction led to Adam being offered Savelugu, which he lost. In retaliation, Adam's friends refused to campaign for Iddrissu, who lost Gulkpeogu–Nanton to the M.A.P. In 1955 Adam's friends got Iddrissu evicted from the vice-chairmanship of Tamale Urban Council. A *modus vivendi* was subsequently established, with Adam running the council and Iddrissu the party. In 1959 Yahaya Iddi defeated Iddrissu's nominee for the post of regional chairman of the C.P.P. and when Iddrissu died in 1960, Adam took his seat in Parliament (won from the M.A.P. in 1956) and subsequently became Regional Commissioner. Factionalism persisted and the chairmanship of the council changed with bewildering frequency. Indeed, the council minutes make continually engrossing reading, with discussions of such topics as how to appease a fetish which was causing fires in the market, what to do about drivers who abandoned their passengers for prayers, and the intriguing item entitled 'The Exploded Latrine' ('The Committee . . . requested the clerk to quicken up with the necessary repairs').

27 *Evening News* (Accra), 12 Jan. 1954.

28 Gold Coast (1951a).

29 *Evening News*, 9 Feb. 1954. The C.P.P., he added, 'was destined to lift all common men from disease, squalor, illiteracy, and poverty'.

30 Ghana, *Parliamentary Debates*, Second Series, vol. 1 (10 Dec. 1969), col. 530.

31 But Allassani, the Ya-Na, and the N.P.P. were agreed on one important issue – the future of the territory under UN (previously League of Nations) supervision, in this case the old Eastern Dagomba district. Both major parties (and a majority of Dagomba) wanted this territory to be fully integrated into the Gold Coast (see Austin (1964), pp. 189–93, 230).

32 Personal communication. His opponent, Eddy-Cockra, was (like Allassani) an ex-employee of the Dagomba Native Authority, though he later described himself as a 'letter-writer and politician'. In January 1954 he was named in the *Evening News* as a member of the C.P.P. executive for the area but he swung over to the N.P.P. and stayed with it until it collapsed in the late fifties (*Gold Coast Gazette*, 28 May 1954; *Evening News*, 12 Jan. 1954).

33 In the Protectorate as a whole, the N.P.P. got 49.6 per cent of the votes and the C.P.P., 44.5 per cent. In the four contested Dagomba constituencies the C.P.P. got 45.6 per cent of votes in 1956, compared to 41.2 per cent in 1954.

34 On relations between the N.P.P., the Council, and the administration, see Austin (1964), pp. 186, 229; charges of administrative support appeared before the 1954 election (*Evening News*, 20 Feb. 1954, 2 March 1954). In 1955 Tarponee Cobla, C.P.P. branch secretary, claimed that 90 per cent of the members of the N.T. council were N.P.P. supporters (*Evening News*, 4 March 1955). The *Evening News*, in a moment of particular inspiration, remarked: 'The N.P.P. . . . is like an isolated mushroom standing confounded in the open fields' (*Evening News*, 20 April 1954).

35 Austin (1964), p. 228.

36 Personal communication. An observer of this election told me that in fact the Tolon-Na won by only four votes – and then only after spoilt papers had been taken from the ground and put into his ballot box. Kumbungu did lose its separate council: in 1962 it was put under the new Tolon Local Council.

37 The Nanton-Na's son, Tia Sulemana, was (on his own account) an active C.P.P. supporter and was at one time considered as a candidate for this seat. In November 1965 he became chairman of the newly founded Tamale Municipal Council.

38 See Austin (1964), pp. 221–2.

39 Iddrissu was the most independent-minded of C.P.P. members. On his later career, see Bretton (1967), pp. 125–6.

217

40 'Rivals to a pro-N.P.P. chief, local leaders who saw the possibility of substantial rewards through support for the ruling party, individuals who were prepared to support a local candidate and who did not mind (or even understand) what particular label they adopted, became "C.P.P.", because their rivals were N.P.P.' (Austin (1964), p. 231). On the manipulation of 'traditional' disputes by the C.P.P. and other parties, see Owusu (1970), p. 31, and Dunn and Robertson (1973), esp. pp. 314–52.

41 *Evening News*, 2 Feb. 1955. Abudulai allegedly said to the N.L.M. representatives that 'he had heard that they were trouble-makers in Ashanti'.

42 The specific charge (made by S. I. Iddrissu) was that the N.P.P. leaders, accompanied by Bafuor Osei Akoto and Dr Busia of the N.L.M., had met the (British) C.R.O. 'and forced the Chief of Savelugu to urge his people to vote for them' (Ghana, *Parliamentary Debates*, First Series, vol. 7, (27 Aug. 1957), col. 263). It is not clear when this meeting could have taken place, for Yo-Na Mahamuru died in February 1956 (five months before the election) and his successor, Abudulai II (Salifu Yakubu's brother), was not enskinned until after the election. If the meeting did not take place before Mahamuru's death, it must have been the *gbonlana* of Savelugu who was intimidated (the then Sanerigu-Na Abudulai presumably needed no encouragement, for he was already backing the N.P.P.).

43 Ghana, *Parliamentary Debates*, Second Series, vol. 1 (10 Dec. 1969), col. 530. Mion province formed the eastern section of the Dagomba South constituency and was separated from the western section (Tolon and Kumbungu) by parts of Gulkpeogu–Nanton and Savelugu constituencies. The western section had a population of 22,824, the eastern section one of 13,120. The intention was obviously to defeat the Tolon-Na by using Mion votes.

44 Ladouceur (1972), p. 102. Ladouceur's article gives a very useful account of events during this period.

45 Cited in letter from regent and six divisional chiefs to Northern Region Committee of Administration, 13 Jan. 1968 (on file, Northern Region House of Chiefs). The signatories included W. H. Wahabu and Dawuda Yahaya, propaganda secretary and chairman respectively of the C.P.P. in eastern Dagomba.

46 Personal communication.

47 *Notice of Appeal ... in the Matter of Deskinment Charges Preferred against the Ya-Na Abudulai III by Dawuda Yahaya* (and others), 4 May 1959 (on file, Northern Region House of Chiefs).

48 The petitioners declared 'that the entire act of the Dagomba State Council was indicative of partisanship'. They asked for the case to be examined by the Appeal Commissioner, under the terms of the Houses of Chiefs Act (1958), s. 28, which provided for appeal against decisions by State Councils.

49 Sibidow remarks that the case against Abudulai was 'so overwhelming' that the Afari Committee 'took only a few days to arrive at a conclusion which of course endorsed the the destoolment of the Ya-Na' (Sibidow (1969), p. 15. Cf. Ghana, *Parliamentary Debates*, Second Series, vol. 1 (9 Dec. 1969), col. 483 (speech by Ibrahim Mahama), and Ladouceur (1972), p. 103).

50 J. H. Allassani to Dr K. A. Busia, 10 Oct. 1970 (on file, Northern Region House of Chiefs). Cf. Sibidow (1969), p. 15.

51 Ghana, *Parliamentary Debates*, Second Series, vol. 1 (10 Dec. 1969), cols.530–1.

52 Yakubu had been a police sergeant until 1956. He had, however, been educated at Achimota where he was a friend of Kojo Botsio, later a leading Minister in the C.P.P. government and a political confidant of Nkrumah. Yakubu's other friends included L. R. Abavana (Regional Commissioner for the new Northern Region from 1957 to 1960) and Joseph Kodzo, who, as Deputy Minister of Health, helped to arrange for the provision of a health centre at Savelugu.

53 Ghana, *Parliamentary Debates*, First Series, vol. 9 (14 March 1958), cols. 252, 254. Yakubu promised to reveal the plans of his former colleagues 'when the time comes': apparently it never did.

54 Interview with Salifu Yakubu, Savelugu, 23 Sept. 1972.

55 Ghana, *Parliamentary Debates*, First Series, vol. 13 (18 Dec. 1958), cols. 595–6; italics in original.

56 'Resident Ministers' were appointed reciprocally by Ghana, Guinea, and Mali after the three states had formed a (largely nominal) union between 1958 and 1960. Yakubu's salary in 1956 as a policeman was £288; as Resident Minister he received, on average, £3,057 per annum. In fact, his turnover was rather higher, a matter investigated by the Jiagge Commission in 1967–8 (see Ghana (1968d), report on Salifu Yakubu, pp. 19–34).

57 Ladouceur (1972), p. 103; personal communication.

58 Ladouceur (1972), p. 104; Ghana (1968e), pt. I, *Report on Mr. Joseph Henry Allassani*, p. 5. As Secretary to the Dagomba Native Authority, Allassani received £240 per annum; nine years later he was receiving, as Resident Minister in Guinea, a salary of £3,000 per annum, plus £3,000 'overseas allowance'. On his activities when employed by the State Housing Corporation, see Ghana (1968b), esp. pp. 70–3.

59 J. H. Allassani to Dr K. A. Busia, 10 Oct. 1970 (on file, Northern Region House of Chiefs). Although such a purge may have occurred in the Yendi area, it was not general throughout Dagomba.

60 Cited in J. H. Allassani to Dr K. A. Busia, 10 Oct. 1970. Allassani claimed that after Nkrumah had rejected the Afari report, the Ya-Na's supporters had 'marched to Mion to hoot at and insult the Mion-lana and his people. The police', he said, 'were afraid to give them protection.'

61 The text of L.I.59 is printed in Appendix 4. It should be noted that the Instrument claimed to have the approval of the Northern Region House of Chiefs and to embody its recommendations. It was later revoked on the technical grounds that it had not been so approved.

62 Legislative Instrument No. 59, para. 5.

63 Calculated on the assumption that the second Andani paramount was born in the year that his father (i.e. the Mion-lana's son) succeeded to Yendi; and that this second king reigned as long as his father. Yakubu Andani, the Mion-lana's eldest son, was in fact 25 when his father died in 1969. A similar point was made to Iddi by the Secretary to the Northern Region House of Chiefs, A. B. Baba: he suggested that after Abudulai died, there should be a simple alternation, each gate taking the skin in turn (Iddi (1969), vol. 2, p. 45).

CHAPTER 9 THE YENDI TRAGEDY

1 The C.P.P. established politically appointed D.C.s of whom there were four in Dagomba in 1960. The most interesting was Miss Ramatu Baba, D.C. for Yendi: Miss Baba was a member of the Yidan Baba, the Yendi butchers' family: she later became an M.P. On relations between the Yidan Baba and the C.P.P., see Ferguson (1972), pp. 27ff. On the formal duties of D.C.s and Regional Commissioners under Nkrumah, see Nsarkoh (1964), pp. 299–300; on their role in local politics, see Owusu (1970), Ch. 9, and Dunn and Robertson (1973), pp. 154–5.

2 Andani said that following a debate on a government White Paper dealing with marriage, divorce, and inheritance, the State Secretary asked council members to sign a paper which, allegedly, contained the conclusions arrived at during that debate: 'Since I understood it to be decision on the White Paper, I stamped it with my stamp. But many days afterwards I heard rumours that that paper which we had endorsed referred to succession to the Yendi skin and not the White Paper' (Mion-lana Andani to Minister of Local Government, 3 July 1961 (on file, Northern Region House of Chiefs)).

3 On file, Northern Region House of Chiefs, Tamale. The text of this document is printed in Appendix 5.

4 The document also said that candidates for Yendi 'should have wide knowledge, and experience and should be ready to support the Government of the day'. As will be seen, the second criterion was taken very seriously, the first rather less so.

5 It denied that there was 'any type of Gate system at all in Dagbon', for 'all the Chiefs, princes, and princesses are from one Great Grand Father – Na Yakuba'.

6 Petition of 'Electoral Committee of the Dagomba State Council', 25 May 1967, cited in Ladouceur (1972), p. 108.

7 Mion-lana Andani to Secretary, Northern Region House of Chiefs, 30 Aug. 1967 (on file,

Northern Region House of Chiefs). Andani also criticised the assertion in the petition that the regent was entitled to be considered an equal of the three royal dukes.

8 Iddi (1968), vol. 1, p. 3. The Yo-Na was accused by some people of having poisoned Abudulai III, a charge made almost casually against any candidate known to have been on bad terms with a king before his death. The Yo-Na, incidentally, was involved in a feud with the secretary to the Traditional Council, who, he said, had been dismissed as a D.C. for having 'toe-printed a Payment Voucher'.

9 The Abudulai family refused to have the king hospitalised during his illness. The superintendent of the Yendi hospital advised the royal family that he would have to be taken to Tamale to receive oxygen (the king had pneumonia). The relatives said that the Ya-Na could not be seen to receive hospital treatment and asked that an injection be given instead. Abudulai III died soon afterwards. There were rumours that he had committed suicide, fearing that the N.L.C. would depose him, but there is no evidence to support this story (Iddi (1968), vol. 1, pp. 1–2).

10 The regent took the issue to the State Council against the opposition of the Mion-lana, who argued that the elders alone were responsible for deciding on such matters (minutes of Dagomba Traditional Council meeting of 21 Oct. 1967; reprinted in Iddi (1968), vol. 1, pp. 16, 55–6). I use the term 'State Council' in this chapter interchangeably with 'Traditional Council' (the official term designated by the Chieftaincy Act of 1961), partly because the term has been used elsewhere in the book and partly because participants apply the terms at random.

11 Iddi (1968), vol. 1, pp. 55–6, 74; vol. 2, p. 13; vol. 3, pp. 42, 54.

12 Letter from the regent, Karaga-Na, Nanton-Na, Gulkpe-Na, Sunson-Na, Kumbung-Na, and Gushie-Na to Regional Committee of Administration, 13 Jan. 1968 (on file, Northern Region House of Chiefs).

13 *Ibid.*

14 Karaga-Na and Yo-Na to Chairman, Regional Committee of Administration, 15 Jan. 1968 (on file, Northern Region House of Chiefs).

15 'It is never true that grandsons are not eligible to the Yendi skin. This statement is based on personal hatred and killing of other gates' (*ibid*).

16 Born 1926, at Gushiegu; attended Tamale Kindergarten School, Yendi Native Authority School, and Government Senior School, Tamale (1941–4); joined Gold Coast Police, 1945; promoted to Inspector, Nov. 1955; subsequently attended Metropolitan Police College, Hendon; Assistant Superintendent, 1958; Deputy Commissioner, Jan. 1965 (details from *Daily Graphic*, 29 Sept. 1969).

17 Sibidow (1969), pp. 20–4; Iddi (1968), vol. 3, p. 10; Ladouceur (1972), p. 107; *Daily Graphic*, 26 Nov. 1968.

18 In January 1968 the Yo-Na accused Yakubu of having told the regent that the N.L.C. was 'solidly behind him' and of telling his colleagues that grandsons were ineligible for Yendi (Yo-Na to B. A. Yakubu, 16 Jan. 1968 (on file, Northern Region House of Chiefs)).

19 J. H. Allassani to Dr K. A. Busia, 10 Oct. 1970. An enquiry into the affairs of the State Housing Corporation discovered that, while deputy chairman of the Corporation, Allassani had embezzled £12,659 by means of letters forged by him in the names of fictitious applicants, whose 'loans' were then used to his profit (Ghana (1968b), pp. 70–3).

20 Zohe-Na and other elders to J. H. Allassani, 30 May 1968 (on file, Northern Region House of Chiefs).

21 'I believe that Yakubu Tali backed the agitators because he says he has all the keys to the gate ways that open into Dagomba and can lock and unlock them as he pleases. I know that he would always unlock them for the Abudulai gate' (J. H. Allassani to Dr K. A. Busia, 10 Oct. 1970). An unedifying exchange of abuse between Allassani and Yakubu followed; the Tolon-Na did not engage in polemics, at least in public.

22 Ladouceur (1972), p. 109; *Daily Graphic*, 9 Nov. 1968. On the factions within the N.L.C., see the excellent study by E. O. Saffu (1973). According to Saffu, Yakubu was originally a 'floating voter' within the N.L.C. but gradually moved into alliance with Afrifa against Ibrahim Mahama, the main supporter of the Andanis. This alliance also served to protect Yakubu against investigations by the security services (led by his colleagues

Harlley and Deku) into certain non-political activities of Yakubu (Saffu (1973), pp. 228, 231). Ankrah's involvement was hinted at by Shanni Mahama in the National Assembly (Ghana, *Parliamentary Debates*, Second Series, vol. 1 (10 Dec. 1969), col. 531).

23 Born 1936, at Tibung; attended Savelugu Primary School, Yendi Middle School, Government Secondary School, Tamale (1956–62); University of Ghana, 1962–6; Commissioner (successively) for Secretariats, Forestry, and Information under N.L.C.

24 Sibidow (1969), p. 20; Ghana, *Parliamentary Debates*, Second Series, vol. 1 (9 Dec. 1969), col. 505. On the politics of the N.Y.A., see Saffu (1973), pp. 269ff.

25 The minutes record that 'the Dagomba Traditional Council . . . had argued that the instrument was enacted by the Nkrumah regime, this alone made it abominable. This was the main argument – no other reasons were given' (minutes of meeting of House of Chiefs, 17 March 1968; reprinted in Iddi (1968), vol. 2, pp. 40ff).

26 Iddi notes that the Yendi elders were 'clearly supporting the Abudu Yili camp', though they were supposed to be neutral in dynastic matters. He attributes their partisanship to two factors. First, that 'the Elders . . . accept implicitly what their overlord says as the only truth'; 'secondly, they are rewarded for standing firm with their overlord'. The Gullana, who spoke up for the regent, told Iddi that 'the *gbonlana* had promised to elevate him to the Balogu eldership' (Iddi (1968), vol. 2, pp. 1ff, 12–13).

27 Ladouceur (1972), p. 109; Des Bordes Acquah (1969), pp. 43, 45. The original instrument was issued while Ankrah was away on a state visit to the Ivory Coast: it was repealed after his return – a coincidence noted by Abudu supporters (Ghana, *Parliamentary Debates*, Second Series, vol. 1 (10 Dec. 1969), col. 531). Cf. the speech by Ibrahim Mahama in the National Assembly which seems to put the blame on B. A. Yakubu (*Parliamentary Debates*, Second Series, vol. 1 (9 Dec. 1969), col. 485).

28 The report was not published. Accounts of its proceedings are given in Sibidow (1969), p. 17; Ghana, *Parliamentary Debates*, Second Series, vol. 1 (10 Dec. 1969), cols. 531, 532.

29 Letter signed by Kuga-Na, Tuguri-nam, Amadu Gomli, and Mahama Kpatia to D.A.O., 4 Nov. 1968 (Ghana (1969a), p. 9).

30 The letter was alleged to be a forgery: the D.A.O. was later criticised for having passed it to his superiors without alerting them to this possibility (Ghana (1969a), pp. 10, 12, 13, 31; Ghana, *Parliamentary Debates*, Second Series, vol. 1 (9 Dec. 1969), col. 495; (11 Dec. 1969), cols. 593–4).

31 J. S. Kaleem, letter in *Ghanaian Times*, 6 Dec. 1968. The Mate Kole Committee of 1969 decided that the king-making elders had met 'three times secretly and consulted oracles under the leadership of the Kuga-Na who claimed to be the principal Kingmaker' (Ghana (1969a), p. 10).

32 The Yo-Na had asked Ankrah to stop members of the N.L.C. from attending the funeral and had protested once more about Yakubu's backing of the regent (Yo-Na to Chairman, N.L.C., 4 Nov. 1968 (on file, Northern Region House of Chiefs)). Allassani and the Tolon-Na were also at the funeral. Afrifa brought his own troop of dancers and drummers from his home town, Mampong-Ashanti.

33 The Special Branch discovered that the Gushie-Na had paid NC.20 (about £7) to the Mion-lana as compensation for his not receiving the nomination (Ghana (1969a), p. 31; Iddi (1968), vol. 3, pp. 23, 25, 65–6). Sibidow alleges that the Gushie-Na had received 'anonymous orders' to convene the selection committee instead of presenting the straw to Andani, and Allassani specifically accused B. A. Yakubu of preventing his brother from handing it to the Mion-lana (Sibidow (1969), pp. 23–4; J. H. Allassani to Dr K. A. Busia, 22 Oct. 1970 (on file, Northern Region House of Chiefs)).

34 Iddi (1968), vol. 3, p. 43.

35 Minutes of a meeting of the selection committee, 8 Nov. 1968 (on file, Northern Region of Chiefs); Iddi (1968), vol. 3, p. 23; Ghana, *Parliamentary Debates*, Second Series, vol. 1 (9 Dec. 1969), cols. 509–10.

36 Ghana (1969a), pp. 31, 34–5. Iddi reports that the Karaga-Na was furious because he felt that he had been tricked by the regent into believing that he would become king. He was threatening to ask for a refund of all the money spent by him on Abudulai III's funeral (Iddi (1968), vol. 3, p. 33).

37 J. S. Kaleem, letter in *Ghanaian Times*, 6 Dec. 1968; Iddi (1968), vol. 3, pp. 37, 57.

38 Iddi (1968), vol. 3, p. 27; *Daily Graphic*, 9 Nov. 1968; Ghana, *Parliamentary Debates*, Second Series, vol. 1 (9 Dec. 1969), cols. 496–9. Mahama denied absolutely having engineered the announcement. For other accusations of interference by Mahama, see *Parliamentary Debates*, Second Series, vol. 1 (9 Dec. 1969), cols. 495–6.

39 Karaga-Na and Yo-Na to Chairman, N.L.C., 12 Nov. 1968 (on file, Northern Region House of Chiefs); *Daily Graphic*, 14 Nov. 1968.

40 Nsaful concluded: 'The fact that the Abudulai gate has had the Ya-Na skins for two consecutive times explains why the elders and in fact the whole Traditional Council signs "Abudulai". It is like packing the House of Lords with supporting Peers to see a controversial Bill through the British Parliament ... the only way to kill the canker which has been destroying the fabric of Dagomba society for over a decade will be to stick to custom ... I am convinced that the old split in Dagomba will be healed with the occupation of the Yani skins by the Mion-lana' (Ghana (1969a), p. 34).

41 The authorisation was given in a letter from the Regional Administrative Officer, Chinery, dated 18 Nov. 1968 (reproduced in Ghana (1969a), pp. 29–30). In view of the blame which was subsequently heaped on Chinery and, especially, Nsaful, it is important that three points be noted here:

    1. Captain Oteng (O.C. the army detachment in Yendi) was called suddenly to Accra on 11 November, reportedly to receive orders from the N.L.C. (Iddi (1968), vol. 3, p. 34);

    2. Nsaful's report of 15 November was intended for the N.L.C.;

    3. Nsaful (according to Iddi) returned to Yendi, on 21 November, from Accra via Tamale. It was said at the time that he had brought with him 'an order from the Inspector-General of Police [Harlley] [which] instructed that the Mion-lana should be installed [as] the new Ya-Na on this same day 21 November 1968' (Iddi (1968), vol. 3, p. 53).

The correspondence printed in the Mate Kole report leaves little doubt that the *final* decision to install Andani was taken in Tamale: two letters from the Regional Office there say as much (Ghana (1969a), pp. 28–30). However, it would have been extraordinarily rash of civil servants to have taken such a decision without consulting their political superiors (especially when the matter was evidently one which so interested several members of the N.L.C.). Equally, it would have been remarkable (given the tussle which had occurred in Accra over L.I.59) if members of the N.L.C. had not during the intervening two weeks discussed the affair with each other and with subordinates and had not expressed opinions about solutions. Nsaful, Chinery, and the Regional Committee of Administration may well have exceeded their powers, since there was a clear procedure for dealing with disputes of this type. Nevertheless, the suspicion lingers that, to some extent, they were made scapegoats for their superiors in the N.L.C.

42 Allassani, Sibidow, and Iddi all suggest that the Gushie-Na was punished for flouting tradition during the selection process in November (J. H. Allassani to Dr K. A. Busia, 22 Oct. 1970; Sibidow (1969), p. 24; Iddi (1968), vol. 3, pp. 65–6).

43 Iddi (1968), vol. 3, pp. 67, 69; *Daily Graphic*, 5 Dec. 1968. *The Graphic* printed a photograph of Andani with three members of the committee, among them Lt-Col. Iddissah, who became Regional Commissioner after the 1972 *coup*.

44 The petitioners stressed that Andani had not undergone the crucial *bolon* ceremony (the presentation to the new king of a wooden sceptre, customarily guarded by Kpati-Na). Indeed, they said, the only rituals performed had been those for which Kuga-Na and Tuguri-nam were responsible. The petition was signed by five divisional chiefs (Gulkpe-Na, Gushie-Na, Nanton-Na, Tolon-Na, and Yelzori-lana) and eight elders (Zohe-Na, Kpati-Na, Gomli, Kpahigu, Mba Malle, Gagbindana, Balo-Na, and Mbadugu); many of the elders refused to attend Andani at court (petition of 24 Nov. 1968 to Chairman, N.L.C. (on file, Northern Region House of Chiefs); Ferguson and Wilks (1970), p. 351; *Daily Graphic*, 29 Nov. 1968).

45 Mate Kole was Konor of Manya Krobo in the Eastern Region and Vice-Chairman of the Constitutional Commission established by the N.L.C. (on his struggles with the C.P.P.,

see Apter (1955), pp. 257–64). Nana Obiri Yeboah was Efutuabahene of Axim-Fosu (Central Region). Kaleo was a former teacher: elected for the N.P.P. in 1954, he later moved to the United Party and under the N.L.C. served on the Siriboe Commission on electoral and local government reform.

46 Terms of reference as printed in *Local Government Bulletin*, 14 Dec. 1968, and in Ghana (1969a), p. 1.

47 The committee's report was dated 8 August 1969; according to Des Bordes Acquah, it was submitted on 22 August. Announcement of the findings was delayed until after the elections of 29 August (Des Bordes Acquah (1969), p. 35).

48 Sibidow (1969), p. 30. Sibidow also said that 'all the members of the Committee were known, at least in private, to share common political views' (*ibid*, p. 26).

49 Saffu (1973), p. 228.

50 It is now clear that Busia had been allowed to set up a 'ghost party' under the aegis of the Centre for Civic Education (of which he was chairman). This process began as early as 1967 and by 1969 Busia had an extensive network ready to be transformed into a party as soon as 'politics' became legal again. On the clandestine formation of Busia's 'proto-P.P.', see Saffu (1973).

51 On the 1969 general elections, see Craig (1969).

52 Ghana (1967), pp. 124, 127. As in 1964, the constituencies were based on Local Council areas (though the councils themselves had gone into abeyance at the time of the *coup*). Chereponi–Saboba is here included as a 'Dagomba' constituency, though in fact the majority of the population in that constituency were non-Dagomba.

53 In the latter case, low registration affected the outcome. The Nanton-Na, a supporter of the Abudu gate and the P.P., told his subjects not to register until he returned from Yendi, where he stayed for several months at the end of 1968: as a result the Nanton villages were never properly enrolled. The Mion villages (supporting Andani and the N.A.L.) were fully registered, a fact which is held to have decided the election in favour of the N.A.L.

54 In Ghana as a whole the turnout was roughly 70 per cent (*West Africa*, no. 2728 (13 Sept. 1969)).

55 In the Dagomba constituencies only 5 per cent of votes went to third-party candidates, none of whom got more than 500 votes.

56 On relations between the N.Y.A. and the parties, see Saffu (1973), pp. 275–82.

57 Sibidow (1969), p. 32. Sibidow remarks that the Abudus supported the P.P. because two (unnamed) members of the Mate Kole Committee identified themselves with the party (one was Kaleo, who became Minister for Labour and Social Welfare in Busia's government). Ladouceur notes that Busia was taken to see Mohamadu Abudulai and that it was generally presumed that they had formed an alliance: 'It was also widely suspected that the Tolon-Na and B. A. Yakubu had persuaded Afrifa and Busia to form an alliance by which the Abudulai representatives undertook to support Busia's party in the forthcoming elections in exchange for Busia's agreement to support the Abudulai cause' (Ladouceur (1972), p. 111).

58 *West Africa*, no. 2727 (6 Sept. 1969).

59 The fight in Yendi was between the followers of the Serkin Zongo (who had been appointed by Abudulai III) and Alhaji Abudu, whose application for the imamate of Zohe Fon in Yendi had been rejected by Abudulai. To make matters worse, Alhaji Abudu's younger brother, Amadu, was appointed imam of Zohe Fon. Alhaji Abudu and his followers therefore gave their support to the Mion-lana (Iddi (1968), vol. 1, pp. 70–1; Ferguson and Wilks (1970), p. 350; letter from regent and five divisional chiefs to Chairman, Regional Committee of Administration, 13 Jan. 1968 (on file, Northern Region House of Chiefs.)). Wahabu had re-emerged, as propaganda secretary of the N.A.L. in Tamale. On other aspects of relations between the Muslims and the parties, see Ferguson (1972), pp. 30–7.

60 One C.P.P. veteran remarked to me that his loyalty was to 'the real Nkrumah': he felt little or none to the Gbedemah wing of the C.P.P.

61 In 1967 Eddy-Cockra, who had moved from C.P.P. to N.P.P. in 1954 and then back again (to become the C.P.P.'s propaganda secretary in the north), was recruited by Busia to help

organise the 'proto-P.P.' in the Tamale area. Cockra became a regional official of the P.P. when it 'went public' in May 1969. Saffu notes that 'P.P. organisers in the north seemed to be particularly anxious to stress that they had captured the influential C.P.P.' Eddy-Cockra told him: 'It would have spoilt things if we hadn't. We persuaded them to go and persuade their people to go with Busia.' Cockra himself 'went with Busia', in another sense: he was jailed in 1972 after the Acheampong *coup* (as he had been in 1966 after the Afrifa *coup*). A similar fate awaited Yahaya Iddi, who had swung from the C.P.P. to Busia's party.

62 Four: the Zangballon-Na in Savelugu; the Lele-lana in Gushiegu; the Tampie-Kukuo-Na in Tolon; and the Tali-Na, also in Tolon.

63 Personal communication. Savelugu has, as may have been suggested in earlier chapters, a distinctive political culture; seedy, but active, even at times manic. A good example of the Savelugu 'style' occurs in the council minutes of 1967. The council noted complaints about the conduct of its typist: 'The Draft minutes of the council are sometimes kept for number of days without being typed and the employee is found often Holidaying about in the town. It is likely, the Clerk continued, that with much regrets the Typist is addicted to drinking and has some time to loose control of the Typewriter' (minutes of Savelugu Local Council management committee, 9 June 1967).

64 The highest N.A.L. vote was in Mion–Nanton (60.2 per cent of votes), followed by Gushiegu (57.2 per cent); the lowest was in Tolon (37.7 per cent). The highest P.P. vote was in Chereponi–Saboba, followed by Tolon (54.4 per cent) and Yendi (49.4 per cent). The pattern of voting thus supports the hypothesis that the vote recorded for a party was a function of the status of the chief supporting it: the bigger the chief, the more efficient the turnout. The case of the Yo-Na was rather special, as we have seen, calling for a supplementary hypothesis to deal with situations in which one party had the support of a chief and one son, another was supported by at least two other sons, while a third was supported by a fourth. The hypothesis eludes me.

65 Ghana (1969a), p. 17. The committee had decided that the *bolon* ceremony was the central rite: 'it is after the Bolon ceremony that a candidate emerges from the Katini Duu as a Ya-Na ... the Bolon or Gbewa ceremony is the final act that makes one a Ya-Na' (*ibid*, pp. 17, 10).

66 *Ibid*, p. 17.

67 *Ibid*, p. 3.

68 'This does not preclude individuals or groups who desired supernatural guidance in discharging this most sacred duty from private consultation of oracles but each consultation could not be final ... the evidence is conclusive that the choice is by the selection committee and therefore whatever choice made by a person or persons other than the accredited selection committee must be null and void' (*ibid*, pp. 5, 11).

69 The Yo-Na (for some reason) had given the committee the names of 'nine previous Ya-Nas who did not occupy any of the three skins of the royal Dukedoms' (*ibid*, p. 4). These names were not given in the report. Tait, as we have seen, knew of 'no recorded instance' in which a regent had become Ya-Na: with the exception of Abudulai III in 1954, all nine Ya-Nas after Yakuba were dukes at the time of their accession.

70 'We have no evidence whatsoever of rotation from "House" to "House" in the right to the skin as alleged by certain persons in petitions and letters to the National Liberation Council and the Chieftaincy Secretariat' (*ibid*, p. 4).

71 The committee described the behaviour of Nsaful and the Superintendent of Police in November 1968 as 'irregular and unreasonable' and Nsaful's report of 15 November 1968 (recommending the enskinment of the Mion-lana) as 'incorrect and fraudulent'. On the decision to install the Mion-lana, the committee castigated both the regional and district authorities for 'attempting to settle such a major chieftaincy dispute by themselves in spite of the Law and Government policy as stated, fully well knowing that they had no jurisdiction or authority so to act' (*ibid*, pp. 14, 15).

72 Ghana (1969b), p. 3.

73 *Daily Graphic*, 5 Sept. 1969, 9 Sept. 1969, 13 Sept. 1969; Des Bordes Acquah (1969), p. 35.

74 Ghana, *Parliamentary Debates*, Second Series, vol. 1 (9 Dec. 1969), col. 487.

75 *Daily Graphic*, 10 Sept. 1969. This statement was also quoted in the National Assembly (*Parliamentary Debates*, Second Series, vol. 1 (9 Dec. 1969), cols. 489, 500, 511).
76 *Daily Graphic*, 10 Sept. 1969. Des Bordes Acquah reported that on 9 September 'five divisional chiefs petitioned the Government to rescind its decision to eject former Ya-Na (son of Mion-lana) from palace "until funeral rites of his father had been performed"' (Des Bordes Acquah (1969), p. 35). Yakubu Andani was not, of course, a 'former Ya-Na'. More important, no government spokesman ever admitted that any such decision had been taken, much less that the troops had entered the palace in furtherance of it.
77 *Parliamentary Debates*, Second Series, vol. 1 (11 Dec. 1969), col. 587. Mr Adade said that at 5.30 a.m. the police and army 'had issued invitation to people in Yendi to surrender weapons'. He continued: 'It is known that because of the reluctance of these people [in and around the palace] to surrender arms, the Police were constrained to do a house-to-house search.'
78 Cited in Des Bordes Acquah (1969), p. 35. Some P.P. members alleged that the Andanis had been responsible for the earlier disturbances in Yendi, by setting fire to the houses of elders and firing poisoned arrows at their opponents (*Parliamentary Debates*, Second Series, vol. 1 (9 Dec. 1969), col. 511; (10 Dec. 1969), col. 533).
79 *Parliamentary Debates*, Second Series, vol. 1 (9 Dec. 1969), cols. 486–7: 'The Government gave prior information to the winning side that they were coming to occupy the skin, so they went round in white cloth celebrating their victory before the victory was actually made known to the public.'
80 *Ibid*, cols. 487–8.
81 J. H. Allassani to Dr K. A. Busia, 22 Oct. 1970.
82 *Parliamentary Debates*, Second Series, vol. 1 (9 Dec. 1969), col. 487.
83 It was said in Yendi that 'in view of the refusal of the command to kill innocent people, the Government was going to ask them to leave the scene in order that they would bring in a new command' (*ibid*).
84 J. H. Allassani to Dr. K. A. Busia, 22 Oct. 1970. Yahaya commented: 'Our later information was that, doubting the willingness of northerners to shoot us, southerners, mostly Asantes, were selected to shoot, and they did it superbly' (*ibid*). In the National Assembly, T. K. Agadzi (N.A.L.) remarked: 'On that day a crowd had been awaiting an Administrative Officer to come to talk to them. It is possible that these people [in front of the palace] had come there because somebody was coming to speak to them and not because they were going to attack' (*ibid* (10 Dec. 1969), col. 537).
85 There was some disagreement about whether tear-gas had been used. The opposition further remarked that not one firearm had been recovered from the crowd (a revolver was found, but at a different time and in a house some way from the palace) (*ibid* (9 Dec. 1969), cols. 488–9; (10 Dec. 1969), cols. 536–8; (11 Dec. 1969), col. 575).
86 The figure of 23 killed was accepted by the Attorney-General in the National Assembly (*ibid* (11 Dec. 1969), col. 590). One obstacle to evaluating the various accounts is that Superintendent Allassan died very soon after the incidents, at the end of November 1969.
87 *Daily Graphic*, 12 Sept. 1969, 13 Sept. 1969, 15 Sept. 1969, 22 Sept. 1969; Ferguson and Wilks (1970), p. 352; Des Bordes Acquah (1969), pp. 35, 37. It was reported that the House of Chiefs had told the government that the Mate Kole report was 'uncustomary' and had urged that Andani should continue to be recognised as a Ya-Na (*Daily Graphic*, 13 Sept. 1969).
88 *Daily Graphic*, 23 Sept. 1969; Des Bordes Acquah (1969), p. 36. Tampion and Pisigu said: 'Our late brother's funeral should be fully observed as for a Ya-Na before we can accept the present one.' This visit gave rise to a bizarre exchange between the two front benches in the National Assembly. The government alleged that N.A.L. members had kidnapped the two chiefs from the State House in Accra (a multi-storey block of offices and luxury suites built for the O.A.U. conference in 1965). Mahama said that the chiefs did not like the plush accommodation at the State House and had asked to stay with him. The Attorney-General then admitted that when the two chiefs had been asked why they had abandoned their official suites, 'all they could say was that there were no coal pots at the State House and that they had been informed that at a certain place they could get what

they described as their own "country chop" and that was why they left' (*Parliamentary Debates*, Second Series, vol. 1 (9 Dec. 1969), cols. 501–2).

89 *Ibid*, cols. 508, 509.

90 *Ibid*, col. 492. Almost every speaker in the three-day debate blamed the troubles upon 'politicians'. Thus Quaidoo, of the minority All People's Republican Party, declared: 'We are seeking to stop the injection of politics, dirty politics, into this kind of situation'; and J. H. Mensah, Minister of Finance, said (in winding up for the government): 'Chieftaincy matters–matters of enskinment–are political matters and we are seeking to ensure that they do not become political parties' football' (*ibid* (11 Dec. 1969), cols. 578, 606). He followed this appeal with an attack on Ibrahim Mahama and the N.A.L. for exploiting the crisis (an attack previously developed at length by his colleagues Amandi, Bayensi, Kaba, and Adade).

91 *Daily Graphic*, 24 Sept. 1969, 29 Sept. 1969; *The Star*, 30 June 1971; Ladouceur (1972), p. 112.

92 In May 1970 he had been appointed Ambassador to Yugoslavia.

93 J. H. Allassani to Dr K. A. Busia, 10 Oct. 1970. Allassani's landlord was his old political colleague, Imoru Ayarna (subsequently condemned to death for involvement in a plot against the N.R.C.).

94 Ferguson (1972), pp. 45–6.

95 The Sang-lana was a younger son of Na Alhassan and a brother of Na Mahama III.

96 As a member of the Regional Committee of Administration, Iddissah was among those blamed by the Mate Kole Committee for the decision to enskin Andani in November 1968.

97 Statement on file, Northern Region House of Chiefs.

CHAPTER 10 CONCLUSIONS

1 Benjamin (1970), p. 38.

2 There are, it seems to me, instances in which responsibility has actually been exaggerated. In particular, as suggested in Chapter 9, there is a *prima facie* case for thinking that the D.A.O. at Yendi in November 1968, Mr Nsaful, was the victim of forces which were far from being either abstract or impersonal.

3 Klein (1968), p. 231.

4 Austen (1968), p. 254.

5 Ferguson (1972), pp. 31–2. Ya-Na Abudulai III supported one butcher, Taribabu, against Yidan Baba. Soon after the 1966 *coup* the king summoned the rivals before him and said to El-Haj Said of the Baba group: 'When your daughter Ramatu Baba was District Commissioner, you, Said, were strong. But now she is no more. Now God is on my side. Some time ago you refused to give up one of your days to Taribabu, but now I have given it to him. Whether you agree or not, Nkrumah's government has fallen, so Taribabu will have his share.' On Ramatu Baba, see Chapter 9, note 1.

6 Leys (1967), p. 104.

7 Kilson (1971), p. 105.

8 Or indeed to Africa. My point is that the special features of West African usage are, first, the dichotomy between 'tradition' and 'politics' and, secondly, the apparent acceptance by many people of the atrophy of the very institutions of representative democracy. The reasons for the latter are not, of course, far to seek.

9 Ghana, *Parliamentary Debates*, Second Series, vol. 1 (9 Dec. 1969), cols. 493, 495.

10 The term 'normative rule' is used in Bailey (1969a and 1969b). It has been criticised as tautological. The term 'jural rule', used by Nicholas in his work on Indian villages, seems to me marginally preferable (see Nicholas (1969), pp. 303–4).

11 Nadel (1942), p. 72.

BIBLIOGRAPHY

Specified Sources

ANDOH, A. S. Y. 1967. *The Development of Local Government in Ghana: Background to the Local Government Ordinance of 1951* (mimeo, Institute of African Studies, University of Ghana).

APTER, David E. 1955. *The Gold Coast in Transition* (Princeton (N.J.): University Press).

AUSTEN, Ralph A. 1968. *Northwest Tanzania under German and British Rule: Colonial Policy and Tribal Politics, 1889–1939* (New Haven and London: Yale University Press).

AUSTIN, Dennis. 1964. *Politics in Ghana, 1946–1960* (London: Oxford University Press).

BAILEY, F. G. 1969a. 'Parapolitical Systems' in M. J. Swartz (ed.), *Local-level Politics: Social and Cultural Perspectives* (London: University of London Press).

— 1969b. *Stratagems and Spoils: A Social Anthropology of Politics* (Oxford: Basil Blackwell).

BALANDIER, Georges. 1972. *Political Anthropology* (Harmondsworth: Penguin Books).

BENING, R. B. 1971. 'The development of education in Northern Ghana 1908–57', *The Ghana Social Science Journal*, I(2).

BENJAMIN, Walter. 1970. *Illuminations*, ed. Hannah Arendt (London: Jonathan Cape).

BENZING, Brigitta. 1971. *Die Geschichte und das Herrschaftssystem der Dagomba* (Meisenheim am Glau: Anton Hain).

BINGER, L. G. 1892. *Du Niger au Golfe de Guinée* (Paris: Hachette).

BOURRET, F. M. 1949. *The Gold Coast: A Survey of the Gold Coast and British Togoland* (London: Oxford University Press).

BOWDICH, T. E. 1819. *A Mission from Cape Coast Castle to Ashantee* (London).

BOYLE, Laura, 1968. *The Diary of a Colonial Officer's Wife* (Oxford: Alden Press).

BRETTON, Henry L. 1967. *The Rise and Fall of Kwame Nkrumah: A Study of Personal Rule in Africa* (London: Pall Mall).

CARDINALL, A. W. 1921. 'Customs at the death of a King of Dagomba', *Man*, XXI (52).

— 1925. *The Natives of the Northern Territories of the Gold Coast* (London: Routledge).

— 1927. *To Ashanti and Beyond* (London: Seeley, Service).

Centre for Civic Education. 1971. *Problems of Local Government in Ghana* (Accra: Centre for Civic Education).

CORNEVIN, Robert. 1962. *Les Bassari du nord Togo* (Paris: Berger-Levrault).

— 1969. *Histoire du Togo* (Paris: Berger-Levrault).

CRAIG, J. A. 1969. 'Ghana's general election', *The World Today*, XXV (10).

DES BORDES ACQUAH, N. (1969). 'Yendi – a "mini" war', *Statesman* (Accra), no. 11.

Bibliography

DUNCAN-JOHNSTONE, A. C., and H. A. BLAIR. 1932. *Enquiry into the Constitution and Organisation of the Dagbon Kingdom* (Accra: Government Printer).

DUNN, John, and A. F. ROBERTSON. 1973. *Dependence and Opportunity: Political Change in Ahafo* (Cambridge: University Press).

DUPUIS, Joseph. 1824. *Journal of a Residence in Ashantee* (London).

EL-WAKKAD, Mahmoud. 1961–2. 'Qissatu Salga tarikhu Gonja; The story of Salaga and the history of Gonja', *Ghana Notes and Queries*, vol. 3–4.

EYRE-SMITH, St J. 1933. *A Brief Review of the History and Social Organisation of the Peoples of the Northern Territories of the Gold Coast* (Accra: Government Printer).

FAGE, J. D. 1959. *Ghana: A Historical Interpretation* (Madison: University of Wisconsin Press).

1964. 'Reflections on the early history of the Mossi–Dagomba group of states' in J. Vansina, R. Mauny and L. V. Thomas (eds.), *The Historian in Tropical Africa* (London: Oxford University Press).

FALLERS, L. A. 1956. *Bantu Bureaucracy* (Cambridge: Heffer/East African Institute of Social Research).

FERGUSON, Phyllis. 1972. 'The Yidan Babas of Yendi: a study in the politics of wealth' in B. Callaway (ed.), *Micropolitics in Ghana* (Cornell (N.Y.): University Press).

1973. 'Islamization in Dagbon: a study of the Alfanema of Yendi' (unpublished Ph.D. thesis, Cambridge).

FERGUSON, Phyllis, and Ivor WILKS. 1970. 'Chiefs, constitutions and the British in Northern Ghana' in M. Crowder & O. Ikime (eds.), *West African Chiefs: Their Changing Status under Colonial Rule and Independence* (New York and Ile-Ife: Africana Publishing Corporation and University of Ife Press).

GAILEY, Harry A. 1971. *The Road to Aba. A Study of British Administrative Policy in Eastern Nigeria* (London: University of London Press).

GHANA. 1957. *Report of the Commissioner for Local Government Enquiries, June 1957* (Accra: Government Printer). ['The Greenwood report'.]

1964. *1960 Population Census of Ghana* (Accra: Census Office).

1965. *Revised Report of the Delimitation Commission, 1964* (Accra: State Publishing Corporation).

1967a. *Parts I and II of the Report of the Commission of Enquiry into Electoral and Local Government Reform* (Accra: Ministry of Information).

1967b. *1964 Statistical Year Book* (Accra: Central Bureau of Statistics).

1968a. *The Proposals of the Constitutional Commission for a Constitution for Ghana* (Accra: Ministry of Information).

1968b. *Report of the Commission Appointed to Enquire into the Manner of Operation of the State Housing Corporation* (Accra: State Publishing Corporation).

1968c. *Report of the Commission of Enquiry into Electoral and Local Government Reform, Part III* (Accra: Ministry of Information).

1968d. *Report of the Jiagge Commission ... Assets of Specified Persons* (Accra: Ghana Publishing Corporation).

1968e. *Report of the Manyo–Plange (Assets) Commission. Assets of Specified Persons* (Accra: Ghana Publishing Corporation).

1969a. *Report of the Committee of Enquiry into the Yendi Skin Affairs* (Accra: Ghana Publishing Corporation). ['The Mate Kole report'.]

1969b. *White Paper on the Report of the Committee of Enquiry into the Yendi Skin Affairs* (W.P. No. 14/69).

228

GILL, J. Withers, [n.d.]. *A Short History of the Dagomba Tribe: Translated from a Hausa Manuscript in the Library of the School of Oriental Studies* (Accra: Government Printer).

GLUCKMAN, Max. 1960. 'The rise of a Zulu empire', *Scientific American*, CCII, no. 4 (April 1960).

　　1963. *Order and Rebellion in Tribal Africa* (London: Cohen and West).

　　1965a. 'The frailty in authority' in M. Gluckman, *Custom and Conflict in Africa* (Oxford: Basil Blackwell).

　　1965b. *Politics, Law and Ritual in Tribal Society* (Oxford: Basil Blackwell).

GOLD COAST. 1922. *Returns of the African Population in Towns and Villages of 1. The Colony, 2. Ashanti, 3. The Northern Territories, 4. The Mandated Area of Togoland* (Accra: Government Press).

　　1928. *Report on the Northern Territories for the Period April 1927 to March 1928* (Accra: Government Printer).

　　1930. *Report on the Northern Territories for the Year 1929–30* (Accra: Government Printer).

　　1931. *Report on the Northern Territories for the Year 1930–31* (Accra: Government Printer).

　　1932. *Appendices Containing Comparative Returns and General Statistics of the 1931 Census* (Accra: Government Printer).

　　1937. *Annual Report on the Northern Territories for the Year 1936–37* (Accra: Government Printer.)

　　1938. *Report on the Northern Territories for the Year 1937–38* (Accra: Government Printer).

　　1950a. *Census of Population 1948. Report and Tables* (London: Crown Agents).

　　1950b. *Record of the Sixth Session of the Territorial Council Held at Tamale on 4, 5, and 6 January 1950* (Tamale: Government Press).

　　1950c. *Record of the Seventh Session of the Territorial Council Held at Tamale on 18, 19, 20 and 21 July 1950* (Tamale: Government Press).

　　1950d. *Report of the Select Committee of the Legislative Council Appointed to Examine the Questions of ... Elections ... and ... the Division of the Country* (Accra: Government Printing Department) ('The Ewart report'.)

　　1951a. *Record of the Tenth Session of the Northern Territories Council Held at Tamale on 31 October, 1 and 2 November 1951* (Tamale: Government Press.)

　　1951b. *A Report of a Committee of the Territorial Council of the Northern Territories Appointed to Make Recommendations Concerning Local Government in the Northern Territories* (Accra: Government Printing Department).

　　1953a. *The Government's Proposals for Constitutional Reform* (Accra: Government Printer.)

　　1953b. *Report of the Commission of Enquiry into Representational and Electoral Reform* (Accra: Government Printer) ['The van Lare report'.]

　　1955. *Report on the Northern Territories, 1955* (Tamale: Government Press).

　　1956. *Local Government Statistics 1954–55* (Accra: Government Press).

GOODY, Jack. 1954. *The Ethnography of the Northern Territories of the Gold Coast, West of the White Volta* (London: Colonial Office).

　　1964. 'The Mande and the Akan hinterland' in J. Vansina, R. Mauny, and L. V. Thomas (eds.), *The Historian in Tropical Africa* (London: Oxford University Press).

　　1966a. 'The Akan and the North', *Ghana Notes and Queries*, no. 9.

　　1966b. Introduction and 'Circulating succession among the Gonja' in J. Goody (ed.), *Succession to High Office* (Cambridge: University Press).

229

1967. 'The Over-Kingdom of Gonja' in D. Forde and P. M. Kaberry (eds.), *West African Kingdoms in the Nineteenth Century* (London: Oxford University Press/International African Institute).

1971. *Technology, Tradition and the State in Africa* (London: Oxford University Press/International African Institute).

Great Britain (Colonial Office). 1949. *Report to His Excellency The Governor by the Committee on Constitutional Reform* (London: H.M.S.O.) (Col. No. 248). ('The Coussey Report'.)

GREENE, Graham. 1971. *Journey without Maps* (Harmondworth: Penguin Books).

HAILEY, Lord. 1938. *An African Survey* (London: Oxford University Press).

1951. *Native Administration in the British African Territories*, pt III (London: H.M.S.O.).

HANLEY, Gerald. 1952. *The Consul at Sunset* (London: Collins).

HANNIGAN, A. St J. J. 1955. 'Local government in the Gold Coast', *Journal of African Administration* VII(3).

HEUSSLER, Robert. 1968. *The British in Northern Nigeria* (London: Oxford University Press).

HILL, Polly. 1970. *Studies in Rural Capitalism in West Africa* (Cambridge: University Press).

HILTON, T. E. 1962. 'Notes on the history of Kusasi', *Transactions of the Historical Society of Ghana*, vol. 6.

HOLDEN, J. J. 1965. 'The Zabarima conquest of North-west Ghana', *Transactions of the Historical Society of Ghana*, no. 8.

IDDI, M. D. 1968. 'The Ya-Na of the Dagombas', Institute of African Studies, University of Ghana/Northwestern University Yendi Project, Report No. 12, 3 vols. [Fieldwork notes.]

ILIASU, A. A. 1970. 'Asante's relations with Dagomba, c. 1740–1874', *The Ghana Social Science Journal*, I(2).

JONES, D. H. 1962. 'Jakpa and the foundation of Gonja', *Transactions of the Historical Society of Ghana*, no. 3.

Journal of African Administration. 1951. 'A note on four recent local and regional government reports from the Gold Coast', *Journal of African Administration*, III(4).

1952. '[Note on] Gold Coast Local Government Ordinance No. 29 of 1951', *Journal of African Administration*, IV(2).

KABERRY, Phyllis. 1957. 'Primitive states', *British Journal of Sociology*, VIII.

KILSON, Martin. 1971. 'The grassroots in Ghanaian politics' in P. Foster and A. R. Zolberg (eds.), *Ghana and the Ivory Coast: Perspectives on Modernization* (Chicago and London: University of Chicago Press).

KIMBLE, David. *A Political History of Ghana: The Rise of Gold Coast Nationalism 1850–1928* (Oxford: Clarendon Press).

KLEIN, Martin A. 1968. *Islam and Imperialism in Senegal: Sine-Saloum, 1847–1914* (Edinburgh: University Press.)

KRADER, Lawrence. 1968. *Formation of the State* (Englewood Cliffs, N.J.: Prentice-Hall).

KUMASI University of Science and Technology. 1969. *Tamale–Kumbungu Survey* (Kumasi: Faculty of Architecture, K.U.S.T.; Occasional Report No. 12).

LADOUCEUR, Paul. 1972. 'The Yendi chieftaincy dispute and Ghanaian politics', *Canadian Journal of African Studies*, VI(1).

LEVTZION, Nehemiah. 1968. *Muslims and Chiefs in West Africa: A Study of Islam in the Middle Volta Basin in the Pre-colonial Period* (Oxford: Clarendon Press).

230

LEYS, Colin. 1967. *Politicians and Policies. An Essay on Politics in Acholi, Uganda 1962–65* (Nairobi: East African Publishing House).

LLOYD, P. C. 1964. 'Traditional rulers' in J. S. Coleman and C. G. Rosberg (eds.), *Political Parties and National Integration in Tropical Africa* (Berkeley: University of California Press).

    1965. 'The political structure of African kingdoms: an explanatory model' in M. Banton (ed.), *Political Systems and the Distribution of Power* (London: Tavistock).

LUCAS, Sir Charles. 1920. *The Gold Coast and the War* (London: Oxford University Press).

MACAULAY, T. B. 1906. *The History of England from the Accession of James II* (London: J. M. Dent.)

MAHOOD, M. M. 1964. *Joyce Cary's Africa* (London: Methuen).

MAIR, Lucy. 1962. *Primitive Government* (Harmondsworth: Penguin Books).

MANOUKIAN, Madeline. 1952. *Tribes of the Northern Territories of the Gold Coast* (Ethnographic Survey of Africa. Western Africa pt V) (London: International African Institute).

MAQUET, Jacques. 1971. *Power and Society in Africa* (London: Weidenfeld and Nicolson).

MENSAH-BROWN, A. K. 1969. 'Chiefs and the law in Ghana', *Journal of African Law*, XIII(2).

METCALFE, G. E. 1964. *Great Britain and Ghana: Documents of Ghana History 1807–1957* (London: Thomas Nelson).

NADEL, S. F. 1942. *A Black Byzantium: The Kingdom of Nupe in Nigeria* (London: Oxford University Press/International African Institute).

NICHOLAS, Ralph W. 1969. 'Rules, resources, and political activity' in M. J. Swartz (ed.), *Local-level Politics: Social and Cultural Perspectives* (London: University of London Press).

NICOLSON, I. F. 1969. *The Administration of Nigeria 1900–1960: Men, Methods and Myths* (Oxford: Clarendon Press).

NKRUMAH, Kwame. 1959. *Ghana: The Autobiography of Kwame Nkrumah* (Edinburgh: Thomas Nelson).

NORTHCOTT, H. P. 1899. *Report on the Northern Territories of the Gold Coast* (London: H.M.S.O.).

NSARKOH, J. K. 1964. *Local Government in Ghana* (Accra: Ghana Universities Press).

OPPONG, Christine. 1965. 'Some sociological aspects of education in Dagbon' (unpublished M. A. thesis, Institute of African Studies, University of Ghana).

OWUSU, Maxwell. 1970. *Uses and Abuses of Political Power: A Case Study of Continuity and Change in the Politics of Ghana* (Chicago and London: University of Chicago Press).

PRUSSIN, Labelle. 1969. *Architecture in Northern Ghana: A Study of Forms and Functions* (Berkeley: University of California Press).

RATTRAY, R. S. 1932. *The Tribes of the Ashanti Hinterland*, 2 vols. (Oxford: Clarendon Press; repr. 1969).

RICHARDS, A. I. 1959. 'The Bemba of North Eastern Rhodesia' in E. Colson and M. Gluckman (eds.), *Seven Tribes of British Central Africa* (Manchester: University Press).

RUBIN, L. 1967. 'Chieftaincy and the adoption of customary laws in Ghana' in J. Butler and A. Castagno (eds.), *Boston University Papers on Africa: Transition in African Politics* (New York: Praeger).

231

Bibliography

RUBIN, L., and P. MURRAY. 1961. *The Constitution and Government of Ghana* (London: Sweet and Maxwell).

SAFFU, E. O. 1973. 'Politics in a military regime: the Ghana case' (unpublished D. Phil. thesis, Oxford).

SCHIFFER, Harriet B. 1970. 'Local administration and national development: fragmentation and centralization in Ghana', *Canadian Journal of African Studies*, IV(1).

SHINNIE, P., and P. OZANNE. 1972. 'Excavations at Yendi Dabari', *Transactions of the Historical Society of Ghana*, no. 6.

SIBIDOW, S. M. 1969. *Background of the Yendi Skin Crisis* (Accra: Yenzow).

SOUTHALL, Aidan. 1956. *Alur Society: A Study in Processes and Types of Domination* (Cambridge: University Press).

TAIT, David. 1953. 'The political system of Konkomba', *Africa*, XXIII.
  1958. 'The territorial pattern and lineage system of Konkomba' in J. Middleton and D. Tait (eds.), *Tribes without Rulers* (London: Routledge and Kegan Paul).
  1961. *The Konkomba of Northern Ghana*, ed. J. Goody (London: Oxford University Press/International African Institute).

TAIT, David, and P. D. STREVENS. 1955. 'History and social organization', *Transactions of the Gold Coast and Togoland Historical Society*, I(5).

TAMAKLOE, E. F. 1931. *A Brief History of the Dagbamba People* (Accra: Government Printer).
  1941. *Dagomba (Dagbane) Dictionary and Grammar* (Accra: Government Printer).

THOMAS, Roger G. 1973. 'Forced labour in British West Africa: the case of the Northern Territories of the Gold Coast', *Journal of African History*, XIV(1).

TRANAKIDES, G. 1953. 'Observations on the history of some Gold Coast peoples', *Transactions of the Gold Coast and Togoland Historical Society*, I(2).

VANSINA, Jan. 1962. 'A comparison of African kingdoms', *Africa*, XXXII(4).

WHITAKER, C. S. jun. 1967. 'A dysrhythmic process of political change', *World Politics*, XIX(2).

WILKS, Ivor. 1961. *The Northern Factor in Ashanti History* (Legon: Institute of African Studies, University of Ghana).
  1962. 'A medieval trade-route from the Niger to the Gulf of Guinea', *Journal of African History*, III(2).
  1965. 'A note on the early spread of Islam in Dagomba', *Transactions of the Historical Society of Ghana*, no. 8.
  1966. 'A note on the chronology, and origins, of the Gonja kings', *Ghana Notes and Queries*, no. 8.
  1971. 'The Mossi and Akan states 1500–1800' in J. F. A. Ajayi and M. Crowder (eds.), *History of West Africa*, vol. 1 (London: Longman).

WRAITH, R. E. 1967. *Guggisberg* (London: Oxford University Press).

Serials

GHANA, *Ghana Gazette*.
GHANA, *Local Government Bulletin*.
GHANA, *Parliamentary Debates*, First Series (1957–66); Second Series (1969–72).
GOLD COAST, *The Gold Coast Civil Service List* (1908–36).
GOLD COAST, *Gold Coast Gazzette*.
Daily Graphic (Accra).
Evening News (Accra).
Ghanaian Times (Accra).
The Star (Accra).

Statesman (Accra).
West Africa (London).

Unpublished Materials

Reports, correspondence, and diaries of officers of the Northern Territories administration, 1899–1956 (National Archives of Ghana, Accra and Tamale).

Reports and correspondence, Northern Region House of Chiefs, Tamale.

H. A. Blair, *Sketches in Sepia* (memoirs of a District Commissioner) and other papers.

H. A. Blair, A. C. Duncan-Johnstone, miscellaneous papers (collected by Oxford University Colonial Records Project and deposited in Rhodes House Library, Oxford).

TAIT, David, untitled manuscript describing election of Ya-Na Abudulai III. Undated manuscripts entitled 'Na Gbewa Bihe', 'History of Ya Nanima, Ya-Na Zirile to Ya-Na Mahamabila', 'Dagomba kings from Na Zajili to Na Al-Hassan' (in library of Institute of African Studies, University of Ghana). (The first two are cited in this work as Tait 'A', the third as Tait 'B').

INDEX

234

237

Index

Saffu, E. O., 220, 224
Said, El-Haj, 226
Sakpiegu, 24, 25, 28
Salaga, 5, 8–10, 11, 45
Salifu, Mion-lana (1899), 63
salt, production of, 5, 34
Sambu, 2, 65–8, 74, 129, 159, 192
Sandule, 61
Sanerigu, 25, 64, 121, 123, 200, 201
Sanerigu-Na, 28, 119, 143, 157
Sang, 25
Sang-lana, 28, 119, 168, 226
Sansanne-Mango, 5, 10, 11, 61, 67
Sansugu, 73
Savelugu, 2, 9, 11, 16, 22, 25, 59–63, 68,
    73–5, 86–8, 92, 106, 110, 112–14, 118–21,
    129, 131, 140–5, 147–9, 155–8, 162,
    166–7, 180, 191, 200, 208, 209, 210, 214,
    218, 224; see also Yo-Na
Segbiri, 73
segmentary state, 36, 194–5
Serkin Zongo, 223
shootings, 164–6, 225, 226
Sibidow, S. M., 122, 136, 155, 156, 213, 218,
    222, 223
Sibie, 4, 28
Singa, 11, 25, 28
Siriboe, Mr Justice J. B., 151
Sitobu, Na, 4, 18, 27, 28
skin dispute, origins, 62–6, 112, 120ff,
    133–4, 136–7, 141, 200
Slater, Sir A. Ransford, 78, 81, 203
slaves, raiding for, 5, 6, 34
social and occupational structure, 14–15,
    34–5, 212
soils, 2, 53
Songhai, 3
Sonni Ali, 3
Southall, A. W., 36
southerners, 50–1, 83, 197
state, functions in pre-colonial society,
    13–14; see also political organisation;
    Ya-Na
State Council (Dagomba), 1, 30, 112, 130,
    144, 149–54, 167, 174, 182, 184, 218, 220
Stewart, Captain D., 10
suffrage, 117, 137
Sugri Issa Yakubu, Gushie-Na, 150–4, 221, 222
Sulemana, Nanton-Na, 141, 217
Sulemana, Mahama, 158
Sulemana, Tia, 208, 217
Sumani, Imorow, 159
Sumani Zoli, Na, 19, 37, 188
Sumner, R. C., 49
Sunson, 25–7, 61, 129, 131, 142–3, 192, 212,
    214
Sunson-Na, 4, 28, 37, 119, 122, 129, 151,
    152, 183

taboos, 16, 30, 208; see also Ya-Na; dynasty
Tait, David, 18, 20, 26, 27, 33, 128, 136,
    188–93, 208, 213, 214, 216, 224
Talbot, R. K., 121
Tali, 25
Tali-Na, 108–9, 119, 208; see also Yakubu
    Tali, Alhaji; Yakubu Tali, Ben Abudulai
Tamakloe, E. F., 6, 11, 18, 20, 30, 32, 51,
    190, 191, 192
Tamale: growth and structure, 1; politics,
    217; Urban Council, 128–9, 131, 217
Tampie-Kukuo-Na, 158, 224
Tampion, 25, 64, 201
Tampion-lana, 119, 166, 189, 210, 225
Tampolensi, 1, 5
'Tarbushi', 100
taremba (people not of royal blood), 26
Taribabu, 226
Tarponee Cobla, A., 217
Tauxier, L., 58
taxation, 12, 35, 44, 54, 72, 79, 81, 92–7,
    115–16, 203, 206, 209; see also indirect
    rule; Native Treasuries
Thomas, Sir Shenton, 78, 80, 81, 203
Thorburn, J. J., 44, 51
Tibung, 25, 29, 209, 221
tindamba (earth priests), 3, 4, 14–16, 186,
    187, 188, 189–90, 192
Togo, 5, 9, 11, 42, 47, 52, 55, 57, 58, 66, 67,
    71, 89, 139
Tohagu, 4
Tohajie ('the Red Hunter'), 3, 24
Tolon, 4, 25–6, 31, 61, 70, 91, 108, 129, 131,
    142–3, 155–8, 162, 192, 214, 217, 218, 224
Tolon-Na, 4, 29, 59, 62, 70, 115, 116,
    119–20, 122, 129, 183; functions of, 26,
    33, 193; see also Yakubu Tali, Alhaji
Toma, 25
Tong, 25, 108
trade school, Yendi, 49, 54, 55
tradition: contemporary meaning, 173–5;
    'fossilisation', 13, 132; 'neo-traditional-
    ism', 127, 132; 'pseudo-traditionalism',
    174; see also chieftaincy
Tuguri-nam, 23, 29, 86, 122, 136, 144, 152,
    162, 163, 178, 183, 184, 222
Tutugri, Na, 5, 19, 20
Twi, 197
Twi Foreigners Arbitration, 51

United Nationalist Party (U.N.P.), 158–60
United Nations (Trusteeship), 217
United Party, 145, 155–6, 223
urbanisation at divisional level, 2

Versailles, Treaty of, 71
village structure, 15; population, 2, 186
Voggo, 25, 28, 201, 209, 210

DATE DUE

8/Jul/76			
GAYLORD			PRINTED IN U.S.A.